Volume 21

DIRECTORY OF WORLD CINEMA
BRAZIL

Edited by Louis Bayman and Natália Pinazza

intellect Bristol, UK / Chicago, USA

First published in the UK in 2013 by
Intellect Books, The Mill, Parnall Road, Fishponds, Bristol, BS16 3JG, UK

First published in the USA in 2013 by Intellect Books, The University of Chicago Press,
1427 E. 60th Street, Chicago, IL 60637, USA

A catalogue record for this book is available from the British Library.

Publisher: May Yao
Publishing Manager: Melanie Marshall and Jelena Stanovnik

Cover photograph: Madame Satã/Madame Satan, 2002, Karim Aïnouz, courtesy of VideoFilmes.
Cover designer: Holly Rose
Copy-edited by Emma Rhys
Typesetting: John Teehan

Directory of World Cinema ISSN 2040-7971
Directory of World Cinema eISSN 2040-798X

Directory of World Cinema: Brazil ISBN 978-1-78320-009-2
Directory of World Cinema: Brazil eISBN 978-1-78320-230-0
Directory of World Cinema epubISBN 978-1-78320-231-7

Printed and bound by Gomer Press, UK.

DIRECTORY OF WORLD CINEMA
BRAZIL

The *Directory of World Cinema: Brazil* is the result of the commitment and enthusiasm of authors and chapter editors from a range of institutions across the globe, and we would like to thank everyone who has believed in and contributed to this volume. We are particularly thankful to the contributors for their efforts in making the volume what it is, and the chapter editors, who have not only written the introductions to each chapter but have played a crucial role in determining the shape of the book. We are very thankful for the opportunity to work on a project that covers the history and ongoing development of Brazilian cinema. We would like to express our gratitude to May Yao and Melanie Marshall for their support and Intellect for creating the Directory of World Cinema and their dedication to the field of film studies. We would also like to extend special thanks to Stuart Smith, and our other friends and family for their support and encouragement.

A note on chapter editors:
A number of contributors have played a particular role in selecting the films and reviewers for their respective chapters and giving them editorial direction. They are credited as follows:

Eliska Altmann, '*Cinema Novo*'
Jens Andermann, 'Documentary'
Jack A Draper III, 'Music'
Regina R Félix, 'Comedy'
Carolin Overhoff Ferreira, 'Literary Adaptation'
Vanessa C Fitzgibbon, 'Afro-Brazilian Identity'
Natália Pinazza, 'Early Years'; 'Representation of the Brazilian Indian';
  'Road Movie'
Cacilda Rêgo, 'Diaspora'
Antônio Márcio da Silva, 'Gender'

INTRODUCTION
BY THE EDITORS

To develop an interest in Brazilian cinema and its cultural roots is to discover a topic in renewed bloom. Its best-known examples portray the country while making important contributions to international cinema: the *favela* (shantytown) life shown in *Cidade de Deus/City of God* (Fernando Meirelles and Kátia Lund, 2002) pushes the gangster film into a new direction, while *Central do Brasil/Central Station* (Walter Salles, 1998) combines the urban realism of its Rio de Janeiro locations with a road trip into the wilderness and to countryside traditionalism. Figureheads of a near twenty-year surge in the domestic industry, these films accompany – and form part of – a no less remarkable transformation in the global position of Brazil, which has overturned its (always disputable) designation of 'Third World' status to emerge as a dynamic economic centre. Dynamism also describes the combination of domestic and international dimensions at work in Brazilian cinema, and its absorption and transformation of traditions. Manifested in ways which are both historical and current, it is such dynamism that this volume exists to convey.

Recently Brazilian cinema has achieved an unprecedented success in its national market with *Tropa de Elite 2/Elite Squad 2: The Enemy Within* (José Padilha, 2010), which newspapers proclaimed 'the most watched Brazilian film of all time' with more than ten million domestic spectators. The film testifies to a topic addressed in this volume: the continued surge in prominence of Brazilian cinema within both national and international markets, discussed in the introductory essays 'The Re-emergence of Brazilian Cinema' and 'Film Festivals in Brazil', as well as in the account of Brazil's most exportable contemporary film-maker, Walter Salles. At the time of writing the growth in national production shows no signs of abating, having increased from fourteen commercially released feature films in 1995 to ninety-nine in 2011 in Brazil.[1]

On the other hand, Frederic Jameson has argued that 'the free movement of American movies in the world spells the death knell of national cinemas elsewhere, perhaps of all other national cinemas as "distinct species".' (1998: 61). Important though they are, Brazilian blockbusters such as *Elite Squad*, *Central Station* and *City of God* cannot overshadow the two remaining forces that affect the national cinema market: the social inequalities that lead to constraints in terms of the size of the potential film audience and hence the number of cinemas, and the domination of the US film industry. Data provided by ANCINE shows that in 2011, 99 out of 339 (29.2 per cent) films screened in Brazil were national productions.[2] What is more, the films which mark the recent success of Brazilian cinema have been criticized as compromising their national culture by offering Hollywoodized entertainment.

Such discussion is not new, and the collection that follows includes an account of the sometimes frustrated attempts to establish a healthy studio system during Brazilian cinema's long-lasting 'Early Years', and the perennial difficulties of the relationship with – and oft-criticized perceived accommodation to – Brazil's main competitor to the north, in the shape of Hollywood. One strategy employed by Brazilian cinema has been to counter Hollywood dominance (and to forge links with Latin American and other cinemas) through a critical rejection of the 'neocolonial' state of film-making described above. This was in particular the strategy adopted from the late 1950s onwards by the *Cinema Novo* film-makers, whose aesthetic and political revolutionary radicalism is the subject of the chapters on *Cinema Novo* and its most famous exponent Glauber Rocha. Another strategy adopted by some Brazilian producers and film-makers has been to appropriate Hollywood production values in films that embrace a popular commercial form of cinema in order to secure a share of their home market. This strategy has led to the development of genres which are distinct to Brazilian cinema such as the carnival-inspired *chanchada* (discussed in particular in the chapters 'Music' and 'Comedy' and in the introductory essay on Carmen Miranda) in the 1940s and 1950s, and has seen the institution of a national studio system based in particular on the companies Atlântida and, most ambitiously, Vera Cruz. Nonetheless, Brazil's many attempts to copy dominant trends have been criticized, notably by Paulo Emílio Salles Gomes who stated: 'We are neither Europeans nor North Americans. Lacking an original culture, nothing is foreign to us because everything is' (1997: 263). The perception by the domestic audience (often articulated by film critics) of national cinema as 'inferior' or a 'copy' has shaped Brazilian film production, as the 'Early Years' chapter shows.

The significance of Brazilian cinema can be appreciated in some of its international and artistic complexity if we take a moment to consider Alberto Cavalcanti, whose name recurs in the pages below. Most Eurocentric approaches to cinema would recognize his canonical status. And yet his integral position in film history, having worked in the European avant-garde and helped establish the British GPO Documentary Film Unit, could tend towards creating an image of a free-floating – or even principally European – cultural figure. This would be to obscure the historical record, for his Brazilian heritage, and his return to Brazil as a film-maker and a producer, are crucial to his development of cinema as an instrument of national representation and of artistic innovation. Cavalcanti thus provides an example of how attention to Brazilian cinema allows a decentring of film history, one which can rethink the historical relationship between avant-gardes and mainstream and documentary modes, and the role of cinema in the absorption and transformation of cultural traditions more generally.

To return to questions of the industry, film distribution and exhibition represent a historical challenge facing Brazilian cinema. Since the late 1990s, cinema-going in Brazil has been dominated by the presence of megaplexes usually located in shopping malls in the main urban centres and surrounded by guards. By way of comparison, according to the UK Film Council statistical yearbook, there were 3,651 screens in the United Kingdom in 2009,[3] whereas in Brazil in 2010 there were 2,206,[4] and given that the Brazilian population is over three times that of Britain, it is clearly apparent that the level of access to cinemas in Brazil is a comparatively major problem. This is especially an issue in a country which has often sought a mass popular basis for cinema, whether for commercial reasons or as part of the political struggles of the engaged radical left and of democratic or dictatorial national governments. Given the middle-class nature of film-making in Brazil, the question of the democracy of self-representation and the ethics relating to the image of a nation emerge as topics in particular in the chapters dealing with 'Afro-Brazilian Identity' and the 'Representation of the Brazilian Indian'. The focus on identity in this collection – with the above mentioned chapters joined by chapters on 'Gender' and 'Diaspora' – serves to put the spotlight on to the variety and diversity within the category 'Brazilian', and to push beyond any viewpoint whether of patriotic chauvinism or stereotyping that would tend towards homogenizing national culture. Such aspects of identity recast the national heritage in terms of the struggles of often marginalized and discriminated groups, suggesting both nation and identity as categories in a continual process of renegotiation – a renegotiation also performed through cinema. In this sense, the chapters dealing with identity can be seen to complement the more established arenas of questions of nationhood in the chapters on 'Documentary' and 'Literary Adaptation'.

Gustavo Dahl, a former president of the Brazilian National Cinema Agency (ANCINE), suggests that in order to enhance the national cinema's market share it is necessary to 'de-elitise' it (2001).[5] With this in mind, film consumption needs to be understood not only as a leisure activity, but also as a social practice. To return to the question of 'First' and 'Third' worlds, the change in positioning in the global system that Brazilian cinema has recently witnessed also informs the reception and production of national films. Nonetheless, literature on Brazilian cinema continues to engage in one way or another with Third Cinema theory, which is still a point of reference for critical debate. For this reason, alongside the chapters on *Cinema Novo* this book dedicates an essay to José Mojica Marins, a central figure for *Cinema Marginal*, which is concurrent with the third, cannibalist-*tropicalista*, stage of *Cinema Novo*. Although classical and important films of this movement that emerged in the Boca do Lixo (Garbage Mouth) in São Paulo such as Rogério Sganzerla (*O Bandido da Luz Vermelha/The Red Light Bandit*, 1968) and Júlio Bressane (*Matou a Família e Foi ao Cinema/ Killed the Family and Went to the Movies*, 1969), *Cinema Marginal* will receive special treatment in a forthcoming volume, *World Film Locations: São Paulo*.

Its awareness of the history in which contemporary Brazilian production stands is one of the reasons for choosing for the Film of the Year *5 × favela, agora por nós mesmos/5 × Favela, Now by Ourselves* (Cacau Amaral, Cadu Barcelos, Luciana Bezerra, Manaira Carneiro, Rodrigo Felha, Wagner Novais and Luciano Vidigal, 2010), a film conscious of its debt to *Cinema Novo*. This collection however reaches back into the silent era and moreover places the popular forms of music, comedy, carnival and romance into the debate on cinema's place in the nation's politics, identity, culture, and, of course, ways of having fun. These popular forms do not institute a binary opposition between Brazil and any other national culture, preferring instead to parody, borrow, and thus transform conventions from within and outside of Brazil. An alternative to the engaged radicalism of the *Cinema Novo*, which however is distinctly subaltern and Brazilian, can be found in the cheap, regionally distributed productions of what Bernadette Lyra terms the '*Cinema de Bordas*', a playful and prolific source of films and a category which it is our pleasure to introduce here for the first time in English-language writing.

The final films considered are those of the road movie, which explore the national territory but point both geographically and generically beyond Brazil's borders. Its characters, not always sure if their movement indicates progress or directionlessness, trace some of the contours of debates over Brazil itself. In the ways outlined above, this volume seeks to act as an introduction for those new to Brazilian cinema and to contain valuable insights for those already well-versed in the topic. The volume is a guide which aims to maintain in its reader the fascination for its subject matter which attended its writing.

Louis Bayman and Natália Pinazza

References

Jameson, F (1998) 'Globalization as Philosophical Issue' in F Jameson and M Miyoshi (eds) *The Cultures of Globalization*, Durham and London: Duke University Press, pp. 54-81.

Salles Gomes PE, 'Cinema: A Trajectory within Underdevelopment', in MT Martin (ed) *New Latin American Cinema*, vol. 1, Detroit: Wayne State University Press, p. 263.

Notes

1. Data compiled from http://oca.ancine.gov.br/media/SAM/ DadosMercado/2102a.pdf. Accessed 20 August 2012.
2. Data compiled from http://oca.ancine.gov.br/media/SAM/ DadosMercado/2108.pdf. Accessed 20 August 2012.
3. UK Film Council Statistical Yearbook 2010, p. 68. Available at: www. birds-eye-view.co.uk/download.php?id=211. Accessed 20 August 2012.
4. Data compiled from http://www.ancine.gov.br/media/SAM/2010/ SalasExibicao/208.pdf. Accessed 13 March 2011.
5. Dahl, 2002, available at: http://www.ancine.gov.br/media/LEITURAS/ arte_ou_industria.pdf. Accessed 3 January 2010.

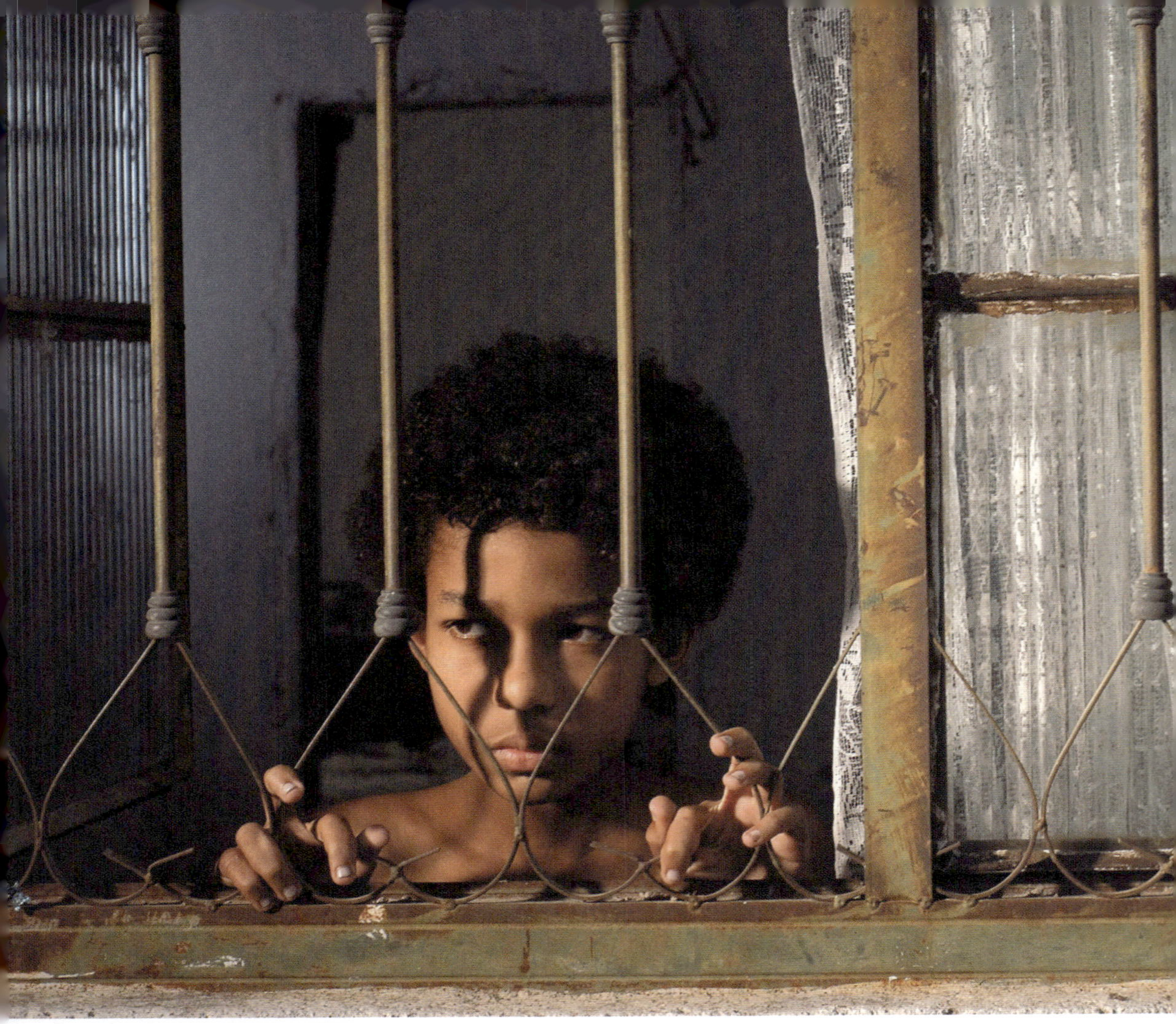

5 x Favela, Now by Ourselves

FILM OF THE YEAR
5 X FAVELA, NOW BY OURSELVES/ 5 X FAVELA, AGORA POR NÓS MESMOS

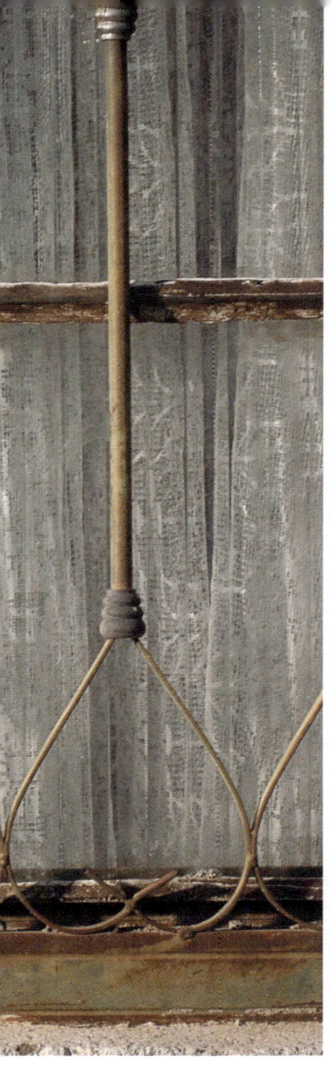

Studio/Distributor:

Luz Magica Produções
Audiovisuais/Globofilmes

Directors:

Cacau Amaral ('Arroz com
feijão')
Cadu Barcelos ('Deixa voar')
Luciana Bezerra ('Acende a luz')
Manaira Carneiro ('Fonte de
renda')
Rodrigo Felha ('Arroz com
feijão')
Wagner Novais ('Fonte de
renda')
Luciano Vidigal ('Concerto para
violino')

The film 5 × *Favela, Now by Ourselves* brings together five short films written, directed and acted by young former dwellers of the *favelas* in Rio de Janeiro. The project revisits the original idea of the film *Cinco vezes favela/Five Times Favela* of 1962, in which middle-class film-makers from the *Cinema Novo* movement, amongst them director and now producer Cacá Diegues,[1] resolved to show the life of the dwellers of the *favelas* in Rio de Janeiro and to intervene politically by renewing the themes, language and characters of Brazilian cinema.

Cacá Diegues's project intends to show how these young people from the slums would nowadays be able to make a film 'by themselves' (the project's original subtitle), and thereby go from being the object to the subject of the discourse. However in order to take on the direction, subject matter and script of the film, they went through an intensive process of training by means of seminars and workshops with professionals in the field.[2]

The outcome of the film reflects this very tension between particularity and convention, a 'producer's film' with real appeal, but also marketable with regards to the project's authenticity and authority originating in the young directors' origins.

The five chapters are a sometimes very schematic demonstration of this purpose, but also an expression of various changes and social and economic impasses in contemporary Brazil,[3] problematizing old oppositions (us and them, legal and illegal, friends and enemies, *favela* and city). The short films also enter into dialogue with the 'favela films' whose discourses around poverty, drug trafficking, politics and slum life oscillate between the demonization of the characters, the criminalization of these areas, and a sort of humanism and paternalism in which the *favela* emerges as a place where poverty is appeased through happiness and solidarity.

In every chapter a small individual or collective drama is unique to each character, this uniqueness becoming their only way out of an impasse. The *favela* is still seen as a place of deprivation and negativity, of individuals who are fragmented and atomized within their social universe, who, whilst strongly marked by collectivism, rely on personal and particular resolutions in order to cope with everyday life. The most interesting aspects of the film are when these individual experiences push social boundaries beyond the clichés which criminalize or romanticize the *favela*.

The boundaries between legality and illegality, idealism and pragmatism, mark the chapter 'Fonte de renda' in which a young black dweller of the *favela* decides to temporarily sell drugs to his colleagues at the law school so as to fund his undergraduate

Producers:

Cacá Diegues
Tereza Gonzalez
Renata Almeida Magalhães
Carlos Eduardo Rodrigues

Cinematographer:

Alexandre Ramos

Art Directors:

Rafael Cabeça
Pedro Paulo de Souza

Composer:

Lucas Marcier

Editors:

Quito Ribero

Duration:

96 minutes

Genres:

Drama
Anthology

Cast:

João Carlos Artigos
Flavio Bauraqui
Zózimo Bulbul

Year:

2010

studies. His attitudes are not condemned within the narrative, but are changed by an affective didactic event that leads him to reverse his decision.

In the chapter 'Feijão com arroz' the same impasse between legality and illegality can be observed but with a looser and fresher narrative, with alternations and turnarounds including the scene in which kids in the *favela* lose money they have made by working for a gang formed by young people in Zona Sul. The cliché of the *favela*-dweller as criminal is inverted and is approached in a comic tone when the kids end up losing a chicken they have tried to buy for their father. In order to please his dad, a *favela* kid commits a petty, justifiable crime and unwittingly ends up repeating the actions of his grandfather, who was humiliated for stealing a chicken from his neighbour in order to feed his hungry family. Once again it is only destiny that enriches the recurrent story of a constituting lack, by opening up different paths, either comic or tragic.

The third chapter 'Concerto para violino' displays a virtuosity of aesthetics, themes and characters that are reminiscent of films such as *Cidade de Deus/City of God* (Fernando Meirelles and Kátia Lund, 2002) or even *Tropa de Elite/Elite Squad* (José Padilha, 2007). Three childhood friends take three different paths: one becomes a policeman, the other a drug dealer and the female of the group, who is a violinist, has a chance to leave the *favela* through the arts. The film, the only one of the five chapters to end in tragedy, institutes other limits, in particular the limits of friendship and allegiances. These are always temporary in a context in which once again determinism and 'necessity' prevail and there are marked contrasts, including in the soundtrack which changes from classical violin to *carioca* funk.

The last two chapters of *5 × Favela* stand out with regards to the difficult balance between determinism and pragmatic necessity, and the uniqueness and strength of these worlds and perspectives: displaying neither necessity nor destiny, nor lack, nor even the eternal repetition of the past, but love and openness towards the world.

In 'Deixa voar' the film reaches a rare level of poetry and lyricism, describing small events in a delicate way. Violence and tension are present in an argument over a kite, heard in the way the characters talk, their tones of voice, their bodies, and their harsh gestures. The chapter explores the past times of wandering and hesitancy on the part of a boy named Flávio, who needs to retrieve a friend's kite which he accidently lets fly into a neighbouring *favela* dominated by a rival faction. Fear, curiosity and naivety are vague feelings keenly felt by the character and the spectator. The space of the *favela* is explored in a sensorial way. The blue of the skies seen from the roofs of the *favelas*, the football courts, gates, bridges, the conquering of another's space, real and imaginary frontiers, create a cinematographically expressive whole in this chapter. The chapter returns us to the time of childhood and adolescence, a loving, conflictual state neither of certainty nor clichéd representation.

This freshness is also seen in the Fellinian chapter 'Acende a luz', which takes place in a vibrant *favela* full of bifurcating and contrasting stories. Communitarianism, consumption, dark humour, happiness and petty, wicked group actions form a complex constellation. It is a couple of days before Christmas and the *favelas* are without light, water and ice. Once again 'deprivation' is a motor for the action, but we quickly leave it aside to share in a richly detailed chronicle of swirling habits, gestures, music, noises. The chapter explores the unique situation of the *favela* as a labyrinth and its distinct bodies, slang and songs (*forró* [north-eastern country music], *carioca* funk, and romantic songs). The *favela* emerges here as a part of city life. 'It is Christmas here too' says a State worker in charge of fixing the lights, removing the last obstacle in the narrative. The *favela* is the city, the *favela* is the world.

By the end, *5 × Favela, Now by Ourselves* makes explicit its central mechanism that goes beyond film or cinema to show the potential and individuality of these young film-makers. It also shows how these peripheral subjectivities are commodities that have been packaged in a film market that requires such worlds, emotions and experiences to sell its products.

Ivana Bentes (trans. Natália Pinazza)

Notes
1. Director of *Bye Bye Brasil/Bye Bye Brazil* (1980) and *Orfeu* (1999) amongst others.
2. The experience of intensive training was formed by audiovisual, theatrical and musical activities as part of the institutions and agreements in operation in the *favelas* and peripheral areas of Rio de Janeiro: Cidadela/Cinemaneiro, CUFA (Central Única das Favelas), Grupo Cultural AfroReggae, Observatório de Favelas and Nós do Morro. These groups have acted independently or with the support of the state and co-operatives, and have established educational projects, autonomous activities, and the inclusion of young people from *favelas* in the urban cultural scene.
3. In the 48 years that separate the two films, Brazil experienced democratic radicalization and advances that resulted in upward social mobility and the end of poverty for more than thirty million Brazilians. Economic, social and also cultural changes, together with the ascension and visibility of cultural/audiovisual production, came from the peripheral areas and *favelas*, and from the dissemination of technologies of communication and digital media.

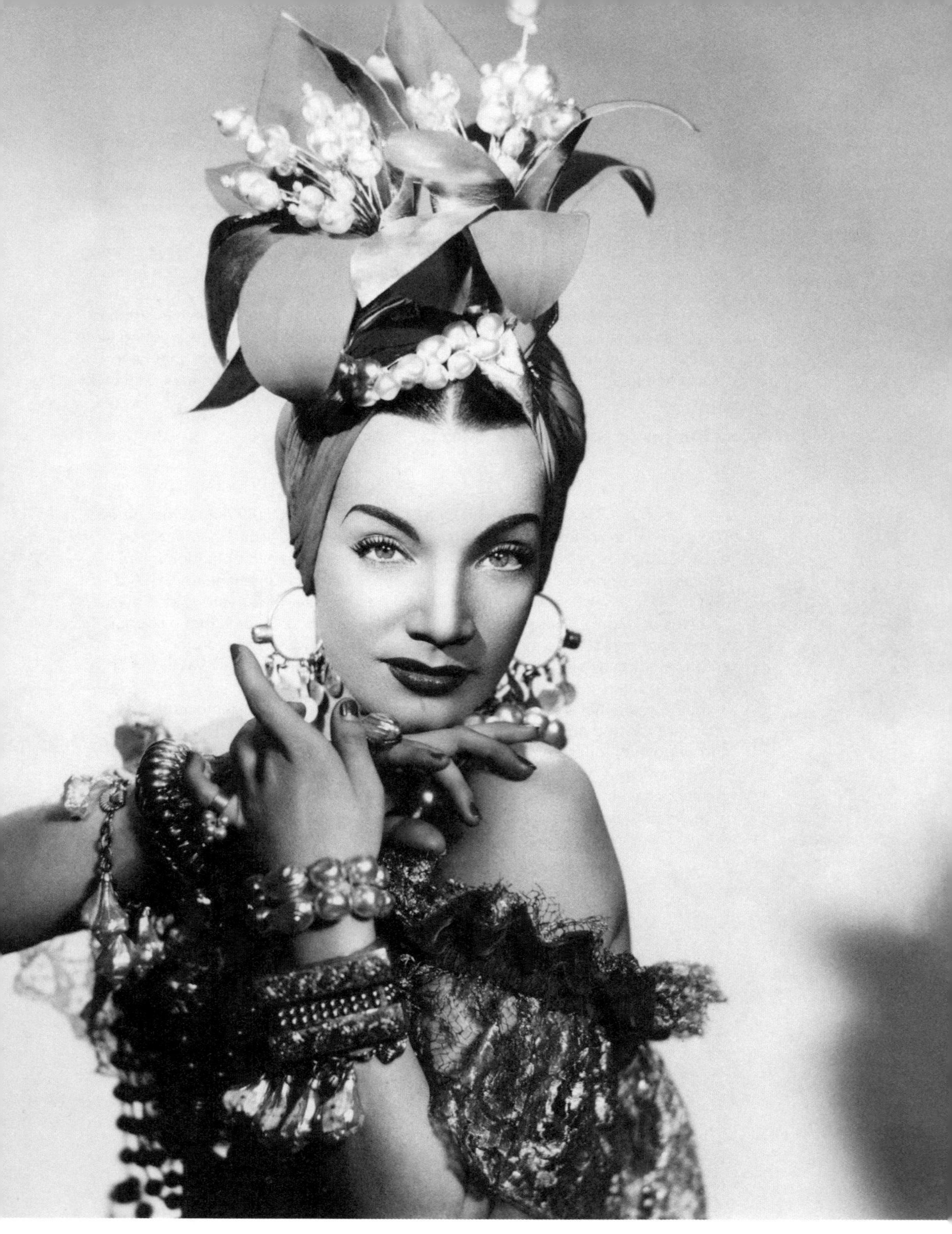

Down Argentine Way

STAR STUDY
CARMEN MIRANDA

Prior to her departure for the United States in 1939 and subsequent Hollywood fame, Carmen Miranda was a well established film star in Brazil, having appeared in six sound films.[1] Lamentably, copies no longer exist of the majority of these films, with the exception of *Alô, alô, carnaval!/Hello, Hello, Carnival!* (Adhemar Gonzaga, 1936), in addition to footage of one of her performances in the film *Banana da terra/Banana of the Land* (João de Barro, 1939). Like many of the first film actors in Brazil, Carmen was already a well established star of popular music and the radio when she made the transition to the screen, and her success in the record industry guaranteed her a place in the first sound films. Her film career in Brazil was closely bound up with the genre of musical films that drew on the nation's carnival traditions, and the annual celebrations and musical styles of the city of Rio de Janeiro, Brazil's then capital, in particular. She performed a musical number in *O Carnaval cantado no Rio/Rio Carnival in Song* (Vital Ramos de Castro, 1932), the first sound documentary on this popular theme, and three songs in *A Voz do carnaval/The Voice of Carnival* (Adhemar Gonzaga and Humberto Mauro, 1933), which combined real footage of street carnival celebrations in Rio with a fictitious plot that provided endless pretexts for carnival musical numbers.

Carmen's next screen performance was in the musical *Alô, alô, Brasil!/Hello, Hello, Brazil!* (Wallace Downey, João de Barro and Alberto Ribeiro, 1935), and her proven star status in the world of popular music was reflected in the fact that she was chosen to provide the closing number of the film, the *marcha* (carnival march) 'Primavera no Rio' ('Springtime in Rio'), which she had recorded on the Victor record label in August 1934. By all accounts, in *Hello, Hello, Brazil!* Carmen stole the show with this performance and the head of the Cinédia studios, Adhemar Gonzaga, decided to make it the musical finale of the film, rather than a number by the leading male singer of the era, Francisco Alves, as had been planned. A few months after the release of *Hello, Hello, Brazil!*, *Cinearte* magazine (Anon. 1935: 10) stated: 'Carmen Miranda is currently the most popular figure in Brazilian cinema, judging by the sizeable correspondence that she receives.' In her next film, *Estudantes/Students* (Wallace Downey, 1935) Carmen was given a narrative role for the first time. In this so-called 'middle-of-the-year' production, released to coincide with Brazil's *festas juninas* ('June festivals'), popular Catholic celebrations with their own musical traditions, Carmen played Mimi, a young radio singer (who performs two numbers in the film), who falls in love with a university student played by the well-known singer Mário Reis.

Carmen was central to the success of the next co-production from the Waldow and Cinédia studios, the carnival musical *Hello, Hello, Carnival!*, which featured a roll call of star performers from the world of popular music and the radio, including Carmen's sister, Aurora. The backstage plot provided the pretext for the inclusion of 23 musical numbers, and by the Brazilian standards of the day *Hello, Hello, Carnival!* was a major production. The set reproduced the interior of Rio's plush Atlântico casino, where some of the scenes were shot, and the backdrops for certain musical numbers, including Carmen and

Aurora's rendition of 'Cantoras do rádio' ('Radio Singers', Alberto Ribeiro / João de Barro / Lamartine Babo, 1935), were art deco designs by the acclaimed illustrator J Carlos. In this musical number, their performance, costumes and the Hollywood-inspired modernist set conspire to create one of the high points of the film, as the two sisters strut 'grandly across a gleaming, tiered stage in silver, sequined tuxedos and top hats' (McCann 2004: 145). Carmen clearly played a pivotal role in attracting mass audiences, as is evidenced by a poster advertising the film which includes just one image, a full-length photograph of her, wearing the high-fashion outfit she wears to perform the *marcha* 'Querido Adão' ('Dear Adam', Benedicto Lacerda, Oswaldo Santiago, 1935), and seemingly supporting a large placard listing the cast members, with her name at the top. It is equally revealing of her star status that the few close-up shots used in *Hello, Hello, Carnival!* are of Carmen. Although in the original 1936 version of the film Francisco Alves provided the musical finale, it was Carmen and Aurora's memorable performance of 'Cantoras do rádio' which won over audiences. When a restored copy of the film was released in 1974, it was precisely their musical number which was chosen to close the film, in recognition of Carmen's enduring star appeal and international fame, as well as the inherent entertainment value of the performance. In the newly restored 2001 version, the Miranda sisters performing 'Cantoras do rádio' continues to provide the film's finale.

Carmen's final Brazilian film was another carnival musical, *Banana of the Land*, in which she performed just two musical numbers but tellingly it is her name and photograph that took centre stage in the production's publicity material. Once again the film's comic plot was essentially a construct to string together the various musical numbers. The story begins on the fictitious Pacific island of Bananolândia, which is faced with the problem of a surplus of bananas. The island's prime minister (played by comic actor Oscarito) suggests that the queen of Bananolândia (played by the singer Dircinha Batista) go to Brazil to sell the surplus, and she promptly arrives in the Brazilian capital in the midst of its legendary carnival celebrations. The action then centres on the cosmopolitan setting of Rio's casinos and radio stations, facilitating the inclusion of a range of musical performances.

It was intended that the two musical high points of the film were to be Carmen's performance of 'Boneca de piche' ('Tar doll' by Ari Barroso and Luiz Iglesias, 1939) in duet with the radio presenter Almirante, and her solo performance of 'Na Baixa do Sapateiro' (the name of a street in the city centre of Salvador, Bahia), also composed by Ari Barroso, 1939. At the eleventh hour, however, Barroso demanded more money for the use of his compositions, it proved impossible to reach an agreement and the songs were pulled from the film, even though the two respective sets had been created, and the costumes and make-up planned. In keeping with the lyrics of 'Tar Doll', Carmen was to adopt the persona of an Afro-Brazilian woman, with both her and Almirante appearing in blackface on the set of a stylized colonial slave quarters. For the performance of 'Na Baixa do Sapateiro' the set was a stylized recreation of the street in Salvador, complete with mock colonial-style facades, palm trees and a large moon. To save both time and money, Wallace Downey, the film's producer, decided simply to use the existing sets and costumes for the performance of two new songs, the *marcha* 'Pirulito' ('Pat-a-cake' by Braguinha and Alberto Ribeiro, the film's scriptwriters) and 'O que é que a baiana tem?' ('What does the *baiana* have?' by little-known Bahian composer, Dorival Caymmi). The only footage from the film that has survived to this day is the sequence in which Carmen performs Caymmi's song, and five still photographs exist of her duet with Almirante of the song 'Pirulito' (João de Barro and Alberto Ribeiro), in which she appears in blackface make-up, as the conventions for the performance of the song 'Tar Doll' dictated.

In keeping with the song's lyrics, Carmen performs 'O que é que a baiana tem?' wearing the costume of the *baiana*, a term which literally means a woman from the north-eastern state of Bahia but more specifically refers to Afro-Brazilian women who since colonial times have sold food on the streets of Salvador in Bahia and Rio de Janeiro, and to the priestesses of the Afro-Brazilian religion, *Candomblé*. Carmen, who had worked as an apprentice milliner and was a skilled dressmaker, stylized the costume herself, adding sequins and a small imitation basket of fruit to her turban, in a playful nod to the baskets of produce that the *baiana* street vendors carried on their heads. This stylized version of the *baiana* costume, with a shortened blouse that exposed her midriff, a figure-hugging, bias-cut, full-length skirt (eschewing the traditional *baiana*'s more respectable white lace blouse and hooped underskirts), and most memorably an elaborately decorated turban, was to become Carmen's iconic trademark for international audiences. The costumes created for her first Hollywood roles, like those she wore on Broadway and in nightclub acts in the United States, would incorporate the same key elements.

Lisa Shaw

References
Bentes, E.M. (1935) *Cinearte*, 15 January 1935, p.11.
McCann, B (2004) *Hello, Hello Brazil: Popular Music in the Making of Modern Brazil*, Durham and London: Duke University Press.

Notes
1. Carmen actually appeared in seven sound films in Brazil if we include the re-use of one of her musical numbers from *Banana da Terra/Banana of the Land* (João de Barro, 1938) in the film *Laranja da China/Orange from China* (Ruy Costa, 1940), a shrewd move by the Sonofilmes studios to be able to use her name in publicity for the latter film. It is also thought that she appeared as an extra in one or possibly two silent films.

FILM-MAKERS
GLAUBER ROCHA

I do not believe in men who wear ties, men committed to the dominant structures. Every day I move more to the left, and the example of my Cuban friends and now the death of the dictator Trujillo, the rebellion in Angola and emancipation across the whole of Africa show that the new countries will be the leaders of the world in a few years: from Brazil, Argentina and Cuba and other Latin countries, fantastic films will emerge. I am already allied with the Cubans, we are very much articulated. They are building an industry there. If we are linked with the Argentineans, we can have an ambitious movement, a South American movement, a powerful and independent movement capable of destroying this damn GEICINES and the stupid slugs who make up our cinematic heritage. It is necessary to 'nationalise' the business and turn the problem into 'reality'. The people must think about our problems. The film-maker has a responsibility which goes beyond what they believe it to be. We need to work hard, including in Brazil. Our group has to be a true motor. We cannot stop making films, discussing and writing.

Rocha, cited in Bentes (1997: 157)

Dated 13 June 1961, Glauber Rocha's letter to the film-makers Gustavo Dahl, Paulo César Saraceni and Joaquim Pedro de Andrade described the strategies that became the foundation of *Cinema Novo* and *Nuevo Cine Latinoamericano*. As a 'new' film-maker, his longing for rupture from the industry of the 1940s and 1950s (represented in Brazil by production companies such as Atlântida – founded in Rio de Janeiro in 1941 and ultimately known for the *chanchada* genre – and Vera Cruz, founded by the Paulista industrial bourgeoisie) was due primarily to the fact that it foregrounded the processes of modernization and urbanization, dismissing the country's rural roots which were valued as authentic by the new crop of film-makers. These film-makers would now conduct a search into history for these roots, which represented the authentic culture of the people. They aimed to construct a modern, decolonized, anti-imperialist and non-alienated nation, populated by a 'new' kind of man.

Glauber Rocha's discourse of rupture did not only belong to the 1960s. In the 1970s he reaffirmed his principles after filming *Barravento/The Turning Wind* (1962), *Deus e o Diabo na terra do sol/Black God, White Devil* (1964), *Terra em transe/Enchanted Earth* (1967) and *Antonio das Mortes/O Dragão da maldade contra o santo guerreiro* (1969), following the *coup d'état* in Brazil, the dismantling of important cultural and artistic movements, as well as the disillusionment of film-makers who had been politically engaged after the disappointment of the revolutionary project. His interview with the newspaper *Última Hora*, dated 27 February 1970, is a good example of the reaffirmation of his ideas:

> Let me get it straight for the last time: decolonised films are ones that refuse to copy the American model and that attempt to re-make national cinema on the basis of our *true cultural roots* [...]. Given that the majority of film criticism is colonised, the public receives false information about Brazilian cinema. The things I denounced in 1960 are still, incredibly, reproduced today. The difference is that since 1960, *Cinema Novo* has emerged, fighting all forms of colonisation and responding to two challenges: to produce de-colonised films and launch the bases of national production and distribution. (Glauber Rocha's interview for *Última Hora*, 1970)

The interpretations of Brazilian and Latin American critics and scholars suggest that Glauber Rocha's preoccupation with themes like underdevelopment, nation or national self-discovery could be related to his own trajectory, as his origins are in 'the depths of Brazil'. Given his development, it would be important to highlight some aspects that make sense of interpretations which associate author and oeuvre. Born in Vitória da Conquista, in the interior of the state of Bahia, in the year 1939, Glauber Rocha began an interest in film from a young age, as a critic on a radio programme in the city of Salvador, where he lived between 1948 and 1962. In a sign of the importance of literature, philosophy and the arts in his formation, the film-maker got involved with theatre and poetry groups, taking part in Cepa (Círculo de Estudos Pensamento e Ação), which gave him a solid intellectual base. Like the many other middle-class youngsters of his generation, Glauber Rocha studied law. In the 1950s, he took part in Clube de Cinema, a cineclub in Salvador, which awakened his critical side, later to be developed in newspapers that he worked for in Bahia (*Diário de Notícias*, *Estado da Bahia*, *Jornal da Bahia* and *Jornal do Brasil*).[1] During this period, the young critic and film-maker got involved with key personalities on the Brazilian cultural scene, testifying to his insertion in the national artistic field. From then onwards in his career, he worked on artistic projects together with friends, producers and film cooperatives such as Difilm[2] and Mapa Filmes. Founded in 1965, this latter group was named after a cultural magazine organized by Glauber Rocha in Bahia, which was a significant arena of debate on new cultural and filmic currents of the time. His education, activities and influences made the connection between intellectuals and artists visible, a cooperation which was characteristic of his time and which aimed at social transformation.

In 1965, after making documentaries and short films such as *Pátio* (1959), *A cruz na praça* (1959) and *Amazonas Amazonas* (1965), he wrote the manifesto 'An Aesthetic of Hunger', in which he states that

> the process of artistic creation in the underdeveloped world is of interest only insofar as it satisfies a nostalgia of primitivism. This primitivism is generally presented as a hybrid form, disguised under the belated heritage of the 'civilised world', a heritage poorly understood since it is imposed by colonial conditioning. (Rocha, cited in Johnson and Stam [1965] (1995:69)

Two years after the writing of the document, the film-maker got involved in a project named 'tricontinental cinema', inspired by the Tricontinental Conference in Havana

(1967), which had repercussions in the field of Latin American political cinema. After seven years in Rio de Janeiro (1962–69), Glauber Rocha went into foreign exile, and, in November 1971,[3] after making the feature film *Cabezas cortadas/Cutting Heads* (1970), he left for Cuba, where he was to live little more than a year, for the duration of his production of the documentary *História do Brasil* (1974). It is also in Cuba that he attempted to produce the film 'América nuestra' ['Our America'], which was to remain unfinished. The mention of this unfinished project is important in regard to the mobilization of the film-maker in representing the historic-continental process. The echo of such mobilization can be heard in a letter dated 3 November 1967 to Alfredo Guevara, the then director of the Instituto Cubano del Arte e Indústria Cinematográficos (ICAIC):

> I hope that you understood why I do not take the risk of going to Cuba now unless you want to involve me in getting a Cuban passport or another identity. I need to have the maximum mobility to make my next film both in Brazil and Peru, and perhaps in Bolivia. I will apply all my resources and take any risk to make *America nuestra*. Finally I have already achieved the ideal phase of the script, with only the final amendments remaining. I have decided to dedicate the film openly to the memory of Che. The film will be a *Practical History of Revolutionary Ideology in Latin America*. It will start as a documentary about the Indians and the historical decadence imposed by 'civilisation', it will explain the phenomena of Bolívar's revolution, the contradictions of the Mexican revolution, the phenomenon of imperialism and of dictatorship, the true Cuban revolution and the current contradictions surrounding the rise and victory of the guerrillas. All aspects of the struggle including American technology, the evolution of the Church, the conflict between romanticism, courage, propaganda, traditional communist strategy, all these subjects are approached in the film. After I make this film, I will definitely be legally outcast in Brazil, because I will make a radical and violent film that openly preaches (and justifies) the creation of many Vietnams. (Rocha, cited in Bentes 1997: 157)

During his iconoclastic trajectory, his preoccupation with the emergence of an authentic Brazilian and Latin American art which would break away from cultural colonization is explicit, and seen as a way to educate and make people aware of their conditions. Largely understood as the product of an auteur, Glauber Rocha's oeuvre is informed by idiosyncratic characteristics, his own personal development and his cinematic techniques. Central to this understanding are the subjective nature of the artistic construction and the presence of an auteurist 'I' as the filmic narrator. Glauber Rocha could thus be defined as an auteur since his characters emerge from real stories (some of which he experienced himself), composing a circuit which leads from and back into Rocha himself, and which is defined through the idea of 'Heustória'.[4] In inserting the term 'eu' (translated as 'I') in the middle of the Portuguese word for 'history', Glauber Rocha seems to de-construct and re-signify his senses, incorporating within himself, or in an opposite movement, incorporating himself into the history of both humanity and cinema.

Eliska Altmann (trans. Natália Pinazza)

References
Bentes, I (ed) (1997) *Cartas ao mundo*, São Paulo: Companhia das Letras.
Gatti, A (2000) 'Difilm', in RAMOS, F Ramos and LF Miranda (eds), *Enciclopédia do Cinema Brasileiro*, São Paulo: Editora SENAC, pp. 171–72.
Johnson, R and Stam, R (eds) (1995) *Brazilian Cinema*, New York: Columbia University Press.

Rocha, G (1963) *Revisão Crítica do Cinema Brasileiro*, Rio de Janeiro: Ed. Civilização Brasileira.
— — (1965) 'A Estética da Fome', in *Revista Civilização Brasileira*, 1: 3.
— — (1978) *Riverão Sussuarana*, Rio de Janeiro: Ed. Record.
— — (1981) *Revolução do Cinema Novo*, Rio de Janeiro: Alhambra/Embrafilme.
— — (1983) *O século do cinema*, Rio de Janeiro: Alhambra/Embrafilme.
— — (2003) *Revisão crítica do cinema brasileiro*, São Paulo: Cosac & Naif.
— — (2004) *Revolução do Cinema Novo*, São Paulo: Cosac & Naif.
— — [1965] (1995) 'An Aesthetic of Hunger' (trans. R Johnson and B Hollyman), in R Johnson and R Stam (eds), *Brazilian Cinema*, New York: Columbia University Press, pp. 68–71
— — (1970) 'Contra direitas e esquerdas o nosso cinema segue em frente', *Última Hora*, 27 February.

Notes

1. The film-maker also wrote for *Pasquim*, *Correio Brasiliense* and *Folha de São Paulo*. As well as this he has written the following books: *Revisão Crítica do Cinema Brasileiro* (1963); *Revolução do Cinema Novo* (1981); *O Século do Cinema* (1983); and the novel *Riverão Sussuarana* (1978).

2. According to André Gatti (2000: 171–72), Difilm was a result of the difficulty faced by Brazilian film-makers in making their films commercially successful, as channels for distribution were rare at the time. In its first phase (1965–69), Difilm had eleven members, amongst them Glauber Rocha, Paulo César Saraceni, Joaquim Pedro de Andrade, Walter Lima Júnior, Cacá Diegues, Leon Hirzman and Luís Carlos Barreto – all of them in some way associated with *Cinema Novo*.

3. In the year of 1971, Glauber Rocha also released the film *Der Leone Have Sept Cabeças*, and wrote the manifesto 'Aesthetic of Dreams', which includes statements such as 'the revolutionary art was the word of order in the Third World in the 1960s and it will continue to be in this decade. I think, however, that many changes in the political and mental conditions demand a continuing development of the concept of revolutionary art [...]. The discontinued existence of this revolutionary art in Year Three is due fundamentally to the repression of rationalism [...]. Rupture with colonising rationalism is the only way out'. The following year, 1972, Rocha released the experimental film *Câncer*, filmed four years before and composed of 27 long takes and actors improvising situations characterized by the theme of violence. 'Psychological, sexual, racial violence exist at an improvisational level' as the director put it. Three years after, in 1975, Glauber Rocha made *Claro*, filmed in Rome over two weeks, which contains stylistic traits which result from the film-maker's intervention. Such traits recurred in two documentaries made in 1977, *Di/Glauber* and *Jorjamado no Cinema*, and a television programme named *Abertura* (broadcast between February and October 1979).

4. As explained by Glauber Rocha in the *Revolução do Cinema Novo* written in 1980, (the year that *A Idade da terra/The Age of the Earth*, his last feature film, was launched) and published in the year of his death in 1981: 'I deal with the cinema movement in the 1960s that saved Brazilian ('brazyleyro' as he writes it) cinema from economic and cultural misery. It is the 'Heuztorya' of a generation of intellectuals (my generation) lacerated by the cruel national process.' In *O Século do Cinema*, published after the death of the film-maker, the expression is used in the following ways: 'Heuztória', 'Heustórya', 'Heuztorya', 'Heuztóryka'. In the last years of his life, the film-maker adopted a new linguistic format that incorporated letters rarely used in Portuguese such as y, k and z.

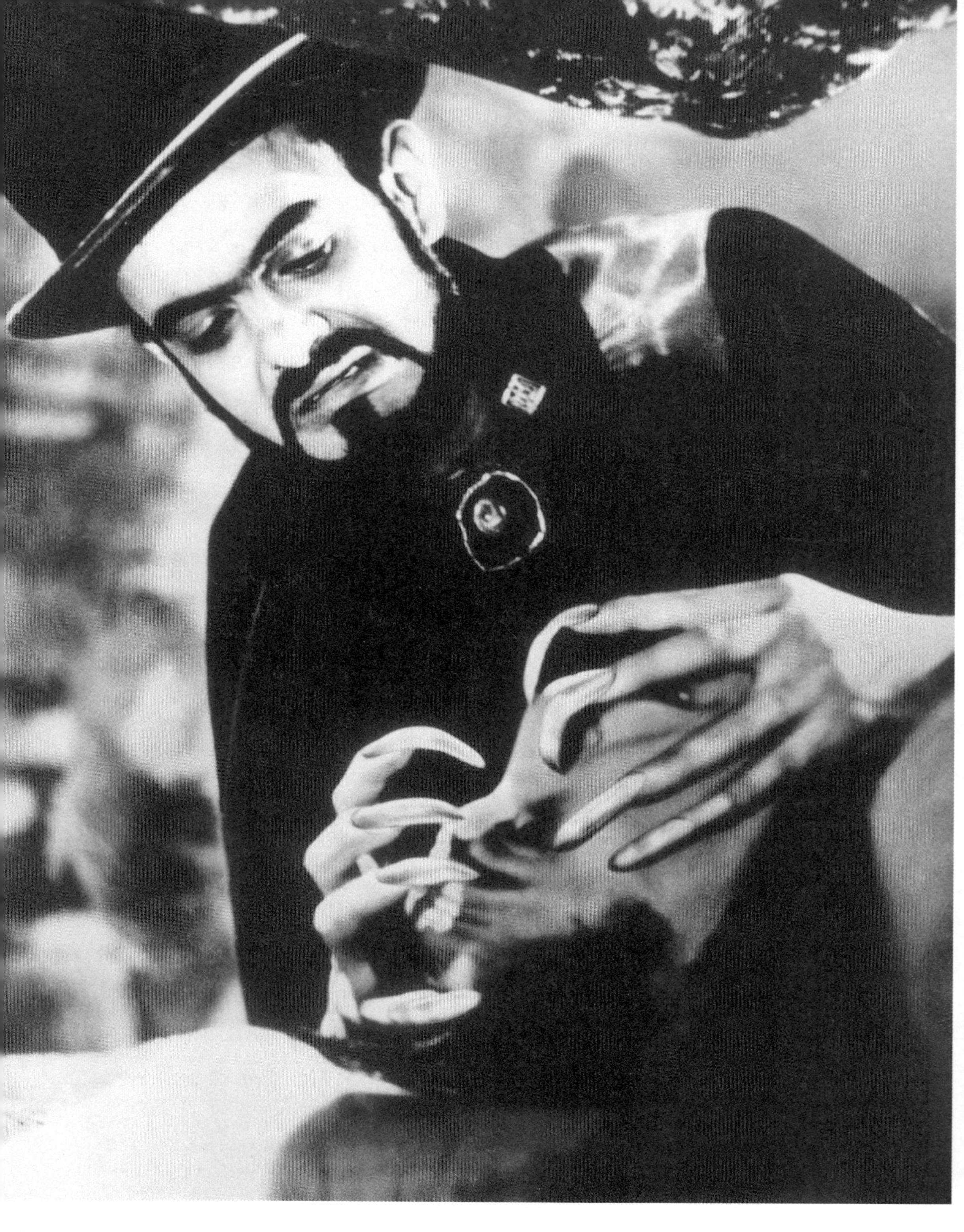

At Midnight I'll Take Your Soul

JOSÉ MOJICA MARINS
A SOUTH AMERICAN AUTEUR

José Mojica Marins is a film-maker surrounded by contradictions. He is the founder of Brazilian horror cinema: a low-budget, low-brow auteur whose work subtly reflects the society in which it was made. Furthermore, 'Zé do Caixão', or 'Coffin Joe', the alter ego from which Marins is at times indistinguishable, is an icon of Brazilian popular culture and, as such, a figure worthy of serious study. And yet Marins is also a creator of exploitative pornography whose work is often discounted as beneath consideration. As Larry Rohter (2011) wrote in the *New York Times*:

> Some admirers see Mr. Mojica, who has directed, written or acted in more than 50 movies, as a kind of South American Roger Corman […]. Others view his work as pure camp – more in the tradition of *Ed Wood* and *Plan 9 From Outer Space* than Luis Buñuel or John Waters – or simply trash.

It is unfair, though, to consider Marins's lesser work as a true indication of his talent or importance. Though films like *O Filho do sexo explicito*/*24 Hours of Explicit Sex* (1985) and *A Estranha hospederia dos prazeres*/*The Strange Hostel of Naked Pleasures* (co-directed with Marcaelo Motto, 1975) are generally without merit, their production was greatly affected by government censorship and the financial hardship it imposed on him. Meanwhile, Marins's best work – the horror films that showcase Coffin Joe, the irreligious undertaker obsessed with conceiving a perfect heir who has become a Brazilian equivalent of Freddy Krueger or Michael Myers – display both a distinctive authorial voice and a comprehensive understanding of the evolution of horror cinema.

À Meia-noite levarei sua alma/*At Midnight I'll Take Your Soul* (1964) and *Esta Noite encarnarei no teu cadáver*/*Tonight I Will Possess Your Corpse* (1967), the first two entries in the Coffin Joe trilogy, recreate the look, and often even the silence, of the horror masterpieces of German Expressionism, as well as the style and sudden shocks of classic American monster movies of the 1930s. What is more, Marins frequently demonstrates an ability to predict future trends in horror films. Coffin Joe's invasion of his victims' dreams, for example, predicts the *A Nightmare on Elm Street* films (Wes Craven et al., 1984–2010), while the sadistic tests he sets prospective mates in *Tonight* and the horrendous 'love or survival' experiment to which a married couple is subjected in *O Estranho mundo de zé do caixão/The Strange World of Coffin Joe* (1968), foreshadow the *Saw* series (James Wan et al., 2004–10). The pseudo-documentary format employed in *O Ritual dos sádico/Awakening of the Beast* (1970) also predates the similar style used in films such as *The Legend of Boggy Creek* (Charles B Pierce, 1972), *The Last Broadcast* (Stefan Avalos and Lance Weiler, 1998) and *The Blair Witch Project* (Daniel Myrick and Eduardo Sanchez, 1999).

Marins seems particularly able to presage important trends in global horror. The general unavailability of his films in the English-speaking world prior to the 1990s makes it unlikely that they had an influence on American films made before, or soon after, them. Nevertheless, in the high points of Marins's oeuvre, we are able to see the past and future of horror films filtered through the abilities and philosophies of a unique, and uniquely Brazilian, film-maker.

And he was at the forefront of a uniquely Brazilian movement: 'Cine da Boca do Lixo' or 'Mouth of Garbage film', centred in São Paulo's Boca do Lixo, or 'Garbage Mouth', area. Although often discussed as a genre, Mouth of Garbage films have diverse subjects and stories. What unites them is, firstly, the location in which they were made; secondly, their exploitative sensibility; and, thirdly, key recurrent features, including cannibalism, explicit sex and shocking violence. 'Cannibalism, Explicit Sex and Shocking Violence' would be an apt title for a Marins retrospective.

Though Marins's work is rarely, if ever, overtly political, *At Midnight* and *Tonight* were enlivened by sub-textual attacks on injustice and his constant depictions of torture at a time when the practice was rampant but unacknowledged in the nation. This, coupled with the controversial themes and explicit images of violence that characterize Marins's work, brought the close attention, and disapproval, of government censors. At first, this hampered but did not derail his films, as when he was required to add an ill-fitting ending to *Tonight*, in which the atheistic Coffin Joe is forced to ask God for salvation at the moment of his death. But Marins's work soon became more violent, and the censors' tolerance of him decreased, culminating in the outright banning of 1970's *Awakening of the Beast*, which dealt specifically with Brazil's drug problem and more generally with themes of sexual violence.

An infamously incompetent businessman, Marins's great fame has never brought him great wealth, and his method of investing the profits of his previous film in the making of his next meant that, after the banning of *Awakening*, he was no longer able to work in the way he had previously. This began the process that forced Marins to work as a film-maker for hire during the 1970s and 1980s, helming projects, often in the popular *pornochanchada* genre (cheaply made films that combined pornography with comedy), that reflected few of his favourite themes and displayed few of his more noteworthy talents.

Beginning in the 1990s, Marins's horror films at last found an audience in English-speaking countries and, by the mid 2000s, international interest was such that he could secure funding to make *Encarnação do demônio/Embodiment of Evil* (2008) and conclude the Coffin Joe trilogy he had begun in 1964. The most fascinating feature of *Embodiment* is that it does not provide a conclusion to the trilogy which is in keeping with the look and tone of the first two films, but keeps pace instead with the evolution of horror films that had occurred since they were first released. The film's extended sequences of convoluted torture recall those that characterize the 'torture porn' films such as *Hostel* (Eli Roth, 2005) that have become prominent in American cinema since the turn of the century and seem, at times, to exist purely to set new standards of excess.

It is this desire to perpetually push boundaries of taste that marks Marins, even in the 1970s, as a film-maker of unusual potency. Just as Coffin Joe positions himself as a character apart from and above society through his aggressive disrespect for religion, superstition and common morality, so Marins, with his talent for creating images that are at once profane, beautiful and sickening, is a film-maker apart from the mainstream and above the average director of exploitation cinema. Whenever a fan, or student, of film is introduced to Brazilian cinema, he or she should be introduced to the work of José Mojica Marins.

Scott Jordan Harris

References

Barzinski, A and Finotti, I (2001) *Maldito – o estranho mundo de José Mojica Marins/ Damned: The Strange World of Jose Mojica Marins.*

Rohter, L (2001) 'A Cult Figure Conjures the Macabre', *New York Times*, 19 October, http://www.nytimes.com/2011/10/23/movies/jose-mojica-marins-brazilian-film-maker-conjures-macabre.html?_r=1., accessed 27/11/2011.

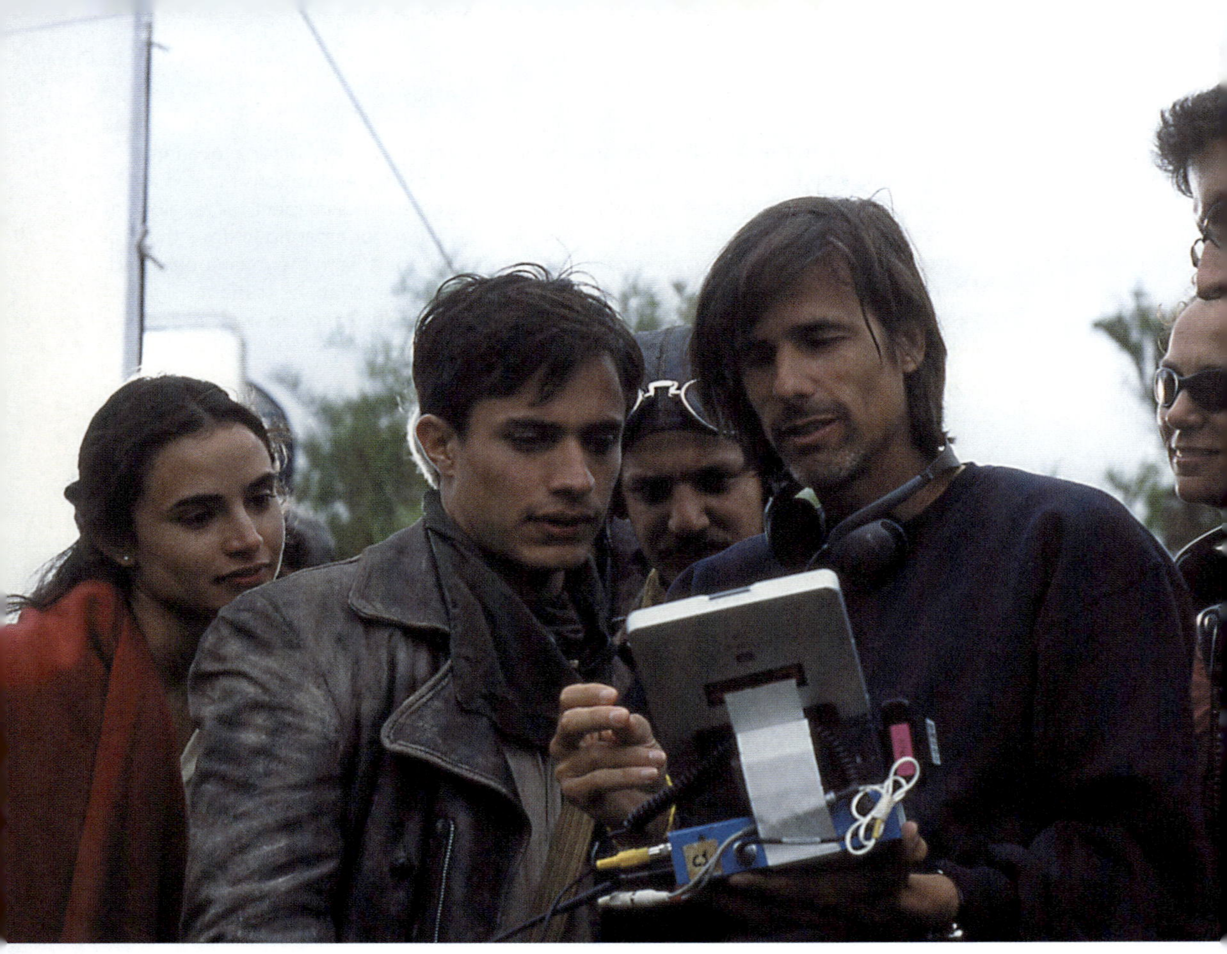

WALTER SALLES

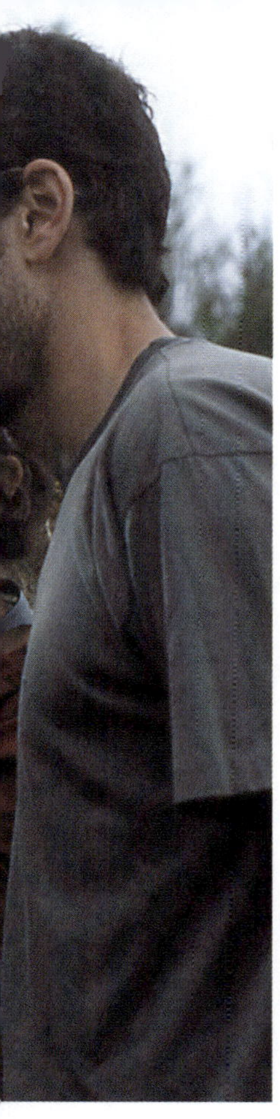

Motorcycle Diaries

Walter Salles is one of a select group of transnational Latin American directors, including Alfonso Cuarón, Guillermo del Toro, Alejandro González Iñárritu and Fernando Meirelles. Like them, he has made films in and secured funding from a range of national and production contexts, and has made critically acclaimed and commercially successful films that address serious social issues. Salles is also a key figure in Brazilian film culture and in 1987 he founded the production company VideoFilmes with his brother João Moreira Salles. VideoFilmes has co-produced important Brazilian films including *Madame Satã/Madame Satan* (Karim Aïnouz, 2002), *Cidade de Deus/ City of God* (Fernando Meirelles and Kátia Lund, 2002) as well as some important documentaries: Nelson Pereira dos Santos's *Casa grande e senzala/The Masters and the Slaves* (2000) and Eduardo Coutinho, *Babilônia 2000* (1999). In addition, the company has co-produced some of the director's own feature films including *Terra Estrangeira/ Foreign Land* (1996), *O Primeiro dia/Midnight* (1998), both co-directed with Daniela Thomas; *Abril despedaçado/Behind the Sun* (2001) and *Linha de passe/Line of Passage* (2008, also co-directed with Thomas).[1]

Despite this prominent position in Brazilian film culture, Salles's global success is also due to the fact that he has looked to other global centres of film production for funding, and made films that have secured wide international release: *Central Station/Central do Brasil* (1998), *Abril despedaçado*, *Los Diarios de motocicleta/The Motorcycle Diaries* (2004), and *Line of Passage*. To this corpus of Portuguese and Spanish language films can be added his first English language Hollywood horror film *Dark Water* (2005), a critically acclaimed remake of Hideo Nakata's Japanese film *Honogurai mizu no soko kara* (2002).

His first international success was *Central Station* which secured its funding on the strength of the screenplay with the story conceived by Salles and written by João Carneiro and Marcos Bernstein, and can be seen as a key film in raising the global profile of Brazilian cinema. The resulting film, shot by his long-term collaborator Walter Carvalho, is a heart warming tale of a young boy Josué (Vinícius De Oliveira) who following the death of his mother and left alone in Rio de Janeiro's main railway station, seeks help from a hardened letter writer who works in the station, Dora (Fernanda Montenegro). The film takes the form of a road movie as Dora eventually softens and accompanies Josué on the journey across the Brazilian *sertão* (backlands) to the north-eastern town of Bom Jesus do Norte, Pernambuco in search of his family. The screenplay won the Sundance Institute International Award and the small prize money was less significant than the exposure the award afforded the project and the international finance which came on board as a result, with Sony Pictures Classic behind the distribution in the United States. The film's producers included the high-profile Swiss Arthur Cohn and Sundance creator Robert Redford.

The Hollywood star was also the driving force behind Salles's best known Latin American and Spanish language film *The Motorcycle Diaries* and its executive producer. As Claire Williams notes (2007: 11), Redford approached Salles to direct the film of the travels of the young Ernesto Guevara through South America in the early 1950s.

This film, based on two sets of travel diaries, those of Guevara, and his travelling companion Alberto Granado, illuminates a number of the central characteristics of the director. As necessitated by the subject, it takes the form of a road movie. Salles favours this format, also used in *Central Station* and *Foreign Land*, and *On the Road* (2012), based on the novel by Jack Kerouac.[2] The format is ideal for the incorporation of documentary techniques; the combination of non-actors with professional actors; the focus on social issues and the plight of marginalized groups; and cinematography which draws its power from the beauty of the landscape, all elements common to Salles's directorial approach throughout much of his corpus.

These characteristics are also seen in *The Motorcycle Diaries* in which viewers travel with Ernesto and Alberto to actual locations across Latin America, visit a leper colony, and meet with locals in Argentina, Chile and Peru. In one scene, the two appear to be interviewing Quechua-speaking women, who describe the difficulties of their life (one of the women speaks Spanish and speaks for her friend). As the director has said in an interview, 'I constantly tried to incorporate what reality was offering us, mixing our actors with the locals we met in the small communities we came across' (Salles 2007). The power of the film comes through a combination of personal connection created with Ernesto and, to a lesser extent, Alberto, and the sense of virtual travel audiences are given as they experience the injustices and beauty of South America through the young protagonists' eyes.

Salles started his career in the media as a director of documentaries and advertisements, and these early career choices help illuminate his unique identity and success as a film-maker. Salles is a director who can tell the stories of the marginalized and the poor to audiences through a focus on protagonists that we care about. Politics, while featuring in all of his films, never stand in the way of the story or the emotional appeal of the characters. He is a transnational director who has worked with cast, crew and production companies from Latin America, Europe and the United States, and is an important Brazilian and global film-maker.

Deborah Shaw

References

Salles, W (2007) 'Notes for a Theory of the Road Movie', 11 November, http://www.
nytimes.com/2007/11/11/magazine/11roadtrip-t.html. Accessed 10 February 2012.
Williams, C (2007) '*Los diarios de motocicleta* as Pan-American Travelogue', in Shaw
D (ed.), *Contemporary Latin American Cinema: Breaking into the Global Market*,
Lanham, MD: Rowman and Littlefield, pp. 11–28.
Xavier, I (2003) 'Brazilian Cinema in the 1990s: The Unexpected Encounter and the
Resentful Character', in Nagib, L (ed.), *The New Brazilian Cinema*, London: I.B.
Tauris, pp. 39–64.

Notes

1. For a dicussion of Brazilian films in the 1990s and Salles's Brazilian films of this period see Xavier (2003).
2. Salles has written an article on the road movie and his approach to it in 'Notes for a Theory of the Road Movie' in the *New York Times* (Salles 2007).

CULTURAL CROSSOVER
CINEMA DE BORDAS IN BRAZIL

The term *Cinema de Bordas*[1] (literally translated as Border Cinema) is used to conceptualize a type of film-making, production and distribution that occupies the periphery of the traditional film history of Brazil. Although a marginalized and excluded cinema, *Cinema de Bordas* is distributed nationally to a specific audience which finds a representation of its habitat, its regional space, and its imaginary within the entertaining narratives of these films.

In between popular and mediatic culture, some *Cinema de Bordas* films display a transgressive intent while others do not, but they all aim to be both funny and engaging. In general, all of them present specific features. The films are made with basic technology, display unsophisticated techniques, and require very low budgets, as they have no principal aim beyond the telling of a story. They focus on fictional narratives in which the subject matter is often the stuff of legend, related to localized traditions, and far-removed from the requirements of documenting reality.

Although they are made in a primarily marginalized and peripheral context, the *Cinema de Bordas* is not part of a 'marginal cinema' or 'peripheral cinema' according to the precise meaning that these terms have acquired in Brazilian film history. These terms are used either to designate a movement of film-makers dedicated to an underground and poetic cinema or to label a body of films made by a person or group at the margins of the cinema industry. Whilst notions of 'marginal cinema' in Brazilian film history are often related to subversive and socially critical film-making, *Cinema de Bordas* films are fictions which aim only to entertain. One of the key characteristics of *Cinema de Bordas* is that it recalls pre-established generic categories. However, in *Cinema de Bordas*, genres are updated and re-combined by including low income groups from the provinces.

In this way, *Cinema de Bordas* films take advantage of situations, scenes, images and sounds that have been used in other films or forms of entertainment. For instance, some films recycle pre-existing images and sounds drawn from comic strips, pulp fictions and old sitcoms and there is a predominance of genres such as the western, police thriller, romantic comedy, pornography, science fiction and horror.

Cinema de Bordas displays two anomalies: (1) certain production peculiarities which are a transformation of traditional forms of genre film-making, making it a conjunction between genre and individual authorship; (2) a fragmented and random collection of images, sounds and narratives. In these films it is as if the genres that characterized the Saturday matinee of the pre-television era such as the western, thriller, comedy and horror had been remixed and reprocessed. Another typical characteristic of *Cinema de Bordas* is that creative solutions to the adversities arising from the precariousness of their production give the films an air of being 'impure', 'mixed' and 'crude', depending on the intention of each film-maker. In this way, some films present an instinctive nature and amateurism while others employ a more refined technique and are more cinematically polished.

The field of *Cinema de Bordas* is heterogeneous, characterized by hybridity and variation in films made in artisanal and independent modes of production. The film-makers are often self-taught and live in small towns or the outskirts of the big cities, and use self-funding to get round the problem of a lack of subsidy and resources provided by outside sources. The *Bordas* film-makers share a sense of cinephilia, and have a predilection for old-fashioned matinees and countryside film showings. These film-makers not only direct, write, and star in their own movies, they are also in charge of the casting, which includes family members, friends and acquaintances. They use cheap cameras, non-professional actors, unsophisticated or natural settings, and they film with different camera support systems. They promote the circulation and exhibition of films in a home-made way and in improvised cinema sessions, festivals and screenings. They also see the internet as a way to get round a lack of exhibition space.

As a whole, it is possible to identify three interlocking axes for the *Cinema de Bordas*. The first one consists of film-makers who in the late 1970s had access to VHS, portable, light and cheap cameras, an innovation that facilitated film-making. In this axis, many self-taught film-makers who had extremely scarce resources made films that were of poor quality but contained a great sense of humour and freedom. What you see in numerous films is a mix of different genres such as westerns, musicals, comedies, melodramas, martial arts, jungle adventures and horror films. In general, there is an appropriation of the soundtrack of other films. This is the case with *O Galo da Madrugada* (1998) made by Sandra Ribeiro from Pernambuco, and with Manoel Loreno (Seu Manoelzinho), a former caretaker for a cinema theatre and builder from Mantenópolis in Espírito Santo, who has made more than twenty films in his small town including *A Vingança de Loreno* (1989), *O Espantalho assassino* (1988), *O Rico pobre* (2002), *O Homem sem lei* (2003), *Amor proibido* (2004), *A Gripe do frango* (2007); Simião Martiniano, a street vendor from Recife, Pernambuco, who has made films including *Traição no sertão* (1979), *O Herói trancado* (1988–89), *A Rede maldita* (1991), *O Vagabundo faixa preta* (1992), *A Valize foi trocada* (2007) and *Show variado* (2008); Francisco Caldas de Abreu Júnior, a land labourer from Pedralva, Minas Gerais, who makes supernatural films including *A dama da lagoa* (1997) and *O farol* (2007); many films produced in the neighbourhood of São Jorge, Manaus in Amazonas featuring the sawmill worker Aldenir Coti, the Amazonian 'Rambo' who adapts Sylvester Stallone's roles in *Rambú III: o rapto do jaraqui dourado* (2007), *Rambú IV: o clone* (2008) and *Roqui, o boxeador da Amazônia* (2010).

The second axis of *Cinema de Bordas* is situated in the context of the golden age of fanzines. This generation of film-makers took not only an anarchic and independent spirit from these publications, which were characteristic of the underground scene in the 1980s, but also the habit of circulating information with others who were interested in subjects like science fiction, pornography, sex and rock and roll. At the same time there was a strong influence from splatter films, and their grim mood, scornful horror and excess of blood. Key film-makers are Gurcius Gewdner from Santa Catarina, director of *O Triunvirato* (2004), *Mamilos em chamas* (2008) and *Viatti arrabbiatti* (2012); Petter Baiestorf, also from Santa Catarina, who made films which were marked by violence, blood and naked women, including *Criaturas hediondas* (1993), *Sacanagens bestiais dos arcanjos fálicos* (1998), *Raiva* (2001), *O monstro legume do espaço* (2006), *Vadias do sexo sangrento* (2008), *Ninguém deve morrer* (2009) and *O doce avanço da faca* (2010); and Coffin Souza, author of *Quadrantes* (2004) and *A paixão dos mortos* (2011). In Rio de Janeiro, Luis Felipe Mano, also known as Pepa, was notable for his urban and suburban fictions such as *Coronel Cabelinho vs. Grajaú Soldiaz* (2002).

The third axis is that of film-makers who are in love with cinema, in particular the low-budget productions of the 1970s and 1980s, who thus employ many intertextual references and use the internet as a site of exhibition. This is the case for Joel Caetano from São Paulo, who made *Minha esposa é um zumbi* (2006), *O assassinato da mulher mental* (2008), *Gato* (2009) and *Estranha* (2010). Also from São Paulo comes Sandro Debiazzi, who made *O tormento de Mathias* (2011), and Gabriel Carneiro, *Morte e morte de Johnnny Zombie* (2011); Igor Alonso from Osasco, *Cyberdoom* (2009); Rubens

Mello from Guarulhos, *A história de Lia* (2010); and Pedro Daldegan from Santa Rita do Passa Quatro, *Vlad* (1989) and *Museu de cera* (1988). Felipe M Guerra comes from Carlos Barbosa, Rio Grande do Sul, and is the maker of films such as *Patrícia Gennice* (1998), *Entrei em pânico ao saber o que vocês fizeram na sexta-feira 13 do verão passado* (2001), *Canibais e solidão* (2007) and *Extrema unção* (2011), while Rodrigo Aragão is from Guarapari, Espírito Santo, and made *Mangue negro* (2008) and *A noite do Chupa Cabras* (2011).

The above sample gives just a few examples of the films that constitute *Cinema de Bordas*. It is impossible to deny the existence of *Cinema de Bordas* and its legitimate place within the current cinematic landscape of Brazil. The films are very successful in the countryside and the regions where they were made. However, they do not enter the national film distribution circuit or gain exhibition across theatres. Thus they are often projected in makeshift exhibition spaces, specific festivals, and in gatherings of friends and associates. Some, in particular those of the third axis, circulate on blogs or are posted online where they can be seen by a public of aficionados. The *Cinema de Bordas* does not focus on originality or novelty, but presents a minimum of information and a maximum of predictability with no other purpose than the audience's entertainment. Perhaps that is the reason for the alternative nature of a group of films which are great to watch.

Bernadette Lyra (trans. Natália Pinazza)

Note

1. The term *Cinema de Bordas* was coined by Bernadette Lyra. Further reading on *Cinema de Bordas* includes: Bernadette Lyra and Gelson Santana (eds) *Cinema de Bordas 1* (São Paulo: Editora A Lápis, 2006) and Gelson Santana (ed.) *Cinema de Bordas 2* (São Paulo: Editora A Lápis, 2009). The webiste of Itaú Cultural is another good source for *Cinema de Bordas*: http://www.itaucultural.org.br/.

THE RE-EMERGENCE OF BRAZILIAN CINEMA
A BRIEF HISTORY

The boom in film production in Brazil at the beginning of the 1990s is also known as the *retomada do cinema brasileiro*, which some critics refer to as the 'Brazilian cinematic renaissance' or 'rebirth of Brazilian cinema'. Nevertheless, the use of the terms 'retomada', 'rebirth' and 'renaissance' is problematic, for 'retomada' derives from the Portuguese verb 'retomar', literally translated into English as 'retake', which implies that Brazilian cinema production was 'retaken' after a period of stagnation. From this understanding, Pedro Butcher (2005) remarks that 'retomada' consists of a process of getting back to something that already has a history, a pre-existing cinema, and thus he argues that 'retomada' is different from 'renaissance' and 'rebirth', as it is not possible to retake something that is dead. In this regard, Luiz Zanin Orichhio (2003) contends that Brazilian cinema production was not 'dead' after the extinction of Embrafilme (The Brazilian Film Company), but almost 'zero'. According to Lucia Nagib (2006), the prevailing view is that Brazilian cinema in the 1990s had to start from 'zero', and this became a motif in some films of the period which represented the nation's quest for self-redefinition.

The administration of Fernando Collor de Mello, the first president democratically elected in 1990, did away with government support for Brazil's film industry. In particular it withdrew funding from Embrafilme, thereby plunging national cinema production into a profound crisis. In fact, the crisis in cinema reflected the general malaise affecting the whole nation in 1992. However, after Collor was impeached for corruption he was replaced by the then vice president, Itamar Franco, whose government implemented the Audiovisual Law (*Lei do Audiovisual*) in 1993, a move which proved to be a crucial factor in the growth of Brazilian cinema. Together with a number of resources coming from the Rouanet Law, which establishes public policies for national culture, the Audiovisual Law has subsidized nearly all Brazilian film production since 1995. Moreover, this law has made provision for tax write-offs for interested corporate investors and encouraged international film distribution companies to invest in national productions. Consequently, major American companies such as Columbia and Warner became involved with national production. Butcher (2005) also cites Riofilmes as one of the contributors to this cinematic revival, as it was the only distributor to work in film between 1992 and 1994, when the public and market rejection of national cinema was still high. The state has played a very important role in the revival of Brazilian cinema, by creating new strategic initiatives and programmes and making a larger proportion of income taxes available for cultural activities as well as refurbishing movie theatres throughout the country.

Since the reformulation of the cultural sponsorship laws, Brazilian film production has increased dramatically. For whilst fewer than twelve films were made in the early 1990s, 155 feature films and more than 100 documentaries were made between

1995 and 2000 (Moisés 2003: 11). The first sign of the national cinematic revival was Carla Camurati's *Carlota Joaquina: princesa do Brasil/Carlota Joaquina: Princess of Brazil* (1995), which attracted viewing figures of over one million. Furthermore, three Brazilian films were nominated for the Oscar for best foreign language film between 1996 and 1999: *O Quatrilho* (Fábio Barreto, 1995; nominated in 1996), *O que é isso, companheiro?/Four Days in September* (Bruno Barreto, 1997; nominated in 1998) and *Central do Brasil/Central Station* (Walter Salles, 1998; nominated in 1999).

Similarly to other Latin American cases, in particular to the Argentine one, the re-emergence of Brazilian cinema in the mid 1990s was due in large part to the appearance of a new generation of film-makers who moved away from the notions of national cinema entrenched by film-makers associated with the avant-garde movements of the 1960s. Perhaps this shift from earlier film-making aesthetics was a result of the experiences that the new crop of professionals had gained in other audiovisual media, for the crisis in national production in the early 1990s forced production companies to turn to different types of media, in particular through advertising. In this context, key figures of the Brazilian cinematic revival, including Fernando Meirelles, Walter Salles and Andrucha Waddington, all worked for important audiovisual production companies in Brazil: O_2, Videofilmes and Conspiração, respectively. Consequently, the films of debut film-makers were heavily influenced by the language of television, advertising and video clips. It is also the case that using a language influenced by the immediacy and viewing of television proved an effective way to attract Brazilian spectators to the cinema, and thus, expand the national cinema's share of the market. Aware of these factors, Globo, the most influential television network in Brazil, created a film subsidiary called Globo Filmes in order to invest in national production. Subsequently, this commercial model of film production often benefited from television merchandizing and featured famous television actors.

Despite the reformulation of the law and the consequent aforementioned changes, the Brazilian film industry still lacked a more systematic organization. As Gustavo Dahl (2006) points out, the tax deduction model privileged production over other equally important sectors of the film industry, including distribution and exhibition. In the light of this problem, the III Brazilian Cinema Congress was held in 2000, gathering film-makers and general representatives of film-making throughout the country with the aim of stressing the pressing need for a more effective film policy (Dahl 2006). It was in response to this call that Fernando Henrique Cardoso's government created the National Cinema Agency (ANCINE). Since its creation, ANCINE has played a key role in the development of a film industry in Brazil, by dealing with private investors and promoting contests that give debut film-makers and scriptwriters an opportunity to make films. Moreover, because of its transparency of data and reports on the film industry in Brazil, ANCINE's website has facilitated research into the Brazilian film industry.

Natália Pinazza

References
Dahl, G (2006) Construindo a ANCINE. [Online]. Available at: http://www.ancine.gov.br/media/
    LEITURAS/construindo_ancine_gd.pdf [Accessed 15/02/2010].
Moisés, JA (2003) A New Policy for Brazilian Cinema in L Nagib (ed) *The New Brazilian
    Cinema*. London: I.B. Tauris, pp. 3-21.
Nagib, L (ed) (2003) *The New Brazilian Cinema*. London: I.B. Tauris.
Oricchio, LZ (2003) *Cinema de novo: um balanço crítico da retomada*. São Paulo: Estação
    Liberdade.

FESTIVAL FOCUS
FILM FESTIVALS IN BRAZIL

As in many other countries worldwide, film festivals in Brazil started during the 1950s inspired by the increasing popularity of post-war European events. Cinematographic festivals opened opportunities to support local film industries, boost tourism, and raise the international profile of the host nation. However, in Brazil the local political and economic situation undermined the events' continuity and their international standing. Thus, the history of Brazilian film festivals is a rather fragmented one. In contrast to well-established European events launched in the wake of World War II, contemporary major film festivals in Brazil are relatively young. São Paulo's 'Mostra International de Cinema' was launched in 1977 and the 'Festival do Rio' appeared only in 1999 as the merger of two festivals originating in the 1980s, namely 'Rio Cine' and 'Mostra Banco Nacional do Cinema'. The earliest attempt to launch an international event in Brazil was the first 'Festival Internacional de Cinema do Brasil' in São Paulo in February 1954. It was a one-off event, complementary to the second 'Bienal Internacional de Artes Plásticas' and part of the city's centenary celebrations. According to local intellectuals' agenda, it was a non-competitive event with a decided emphasis on educational films, conferences and retrospectives. Despite Brazilian critics' intentions of hosting a more serious and culturally-oriented festival, the international celebrities, especially from France, the United States and Italy, caused great excitement grabbing the attention of the media and audiences in São Paulo.

After the event, the idea of hosting a regular festival never took off because of cost considerations and competition from major festivals which got preference over the most coveted world premieres. In this sense, festival organizers faced a recurrent dilemma of film festivals: are they aimed at local festival-goers or at their international guests? The Brazilian press criticized the festival's elitist practices and excessive budget as it remained unclear how it benefited Brazilian audiences or film-makers. Moreover, both local and international critics bemoaned the low quality of the programme as the good films had already been seen in Europe, whilst the new ones were deemed to be rather mediocre. For *Cahiers du Cinéma*, the situation was that producers preferred to premiere their best films at more prestigious European events.

Similar difficulties hampered the subsequent attempt to launch the first 'Festival Internacional do Filme' (FIF) in Rio de Janeiro in September 1965. The competitive event attracted several international film magazines and guests enthused by the rising visibility of the *Cinema Novo* movement in European festivals in the preceding year. That was especially at Cannes in May 1964 with *Deus e o Diabo na terra do sol/Black God, White Devil* (Glauber Rocha, 1964) and *Vidas secas/Barren Lives* (Nelson Pereira dos Santos, 1963) and during a short-lived festival in Genoa in January 1965 where Rocha presented his celebrated essay 'An Aesthetic of Hunger'. Yet, despite successfully attracting international attention, the first FIF had programming difficulties. As the British *Films & Filming* (Baker 1965) reported, Rio's line-up mainly consisted of films already seen by most European festival-goers. Thus, although the films were 'new' for Brazilians, the programme was unappealing for foreign participants.

Additionally, the Rio festival faced a broader problem: the instalment of a military regime in March 1964 and its existence for the next two decades. While the changing political landscape noticeably encouraged some international protests against the festival in 1965, it did not arouse an immediate rejection from the *Cinema Novo* group. However, the differences between the Brazilian film-makers and the increasingly repressive government would create serious problems for the second and last FIF in March 1969. Amidst the political effervescence of the late 1960s, the Brazilian film movement became well-known in international cinematic circles that praised its commitment to left-wing politics. For prestigious European festivals the political agitation that peaked in May 1968 meant events' disruption, demonstrations and later organizational changes. For Rio's festival the political tensions were translated into an active attempt at the sabotage of its second edition by the *Cinema Novo* group. They not only refused to present any films at the event, but tried to convince foreign delegations to do the same. During the festival, they staged demonstrations that concluded with the imprisonment of some Brazilian film-makers. Local and international media highly criticized the absence of the *Cinema Novo* group and the overall conclusion was that the festival had been a failure. While headlines in the *Jornal do Brasil* remarked that the '2nd FIF was unappealing to half of Rio' (1969: 33), international specialized magazines tended to ignore the event altogether. In a short but highly critical note, *Sight & Sound* (Stein 1969) condemned it with the already familiar argument that its programme did not contain enough world premieres of high-quality. Lacking the support of local film-makers and the international critical establishment the discredited festival was cancelled.

Although launching high-profile international film festivals had proved a difficult enterprise in Brazil, local authorities and cinephile groups still organized national cinematic encounters. The most visible and long-lasting events have been those in Brasília, launched in 1965, and in Gramado, started in 1973. The first 'Semana do Cinema Brasileiro' in Brasília commenced as a modest showcase of local non-commercial films. Becoming the third 'Festival de Brasília do Cinema Brasileiro' in 1967, it soon gained a reputation among Brazilian film circuits for being a cultural event promoting independent cinema. In the mid 1970s the revamped national film institute, Embrafilme, took control of the festival and unsuccessfully tried to use it as an international springboard for Brazilian cinema. It invited a handful of foreigners and screened a selection of recent local films. Yet, as reported by *Film Comment* (Riley 1976), there was a considerable mismatch between local programming taste and foreign expectations. Thus, although it became a key hub for the local film industry in the late 1970s, its geographical influence remained limited because its Brazilian programming was unappealing to international observers. By the end of the 1970s the festival's legitimacy was strongly questioned by local film-makers and in the early 1980s reports declared it to be in 'a state of coma'. Not only was it criticized for lacking transparency, but it also faced the competition of a well-run event in the southern city of Gramado.

Launched in 1973, the festival in Gramado promptly established a good reputation and during the 1980s it took the lead as the main national cinema showcase. The event, however, never captured international attention. Like Brasília's festival, Gramado's Brazilian exclusive focus limited its influence to the domestic market, thus making it an unsuitable launching pad for films with international ambitions. Moreover, both Brazilian-themed festivals faced huge difficulties in the early 1990s when Embrafilme was closed down and film production almost stopped completely. They not only lost a key funding source but they also literally ran out of films for their competitions. The rivalry between the two festivals turned fiercer than ever. In 1991 Brasília's organizers made an aggressive change of dates from October to July to step ahead of the August festival in Gramado. Instead, Gramado expanded its programming choices by hosting an Ibero-American competition for a few years until Brazilian film production increased with the phenomenon known as *cinema da retomada*. In 1996, the festival split its competitive section into a Brazilian and an Ibero-American one. Yet again, Gramado's lower status in the festival hierarchy brought limited international coverage and programming difficulties. As reported by *El Amante Cine* in 1997 (Quintin 1997), despite having good organization and friendly staff, the festival had far too many guests but rather too few interesting films.

Both festivals in Brasília and Gramado can currently claim a lengthy tradition since the 1960s and 1970s. However, their influence has never reached far beyond Brazilian frontiers. Moreover, in the past decade they have faced competition from other regional festivals and, most noticeably, from the axis Rio-São Paulo which has historically concentrated most of Brazilian cinematic activity. With a decidedly cinephile profile, São Paulo's Mostra International de Cinema was launched in 1977 as a showcase of experimental and arthouse world cinema. Over the years, the Mostra has crafted a reputation of having both a rigorous selection of the best films from other international festivals, and a strong support from São Paulo's audiences. Programming more than 300 films every year, a competition for first and second feature films, and comprehensive retrospectives of celebrated auteurs, it is the biggest and most prestigious cinephile event in Brazil. Every October, the festival offers conferences, seminars, a Brazilian film market, and innovative strategies such as a free bicycle scheme and online screenings.

Regularly held in late September, a few weeks before São Paulo's Mostra, the more industry-orientated Festival do Rio results from multiple festival initiatives including the ill-fated 'FestRio' – held 1984–89 – as well as Rio Cine and the Mostra Banco Nacional do Cinema – two festivals also launched in the 1980s that merged in 1999 to form the present Festival do Rio. Despite being a relatively young festival, it concentrates most of Brazil's film industry activity with hundreds of international and local film professionals attending one of the busiest markets in Latin America. Moreover, the festival programmes around 350 films spread across 40 venues accompanied by several free outdoor screenings, taking over the city to create a true sense of cinematic celebration. Differing in profile, both Rio and São Paulo film festivals emerge during the September–October season and are generally considered as key festival players at both national and regional level.

Laura Rodríguez Isaza

References

Anon. (1981) 'Brasília entró en estado de coma [sic]', *Cinemateca Revista*, 29, pp. 31–32.

Anon. (1983) 'Brasília já está na historia do cinema nacional', *Jornal da Tela*, 11, pp. 6–7.

Baker, P (1965) 'Festival: Peter Baker in Rio', *Films & Filming*, 12: 3, pp. 17–20.

Bazin, A (1954) 'Un Festival de la Culture Cinématographique', *Cahiers du Cinéma*, 34, pp. 23–29.

Bresser-Pereira, LC (1954a) 'Ataques ao Festival', *O Tempo*, 22 February.

— — (1954b) 'Balanço do Festival', *O Tempo*, 9 March.

— — (1954c) 'Festival Internacional de Cinema do Brasil', *O Tempo*, 11 February.

Caetano, MR (1997) 'Festivais', in F Ramos and LF Miranda (eds), *Enciclopédia do Cinema Brasileiro*, 2nd edn, São Paulo: Editora Senac São Paulo, pp. 238–41.

Cajueiro, M (2009) 'Populist Platform', *Variety*, 19–25 October, p. 4.

— — (2010) 'Rio's Window', *Variety*, 20-26 September, p. 19.

— — (2008) 'Populist Event Pulls in Paulistas', *Variety*, 22-28 September, p. 37.

Figueirôa, A (2004) *Cinema Novo: A onda do jovem cinema e sua recepção na França*, São Paulo: Papirus Editora.

Jonald, D (1954) 'Como foi Inaugurado o Festival em S. Paulo', *A Cena Muda*, 8, pp. 6–8.

Jornal do Brasil (1969) 'II FIF nao interessou a metade do Rio', 31 March, p. 33.

Marcorelles, L (1965) 'Rio: Bravo', *Cahiers du Cinéma*, 172, p. 8.

Quintin (1997) 'Una empanada sin relleno', *El Amante Cine*, 67, pp. 46–49.

Ramos, F, and Miranda, LF (1997) *Enciclopédia do Cinema Brasileiro*, 2nd edn, São Paulo: Editora Senac São Paulo, pp. 238–41.

Ribas de Faria, M (1970) 'Brasília 70: O ano do impasse', *Filme Cultura*, 18, pp. 63–65.

Riley, B (1976) 'Journals: Brooks Riley from Brasília', *Film Comment*, 12: 5, p. 6, 71.

Stein, E (1969) 'Rio Festival', *Sight & Sound*, 38: 3, pp. 122–23.

V.B.O. (1975) 'Gramado 1975: Maturidade de um festival', *Filme Cultura*, 27, pp. 50–57.

Valente, E (1999) 'Orgia Cinéfila', *Contracampo*, 11–12, http://www.contracampo.com.br/11-12/orgiacinefila.htm. Accessed 26 September 2011.

— — (2000) 'Brevíssima História dos Festivais: ou alternativas aos alternativos', *Contracampo*, 22, http://www.contracampo.com.br/22/brevissimahistoria.htm. Accessed 26 September 2011.

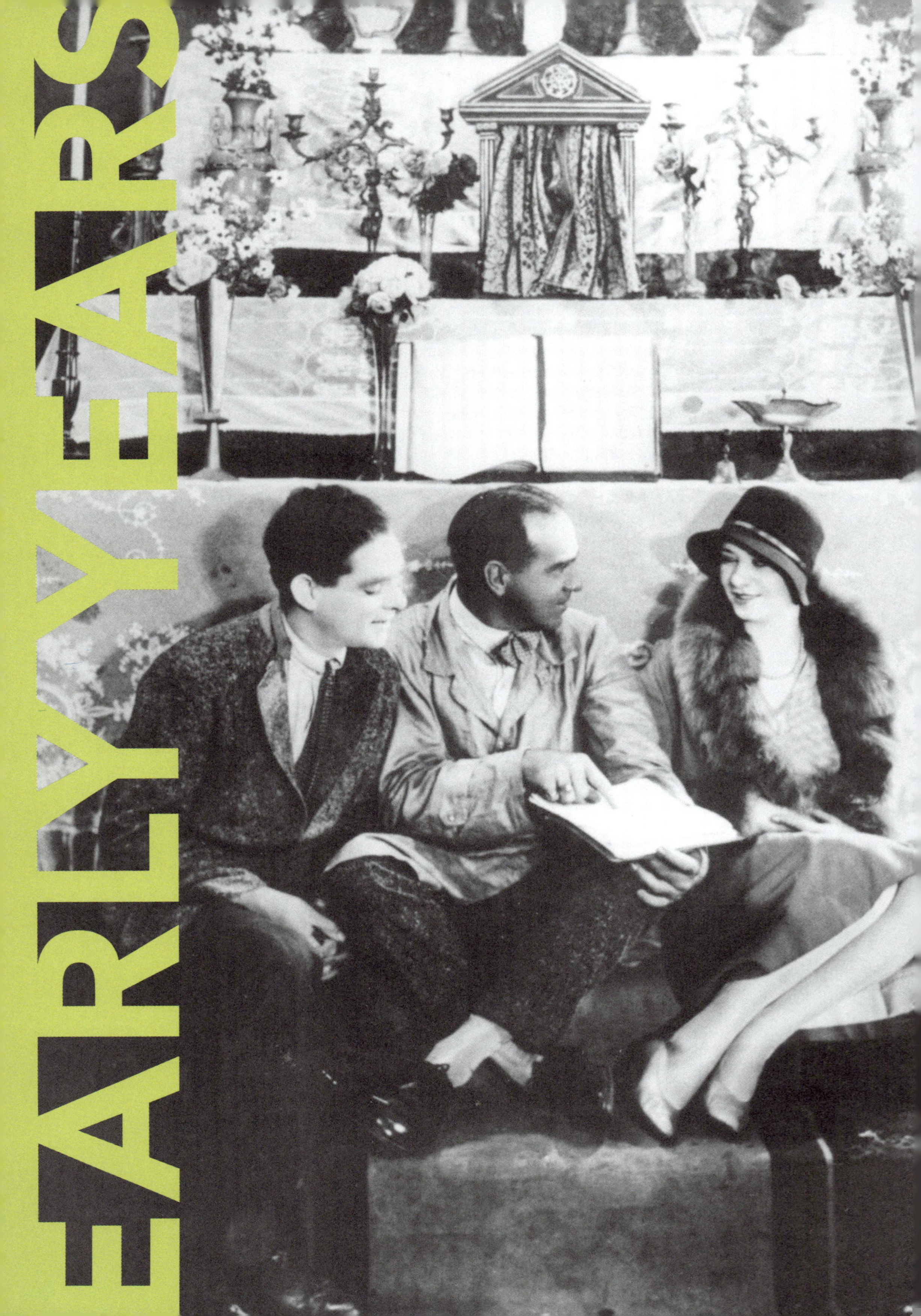
EARLY YEARS

The first 50 years of film-making in Brazil were marked by one important fact: Brazilian cinema was not what the country's spectators saw on-screen. This fact not only inscribes the difficulties facing Brazilian cinema historically with regard to its audience, but it also marks the dialogues, aesthetic forms and narratives found on-screen. Brazilian film-making started in 1897 but, except for the period between 1908 and 1912, national theatres were dominated by foreign productions. Until then, the majority of Brazilian films produced were reportage, propaganda or documentary films. In 1908, one of these film-makers, Júlio Ferrez, made his first fiction film, *Nhô Anastácio chegou de ciagem*, which adopted a plot common to the theatre and the circus: the country dweller who arrives in the Federal Capital and is seduced by its enchantments, gets infatuated with a singer and then is caught by his wife, and after much confusion returns to his hometown. This was also the period when the French-style *phonoscénes*[1] were replaced by films of popular arias or, as is the case with Brazilian cinema's first popular success, *Paz e amor* (William Auler, 1910), in which performers recite and sing from behind the cinema screen.

During the early prevalence of foreign films in the Brazilian market, *cinejornais* [newsreels] and documentaries were a niche which enabled the production and exhibition of Brazilian cinema to progress. Fictional production was scarce up until the mid 1920s and was concentrated in Rio de Janeiro and São Paulo, where European immigrants dominated film-making and attempted to attract audiences with national epopees such as *O Guaraní* (Vittorio Capellaro, 1916) or *Pátria e bandeira* (Antonio Leal, 1918). When Humberto Mauro produced *Valadião o cratera* in 1925 in Cataguases, Minas Gerais, he considered himself a pioneer. In fact, he was not aware of what had been produced up to that moment in Brazil since the country's scarce film production was not distributed in regions aside from the ones in which they were produced.

It was at this moment that interesting productions began to emerge in different locations across Brazil, conferring on this period the name of the 'Regional Cinema Cycle'. The films include those from Rio Grande do Sul by Francisco Santos and Amazonas by Silvino Santos, and his documentaries and propaganda films which are not without artistic interest. From 1923 to the emergence of sound cinema in 1930, 50 films, including short and feature films, were made by twelve production companies in Recife. At the time, the link between government-sponsored documentary propaganda cinema and fiction film production was fundamental since the sponsorship of propaganda enabled the financing of films with fictional plots. The film-makers were passionate about cinema and their films, influenced by serial productions, were modelled on successful US genres such as adventure and melodrama. In this way, local reality would be transformed and conventionalized according to genre, with examples found in *Jurando vingar* (Gentil Roiz, 1925) or *A Filha do advogado/The Lawyer's Daughter* (Jota Soares, 1926). At the same time, however, these films often featured Afro-Brazilian characters who were committing crimes of which they either were not really guilty, or had been forced into due to their subaltern position. These features can be read for their aesthetic hybridity, but above all, for their social and cultural complexities.

Humberto Mauro also engages with Brazilian cinema's dialogue with Hollywood influences. However, his treatment of nature and landscape, lighting choices, and the sensuality in his films make him a film-maker differentiated in terms of quality and who was to remain active (he is the director of the important *Ganga bruta* [1933]) despite the arrival of sound cinema and the lack of distribution and exhibition structures which made the existence of regional cinemas difficult. Amongst regional film productions, *Limite* (Mário Peixoto, 1931) is an exceptional work in Brazilian cinema history: film essay and poem, inspired by both the European avant-garde and Charlie Chaplin, Peixoto made a film that is non-narrative but that is marked by the rhythm of images, of montage, of songs, according to the ideas of the Chaplin Club: the gathering of young people in Rio de Janeiro who opposed talkies.

It was not only the arrival of sound cinema that engendered change in the 1930s. Getúlio Vargas and the 1930 Revolution would also determine the end of the Old Republic's regionalization and liberalism, starting authoritarian and centralizing projects of national construction which encompassed film. This period saw the creation of the Instituto Nacional de Cinema Educativo (1936–66) where Humberto Mauro made a significant number of classic Brazilian documentaries, films which worshipped the nation's great men, its bounteous nature and the sciences that would transform it. In fiction this ideal appears in consonance with the ideals of the Estado Novo and its fondness for teachers and doctors in the country, as seen in *Aves sem ninho* (Raul Roulien, 1939).

Cinédia emerged in 1930 as a result of the endeavours of Adhemar Gonzaga. With a view to elevating the artistic quality of Brazilian films, the studio produced well-made films and aimed to attract a literate public with strong plots that approached the feminine universe by dealing with love, women's difficulties and intrigues occurring in the *favela*, as is seen in *Mulher* (Octávio Gabus Mendes, 1931). However, the failure of this type of film to receive public and critical acceptance made Cinédia turn to reportage and educational documentaries encouraged by the State as well as to the musical *carnavalesque* film *Alô, alô, Carnaval!/Hello, Hello, Carnival!* (Adhemar Gonzaga, 1936), in which the attractions were radio singers and parodies of American cinema, producing a creative and affirmative legacy in Brazilian cinema.

The resort to musical comedy and parody intensified in the 1940s, culminating in the *chanchada*, a genre with great popular appeal that coincides with the strengthened influence of US culture in Brazil brought about by World War II. The success of this genre was facilitated by a decree in 1946 that established that three Brazilian films would have to be exhibited per year. In this context, *chanchada* became a successful aspect of national film production that would continue until the late 1950s. It was part of an industrial strategy based on simple techniques and reduced costs brought about by the alignment of the interests of Brazilian producers, distributors and exhibitors. Despite criticism, the Atlântida studio had much popular success, including *Carnaval atlântida* (Watson Macedo, 1952), *Matar ou morrer* or

Nem Sansão nem Dalila/Neither Samson Nor Delilah (Carlos Manga, both 1954), each parodies of US films.

The post-war era in São Paulo was a moment of great cultural ferment. Production companies established by Italian immigrants invested in 'quality' cinema made in big studios. Not entirely aware of the lack of mechanisms for distribution and exhibition of domestic cinema, the Vera Cruz Cinematography (Company Cia. Cinematográfica Vera Cruz) imported state-of-the-art machinery and recruited numerous European professionals under the stewardship of Alberto Cavalcanti (who at that point was based in England). Cavalcanti started the studio up but was dismissed before filming his second film there. Between 1949 and 1954, sixteen films were made, amongst them melodramas with neo-realist influences such as *Caiçara* directed by Italian actor Adolfo Celi (1950) or grand historical reconstructions like *Sinhá Moça/The Plantation Owner's Daughter* directed by the Argentine film-maker Tom Payne (1953). The film *O Cangaceiro/The Bandit* (1954, Lima Barreto) marks a convergence between Mexican cinema, westerns and a national historic figure, to create a genre whose echo is still found in Brazilian cinema today. This experience engendered similar attempts in smaller productions by studios such as Maristela and Multifilmes, two studios which were also based in São Paulo. Despite being produced in a moment of economic expansion, films such as *O comprador de fazendas* (Alberto Pieralise, 1951), *O Homem dos papagaios* (Armando Costa, 1953) and *Simão, o caolho* (Alberto Cavalcanti, 1952), amongst others, centred on stories of economic failure, dramatic events, and wives that were constantly unsatisfied with the economic status of their husbands. However, this is the moment that social concerns are foregrounded on-screen. This occurs in *O Canto do mar/Song of the Sea* (Alberto Cavalcanti, 1952), which deals with the drought in the Brazilian north-east and the consequent migration of the region's inhabitants, and oscillates between documentary, a genre appreciated by Cavalcanti, and the melodrama that interweaves the characters' destiny.

With the existence of large and small studios, Brazilian cinema received unprecedented investment which engendered technological improvements. This, however, did not guarantee a substantial change in its standing with the public. Instead, it made evident the difficult situation which led to the failure of many companies. Without distribution and without access to theatres, it was not possible for the studios to continue.

Between 1951 and 1952, two conferences were held to gather together industry professionals to discuss the future of Brazilian cinema. As a result of left-wing political influence, communism in particular, the conferences discussed national cinema as a vehicle to also debate the Brazilian situation more generally. Amongst the many unmet demands they made on the government was a request for a limitation on the importation of US films as well as measures to benefit national production.

Amidst studio failure and the influx of neo-realism, film-makers would turn to independent and inexpensive production schemes that would shift the focus of their films, considering them a reflection on social reality and underdevelopment. The exploited boys in *Rio, 40 graus/Rio, 40 Degrees* (Nelson Pereira dos Santos, 1954) replace the streetwise characters that marked the *chanchada*. As a consequence, Brazilian cinema began to search the country and its own aesthetics.

Sheila Schvarzman (trans. Natália Pinazza)

Notes

1. A pre-sound form of technology in which actors would lip-synch to a sound recording played simultaneously to the silent filmed image.

Aves sem ninho

Studio/Distributor:

DFB

Director:

Raul Roulien

Producer:

Raul Roulien

Screenwriter:

Raul Roulien (adapted from the play Nuestra Natacha [Alejandro Casona, 1935])

Cinematographer:

Moacyr Fenelon

Art Director:

Ruy Costa

Composer:

Lyrio Panicalli

Editor:

Nelson Schultz

Duration:

98 minutes

Genre:

Drama

Cast:

Déa Selva
Rosina Pagã
Lídia Matos
Darcy Cazarré
Celso Guimarães

Year:

1941

Synopsis

The girls in a female orphanage are ill-treated and exploited by their principal, who makes them work as slaves. One of the orphans, Vitória manages to escape after being locked in a contaminated 'reflection room' as a punishment. Ten years later, Vitória, who was adopted by a teacher and his sister, has become an outstanding and popular university student. Amongst her friends is the funny and shallow medicine student Léo. After graduating as the country's first doctor of 'social and educational sciences', she is invited to become the principal of the same orphanage from which she had previously escaped. Vitória provokes a revolution in the place with a new educational philosophy, earning the affection of the girls, the hatred of the other principals and general incomprehension. However, her efforts and commitment to her work are ultimately rewarded.

Critique

Aves sem ninho is a key film of Brazilian cinema in the period that marks the 1930s/40s. On the one hand, it is a nationalist melodrama, in tune with the general mindset of the Estado Novo, which encouraged citizens to create a modern Brazil primarily through education and hygiene. This film was thus in line with other productions such as Favela dos meus amores (Humberto Mauro, 1935), O Grito da mocidade (Raul Roulien, 1937) and Romance proibido (Adhemar Gonzaga, 1944), amongst others, whose protagonists are young doctors, nurses and idealist teachers, who renounce their passions and desires in order to contribute to the cause of progress in Brazil. On the other, Raul Roulien's film stands out as one of the most aesthetically interesting productions of the era. The Brazilian singer and actor, who was also fluent in Spanish, had worked in Hollywood at the beginning of the sound era, acting alongside stars such as Janet Gaynor (Delicious [David Butler, 1931]) and under the direction of John Ford (The World Moves On [1934]). Upon his return to Brazil as a big star in 1935, he became a film producer and director along with the re-establishment of his successful career in the theatre. His second screened film – the second he directed, 'Asas do Brasil', was destroyed whilst being edited in a fire on 21 November 1940 – Aves sem ninho was filmed in a makeshift studio with sparse resources. However, the film crew gathered together some of the best Brazilian practitioners, including Moacyr Fenelon, Ruy Costa and Nelson Schultz.

In contrast to the rest of contemporary Brazilian sound cinema (which has been criticized for its excessive influence from the radio and theatre, as manifested in particular by the frontality of its staging and the immobility of the camera and in the long and static musical numbers, especially in the underrated carnivalesque films), Aves sem ninho is marked by extremely dynamic montage and camera angles which reveal Roulien's full control over the language of classical cinematic narration. The film does also show a sort of exhibitionism, as it had the purpose of affirming for definite the director's film-making talents, which had fed numerous conflicts in Brazilian cinematography – it makes explicit references to films such as *Bronenosets Potyomkin/Battleship Potemkin* (Sergei Eisenstein, 1925) and *Godless Girl* (Cecil B DeMille, 1929).

The film's message and aims become most clear towards the end of the film, when fiction and reality interweave in the presentation of Dona Darcy Vargas, the first lady of the Estado Novo. *Aves sem ninho* reveals itself as one of the most skilful filmic expressions of the imaginary of national unity in the process of a modernization which is fundamentally white and urban. Certainly, this was one of the key reasons for its enthusiastic reception by Brazilian film critics at the time of its release.

Rafael de Luna Freire (trans. Natália Pinazza)

Caiçara

Studio/Distributor:

Vera Cruz

Director:

Adolfo Celi

Producer:

Alberto Cavalcanti

Screenwriters:

Adolfo Celi
Alberto Cavalcanti
Ruggero Jacobi

Cinematographer:

Henry Chick Fowle

Art Director:

Aldo Calvo

Composer:

Francisco Mignone

Editor:

Oswald Hafenrichter

Duration:

100 minutes

Genre:

Drama

Cast:

Abílio Pereira de Almeida
Eliane Lage
Carlos Vergueiro
Mário Sérgio

Year:

1950

Synopsis

Marina is a beautiful lady who has lived most of her life in a charitable institution, as her parents suffered from Hansen's disease, which carries a heavy social stigma. Marina was isolated from an early age from her family leading to a difficult childhood and leaving her a fragile and timid figure. In order to escape this situation, Marina agrees to a marriage with the widower José Amaro, arranged by the orphanage managers. However, José Amaro is an arrogant man with social status. Amara owns a small shipyard by a paradisiacal island called Ilhabela. The island is the setting of the action, made up of a web of complex relationships full of jealousy, superstitions and torrid passions. Marina is the centre of the drama and she becomes a kind of icon of beauty and an object of desire. Her marriage with José Amaro is never consummated because Marina rejects his every attempt, which culminates in harassment, and almost rape. This becomes public knowledge and the subject of gossip and jokes. Nevertheless, the arrival of a sailor results in a change to the unresolved situation.

Critique

Caiçara's importance to Brazilian film history lies in the fact that it was the first film made by the Vera Cruz studios (Companhia Cinematográfica Vera Cruz), and was the biggest investment made by a company in the history of Brazilian cinema. Vera Cruz aimed to implement an international standard of quality for their films and, in order to achieve this standard, imported equipment, technicians and artists from various parts of the world, amongst them Italy, Denmark, the United Kingdom and others. However, although there were many Italians due to the origins of the studio owners (Cicillo Matarazzo and Franco Zampari), the best technical-artistic contribution came from Britain, in particular technicians that had previously worked with Alberto Cavalcanti in British films. Amongst the most important contributors is the director of photography Chick Fowle, who was best known for his black-and-white still photography and whose style was copied by many Brazilian photographers. Brazilian film-maker

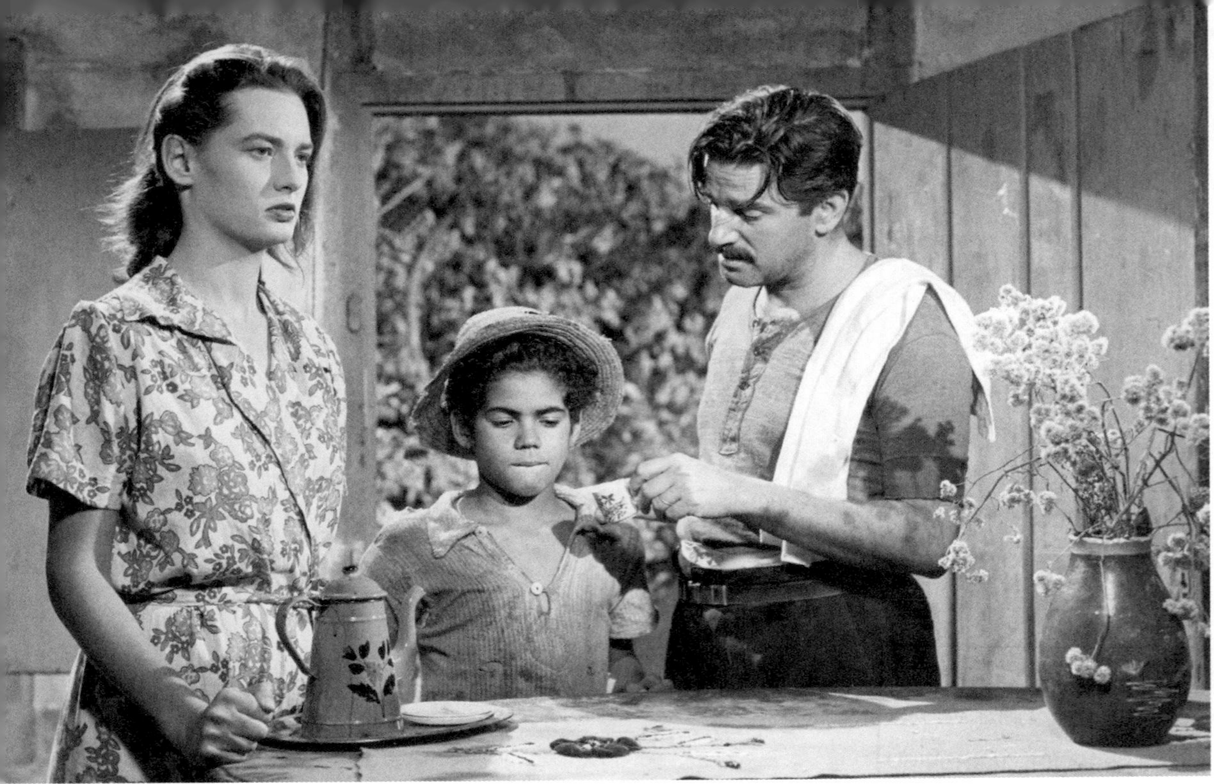

Caiçara

Roberto Santos paid tribute to him in the short film entitled *Chick Fowle, faixa preta de cinema* (1981). There was a great desire at the time for filming entirely on location whilst the Vera Cruz studios were still being built in São Bernardo do Campo. The critic Walter George Durst considered shooting the film 'a picnic in Ilhabela' due to the fact that the crew spent a long time on fieldwork so as to be able to finish the shoot, which was marked by a series of accidents, technical problems and difficulties in filming with a large crew in such an isolated location. The film attempts to set up a delicate balance, oscillating between a realistic tone and an aura of exoticism and mystery, and its resolution concerns the Pedra do Sino (Bell Stone), a mythical stone located at the Bell Stone Beach, Ilhabela, that makes a particular noise when touched. On the other hand, the director, Adolfo Celi, lacked experience in direction and his arguments with the film's editor Oswald Hafenrichter became legendary, as it was the editor who controlled the quality of the Vera Cruz studio. However, when the film was exhibited, the public was very receptive and the critics admired the international standard that the film had set. Moreover, *Caiçara* revisits the coast, reinforcing a Brazilian tradition both in documentary and in films set by or on the sea (*Limite* [Mário Peixoto, 1930–31], *Aitaré da praia*, (Gentil Roiz, Ary Severo, 1925) and more), which is consolidated later in *sertão-favela-sea*,[1] the trinomial ideology of *Cinema Novo*. Upon its release in São Paulo, the film was screened in more than twenty movie theatres by the US distributor

Universal, granting Vera Cruz what could be termed a triumphant entrance on to the film market. In terms of critical reception, there were positive reviews, particularly notable being the one by Almeida Sales, the most prestigious critic then working in São Paulo, who, at first, was sceptical about Vera Cruz.

André Gatti (trans. Natália Pinazza)

Note

1.   The film-maker also wrote for *Pasquim*, *Correio Brasiliense* and *Folha de São Paulo*. As well as this he has written the following books: *Revisão Crítica do Cinema Brasileiro* (1963); *Revolução do Cinema Novo* (1981); *O Século do Cinema* (1983); and the novel *Riverão Sussuarana* (1978).

Fragmentos da vida

Studio/Distributor:

Rossi Filme
Medifer

Director:

José Medina

Producers:

Gilberto Rossi
José Medina
Carlos Ferreira

Screenwriter:

José Medina (adapted from the story 'The Cop and the Anthem' [O Henry, 1904])

Cinematographer:

Gilberto Rossi

Duration:

38 minutes

Genre:

Drama

Cast:

Carlos Ferreira
Alfredo Roussy
Áurea de Aremar
Medina Filho

Year:

1929

Synopsis

In the first years of the twentieth century in the city of São Paulo (undergoing urbanization) a worker from a civil construction company falls from scaffolding and, in a final effort prior to his death, pleads his son to live an honourable life dedicated to work. Fifteen years later, as an adult, the son has turned out to be the opposite of his father's wishes. Transformed into a tramp and accompanied by a friend who makes a living out of petty theft, he hatches a plan that would involve him going to prison to protect himself from the cold weather that grips São Paulo. His plan, however, does not work. In a restaurant, when he tries to be arrested for eating without any money to pay for it, an unknown man decides to settle his bill. After an unsuccessful attempt to steal an umbrella, he throws a stone at a grocery shop, breaking its glass. However, the blame falls on an innocent man who was running to get the bus. He tries again to be arrested by hassling a girl. However, he ends up helping her to run away from two men who were after her. In a final effort, he goes into a church planning to cause a scandal, but ends up moved by the religious atmosphere, especially after the preacher's assertion that 'the advice to the sons comes from the experience of the parents'. He decides to redeem himself and look for a job, but a twist of fate intervenes.

Critique [warning: this Critique necessarily includes a spoiler which gives away the twist at the film's ending]

As a director in the 1920s, José Medina was influenced by North American cinema in the tradition of David W Griffith. According to an interview with Maria Rita Galvão in *Crônica do cinema paulistano* (1968), he learnt the conventions for how to construct the *mise-en-scène* as a spectator of the work of Thomas Ince, Ernst Lubitsch and Erich Von Stroheim. His preference for this sort of cinema would also stimulate him to the construction of dramatic narratives characterized by emotional appeal and moral messages. In *Fragmentos da vida*, he rigorously followed the classical rules of continuity, as can be seen in

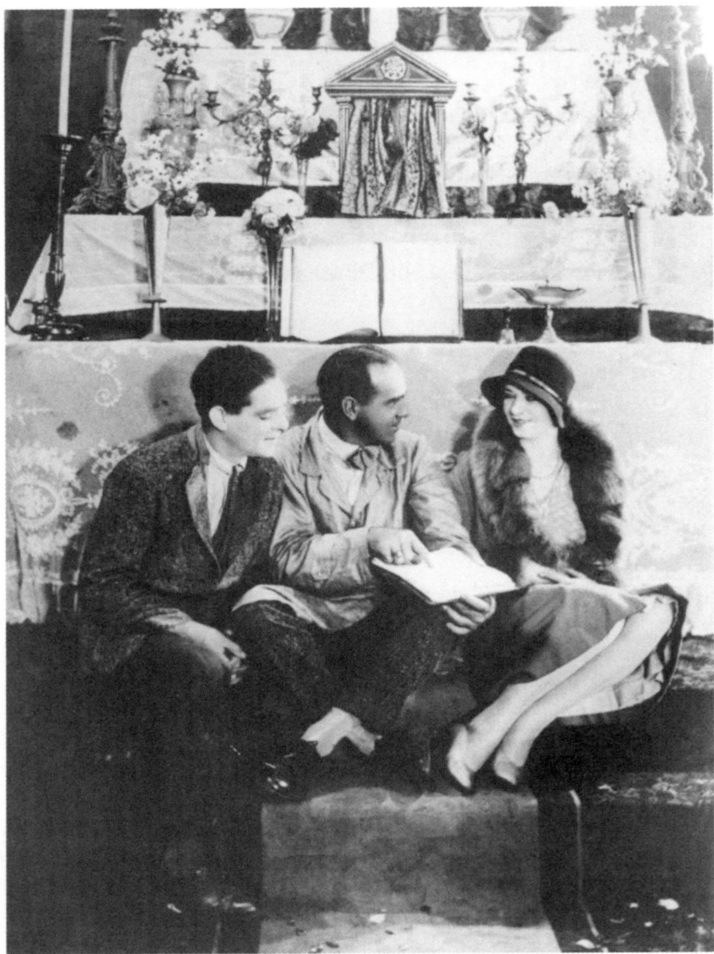

Fragmentos da vida

the sequences in the park or in the restaurant. Medina represented the city of São Paulo as a place of progress and economic mobility, where virtue is a consequence of hard work. As an antithesis of such a moral presumption, both central characters are deviant to this world as seen from a bourgeois perspective: while one is hopelessly crooked, the other is a tramp who, moved by a religious act, feels guilty for not having followed his late father's advice and ends up committing suicide in prison.

It is interesting to note that the remorse experienced by the protagonist will not lead him towards his redemption. Moralism is recurrent in Medina's oeuvre and is also present, farcically, in the short film *Exemplo regenerador* (1919), which narrates how a wife pretends to have an adulterous relationship with a butler so as to set her hedonistic husband straight. In contrast, in *Fragmentos da vida* the moral lesson is more pungent as the character abruptly takes his own life due to remorse. Similarly, in *A culpa dos outros* (1922), a missing film by Medina, the alcoholic father has to deal with remorse for causing his wife and son's deaths at the end of the film. Significantly, together with the moral lesson associated with work, *Fragmentos da vida* also presents a naturalistic approach to the fictional construction of popular characters in São Paulo during the 1920s.

Most of the settings are filmed on location, presenting an urban space deteriorated by neglect. The film represents Brazilian types often associated with the *malandro*, a streetwise character who lives a life of idleness and more often than not theft. Although the protagonist's friend fits into this stereotype and exposes the vices of society, as conducted by the ideals of a bourgeois viewpoint, the figure of the *malandro* also offers the most charismatic moments of the film partly due to the performance of Alfredo Roussy, an actor who had previously worked in amateur theatre. As Medina wanted, and in line with US films of the time, the film succeeded in synthesizing comic and dramatic elements.

Reinaldo Cardenuto (trans. Natália Pinazza)

Ganga bruta

Studio/Distributor:

Cinédia

Director:

Humberto Mauro

Producer:

Adhemar Gonzaga

Screenwriters:

Octavio Gabus Mendes
Humberto Mauro

Cinematographer:

Aphrodisio P de Castro

Editor:

Humberto Mauro

Duration:

85 minutes

Genre:

Drama

Cast:

Déa Selva
Durval Bellini
Décio Murillo
Lu Marival
Ivan Villar
Carlos Eugenio

Year:

1933

Synopsis

In Rio de Janeiro, the then capital of Brazil, a young and rich engineer, Marcos Rezende, kills his wife on their wedding day. He is legally decreed innocent as the bride had only confessed to not being a virgin after their marriage ceremony. So as to forget his personal tragedy, the engineer goes away to the countryside with his secretary Guimarães where he tries to find distraction by focusing on building a factory. He stays in a residence along with two other young people – Décio and Décio's adoptive sister Sonia – where they live out a childlike romance in the vast gardens of the house. Obsessed with his past memories, Marcos is also treated with hostility by a group of workers revolted by the frenetic rhythm of work he has imposed. Sonia, fascinated by Marcos, involves him in a conspiracy which is marked by temptation and rejection.

Critique

This film took almost three years to make, in a period which was marked internationally by the impact of sound cinema. Sound equipment was too expensive for the precarious economic conditions in which Brazilian cinema struggled to survive, and it was released in 1933 on Vitaphone.[1] The soundtrack to *Ganga bruta* was outdated, featuring only music and some synchronized dialogues, and thus underwent public and critical rejection. It was not until the 1960s that the young film-makers of *Cinema Novo* consecrated Humberto Mauro as a pioneering auteur. Restoration and re-synchronization in 1972 and 1987 made *Ganga bruta* once again available to be seen in full.

The film revolves around sexual tension, which can be understood from a dramatic, historical or cultural perspective. However, one must take into account that *Ganga bruta* consecrates sex in its different manifestations. From the wedding, whose major consequence is supposed to be the defloration of the bride, the theme of sex develops in a way that resembles the movement of the biblical serpent. His male chauvinist expectations of being the first to have sex with the bride frustrated, the engineer shoots her and kills her. Being declared innocent by an equally male chauvinist justice, he cannot stand to be in a city in which everybody knows that his honour was tainted. He finds refuge in the countryside, and dedicates himself to the hard work of constructing a factory while living in a bucolic bungalow with a paralytic old lady, her son Décio (Décio Murillo), and the adopted Sonia (Déa Selva) – both just past adolescence.

This new environment is, however, only apparently Edenic: there is erotic intimacy between Décio and Sonia; the workers are hostile to Marcos (Durval Bellini) who makes the building work go faster. Sonia, on the other hand, is excited about the presence of an older man who has come from the metropolis, and she employs childish tricks to draw his attention. She is at the same time child and woman, and it is the latter aspect which attracts Marcos. It would thus be an overstatement to call it paedophilia, but voyeurism describes the way in which Marcos observes the near-siblings lying together in a chair or a swing, or rolling on the lawn at night, exchanging the hot air of their mouths and voraciously brushing together their bodies which are full of a near-explosive energy. The provisory repression of desire is channelled in the violence executed by the engineer towards the workers in a local pub, hitting them and even submitting them to humiliating practices, while Guimarães (Ivan Villar) watches to his own sadistic delight. Resistance, however, has its limits. Marcos succumbs to the temptation of Sonia's lips, and after looking at her thigh, exposed by a dress which has been ripped by a bush, he takes her in his arms and consumes her virginity amongst the brackens and the big trees (turbulent objects such as jackhammers, drilling stones and squirting water act as metaphors in place of turgid members, scandalously at the time of the film's release and whose daring continues to shock today). Eros and Thanatos: Marcos only continues to possess Sonia with the death of Décio, which occurs 'accidentally' in a waterfall. A sequence of crosses in a funeral precedes the final wedding, when Marcos Rezende, ironically, gets married for the second time to a deflowered bride.

Carlos Roberto de Souza (trans. Natália Pinazza)

Note

1. Vitaphone was a short-lived technology in which film was projected alongside a soundtrack that was played on shellac record, and made obsolete by synchronous sound recording.

Hello, Hello, Carnival!

Alô, alô, carnaval!

Studio/Distributor:

Cinédia

Synopsis

Originally entitled 'The Big Casino' ('O grande cassino') the film centres on two tramps who try to have fun at the Cassino Mosca Azul ('The Blue Fly Casino') at the expense of a gullible drunkard played by Oscarito. Later in the film, they propose putting on a play called 'Banana da Terra' [Banana of the Land] to the Casino manager, which he turns down straight away. However, an opera company from Europe cancels their performance at the last minute, leaving the

Director:

Adhemar Gonzaga

Producers:

Adhemar Gonzaga
Wallace Downey

Screenwriters:

Ruy Costa
Adhemar Gonzaga

Cinematographers:

Antônio Medeiros
Edgar Brasil
Vitor Ciacchi

Art Director:

Ruy Costa

Composer:

Alberto Ribeiro and others

Editor:

Ruy Costa

Duration:

75 minutes

Genre:

Film-Revue

Cast:

Barbosa Júnior
Pinto Filho
Jayme Costa
Oscarito

Year:

1936

manager no choice but to resort to the pair. The musical numbers are triggered by jokes about the efforts made by the writers from the theatre magazine to make the performance happen. The film includes two numbers sung by the Brazilian musical star Carmen Miranda.

Critique

This is the oldest integrally preserved talkie filme-revista. Cinédia, one of the main Brazilian studios at the time, formed a partnership with Sonofilms, a company related to the radio and recording industry, made three musicals in two years: *Alô, alô, Brasil!/Hello, Hello, Brazil!* (Wallace Downey, João de Barro and Alberto Ribeiro, 1935), *Estudantes/Students* (Wallace Downey, 1935) – both are lost – and *Hello, Hello, Carnival!* (1936). Both *Alôs, Alôs* were produced to come out near Carnival time and they pioneered the *carnavalesco* (*carnivalesque*) genre, which would be consolidated by the end of the 1930s and remain the most popular genre in Brazilian cinema for two decades despite its rejection by the elite.

Such disapproval for the *carnavalesco* was largely due to a much discussed excessive influence of – or submission to, as some critics would argue – the radio on national cinema. However, unlike *Hello, Hello, Brazil!* and other pioneer sound films such as *Como Coisas Nossas* (Wallace Downey, 1931), *Hello, Hello, Carnival!* pays more attention to its filmic aspects thanks to its scriptwriters Ruy Costa and Adhemar Gonzaga who concentrated on the backstage story. Their narrative enables a complete insertion of the musical numbers into the diegesis.

Moreover, in showing the very distance between the artistic ideal, including the filmic ideal, and the reality of the country, the film explores the relationship of the carnivalesque to high and low culture and to foreign and national culture. This would become one of the main features of *chanchadas*, which formed part of the comedy genre – whether in carnivalesque musicals or not – and which was definitively consolidated in the 1940s and 1950s, making *Hello, Hello, Carnival!* a significative precursor. The film is also the oldest work featuring the then young Oscarito, the comedian who would become the main star of the *chanchadas*.

Other reasons why this film production stands out from the filmic context of its time are: the use of more than one camera to film the musical numbers, making the film more dynamic, the modernist settings created by Ruy Costa with illustrations by the brilliant cartoonist J Carlos as well as scenographic disguises for the microphones. Above all, it features some of the biggest Brazilian music stars of the time. The film brought crowds to the cinema who wanted to see and listen to a potpourri of successes by big stars of the phonographic and radio industries, amongst them Francisco Alves, Mário Reis and the sisters Aurora and Carmen Miranda. Originally 'Chico Viola' (Francisco Alves's nickname) ended the film. However, the ending was altered for the film's re-launch. In its later cut the film ends with the Miranda sisters singing the samba 'Cantoras do rádio' (translated as 'Singers of the Radio', Alberto Ribeiro / João de Barro / Lamartine Babo).

Rafael de Luna Freire (trans. Natália Pinazza)

In the Land of the Amazons

No paiz das amazonas

Studio/Distributor:

JG Araújo & Cia

Directors:

Agesilau de Araújo
Silvino Santos

Producer:

Joaquim Gonçalves de Araújo

Cinematographer:

Silvino Santos

Duration:

128 minutes

Genre:

Documentary

Year:

1922

Synopsis

In the Land of the Amazons is a mix of commercial inventory and travelogue, displaying the productive potential of the Amazon region. Shot from a variety of perspectives on boats, along roads and from a train, the film provides a fascinating tour through the region. Having opened with a scene in the port city of Manaus including a series of views of its public buildings, the camera leaves the city behind in order to embark upriver on a journey in which images of places, peoples and products actively intermingle. Film technique and narrative structure are used effectively so that the organization of labour in the Amazon region itself becomes the main subject of the film. A variety of devices, including close-ups, long takes and continuity editing, are used to capture both the density of the forest and the dynamics of people at work in a wide range of economic activities, such as the hunting of the manatee, the fishing of the pirarucú, the productive cycles of the Brazil nut, tobacco, rubber, *guaraná* and balata. The film also shows scenes of the ill-fated Madeira-Mamoré railway, finally concluding in the cattle ranches of the region.

Critique

Produced for the 'Centennial International Exhibition' in Rio de Janeiro, which opened in 1922, *In the Land of the Amazons* constructs an image of Brazilian nature quite literally for external consumption, displaying to Europe and the United States its potential for future investment. At the same time, it brings urban spectators in Brazil much closer to the everyday life of a region that has conventionally been imagined as a huge, thinly populated wilderness, inhabited only by nomadic indigenous groups. In the film Silvino Santos refuses exoticism: instead, he dares 'to make a documentary about work, about capital and about the possibilities of profit' (Souza 1999: 231) in one of the most remote regions of the country. While the film might at first seem to endorse the nineteenth-century evolutionary narrative of progress (in which indigenous nature is subject to the power of civilization), Santos's enthusiastic embrace of the cinematic medium brings something new to that static picture, making the most of the kinesthetic experience offered by cinema. It provides a remarkable contrast to the outdated language used in the intertitles by Agesilau de Araújo (son of the businessman JG Araújo), which reiterates the mythic image of the Amazon region.

Santos's camera enters a factory where hundreds of women undertake the monotonous task of shelling Brazil nuts, providing a subtle comment on the working conditions created by the intensification of modern industrialization in Manaus. The detailed, close-up shots of the shelling process follow the rhythmic and coordinated activities of hand, body and machinery at work; meanwhile a scene of a monkey shelling nuts in the forest forms a comic counterpoint. A scene of the workers leaving the factory, which was already a cinematic cliché even in 1922, gains momentum through skilful editing: first the standard frontal view of the crowd of workers making their way out, then a cut to the view from the back, before returning to the frontal view once more, this time with the camera much closer to the workers.

In the Land of the Amazons also reveals something of ordinary people's lives; workers look at the camera, they smile, they bathe, they drink, they cook, they eat. Combining the spatially unfolding structure of early 'place films', with the temporal strategies of films of the labour process, Santos's editing displays a considerable degree of sophistication, furnishing the Amazon with both spatial variety and temporal depth. It is this very dynamism, capturing the energy brought by capital investment through the moving image, that saved the film from being dismissed as mere travelogue: more than simply another portrayal of a journey into tropical nature, the film seemed to harmonize with the efforts of the organizers of the 1922 exhibition to project a new image of Brazil as a modern nation.

Luciana Martins

Referemce

Souza, M (1999) *Silvino Santos: O cineasta do ciclo da borracha*, Rio de Janeiro: Funarte.

Limite

Studio/Distributor:

Produção independente, with the aid of Estúdios Cinédia

Director:

Mário Peixoto

Producer:

Mário Peixoto

Screenwriter:

Mário Peixoto

Cinematographer:

Edgar Brazil

Duration:

120 minutes

Genres:

Experimental
Drama

Cast:

Olga Breno
Taciana Rei
Raul Schnoor
Brutus Pedreira
Carmen Santos
Mário Paixoto

Synopsis

Three shipwrecked people drift on a boat. At the limit of their strength, a man and two women, each nameless, tell their life stories in flashback. 'Woman number one', a former prisoner, narrates her condition after her escape: a fugitive, she found work as a seamstress, leading a monotonous life with no expectations or freedom. 'Woman number two' tells the others about her unhappy marriage with an alcoholic pianist who plays at movie theatres. Out of desperation, she broke free from her miserable existence. 'Man number one', a widower, remembers the anguish he felt after discovering his lover was dying of leprosy, leaving him no choice but to escape from a life of false promises of happiness. Meanwhile, the shipwreck gets worse: the oars do not make the boat move and the drinkable water runs out. The melancholia and impossibility of escaping fatality mirrors the situation represented by the drifting boat, which evokes the imminence of death. In anxiety for the absolute, humans are forced to face, hopelessly and fearfully, the inevitable end of their existences. The image at the beginning of the film is of two arms handcuffed behind a woman's neck, symbolizing anguish at being imprisoned by life. In the final moments of the film, a storm looms on the horizon: the shipwreck is a metaphor for the human condition, in which, perhaps, all that can be done is to wait for death.

Critique

An atypical film in the history of Brazilian cinema, *Limite* is the only film made by Mário Peixoto (1908–92). With the support of the Cinédia studios, the film is an independent production made during

Edgar Brazil

Year:

1930–31

Brazil's attempt to create a film industry in emulation of the US model. *Limite*, a silent feature film apparently influenced by the modernism of the French avant-garde of the 1920s, was a different project. Scholars like Rubens Machado in the *Enciclopédia do Cinema Brasileiro* (1997), have even compared the film to those of Abel Gance, Germaine Dulac and Jean Epstein. Due to the particularities of *Limite* and the rather obscure intentions of its reclusive maker, Peixoto, these comparisons have been made by others aiming to better understand a film that does not seem to belong to its time and place, completely isolated from the film culture of Brazil in the 1930s.

The narrative of *Limite* concerns melancholic stories of daily life and the film's poetics emerge from a realist use of natural light and real locations in nearly the entire film. However the extreme situation of the shipwreck victims symbolizes humanity being adrift and facing imminent death, and thus places the film on to a metaphysical level. As metaphors of the unfortunate condition of humanity, the characters on the boat, all nameless, despair in the face of mortality and the distressing perspective of their own finitude. Together, they symbolize the diverse (and adverse) reactions to the impossibilities of escaping the imprisonment of life and the inevitability of death: 'woman number two' is lacerated, a melancholic body that does not react any longer, 'man number one', upset, accepts whatever destiny has in store; 'woman number one' is the only one to react, trying, for example, to use the oar to move the heavily symbolic boat. However, she soon feels the frustration of not being able to control her own destiny. The terrible human realization at the end of the film, and the unhappiness of life, are themes that inform *Limite*. They are triggered by a highly inventive aesthetic in which Mário Peixoto, in partnership with photographer Edgar Brazil, creates a visual and plastic impact through a slow and contemplative rhythm which alternates with fast and sudden camera movements. The oscillation established in the film style in combination with a musical score by Erik Satie, Debussy and Prokofiev, among others, seems to reinforce the adriftness and melancholia of these characters at the limits of their existence.

Partly due to its uniqueness, *Limite* was barely screened in Brazil at the time. Apart from some special exhibitions such as the session organized by the Chaplin Clube cineforum on 17 May 1931, the film of Mário Peixoto was unknown to the Brazilian public, resurging only sporadically in the following decades at university screening sessions organized by the physics lecturer Plínio Sussekind Costa. It was only in the 1970s, with the supervision of Plínio and help from Saulo Pereira de Mello, that the film was restored. Thanks to the film's distribution on video in the 1980s, researchers in Brazilian film history managed to bring Peixoto's oeuvre to prominence, one of the main publications being the book entitled *Limite* published by Pereira de Mello in 1996.

Reinaldo Cardenuto (trans. Natália Pinazza)

Mulher

Studio/Distributor:

Cinédia

Director:

Octávio Gabus Mendes

Producer:

Adhemar Gonzaga

Screenwriter:

Octávio Gabus Mendes

Cinematographer:

Humberto Mauro

Art Director:

Alcebiades Monteiro Filho

Editor:

Octávio Gabus Mendes

Duration:

77 minutes

Genre:

Drama

Cast:

Carmem Violeta
Celso Montenegro
Ruth Gentil
Alda Rios

Year:

1931

Synopsis

Mulher is the second production of Cinédia, Adhemar Gonzaga's studio founded in 1930 in Rio de Janeiro, which would become the largest film studio of Brazil in the early years of sound cinema. It tells the story of a young woman from a Rio de Janeiro slum who becomes the lover of a writer after being kicked out of home, and therefore gets to know the daily life of the upper class. One of the highlights of the movie is the bold choice for the leading role of actress Carmem Violeta, whose dark skin caused prejudiced comments from the Brazilian movie critics of the time, as well as the no less daring choice to shoot in the Morro da Providência slum. *Mulher* is an example of the first results of the transition from silent to sound film in Brazil, containing music but not spoken dialogues. Humberto Mauro, soon to be recognized as the most important Brazilian director of the period, is the cinematographer and has a small role as an actor.

Critique

After the debut of the Cinédia studio with *Lábios sem Beijos*, released in 1930, the founding year of the company, the producer Adhemar Gonzaga commissioned Otávio Gabus Mendes to direct *Mulher*. This means that a critic recognized since the end of the previous decade for his work in the *Cinearte* magazine – the main publication about cinema in Brazil of the period – had begun to direct his own movies. Filming would begin 19 January 1931, and the film would be released 12 October at the Capitólio movie theatre in Rio de Janeiro. The sound was pre-recorded for the premiere. Luis Steel was in charge of recording the discs, as in all films of the company which used the Vitaphone sound-on-disc process. The music composed for the film was dedicated to the maestro Alberto Lazzoli, who had worked with film sound in *Barro humano/Human Clay* (Adhemar Gonzaga, 1929). This music simulates synchronization with steps and other actions, in harmony with the editing of the sequences. The combination of image and music is evident, for example, in the detail shot of a guitar string breaking, in which a sharp stop in the music reinforces the rupture. Such a use of music can be perceived as an exemplary moment of transition from silent to sound film. While the music is present at all times over the images, it is no longer a type of music that simply accompanies the film while being external to it, played by musicians simultaneously to the exhibition and succeeding to establish a connection with the projection. In this case, the closer relationship with the images through the discs, and the fact that the music was made to fit these images, allowed a certain refinement in the synchronization that would be one of the necessary steps to the achievement of sound film.

The lack of dialogue and the choice of synchronizing only the music, even in 1931, can be explained by the combination of conceptions of both the director and the producer about the function of sound. Mendes had already revealed in *Cinearte* that he did not favour talking pictures. At the time, Gonzaga was aligned with the supporters of the intermediate solution: 'sound film yes, but talkies never.' As in other countries' cinemas, however, the choice of music as the preferred accompaniment to early sound cinema was soon to lose ground to the voice. Spoken dialogues would still not be central to the narrative of the company's next film, *Ganga bruta* (Humberto Mauro, 1933), but would dominate the screens in the carnival musicals produced from 1933 onwards.

Fernando Morais da Costa

São Paulo, Symphony of a Metropolis

São Paulo, a sinfonia da metrópole

Studio/Distributor:

Rex Film
Paramount

Directors:

Rodolpho Rex Lustig
Adalberto Kemeny

Producers:

Rodolpho Rex Lustig
Adalberto Kemeny

Screenwriters:

Rodolpho Rex Lustig
Adalberto Kemeny
Niraldo Ambra

Cinematographers:

Rodolpho Rex Lustig
Adalberto Kemeny

Art Directors:

Niraldo Ambra
João Quadros Júnior

Duration:

90 minutes

Genre:

Documentary

Persons:

Real-life participants

Year:

1929

Synopsis

The film centres on the daily life of a thrilling and pulsating city, where the economic development that has characterized São Paulo since the early 1920s vibrates. Employing various techniques, including hidden camera, the film-makers Lustig and Kemeny record daily life in the streets of the city from dawn to sunset. The film manages to capture the main social fluxes during the period of Paulistano[1] progress. The city awakes and sleeps, showing different faces and characteristics. The process of urbanization accelerates and electricity is shown as shaping modern life. What we see is a clear attempt to overcome chronic underdevelopment, conveyed in a direct and nationalist way. We also notice details of the habits and customs of the time through the portrayal of fashion, schools, the financial centre, the presence of the State, commerce, industry, traffic and architecture. The documentary is the most important cinematographic record of the process of urban and social renovation of the time in the city of São Paulo.

Critique

São Paulo, Symphony of a Metropolis emerges from the tradition of the European avant-garde documentary of the 1920s. The film is notably influenced by Soviet (Dziga Vertov), French (Alberto Cavalcanti) and German (Walter Ruttmann) cinema. Here, the Hungarian film-makers were able to make a film which is impressive for its use of techniques that were new to Brazilian cinema as well as for its accelerated rhythm and rich imagery. The film has an atypical narration for a documentary due to its use of montage, which was not characteristic of Brazilian film-making in this period. At the time, other Brazilian film-makers such as Mário Peixoto and Humberto Mauro were only making their first contributions to the avant-garde. Moreover, the plastic qualities of the images were brought out in the skilful framing of the foreign gaze of its film-makers. The film marks a moment of maturity in Brazilian photography through the work of Edgar Brazil, who together with Kemeny and Lustig raised the quality of the image in Brazilian cinema. The film has the status of a definite classic in Brazilian cinema, because it introduces new ways of filming, framing and organizing documentary footage. The critic Otavio de Faria spoke highly of it at a time when São Paulo only produced weak films, poorly made and lacking good subject matter. Although the film's style was not much copied, the film remains a seminal piece and a point of reference in the national documentary tradition. Furthermore, the film is one of the very few Paulistano[1] films that has stood the test of time, artistically and physically. The film also benefited from the unprecedented participation of Paramount, who in the figure of Niraldo Ambra, their publicist at the time, was responsible for the beautifully written and presented intertitles. The filming took around a year to make and the richness of the material allowed it to circulate in both silent and sound versions.

André Gatti (trans. Natália Pinazza)

Note

1.   A term meaning belonging to the city of São Paulo.

Song of the Sea

O Canto do mar

Studio/Distributor:

Kino Filmes SA

Director:

Alberto Cavalcanti

Producer:

Alberto Cavalcanti (Kino Filmes SA)

Screenwriters:

João Mauro de Vasconcelos
Hermilo Borba Filho

Cinematographer:

Cyril Arapoff

Art Director:

Ricardo Sievers

Composer:

Guerra Peixe

Editor:

José Cañizares

Duration:

87 minutes

Genre:

Drama

Cast:

Margarida Cardoso
Cacilda Lanuza
Rui Saraiva
Aurora Duarte

Synopsis

In the *sertão* (backlands), in the Brazilian State of Pernambuco, a voice-over tells us why the region has been depopulated. A portrait of the *sertão* is outlined: the dryness of the vegetation, some animals, two groups of people, one on foot and another by truck, leaving their homes because of drought, hunger and misery. The ones in the truck arrive at a beach, the first time they see the sea. In Recife, Raimundo has only one dream: to begin a new life in the south-east of Brazil to escape his hard existence. His father Jozé Luiz, an elderly sailor, the victim of an accident that has left him mentally deranged, tells his son of his travels on the seas so enthusiastically that he not only motivates Raimundo but also makes him believe that a better life is possible. The mother Maria, a laundress, supports the family, formed by the young man and woman, Raimundo and Ponina, who both give her a little help, and the child Silvino. Maria´s statement that 'The sea is treacherous […] it only brings disgrace, drives us crazy' introduces the two main lines of the plot about the drama of a family which will tend to disintegrate.

Critique

An auto-remake of Alberto Cavalcanti´s French avant-garde film *En rade/Sea Fever* (1927), *Song of the Sea* represents the best of Alberto Cavalcanti's work in Brazil. Both director and producer, he had full creative freedom on this film, and reinvents the original script substantially. In *Song of the Sea* new elements are introduced, which can be noticed already in its title which accords importance to the use of sound. In the 1950s, Cavalcanti adopted a pioneering approach to the representation of the Brazilian north-east, its customs and its social problems, employing professional and non-professional actors and location shooting.

With this film, the director aims to denounce the misery of the region. For this reason he invents a particular way of dealing with the theme of the dream: the protagonist Raimundo´s (Rui Saraiva) wish to start a new life in the south-east of Brazil. Making use of a documentary approach, *Song of the Sea* reminds us of the exodus of the rural population from

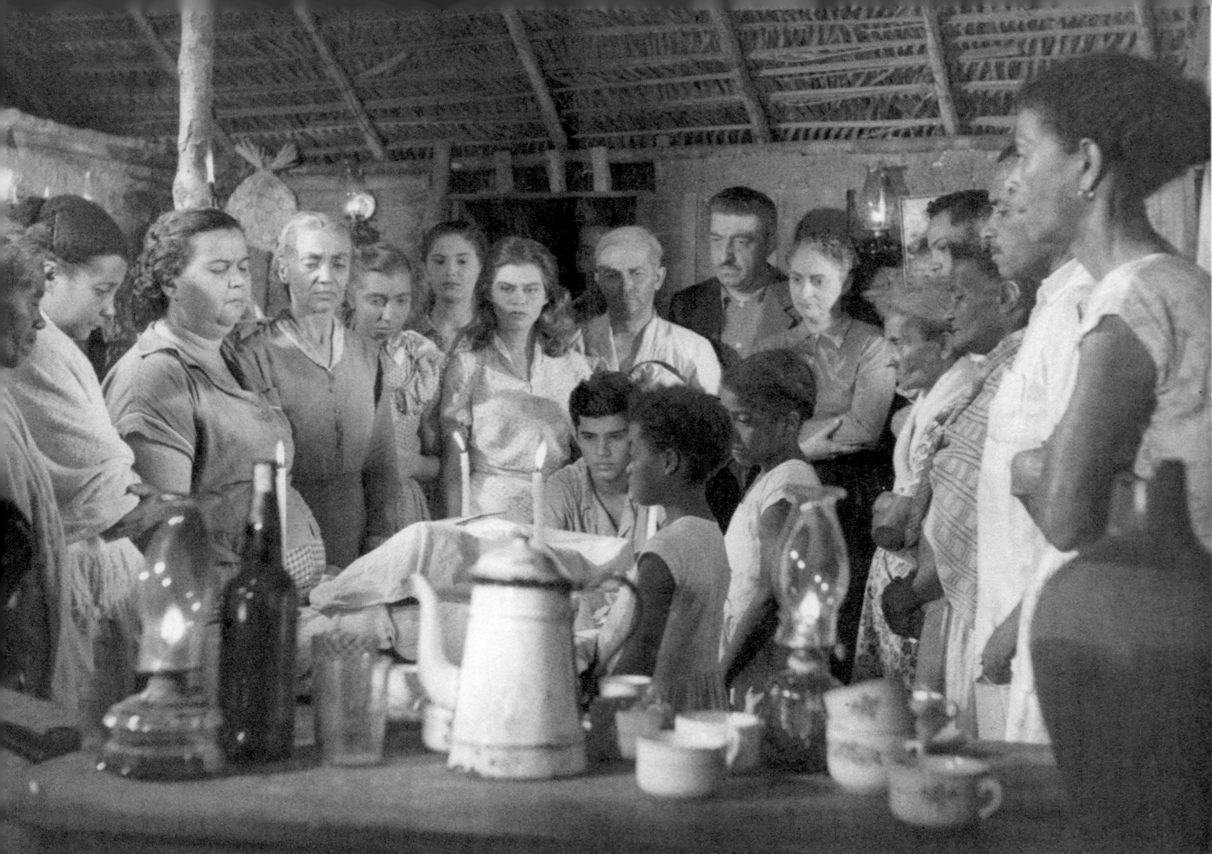

Song of the Sea/O Canto do mar

Alfredo Oliveira
Alberto Vilar
Fishermen
sertanejos from Pernambuco

Year:

1953

the *sertão*, a space that is both mythic and harsh, a vast area subject to terrible droughts in addition to its semi-arid climate.

Like *Sea Fever*, the story takes place in a coastal city. This time Recife replaces Marseille with its beaches, buildings and ruins, its port and surroundings, and shows a great interest in regional popular culture, its folklore and traditions, its beliefs and rituals, including a focus on the particularities of the spoken language. Because of its documentary approach, its use of non-actors, location shooting and dialect, *Song of the Sea* can be compared to Italian neo-realism, in particular Luchino Visconti´s *La Terra Trema* (1948) and its reference to the sea. As in Cavalcanti´s film, a female character says that 'the sea is bitter', similarly to Maria (Margarida Cardoso) here. Despite this comparison, Cavalcanti´s status as an avant-garde film-maker cannot be forgotten. The photographic style of silent film, some framings and superimpositions may be related to his work on French avant-garde films of the 1920s. The use of editing is also worthy of attention. The influence of Soviet Montage and its concept of a 'creative geography' is noticeable as well as the fast rhythmic editing characteristic of French Impressionism.

In its title 'Song of the Sea', an ambitious use of sound is immediately announced. The music possesses a narrative function, aiding the sense of evocation to which the narrative is dedicated. Throughout the film, this 'song of the sea' has a tragic dimension: that of an opposition between the unfortunate present of the characters and the memories of their happy past. If on the one hand the music is omnipresent, and plays an essential role in the soundtrack, on the other, a potential towards musicality can be noticed in the film images themselves. Within this original work relating the film images to music, some sequences exploring Pernambuco's popular culture such as Frevo, Xangô and Maracatu merit attention. But it seems to be 'the singing (song) of the sea' which prevails and becomes definitely integrated into the film images. It evokes the geographical reality of the environment, Recife's coral reef near the surface of its sea, and more obviously the theme of the dream and despair, the characters being taken in a mechanism which exceeds them. If the geographical reality of the environment, Recife's coral reef near the surface of its sea, may have inspired *Song of the Sea*'s script, the truth is the characters seem to be taken in a mechanism which exceeds them during the whole film.

Fernanda Aguiar Carneiro Martins

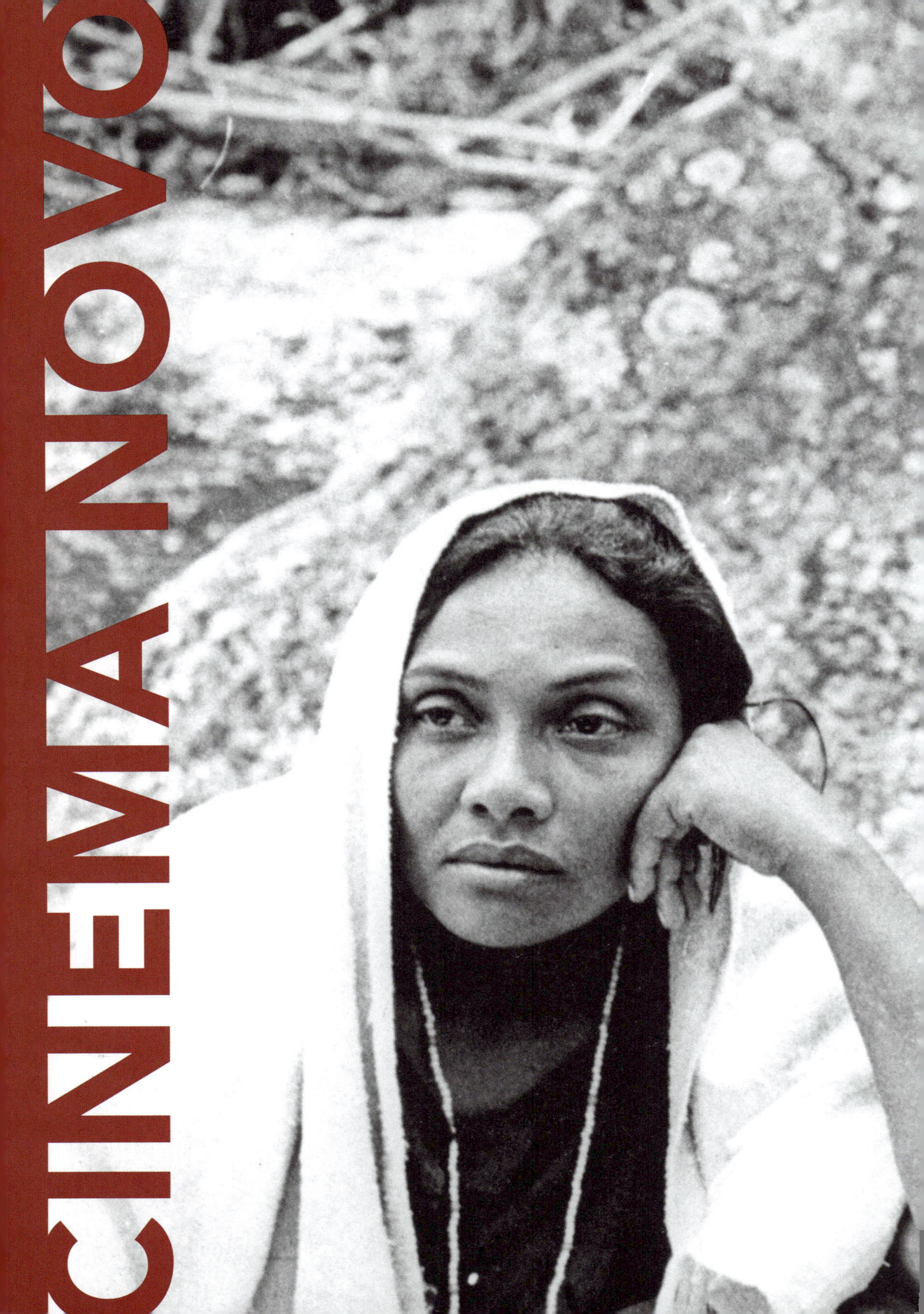
CINEMA NOVO

Although it is one of the most studied and celebrated movements of Brazilian cinema, finding a strict definition of the *Cinema Novo* (Brazilian New Wave) is not an easy task. As Glauber Rocha, one of its main ideologists, declared in 1980, one year prior to his death: 'the "thousand faces of the *Cinema Novo*" confound the (inter)national critics that seek the typical "coherence" of the rich cultures, unaware of Brazil's multiracial and economic complexity' (Rocha, 1981: s/r). This assertion hints at the major goals of this group of film-makers, which is especially guided by ideals of rupture with industrial cinema, cultural decolonization and anti-imperialism. Widely known as one of the most important political film movements of the 1960s, the *Cinema Novo* began to be conceived at the end of the 1950s, when, still according to Glauber Rocha, in 1957–58,

> I, Miguel Borges, Carlos Diegues, David Neves, Mario Carneiro, Paulo Saraceni, Leon Hirszman, Marcos Farias, and Joaquim Pedro (all of us in our early thirties) used to gather in the bars of the Copacabana and Catete neighborhoods to discuss the problems of the Brazilian cinema. A revolution was taking place in the Theater, Concretism was stirring Literature and Fine Arts, in terms of Architecture, the city of Brasília showed that the country's intelligence was not aground. What about the cinema? (Rocha, 1981: s/r).

These were the 'heads' of the movement. At that time, the formation of a unique art circuit, the inspiration of the Cuban Revolution and some European cinema movements contributed to the formation of a generation that prioritized direct dialogue with the people by means of an activist art. Regarded as 'artistic *intelligentsias*', the *cinemanovistas* were committed to cultural projects that sought to promote reflections on national identities. Although cohesive, the group did not intend to create a model or an aesthetics of its own, given the plurality of its authors.

Under a continental perspective, the *Cinema Novo* would establish a direct dialogue with the *Nuevo Cine Latinoamericano* in the 1960s. This period, which was particularly fruitful for Latin America's film production, saw the emergence not only of the Brazilian *Cinema Novo*, but also of movements such as the Argentine *Tercer Cine* – which had Fernando Solanas and Octavio Getino among its exponents – and the *Cine Imperfecto*, envisioned by the Cuban Julio García Espinosa. This group of regional film-makers aimed to build, based on their national cinemas, the idea of a 'great native land'. The proposal to create a unity – or Latin American identity – in the midst of diversity would arise from consideration of the following common factors: hunger (in the context of social inequality), violence (and forms of authoritarianism), and the need for cultural decolonization (to be performed by the artist-intellectual).

As for the Brazilian historical context, the first signs of the *Cinema Novo* appeared mainly due to the following factors: (1) the failure of industrial cinematographic experiences such as the Vera Cruz Cinematographic Company – known as the 'Brazilian Hollywood'; (2) the death of the Brazilian President Getúlio Vargas in 1954 and the attachment of Juscelino Kubitschek's (Brazil's President from 1956 to 1961) developmental government to the ISEB (Higher Institute of Brazilian Studies) – an agency under the Ministry of Education and Culture that involved intellectuals from several fields of Social Sciences and was primarily concerned with questions of nationalism and populism; and (3) the filming of Nelson Pereira dos Santos's *Rio, 40 graus/Rio, 40 Degrees* (1954) – a film that established the possibility of a Brazilian independent cinema against the rules of the industry. This debut would trace the heritage of the *Cinema Novo* and of the *Nuevo Cine Latinoamericano* to Italian neo-realism as cinemas originating from periods of socio-historical crisis.

Moreover, the struggle for nationalization not only of film production, but of a much broader range of activities, as well as the denunciation of Brazil's cultural dependence on the main urban centres, were matters of discussion among critics and thinkers such as Paulo Emílio Salles Gomes, for whom the impregnation of the American cinema was so general and has occupied in such a way the collective imagination of both occupiers and occupied – except in the case of those at the lower end of the social ladder –, that it has acquired a quality of a thing of our own, in the sense that nothing is foreign to us because everything is foreign to us. (Salles Gomes, 1996: 90-93)

Sharing a similar opinion, Jean-Claude Bernardet indicates that the intellectual elites, as if ashamed of belonging to a country with no cultural tradition and fed by sciences and arts coming from more cultured countries, would recognise only in the latter ones the authentic mark of culture. Brazilian cultural products were not denied: for them, they simply never came to exist. (Bernardet, 1976: 20-21)

It was a certain denial of Brazil itself that would establish the issue of identity construction as one where the concern was that what was ours did not belong to us. In this case, what meaning was to be found in national identity?

By resorting to ideas such as decolonization, cultural heritage, national cinema and popular culture, this group of film-makers set out to make pictures of a political and social nature to express identity through the retrieval of elements that were supposedly authentically national. The key point is that the interest in illustrating a genuine identity through tradition was part of a context that sidelined mass culture, even when some studies were addressing aspects of Brazilian culture. The objection to mass culture in favour of the exaltation and legitimating of national roots resulted in an emphasis on images of traditional rural Brazil, as in the case of the *Cinema Novo* movement and its period – modernity – that, in turn, was represented by a critique of underdevelopment and an emphasis on the backwardness and misery that resulted from it. Such critique inspired hope in a modern alternative based on the prominence given to the 'pure' elements of the people. The underdeveloped and colonial country would have to take advantage of its true and genuine characteristics to develop itself. Through films that denounced modern underdevelopment, the *cinemanovistas* sought to find models to overcome the reality experienced by a great portion of the population. One of their goals was to spread awareness of the unique destiny of the country.

The origins of *Cinema Novo* can be traced, in fact, to the early years of the 1960s, when intellectual agitation brought together various art forms. For the thinker and literary critic Robert Schwarz, at that moment Brazil was 'unrecognizably intelligent', as well as experiencing an 'independent external politics', 'structural reforms', 'national liberation' and 'combating imperialism and latifundium'. The government of João Goulart had allowed progressive forces to achieve some political power. Thus, in cities, students and intellectuals began to argue in favour of structural reforms, developing an intense cultural and political militancy. The city of Rio de Janeiro saw the emergence of the Center for Popular Culture (CPC), an institution related to the Nation Students Union (UNE) that sought to implement strategies to build a national, popular and democratic culture. In the rural areas, especially in the north-eastern region, the Peasants Leagues (social organizations composed of agriculturalists, originally organized by the Brazilian Communist Party – PCB) started to achieve country-wide renown. Regarding these events, two significant facts should be emphasized: (1) the methodological controversy between the CPC and the *Cinema Novo* movement, and (2) the geographic region of origin of the latter.

It is possible to say that the 'author's politics' were the focus of this controversy. Adopted in Brazil in a different fashion than its French original form, the authorial conception of the *cinemanovistas* was used as a political way to analyse the history and the contradictions of the country. Contrarily to the collective proposal of the CPC, which was subjected to a state agency, Glauber Rocha affirmed that 'the author holds the greater responsibility for the truth: his aesthetics is an ethics, his *mise-en-scène* is a politics' (Rocha: 2003: 36). Moreover, the disagreement referred to a certain paternalistic cultural vision of the CPC, which practised the very populism attacked by the *Cinema Novo* in order to promote a new language. This new language, in turn, was made possible by the emergence of new technologies, which lead Paulo César Saraceni to create the following motto: 'a camera in the hand and an idea in the head.' (Saraceni and Caetano, 2007: 7) As for the 'original' geography of the *Cinema Novo*, it appears that, despite its origins in the north-eastern region, notably the state of Paraíba (with Linduarte Noronha's documentary *Aruanda* [1960]) and the state of Bahia (especially with Roberto Pires's *A grande feira* [1961], and Glauber Rocha's *Barravento/The Turning Wind* [1962], as well as the central figure of the latter), the movement happens, in fact, in Rio de Janeiro, which justifies the statement of Nelson Pereira dos Santos: 'the *Cinema Novo* is when Glauber Rocha is in Rio de Janeiro.' (Pereira dos Santos and Caetano, 2007: 7)

The first steps of arguably the most important Brazilian cinematographic movement of the intellectual vanguard of the twentieth century took place exactly in the aforementioned context, with the production of the short films *Arraial do cabo* (1959), by Paulo César Saraceni and Mario Carneiro – awarded a prize in 1961 in the Santa Margherita Festival – and *Couro de gato* (1961), by Joaquim Pedro de Andrade, which would later become one of the episodes of the feature film *Cinco vezes favela/Five Times Favela*, the only cinematographic production of the CPC. In 1962 Glauber Rocha's *The Turning Wind* and Paulo César Saraceni's *Porto das Caixas* were released, while Anselmo Duarte›s *O Pagador de promessas /The Given Word* won the Palme d'Or at the 'Cannes Film Festival'.

Prior to the military coup of 1964 the trilogy of the hinterland was produced, an example of the maturity of the movement, composed of Nelson Pereira dos Santos's *Vidas secas/Barren Lives* (1963), Ruy Guerra's *Os Fuzis/The Guns* (1964), and Glauber Rocha's *Deus e o Diabo na terra do sol/Black God, White Devil* (1964). One year after the latter film was completed, Glauber Rocha, as the main coordinator of the *Cinema Novo*, produced in manifesto form an account of the hunger, the poverty and the underdevelopment of the country in the Latin American context. In 'An Aesthetic of Hunger' [1965] (1995) he declared that it was precisely because of their hungry and miserable condition that colonized people possessed the potential to create a genuinely revolutionary culture. It is important to remember that the document, presented for the first time in Genova, Italy, on the occasion of a retrospective of Latin American Cinema, was explicitly directed at Europeans as a provocation that would demonstrate the misunderstanding of the colonizer regarding the experience of 'The Third World'.

Films produced after the shift of political power in the country, such as Paulo César Saraceni's *O Desafio/The Dare* (1965), Glauber Rocha's *Terra em transe/Enchanted Earth* (1967), Arnaldo Jabor's *A Opinião pública/A Public Opinion* (1967) and Gustavo Dahl's *O Bravo guerreiro/The Brave Warrior* (1969), reveal a self-examination of the intellectuals due to their disenchantment brought about by the dictatorship of Marshal Castello Branco. As stated by Gustavo Dahl when submitting his film to the press:

> My generation, formed between the death of Getúlio Vargas and the rise to power of Castello Branco is the last who believed in political solutions. As it reaches the age of thirty, it casts a pessimistic look on Brazil. Its characters, torn between the conscience of the tricontinental poverty and of their impotence, of the impossibility to surpass it, to surpass themselves, see suicide as the only solution. (Dahl, n/d, s/r)

This symbol, however, would not mark the 'end of the process of the *Cinema Novo*, which, between 1967 and 1973, would start an ideological conflict between the iconoclastic *Cinema Marginal* and a flirtation with Tropicalism, a movement of rupture that was primarily based on popular music. One year after the implementation of the most repressive period of the dictatorship, the Institutional Act no. 5 of 1968, Joaquim Pedro de Andrade films *Macunaíma* (1969) as the result of a mixture of languages and traditions, of the return of Oswald de Andrade's modernism and his anthropophagic ideal. Three years later, concerned with guaranteeing the continuity of a national and authorial cinema, however less committed to a revolutionary dream, Leon Hirszman films *São Bernardo* (1972).

Obviously the films mentioned in this introduction and discussed in the chapter cannot provide a full account of this vast movement, which still includes titles such as Leon Hirszman's *A Falecida* (1965), Cacá Diegues's *A grande cidade* (1966) and *Ganga zumba* (1964), Joaquim Pedro de Andrade's *Garrincha, a alegria do povo/Joy of the People* (1963) and *O Padre e a moça* (1966), Nelson Pereira dos Santos's *Fome de amor* (1968), Walter Lima Jr's, *Menino de engenho* (1966) and David Neves's *Memória de Helena* (1969). Not to mention seminal documentaries such as Leon Hirszman's *Maioria absoluta/Absolute Majority* (1964), Paulo Gil Soares's *Memória do cangaço* (1964), Geraldo Sarno's *Viramundo* (1964) and Glauber Rocha's *Maranhão 66* (1966), among others.

Due to the great scope of the movement, it would be interesting to conclude this brief introduction with the analysis written by Paulo Emílio Salles Gomes in the 1970s in which the critic states that

> the *Cinema Novo* is part of a broader and deeper current that also expressed itself through music, theater, Social Sciences and literature. This current – composed of spirits that reached a brilliant maturity and enriched by the continuous explosion of young talent – was, in turn, the most refined cultural expression of a vast national/historical phenomenon. Everything still is very close to us. There were no fundamental changes in the state of things and it is difficult nowadays to reach a balanced perspective on what happened. There remains the possibility of a general overview in terms of occupier and occupied that could, in the process, bring us closer to the meaning of the *Cinema Novo* (Salles Gomes, 1996: 38)

Even today, given the various interpretations of the *Cinema Novo* movement, it is possible to affirm the validity of that process.

Eliska Altmann

References

Bernardet, JC (1976). *Brasil em tempo de cinema*. Rio de Janeiro: Paz e Terra, p. 20-21.

Dahl, Gustavo (n.d.) Apresentação. Kit de imprensa de *O Bravo Guerreiro*.

dos Santos, NP and Caetano, D (2007) 'O velho e o novo' in *Revisão do Cinema Novo* (Catálogo), p. 7.

Salles Gomes, PE. *Cinema: trajetória no subdesenvolvimento*. Rio de Janeiro: Paz e Terra, 1996, p. 38.

— — (1996). *Cinema: trajetória no subdesenvolvimento*. Rio de Janeiro: Paz e Terra. pp. 90-93.

Johnson, R and Stam, R (eds) (1995) *Brazilian Cinema*, New York: Columbia University Press.

Rocha, G [1965] (1995) 'An Aesthetic of Hunger' (trans. R Johnson and B Hollyman), in R Johnson and R Stam (eds), *Brazilian Cinema*, New York: Columbia University Press, pp. 68–71

— — (1981) 'Prefácio de uma revolução' in *Revolução do Cinema Novo*. Rio de Janeiro: Alhambra/Embrafilme. no page

— — (1981) *Revolução do Cinema Novo*. Rio de Janeiro: Alhambra/Embrafilme, p. 15.

— — (2003). *Revisão crítica do cinema brasileiro*. São Paulo: Cosac & Naif, p.36.

Saraceni, PC and Caetano, D. (2007) 'O velho e o novo' in *Revisão do Cinema Novo* (Catálogo), p. 7.

Barren Lives

Vidas secas

Studio/Distributor:

Luiz Carlos Barreto Produções
Cinematográficas, Sino Filmes

Director:

Nelson Pereira dos Santos

Producers:

Luis Carlos Barreto
Herbert Richers Nelson Pereira
dos Santos
Danilo Trelles

Synopsis

Sinhá Vitória, Fabiano, their two boys and dog Baleia are the protagonists of this film which takes place in the north-eastern backlands of Brazil in the 1940s (the film is an adaptation from the homonymous novel by Gracialiano Ramos). The film tells the story of a family of *retirantes* (migrating people in the droughty backlands of the Brazilian north-east who search for work during the dry season). Always on the lookout for a place to live, they find shelter and labour on the property of an important landowner in the region, the colonel. The action begins when the family arrives at the property of the colonel, the time when the first rain falls, and ends when the first signs of a new drought become visible and oblige the family (having lost one of its members, the dog Baleia, which had to be sacrificed) to leave their house and become nomads again.

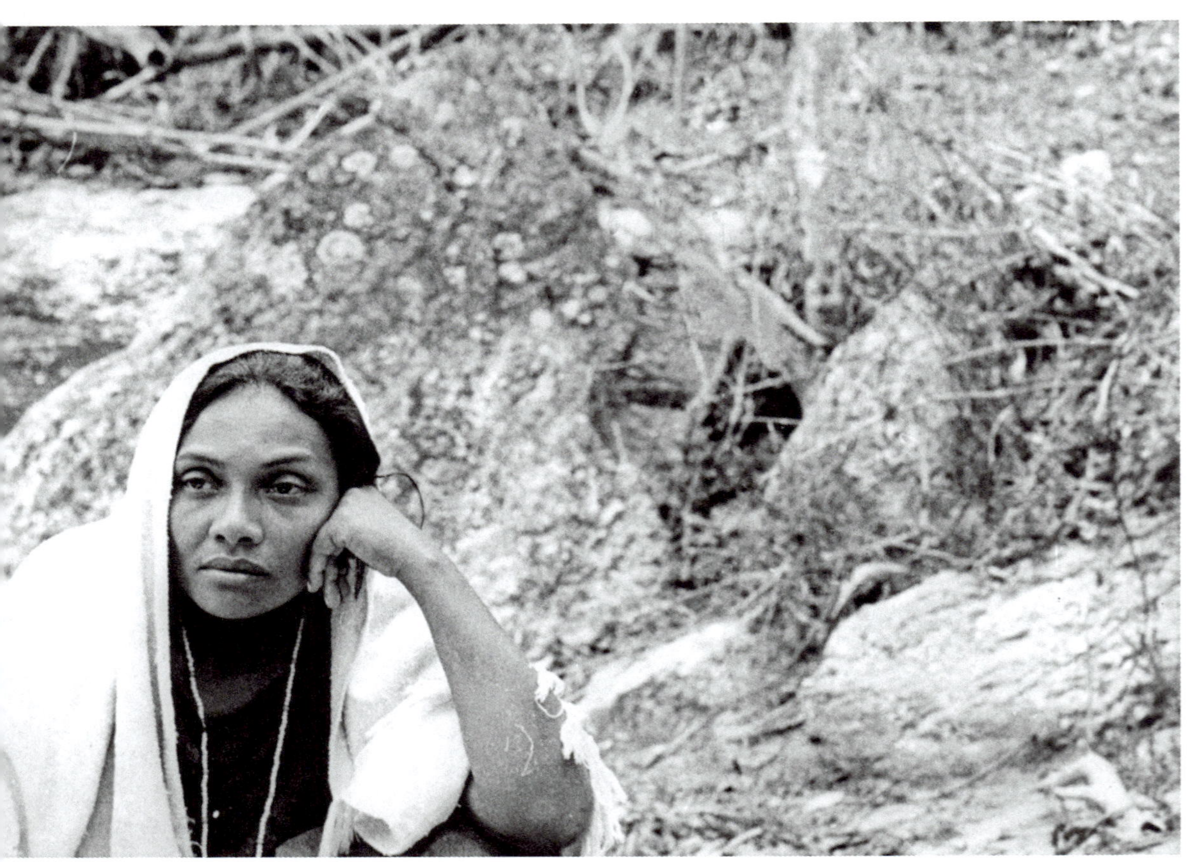

Barren Lives / Vidas secas

Screenwriter:

Nelson Pereira dos Santos
(adapted from the homonymous
novel by Gracialiano Ramos
[1938])

Cinematographers:

Luis Carlos Barreto
José Rosa

Composer:

Leonardo Alencar

Editor:

Rafael Justo Valverde

Duration:

103 minutes

Genre:

Drama

Cast:

Átila Iório
Maria Ribeiro
Orlando Soares
Jofre Soares
Gilvan Lima
Genivaldo Lima
the dog Baleia

Year:

1963

Critique

Shot in black and white, the film explores the extreme light of the radiant sun through overexposure, contrasting it with the calming dark of the shadows, in order to underline the harshness of life in this inhospitable landscape. Its inhospitality is not only a result of the long periods of drought still common today, but serves as a metaphor for the accentuated authoritarianism that dominates social and working relationships. In fact, the bonds established between the characters derive from a patriarchal power structure which takes its toll on those who should be treated with affection. The faltering dialogue between husband and wife, and with their children, is but one sign of its effects. Moments of spontaneous affection only take place when nature offers a truce, as for example, at the beginning of the film when the long-awaited rain triggers off conversations and the making of future plans, and even caresses for the dog Baleia when he proves a skilful hunter of guinea pigs.

During the opening sequence a fixed shot shows the sky, the low vegetation, and in the left corner a tree without leaves. Gradually we start to identity a dog and four people who arise from the lower border of the screen. On the soundtrack we hear an ox-cart, which is still out of sight. The sound of the cart is a recurring theme, present in other moments of the film. In the beginning its slow and heavy rhythm serves as a foreboding of the many difficulties that the family will face.

The shots focus on the harsh environment and its dry vegetation under the gliding sun that appears merciless in more than one situation. The unforgiving nature is shown in subjective shots (for example, when the older boy looks at the sky before collapsing exhausted at the beginning of the film), or in shots that frame it like an imposing force that exceeds everyone.

Nelson Pereira dos Santos's film calls attention to the way in which power relations are reproduced by representatives of the local government to which the other characters are subservient. The sequences of a popular celebration in the city are worth mentioning in this context, first of all due to the hierarchy revealed on-screen between men and women's labour, between adults and children, working and holiday clothes, between city and countryside, between the colonel and the local population, the police force and the gang members, the priest and the folk healer. The inflexibility of this hierarchy, which structures social life, seems to find affinities with the harsh conditions in which the people of this landscape produce their living. Second, they are worth mentioning because the popular celebration is a moment of respite between the people and the nature they live in. In fact, it is less an expression of local culture than a diegetic sequence in which the hierarchy mentioned above is expressed most strikingly in the parallel montage of close-up shots of Fabiano's (Átila Iório) face in prison and shots of the colonel (Jofre Soares) who receives the performance of popular dancers on his doorstep.

Another counterpoint that organizes people's lives is the oscillation between celestial forces and everyday life. The first one invokes spiritual forces like 'God' or the 'Holy Virgin'. On the other hand, everyday and physical life point towards the existence of hell. Reference to it appears repeatedly in the opening sequences when Fabiano talks to his oldest son ('keep walking, damned of the devil'), and further into the film, when the mother defines hell as 'the place where the damned go' and her life as 'miserable and unhappy'. It is also present in the camera movement that follows the older boy's gaze as it moves from the house to the son, while he repeats his mother's words, ('horrible place') and utters more than once 'Hell'.

The last shot is again fixed, pointing towards the trail in the background that the characters are now taking in the opposite direction from where they came in the beginning. While Baleia is no longer among them since he was sacrificed by Fabiano, we again hear the unseen ox-cart. This resolution seems to reinforce our urban and distanced outlook on Fabiano, Sinhá Vitória (Maria Ribeiro), and the boys. The camera had been waiting for them at the opening of the film, accompanied them throughout up until the edge of the abandoned house; now it stands still, as though saying goodbye, watching them leave.

Mauro Rovai

The Brave Warrior

O bravo guerreiro

Studio/Distributor:

Gustavo Dahl Producoes Cinematograficas, Joe Kantor Produções Cinematográficas, Saga Filmes

Director:

Gustavo Dahl

Producers:

Gustavo Dahl
Joe Kantor

Screenwriter:

Gustavo Dahl

Cinematographer:

Affonso Beato

Art Director:

Alexandre Horvat

Composer:

Remo Usai

Editors:

Gustavo Dahl

Synopsis

The Brave Warrior starts with an epigraph by Nietzsche: 'I love the one who tries to create something better than himself and succumbs for this art.' The action begins when the young politician Miguel Horta, newly elected, changes from a radical leftist party to a more conservative one, joining the government party to approve his social-care projects; inside it, he believes, there will be more chances to 'create something better'. Soon he discovers how wrong he was – but Horta doesn't fall defeated: he keeps on fighting, using his voice as a weapon for which he is even willing to die.

Horta looks for his own space through the dialectics of political negotiations; he believes that 'nobody does anything without getting their hands dirty'. But then Horta realizes that, when some concessions are made, there is no progress at all; that the price paid to get the power to change things in society is greater and harder than the small political victories. So he goes back to the leftist party and, in a union meeting, makes a rousing speech for a big general strike.

Critique

The Brave Warrior was one of the films of *Cinema Novo*'s so-called urban phase, driven by one question presented by Paulo César Saraceni's *O Desafio/The Dare* (1965) and *Terra em transe/Enchanted Earth* by Glauber Rocha (1967): how should intellectual activists respond to the new Brazilian dictatorship and the old social inequality? However, if the films by Glauber and Saraceni were vibrant and baroque, this film directed by Gustavo Dahl has a slower rhythm, suitable for the clarity of reflection. There is something

Roberto Marinho de Azevedo
Neto

Duration:

80 minutes

Genre:

Drama

Cast:

Paulo César Pereio
Mário Lago
Ítalo Rossi
Maria Lúcia Dahl
Paulo Gracindo
Hugo Carvana

Year:

1969

solemn and martial about it, as if within it we could witness the intense struggles in our system of political and social representation. We could substitute the party labels invented by the film (the Radical Party, National Party and Reform Party) for the names of the parties of today. If we do, the film seems to offer a clear diagnosis of the problems of the Brazilian political landscape of 2011.

This scenario, both pessimistic and militant, is seen in scenes soberly presented with no space for excess – until the final speech, driven by the desire for action. This melancholy atmosphere is achieved in scenes where the actors are so strong and serious that their conflict seems about to explode.

The film succeeds in posing an issue that first arose in the nineteenth century and is still relevant: the failure of so-called 'dialectical overcoming' and the tragic alternative to it. In a regime in which strong conservatism has always prevailed, the whole environment succumbs to a sickness and renewal can only come from the clash between social forces that cannot be reconciled. It is no accident that the film's epigraph comes from Nietzsche, a critic of the dialectical tradition. However, this philosophical question is not represented abstractly, but concretely – as is said in the film, society is not an abstraction, it is a collective formed by people who actually exist, so there is no synthesis that could be historically fair. Aware of this, *The Brave Warrior* refuses to succumb.

It is possible to see *The Brave Warrior* as a premonitory Gustavo Dahl looking forward to his vocation and his destiny. A few years after Dahl directed it, he moved away from film production and began to work on the organization and management of film production. In a sense, this film shows how he was aware of the political struggles (which were at the same time not hopeful, and stubborn) when he started work on creating a positive structure for film production (being responsible first for the film distribution of Embrafilme, in the 1970s, then for the creation of ANCINE, in the 1990s). When you have a good reason to fight, *The Brave Warrior* proves to us, it is worth continuing the fight, no matter how serious the difficulties and consequences.

Daniel Caetano

The Dare

O desafio

Studio/Distributor:

Mapa Filmes, Produções
Cinematográficas Imago

Director:

Paulo César Saraceni

Producer:

Synopsis

Ada and Marcelo are lovers. She is the wife of an industrialist and he is a young journalist. But their relationship is not going well: Marcelo has become depressed by the political turmoil that led to the 1964 Brazilian military coup and has stopped caring about personal problems, wanting to get in on the action and take a stand. Even his ambition to become a writer is shaken in the process. And although Ada tries to convince Marcelo to overcome his crisis, she feels all the more estranged from him.

Some scenes are in flashback: they focus on the beginning of the affair between Ada and Marcelo before the military coup. The memories also have a melancholic tone. Ada ends up isolated in her

Sérgio Saraceni

Screenwriter:

Paulo César Saraceni

Cinematographer:

Guido Cosulich

Art Director:

José Henrique Bello

Editor:

Ismar Porto

Duration:

93 minutes

Genre:

Drama

Cast:

Sérgio Britto
Oduvaldo Vianna Filho
Isabella
Luiz Linhares
Joel Barcelos
Maria Bethânia

Year:

1965

bourgeois ambience with her husband, who insistently reminds her which social class she belongs to. As for Marcelo, he has to choose between conformism and political struggle, but the future looks bleak.

Critique

The 1964 military coup was a traumatic rupture for the generation of Paulo César Saraceni. From that moment on, the idea of the *future* could no longer follow lines previously envisioned. History was unable to offer reassurance to left-wing intellectuals, for whom it was now clear that they did not have control over things – as they never really had. The bourgeoisie and the liberal industrialists did not celebrate their supposed 'noble pact' with the revolutionaries either. Their illusions were over and all they could do was look to the future, no matter how tragic it may have appeared.

No doubt *The Dare* is an uneven film, but the limitations of this unbalanced work are what make it so endearing. *The Dare* is a response to its time, to history being stolen from the people. Furthermore, it contains the sense of intimacy that has characterized Saraceni's work since at least *Arraial do cabo* (co-directed by Mário Carneiro in 1959), adding another rupture to the one imposed by the military: that of the relationship between two lovers.

But that is not to say that the film employs metaphorical parallelisms or a traditional hierarchy of the main characters' relationship troubles against a political backdrop. For the narrative is poised between the concreteness of the bodies (hands, eyes, mouths) and the abstraction of the mind (love, freedom, death). In a certain sense, it tries to build a bridge between the lyricism of *Porto das Caixas* (1962) and the objectivity of *Integração racial/Racial Integration* (1964), but ends up making a further leap into eliminating the distinction between these two points of view. This is because the actual main object of *The Dare* is *time*; time is the very element responsible for its complexity, calling to mind Andrei Tarkovski's concept of the cinematographic image: the image becomes true not only when it lives through time, but also when time remains alive inside of it, 'inside the very photograms' (Tarkovski 1990: 78).

So this is a film about time. At first this may seem quite vague as a statement, but we have to think of 'time' not as the mere duration of an action, but as the *historical* and *aesthetic* material for building a discourse about passion. It's a rather radical political option: for both the film-maker Saraceni and his character Marcelo, to fight is to face not only their own time, but also the times which are behind and ahead of them. For *The Dare* transforms the subjective gaze of the poet into the heart of history itself.

Luís Alberto Rocha Melo

Reference
Tarkovski, A (1990) *Esculpir o tempo*, São Paulo: Martins Fontes.

The Given Word

O Pagador de promessas

Studio/Distributor:
Cinedistri
Director:
Anselmo Duarte
Producer:
Oswaldo Massaini
Screenwriter:
Anselmo Duarte

Synopsis

Zé do Burro, a simple Brazilian north-eastern man with solid moral values, tries to keep the promise he has made to save the life of his pet donkey, Nicolau. He goes to a *candomblé* temple and makes a promise before the image of the goddess *Iansa* (*Orixá*), whom he supposes to be Saint Barbara, to take a Christ-like wooden cross to the altar of the church of Saint Barbara in Salvador. Along with his wife Rosa, he walks seven miles from the backcountry to the inner city carrying the huge cross on his shoulders. Father Olavo, who is responsible for the church, interprets Zé do Burro's behaviour as heresy and prevents his entry and thus the fulfilment of the promise. However, Zé do Burro does not give up and stays on the church steps. His attitude is interpreted differently by a range of people: Rosa, who gets involved with a pimp, a journalist who intends to exploit the

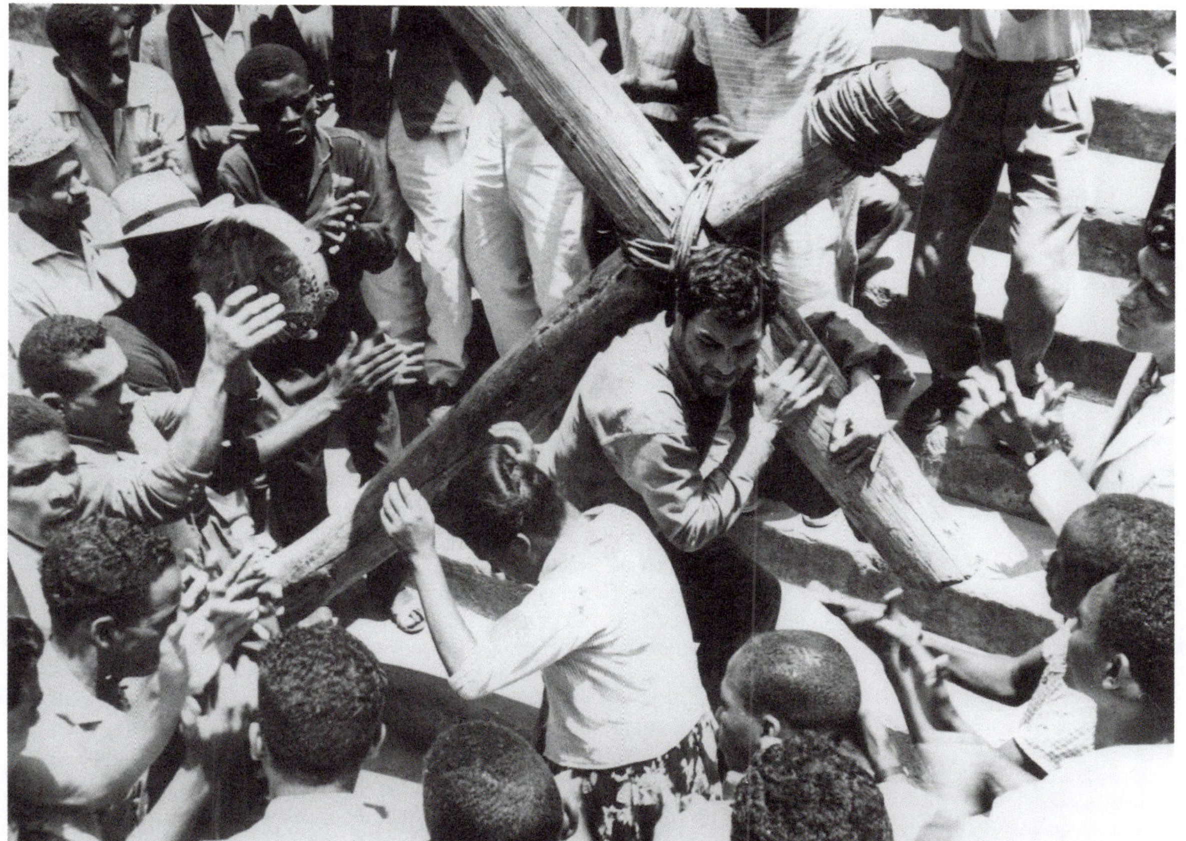

The Given Word

Cinematographer:

Chick Fowle

Art Director:

José Teixeira de Araújo

Editor:

Carlos Coimbra

Duration:

95 minutes

Genre:

Drama

Cast:

Leonardo Villar
Glória Menezes
Geraldo Del Rey
Dionísio Azevedo
Othon Bastos

Year:

1962

event, representatives of the church and the police. The increasing social tension culminates in a tragic turn of events revolving around the possibility of his final entry into the church.

Critique

The historical importance of *The Given Word* lies only partly in the fact that the film is, to date, the only Brazilian film to have won the Palme d'Or at the Cannes Film Festival. Much more important are the tensions and debates surrounding the film and its award, controversies it provoked summarising the sense of a "moment of transition" that marked the period.

In May 1962, news of the award was received positively. The film beat major competitors and was to be highlighted at the festival.

The film achieved the status of a model for the future of Brazilian cinema and thus faced more difficulties than if it had not received the award. What, for some, should have been understood as a positive event in the development of Brazilian cinema became a reason for others, both conservative and "progressive", to criticise.

Some pointed to the academic style of the narrative, or the "ambiguity" and the artificiality of the film in dealing with political and social issues. The treatment given to Brazilian social reality was considered to be close to that of a traditional and commercial cinema.

Another debate concerned the recognition of *The Given Word* as an example of a "renewal" that was underway in Brazilian cinema. With the coining of the expression *Cinema Novo* and the attention given to it in the press between late 1961 and early 1962, *The Given Word* was understood by some as part of the young movement, despite of the advanced age of its director. This assumption intensifies the debate about the movement's boundaries and the differences between "trends" and "authors". For Glauber Rocha, the problem was Brazilian critics who needed a definite term to justify the upsurge of a new cinema. *Cinema Novo* was then disturbed by the fact that a variety of films were for superficial reasons seen as belonging to the movement, whose sense of renewal they did not merit.

Glauber Rocha sought to establish lines of division in what was called "new cinema". In texts of 1961 and early 1962, Rocha and other directors of his group praised the works of authors who were now part of the "dead phase" of the "new cinema". In a previous text which discussed "Movement 62" and not yet *Cinema Novo*, Rocha cites *The Given Word* as part of a movement of 'renewal and rehabilitation of veterans like Anselmo Duarte'. Later, Duarte passes to the group of film-makers who were 'worried about a movie spectacle that gives money and gets awards'. Other critics would admit that *The Given Word* did not really display a concern with the renovation of film, but would also highlight the film's effort to break with the devastating block of "useless films" produced so far in Brazil. For some, Anselmo Duarte legitimately belonged to a movement of renewal in Brazilian cinema. He could be seen, therefore, as a film-maker politically engaged with the progressive and reformist tendencies of the period. However, the traditional and classical narrative was unacceptable to the proponents of a deeper aesthetic break with cinema studios. For this reason, the Cannes award has made clear the disputes amongst those proposing tendencies of renewal. In this debate, the various similarities among these tendencies were more often ignored, while the differences grew and deepened.

The Given Word is certainly not a film that can be completely identified with aesthetic and political renewal. Nevertheless, the debates around the film reveal in a clear way the aesthetic and political divisions that had already been underway for at least a decade in Brazilian cinema. After that, and more so than before, it was no longer possible "to dream" about Brazilian cinema as a unity of ideas, values, goals or directors. Not everyone wanted the same for Brazilian cinema.

Luiz Augusto Rezende

The Guns

Os Fuzis

Studio/Distributor:

Copacabana Filmes, Daga Filmes, Inbracine Filmes

Director:

Ruy Guerra

Producer:

Jarbas Barbosa

Screenwriters:

Miguel Torres
Ruy Guerra

Cinematographer:

Ricardo Aronovich

Art Director:

Calazans Netto

Editor:

Raimundo Higino

Duration:

80 minutes

Genre:

Drama

Cast:

Átila Iório
Nelson Xavier
Paulo César Pereio
Hugo Carvana
Joel Barcellos

Synopsis

The Guns tells a story of hunger in the north-eastern Brazil in the 1960s. A group of soldiers is sent to a small town in this poor region of Latin America during a strong drought. Their duty is to prevent the starving population of the backlands of Bahia from invading and looting a food warehouse, owned by a local politician. When the soldiers arrive, everything seems to be under control. But things are getting worse. In the countryside, near to the town, peasants involved in a religious cult worship a sacred bull. Maybe the hunger is driving the population mad. The soldiers can no longer cope with the tensions and start arguing between themselves. Gaucho, a truck driver, questions the government: 'why, instead of sending us food, do they send us soldiers?' When a man comes to the bar where Gaucho drinks *cachaça*, asking quietly for a box to bury his son in, the truck driver decides that he cannot take it anymore. He starts an uprising.

Critique

The year 1964 was a landmark year for Brazilian cinema. *Vidas secas/ Barren Lives* (Nelson Pereira dos Santos, 1963) and *Deus e o Diabo na terra do sol/Black God, White Devil* (Glauber Rocha, 1964) were both nominated for the Palme d'Or at Cannes. A pioneer of neo-realist aesthetics in Brazil, Nelson Pereira dos Santos directed the former, while the most famous Brazilian film-maker of all-time Glauber Rocha, having started his career as a film critic, made the latter. Despite their good critical reception, they both returned home without an award. But in the same year a third Brazilian film called *The Guns* made an even greater impact in Europe. The film won the Silver Bear Award in the 1964 Berlin Film Festival. The director of *The Guns*, Ruy Guerra, was a Mozambican immigrant to Brazil and also the only one of this young generation of directors with a formal degree in film studies.

The three men had different backgrounds but their movies mark an important moment of worldwide consecration of the *Cinema Novo*.

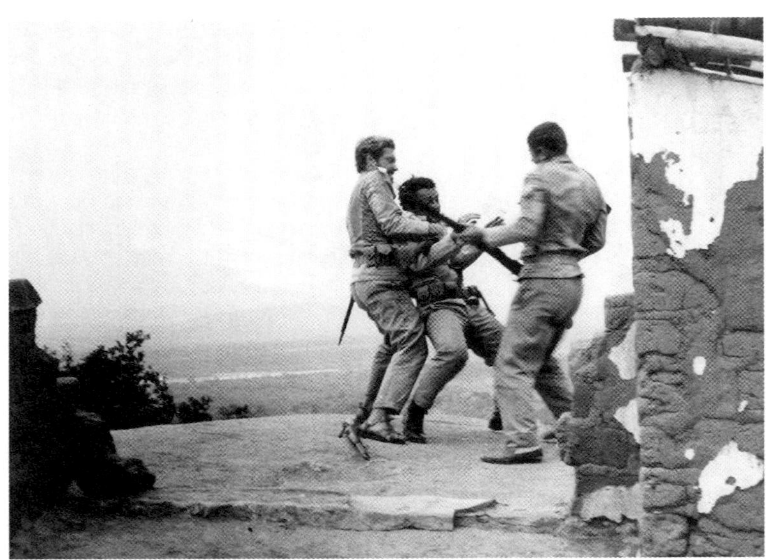

Os fuzis/The Guns

Ivan Cândido
Maria Gladys
Year:
1964

The films have a lot of things in common, a factor contributing to the belief that together they were part of the same artistic movement. Brazilian film scholar Fernão Ramos calls it the 'Trilogy of the *sertão*', '*sertão*' being the name of the region in north-eastern Brazil where these movies were shot, and whose history of social turmoil inspired their plots. A similar conception of cinematography is also shared. The sunny and dry climate of the *sertão* is visually represented by non-filtered light, which literally burns the negative. This avant-garde procedure was a visual trademark of all three films. Now let's come to the particularities of *The Guns*.

Ruy Guerra's first feature film, *Os cafagestes*, released in 1962, was also the first Brazilian film to adopt the sophisticated editing techniques of the French New Wave. *The Guns* goes further in that direction having the most complex *mise-en-scène* of the trilogy. Glauber Rocha criticized Guerra's ability to direct in a more modern fashion, but both Guerra and Rocha received good reviews in the European press. Michel Ciment (1967) wrote in *Positif* that their films were complementary besides their differences while Brazilian critics stressed the different fates of the main characters. The cowboy Manuel defies his boss and his religious guru to turn into a bandit in *Black God, White Devil*. In *The Guns* we get instead the history of a wild bunch of undisciplined soldiers in charge of protecting a warehouse full of food, owned by a corrupt politician during a time of great famine. They are anti-heroes, urban men lost in the wilderness of the *sertão*. The only heroic character is a truck driver who dies at the end of the movie trying to defend the poor against the powerful. Gaucho starts as a sceptical guy who just wants to get his job done and then get out of the god-forsaken place. The general pace of the narrative is similar to Anotonioni's and Bergman's representations of incommunicability which convey the sad boredom of those who pity the poor but cannot do anything about it. But the state of mind of this character changes suddenly, and so does the pace of the film. In the last scene we see real action. A revolting Gaucho starts shooting at the soldiers. Then we see a vibrant combination of the jump-cut edits pioneered by Godard with the re-enactment of a cowboy duel as depicted in a Hollywood western. The duel in this case takes place in the untamed frontier of the Brazilian north-east, where we can also see isolated small towns and open landscapes, as well as cowboys and gunmen. This film is a typical *Nordestern*, a genre of modern Brazilian cinema which combines European and American styles of film-making with Brazilian cultural, political and aesthetic requirements. Our hero, caught up in Brazil's social conditions, dies in the end, and everything remains the same. So, for the French-Brazilian author Jean-Claude Bernardet, the ending of *The Guns* makes us think about how left-wing middle-class intellectuals were wrong about their methods of fighting social injustice in Brazil in the 1960s. We cannot understand poor country people because the tragedy of their hunger is too vast and incomprehensible for an urban audience. Unfortunately, we are only able to identify ourselves with the villains, who were in fact only doing their jobs.

Simplício Neto

Reference
Ciment, M (1967) 'Le Dieu, le diable, e les fusils', *Positif*, May 1967, pp.25-32.

Macunaíma

Studio/Distributor:

Condor Filmes, Filmes do Serro, Grupo Filmes

Director:

Joaquim Pedro de Andrade

Producer:

Joaquim Pedro de Andrade

Screenwriter:

Joaquim Pedro de Andrade

Cinematographer:

Guido Cosulich

Editor:

Eduardo Escorel

Synopsis

Macunaíma is born ugly, the son of an old lady, and drops fully grown from his mother's belly on to the dirt floor of a hut in the Amazon. He is black, she is white. He is raised there alongside two brothers, one black and one white, who don't care much about him. One day when he is being looked after by a woman in the middle of the jungle he is magically transformed into a handsome white prince. After a short interlude, he changes back into a black man. Following the death of their mother, he and his brothers move to the city. Macunaíma is permanently transformed into a white man after stepping into a gushing spring. After wandering through the busy streets of the big city, he falls in love with Ci, a revolutionary woman who kills many government agents who try to capture her. She wears a magical amulet around her neck which is supposed to bring her good luck. Ci and Macunaíma (now white) have a black child. But she and the baby die when a bomb that she is carrying in the baby carriage explodes. Macunaíma then learns that a wealthy industrialist now has the

Duration:

110 minutes

Genre:

Comedy

Cast:

Grande Otelo
Paulo José
Jardel Filho
Dina Sfat
Milton Gonçalves Joana Fomm
Zezé Macedo

Year:

1969

magical amulet that once belonged to Ci. So he decides to dress up like a woman and tries to seduce the villain. But he does not succeed and is made a prisoner in a big feast where he will be the next 'plat du jour'.

Critique

To understand why, as well as being a highlight in the history of *Cinema Novo*, *Macunaíma* is always chosen by critics as one of the best Brazilian movies of all time, it is necessary to show the context to the story of the 'Brazilian hero with no principles' and how its director adapted a literary work that was considered 'unfilmable'.

First of all, Joaquim Pedro de Andrade's work shows an understanding of the similarity between *Cinema Novo* and the Brazilian Modernist movement of the 1920s. *Macunaíma*, first published in 1928, was written by Mario de Andrade, one of Modernism's leading exponents. Both Modernism and *Cinema Novo* had intentions to decolonize Brazil's culture through a critical and nationalist approach to art. Unlike the book, a rhapsody that carries a sense of optimism in its poetic finale, in the movie the hero is devoured by Brazil – 1969 was one of the harshest years of military dictatorship. The movie can be interpreted as a denunciation of the exploitation that, in the vision of the *Cinema Novo* director, would lead inevitably to the country's destruction as an independent nation.

Joaquim Pedro's *Macunaíma* represents the beginning of *Cinema Novo*'s third phase. Like Glauber Rocha in his masterpieces from the previous period, *Deus e o Diabo na terra do sol/Black God, White Devil* (1964) and *Terra em transe/Entranced Earth* (1967), he made use of a radical and liberating aesthetic that contrasted with the cinematic conventions imposed by American narrative models. Through the use of intelligent allegories (not noticed by the bureaucrats who were in charge of censorship in those days), the movie depicts a deep political and social critique of the Brazilian government. The difference between Glauber Rocha's cinema and that of Joaquim Pedro is that the latter aimed for his movie to reach the hearts and minds of the Brazilian people in general, not only the intelligentsia, teaching them how to have a deeper critical view of their own reality.

In order to reach his target, he used comic elements from the *chanchada* (a popular Brazilian cinematic form from the 1940s and 1950s), a visual design that used vibrant colours (including the film's costumes), and a musical selection that places carnival songs alongside popular singers like Roberto Carlos. By doing so, Joaquim Pedro de Andrade broke the curse on the elite intellectuals that surrounded *Cinema Novo* and *Macunaíma* became not only a critical success, but a big hit at the box office.

Marcelo Janot

Porto das Caixas

Studio/Distributor:

Equipe Produções
Cinematográficas, Everon
Filmes

Director:

Paulo César Saraceni

Producers:

Davi Conde
L Carlos Miéle

Screenwriter:

Paulo César Saraceni

Cinematographer:

Mário Carneiro

Art Director:

Mario Carneiro

Composer:

Antonio Carlos Jobim

Editor:

Nelo Melli

Duration:

80 minutes

Genre:

Drama

Cast:

Irma Álvares
Reginaldo Faria
Paulo Padilha
Joseph Guerreiro
Margarida Rey
Sérgio Sanz

Year:

1962

Synopsis

The story is based on a crime that takes place in the city. A woman is abused by her husband. He is simple-minded and rough, but stunned by his wife's mysterious beauty. One day, she decides to kill him. In search of someone who can put her plan into action, she does not hesitate to use all her womanly attributes and feminine charms. The lad from the grocery store, a private soldier, the barber, are each at one point involved with the beautiful Irma. In a trip to the city's fair, destiny confronts her with two images: birds flying and cattle killed out in pasture. The 'animal-woman' must, then, choose between dying in town and taking flight … Lean, with deep and mysterious eyes, she is as dry and empty as the city itself.

Critique

One of the main developments of post-war cinema across the world was the rejection of a continuous narrative development based on a cause and effect relationship. It was no different in Brazil. What would by the beginning of the 1960s turn into the *Cinema Novo* was already largely driven by these processes of narrative dissolution. *Porto das Caixas*, directed by Paulo César Saraceni in 1962, is a film that takes its place among a variety of strategies that transformed (and disturbed) a certain way of making cinema. In addition, its roots are those of a cinema interested in reinventing itself through the representation of the history, and experience, of being Brazilian.

In 1962, Saraceni was not exactly an 'apprentice'. Along with many other directors from *Cinema Novo*, *Sarra* (a nickname he received from Glauber Rocha) began making films after several years as a critic for magazines, newspapers and cinema conferences in the 1950s. As did the French *nouvelle vague*, *Cinema Novo* arose from the personal and intellectual involvement of a group of youths crying out for an urgent renewal of their country's cinema. In 1959, with the noted Brazilian cinematographer Mario Carneiro, Saraceni had already shot *Arraial do cabo*. This film was a short documentary that depicted the social life of a fishing community on the verge of extinction because of the arrival of a nearby industry, a film that is considered one of the main predecessors of the *Cinema Novo*. In early 1960, Saraceni went to Italy with a scholarship to the Centro Sperimentale di Cinematografia in Rome. There, he had full contact with a cinema industry that had been revitalized by neo-realism and a wealth of major post-war works. *Porto das Caixas* is unique in that it promotes the encounter between the language of neo-realism and the reinvention of the image in Brazilian cinema promoted by the *Cinema Novo* group.

The film was shot entirely on location in the small Porto das Caixas, a village located in Itaboraí, close to Rio de Janeiro. At the end of the nineteenth century, due to a privileged location next to the navigable Macacu river, the community became a point of convergence for neighbouring regions. This stimulated population growth and local business, and transformed the place into a political, commercial and religious centre. However, all this already forms part of the past in

Saraceni's film. The Porto das Caixas in this story is almost a ghost town, haunted by the loneliness of its inhabitants, and by a deep sense of disappointment and indifference. Framed in a distant time, it survives to the rhythm of religious processions and local products. The only sign of modernity, the train, serves as a marker that, if there is progress, it leads away from Porto das Caixas.

The unique cinematography by Mário Carneiro is essential in creating the feeling of oppression that surrounds the characters. They do not live under the abundant tropical sunlight so common to images of Brazil in the cinema, but are illuminated by a kind of a firefly, light, small, fragile and fleeting, that hides more than it shows. Inspired by the engravings of the Brazilian artist Oswald Goeldi, the cinematography of *Porto das Caixas* emphasizes the contrast between light and dark, opacities and transparencies, and gives the tone of relationships structured by doubt, uncertainty and insecurity. The music of the celebrated performing artist Antonio Carlos Jobim underlines the mood of seduction and primitive erotica very subtly. One of the most sublime sequences of the film is in the woman's passage by the city's fair. In the best style of Direct Cinema, it is the moment where film blends with the world it records: walking among the crowd, interacting with local natives, the audience witness the story unfold while cinema is being made. This aesthetic and political choice of directness is revealed in the images of the village people who look directly at the camera, breaking the illusion of truth. And challenging cinema, that strange element that walks between them.

Patrícia Rebello da Silva

A Public Opinion

A Opinião Pública

Studio/Distributor:

Film-Industria, Verba Filmes

Director:

Arnaldo Jabor

Producers:

Jorge da Cunha Lima
Luiz Fernando Goulart
Arnaldo Jabor
Nelson Pereira dos Santos

Screenwriter:

Arnaldo Jabor
Carlos Drummond de Andrade_
(poem)_

Synopsis

The film is introduced by images of an apartment building in Copacabana and some narration of ethnographic tastes which intends to discuss the mentality of the middle class in Rio de Janeiro. In a *cinéma-vérité* style, the camera goes down to the streets, the beachside and up back to apartments, interviewing students about their plans for the future; young ladies about their dreams of romance and consumption; passersby about the events going on at that time.

In order to get a broader array of 'public opinion', Arnaldo Jabor also takes us to the backstage of a live TV show, a crowded nightclub, a dirty dorm room in downtown Lapa, a *candomblé* temple and the house of suburb where a woman is said to perform miraculous healings.

In individual interviews, group discussions and public events, ordinary people talk freely about topics such as youth, bourgeois family, sensational phenomena, mysticism, politics, and the mass media.

Critique

Two years after the 1964 military coup that lead to 26 non-democratic years in Brazil, this documentary tried to examine the dreams and

Cinematographers:

Ivo Campos
João Carlos Horta
Dib Lutfi, and others

Editor:

Arnaldo Jabor
Gilberto Macedo
João Ramiro Mello

Duration:

65 minutes

Genre:

Documentary

Persons:

Fernando Garcia
Wanderley Cardoso
Chacrinha, Leila Diniz

Year:

1967

plans (or lack thereof) of a vast human variety for whom the movie camera on the streets was still a novelty.

Unlike most films about Rio de Janeiro in the 1960s, *A Public Opinion* is not interested in landscapes or stereotypes of the city. Rather, Dib Lutfi's camera ends up catching the absurdity that lies behind everyday life and social interactions, in doing so anticipating what Arnaldo Jabor would later explore in his fiction films.

More than an image of the city, this landmark of the Brazilian documentary goes in search of the expression of a social class. It is the middle class, seen as largely responsible for the contradictions exposed by the films of *Cinema Novo*. Political paralysis in exchange for social mobility, the cult of celebrity, the dearth of bigger projects, all of which Jabor detected in middle-class Rio, certainly formed part of previous diagnoses made by the film-maker. Although *Cinema Novo* emphasized the most dramatic dichotomy between the poor and the bourgeoisie, this intermediate social group was a prime target in the minds of film-makers, almost all of whom came from the middle class itself.

Obviously, there is a strategy of inclusion/exclusion that builds on the irony of Arnaldo Jabor's usual arguments. Even in his recent writings for the press, Jabor severely criticizes the social behaviour of the average Brazilian by including himself amongst the targets. In the opening scenes of the film, the commanding voice of the narrator talks about 'us'. However, this demonstration of awareness of the problems creates a nuance in the inclusion of those who made the film. Basically, when he says 'we', he means 'they' – the ones whom he accuses of alienation and passivity. Jabor's first feature film serves the dual agenda of *Cinema Novo*. On the one hand, it delves deep into the country, while on the other it tries to tune Brazilian cinema into the practices of modern film-making. *A Public Opinion* is one of the best echoes, in Brazil, of the revolution that took place in documentary film-making around the world at the dawn of the 1960s. The enormous influence of Jean Rouch and Edgar Morin's *Chronique d'un été/Chronicle of a Summer* (1960) accounts for this new concept of *cinéma-vérité* in which opinions are provoked by the acknowledged presence of the camera, instead of just being observed or retold.

It is indeed the presence of the camera that triggers in people the desire to speak and promotes the relationships that are briefly established within the framework of the screen. It is the camera that stimulates a mischievous boy to grimace while his grandfather speaks seriously, in a deconstruction of solemnity that has become a classic scene. The camera is an expository, ruthless eye in front of which so-called public opinion is produced.

Carlos Alberto Mattos

São Bernardo

Studio/Distributor:

Embrafilme, Mapa Filmes, Saga Filmes

Director:

Leon Hirszman

Producers:

Marcos Farias
Márcio Noronha
Henrique Coutinho
Luna Moschovitch

Screenwriter:

Leon Hirszman

Cinematographer:

Lauro Escorel

Art Director:

Luis Carlos Ripper

Composer:

Caetano Veloso

Editor:

Eduardo Escorel

Duration:

110 minutes

Genre:

Drama

Cast:

Rodolfo Arena
Othon Bastos
Luiz Carlos Braga

Year:

1972

Synopsis

São Bernardo, based on the eponymous novel by Graciliano Ramos published in Brazil in 1934, tells the story of a man born on the farm of São Bernardo, located in the state of Alagoas, in the north-east region of Brazil. Later, in his adult life, he becomes the owner of the property. Paulo Honório meets Madalena, a woman he hires to teach his employees. Soon they are married, although she is not convinced about the possibilities of happiness that this marriage could bring. Paulo Honório needs an heir. However, the differences between his authoritarian personality and the libertarian ideas of his wife will eventually derail the marriage, and consequently the progress of the farm and the very life of its owner.

Critique

In the opening sequence we are immediately presented to the main character and narrator, Paulo Honório, through his voice and images subtly separated in time. We see him sitting at the table on which he writes his memoirs, while his voice-over begins to tell us the story of the man who went from a menial worker to become the owner of the farm where he used to work. As Hirszman's biographer, Helen Salem, notes, the voice of Paulo Honório in the film actually reproduces whole paragraphs of the novel. The film, however, begins with the third paragraph of the book, transforming a phrase that begins with 'Let's continue' into a curious starting point.

From this point on, we watch a film marked by a clear preference for long takes, a still camera, minimalist editing, and the denial of the ordinary use of over-the-shoulder shots in dialogue sequences. In *São Bernardo* the characters talk with their backs to the camera – as in the sequence in which Paulo Honório meets his future wife Madalena at the train station – and in the shadows, as in the sequences in the farm's chapel. These shots all have something in common. Elements such as the distance of the camera, the position of the actors, and the use of backlighting break one of the greatest, if not the greatest, contract made between classical narrative cinema and the spectator: the need to confirm the synchronization of the image of the characters' mouths with their voices. In classical cinema, the spectator is unaware that the effect of synchronization is achieved after shooting, but this concern is ignored by the editing of *São Bernardo*.

Regarding the stillness of the shots, Hirszman himself gives an explanation which is fundamental to understanding some of the relationships between sounds and images in the film. The director reveals that 'the movement comes mainly from the editing, from the conflict between images and sounds'. In some shots, he explains, the image is fixed but the sound moves, changing its point of enunciation within the frame; likewise, in the shots in which the sound is fixed – for instance, when it comes from a voice-over – it is the image that moves.

São Bernardo also features one of the most commented-upon musical soundtracks of modern Brazilian cinema. Leon Hirszman would show Caetano Veloso recordings from the singing of the farm workers on the outskirts of Viçosa, Alagoas where the film was shot.

The director asked the musician to compose a simple theme similar to the singing. Caetano Veloso would then improvise melodic lines while the film was projected. Repeated on four channels, the 'groans', as the musician himself defines them, would create a harmony at the same time modern and closely linked to the original cries of the farm workers.

Fernando Morais da Costa

The Turning Wind

Barravento

Studio/Distributor:

Iglu Filmes

Director:

Glauber Rocha

Producers:

Rex Schindler

Braga Neto

Screenwriters:

Glauber Rocha

José Telles de Magalhães

Cinematographer:

Tony Rabatoni

Composer:

Canjiquinha

Editor:

Nelson Pereira dos Santos

Duration:

80 minutes

Genre:

Drama

Cast:

Antônio Pitanga

Luíza Maranhão

Aldo Teixeira

Lucy Carvalho

Lídio Cirillo dos Santos

Year:

1962

Synopsis

The Turning Wind is the first feature film by Brazilian film-maker Glauber Rocha. The film takes place in a fishing village in Bahia, Rocha's home state. In this village, the arrival of Firmino, a former dweller who comes from the big city, brings a series of transformations to the emotional, economic, political and religious life of the village, where the Afro-descendent cults remain alive and poverty and exploitation rule. In the words of the Director: 'Our film, Barravento, centres on the social problems facing the black fishermen on Bahia's coastline, existing in a terrible situation of exploitation like many others classes in Brazil.' In his film, Glauber, a debut film-maker, already presents some of the themes that will mark his oeuvre such as politics, social unrest, exploitation and mysticism, all characterized by a narrative and a series of formal choices that do not set up the dichotomies and ideological simplifications which these themes might otherwise motivate.

Critique

In 1962, renowned Brazilian critic Alex Viany published an article about *The Turning Wind* entitled '*Barravento*: um problema de comunicação', in which he indicates that to his understanding, the main problem of the film is its 'deficiency of communication'. In this same article, Viany mentions the relationship that Rocha's first feature film has with the documentary tradition, citing *Tabu* (1930) by Robert Flaherty and *Redes* (1936) by Fred Zinnemann.

Time has perhaps allowed enough distance for us to return, with more openness, to the elements considered by Viany as a problematic relationship with the documentary tradition. In a letter to Paulo Emilio Salles Gomes, Glauber Rocha talks about how his *mise-en-scène* is fused with the actors and what was already at large in the environment where *The Turning Wind* takes place. 'I am using black, fabulous, lively, attractive actors who are full of plastic violence and sensuality. The *mise-en-scène* is based on the popular routine of swings and steps of those latent *capoeiristas*.' From his first film, Glauber Rocha sought an image of the world on film, one which would recognize the aesthetic autonomy of this world whilst simultaneously looking for an image capable of linking various national questions such as class struggle and exploitation. To this extent, *The Turning Wind* is the starting point to an excessive cinematographic style.

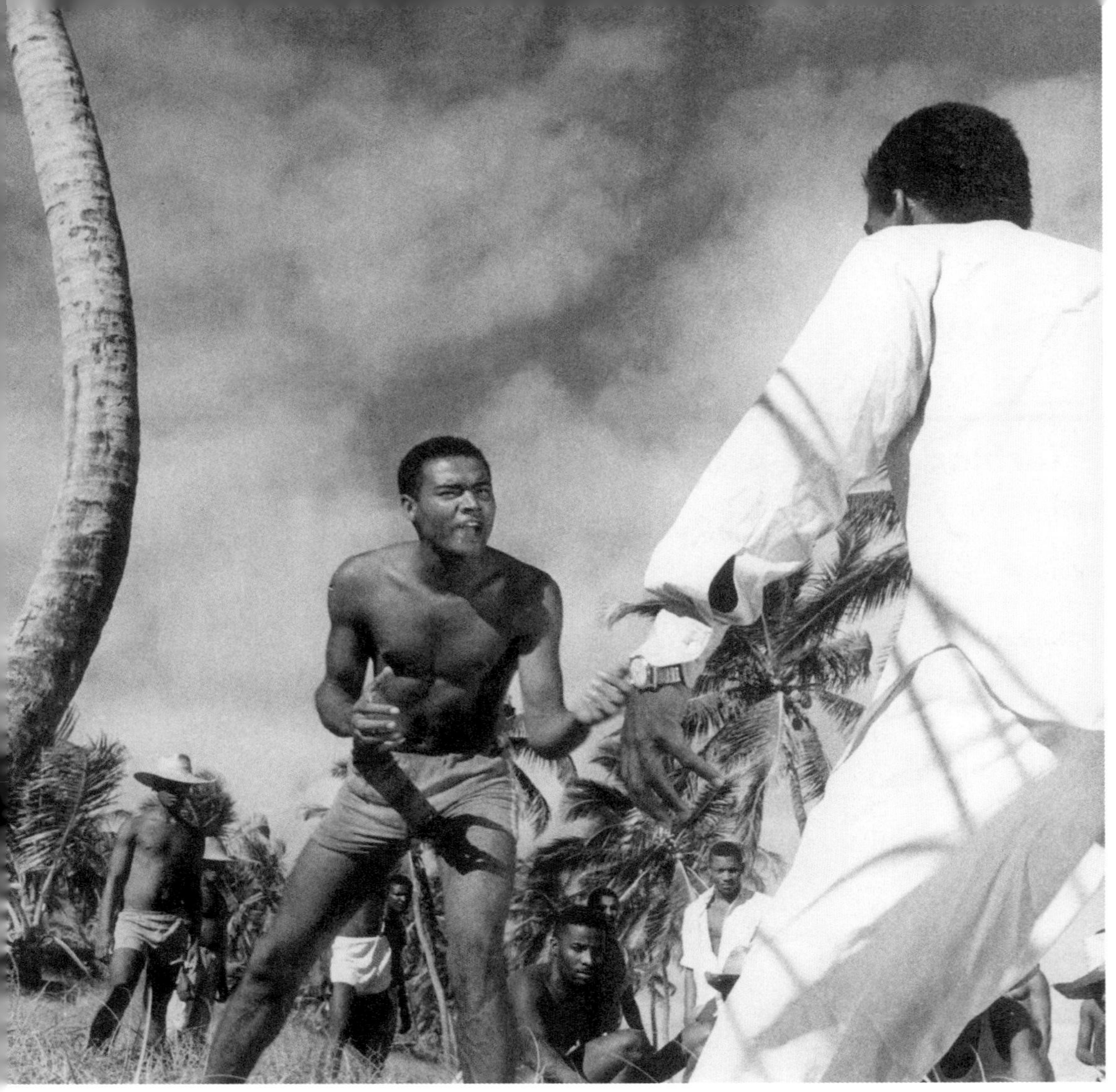

Barravento

Distanced from such ambiguity on the part of Glauber Rocha, the critic Jean-Claude Bernardet wrote in 1979 that *The Turning Wind* 'condemns religious practices and, through its characters, recommends another type of action. [Its director] embodies an intellectual position that judges people from on high in a position of superiority from which he proposes rules' (Bernardet 2009). What Bernardet has perhaps missed is precisely the 'communication problem' identified by Viany. In fact, the film's ambiguous communication, which is more of a characteristic rather than necessarily being a problem, is truncated and strongly attentive to the aesthetic of the world narrated in *The Turning Wind*, allowing Glauber to maintain fidelity to this world as well as to corroborate his critical outlook. The intellectual's position is disturbed by the film's own *mise-en scène*, which balances human relationships in ways which are irreducible to the dichotomies of people/intellectuals, exploiter/exploited, ignorant/enlightened.

Together with the documentary force of *The Turning Wind*, Glauber Rocha brings to 'them' – the fishermen – an excessive subjective and aesthetic knowledge about Afro-Brazilians and Brazil. There, everything was about to be changed, but the film was also facing another element of excess, disturbing the thesis, its messages and discourses. Fortunately, Viany was right; *The Turning Wind* is a problem of communication.

Cezar Migliorin (trans. Natália Pinazza)

Reference
Bernarddet, JC (2009). *Cinema Brasileiro: Propostas para uma história*. São Paulo: Cia das Letras. p. 93.

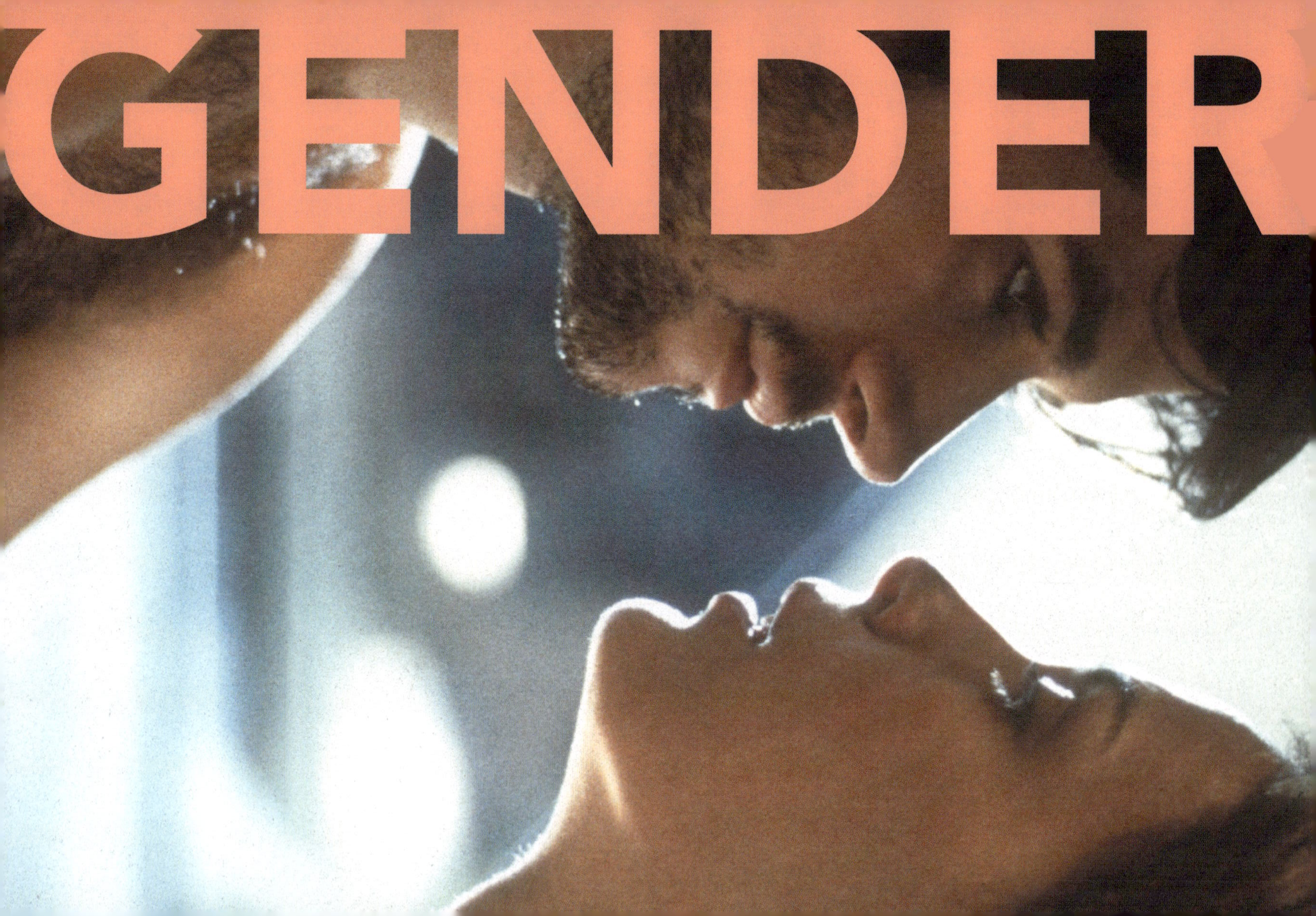
GENDER

Brazilian gender relations have been prominent in the country's prolific film production since its early years. Regardless of the period the films are made, the social imaginaries related to gender identities that are evident in them provide important information about Brazilian society. For instance, many of the films repeat the gender roles and identities dictated by patriarchal society that have been reinforced since Portuguese colonialism, especially the ideal binary genders that propagate heteronormativity, that is, hegemonic masculinity and femininity. In so doing they bring to the fore 'the perceived salience of the patriarchal family in Brazilian history' (Parker 1991: 34). This means that the man has to be powerful and tough (i.e. a proper *macho*), whereas the woman must be feminine, honest and submissive. These have been the two models on which various films based their characters' gender (and sexual) identities over the years.

Nevertheless, other genders have also appeared in the country's film-making. These gender identities transgress patriarchy's binary frame, and they have been depicted in Brazilian cinema from as early as the 1920s (Moreno 2002). Such hegemonic gender transgressors have particularly been represented in the figure of the male homosexual, especially suggested through cross-dressing up to and during the 1960s. But these cross-dressed characters were meant to be comic (e.g. the black comedian Grande Otelo wearing a blonde wig and a dress while playing Juliet in *Carnaval no fogo/Carnival on Fire* [Watson Macedo, 1949]) rather than addressing homosexuality itself. However, other representations have also become prominent, mainly from the 1970s onwards, including the effeminate homosexual (denominated *bicha*/'fairy') (e.g. *Bacalhau/Codfish* [Adriano Stuart, 1975]), the 'straight-acting' homosexual (e.g. *Aqueles dois/Those Two* [Sergio Amon, 1985]), male prisoners (e.g. *Barrela: escola de crimes/Barrela: School of Crimes* [Marco Antonio Cury, 1990]) and married men (e.g. *Barrela: escola de crimes/Kiss on the Asphalt* [Bruno Barreto, 1980]), among others.

It is fair to argue that such portrayals emerged not from the film-makers' interest in portraying homosexuality as such (i.e. as an identity), at least in the past, but to contrast to or indeed suggest homosexuals' degeneration from the models that patriarchal Brazilian society prescribes to its citizens. This is well illustrated by the representations of male and female homosexuals in the second half of the last century, who were mostly depicted in negative ways and often explored either as a source of 'laughter' – concerning male homosexuals – or as sexual 'stimulators' in the case of women (especially the 'heterosexuals') involved in lesbian sex. The films portraying lesbianism were indeed more interested in titillating the heterosexual male audience than presenting it as an identity. Regarding the male homosexual, Moreno (2002) argues that it is during the 1970s that a gay pattern for the subsequent decades was established in Brazilian cinema, and that this would be expanded into television and radio.

Putting these issues aside, such representations, as well as those of the heterosexual binary, although repeating the prescribed patriarchal formula, do indeed indicate that while these identities are repeated on screen, their depictions indicate that gender is a 'situation' – it is a performance rather than a trait based on

the biologically born body or the preferences of patriarchy. Hence, although gender
identities in Brazilian cinematic production repeat the socially constructed gender
roles (*macho/bicha*; woman/*sapatão* [dyke]) that populate the Brazilian popular
imaginary, such representations echo Butler's (1990) assertion that gender identity is
performatively constituted.

The construction, or better phrased, the performance of gender thus responds
to patriarchy's demands and is associated with the social context, illustrated, for
example, in its connection to politics and religion. As is commonly known, Brazil has
a strong Catholic background (and still is predominantly Catholic) and has had two
dictatorships, which have considerably influenced the development of gender and
sexual politics in the country and this is echoed in its cinematic production. A good
example of this is the role of women as the *mulher direita* (an honest woman) – the
'Virgin Mary type', from a Catholic viewpoint – to which every woman should aspire
in Brazil, which means retaining virginity in the case of unmarried women and being
good housewives and mothers for the married ones. If a woman does not follow this
model, she is considered loose, attracting much condemnation from conservative
Brazilian society.

Many films played on the imaginaries related to women and the consequences of
their behaviour for patriarchal males. For example, various sexploitation films in the
1970s and the 1980s, known as *pornochanchadas*, exploited many issues that were
connected to women's identity, particularly virginity (e.g. *Mais ou menos virgem/
More or Less Virgin* [Mozael Silveira, 1974]), and males' concerns with betrayal (e.g.
O Clube das infiéis/The Unfaithful Females' Club [Cláudio Cunha, 1975]). They
also suggested males' fear of impotence and castration (e.g. *As Mulheres do sexo
violento/The Women of Violent Sex* [Francisco Cavalcanti, et al. 1976]), among
other anxieties. Moreover, the titles of various *pornochanchadas* gave attributes
to the women in the films, including the way they behaved and their race, and
mentioned taboos such as virginity, sodomy, orgies, interracial sex, homosexuality
and sadomasochism. They also presented religious judgments, especially regarding
sexuality, amongst others. However, even if unaware of doing so, these sexploitation
films documented a sexual revolution for women within the dictatorship that was
mostly absent from 'mainstream' cinema. But because commercial purposes were
the core of such films, as they were in other contexts, these films were consequently
ignored and 'deemed unworthy of serious critical attention' (Cook 2005: 56). As a
result, they have since been treated like 'a dirty little secret' (Schaefer 2005: 80).

Hence, women's identity has been depicted in Brazilian cinema in different ways
and explores various topics, for example rape, which symbolizes gender violence: a
crucial aspect to 'any full understanding of the relations between men and women in
patriarchal Brazil' (Parker 1991) – as illustrated in *A Filha do advogado/The Lawyer's
Daughter* (Jota Soares, 1926), *À Meia-noite levarei sua alma/At Midnight I'll Take
Your Soul* (José Mojica Marins, 1964) and *Fêmeas em fuga/Women in Fury* (Michele
Massimo Tarantini, 1984). Women's identity also covers issues concerning female
sexuality such as bisexuality and/or lesbianism, as in *Gisele/Giselle* (Victor Di Mello,
1980), *Women in Fury* and *Vera* (Sérgio Toledo, 1986), and, of course, the ideal
Brazilian female type (e.g. *A Super fêmea/Super Woman* [Aníbal Massaini Neto, 1973]).
Just in the small selection of films discussed in this chapter, one sees that despite the
themes repeated across genres, the films still have many particularities of their own
and show the plurality of gender representations in the country's cinematic production.

As far as concerns men's identity, the *macho* (the alpha male) has been desired and
propagated as the ideal type in various films over the years (e.g. the womanizer, the
gangster). But despite many films promoting this male type, such a masculine ideal
is mocked in some films, as illustrated in many *chanchadas* such as *Nem Sansão nem*

Dalilah/Neither Samson Nor Deliliah [Carlos Manga, 1954]) and in various films of other genres (e.g. drama, comedy) such as *Se eu fosse você/If I Were You* (Daniel Filho, 2006). Even if some films do not directly 'mock' this type, they question its prescribed identity, especially in relation to sexuality (more specifically concerning the sexual roles that define gender identities in the Brazilian social imaginary) to show that gender can and does go beyond the heteronormative binary male/female, as suggested in *Amores possíveis/Possible Loves* (Sandra Werneck, 2001). Or they indicate that these hegemonic types of masculinity are troubled, archaic and need challenging, as happens in *Deus e o Diabo na terra do sol/Black God, White Devil* (Glauber Rocha, 1964) and *At Midnight I'll Take Your Soul*.

Nevertheless, changes in portrayals of gender, particularly concerning homosexuals, have happened only more recently, mostly in the current century, in which a considerable number of films have gay characters in them. These characters are portrayed in ways that differ from the previous century, but the features present in the latter are also evident in the current century's cinematic production, without showing much progress in the depictions of certain characters. Some types of homosexual characters, for example the *bicha louca* ('crazy fairy'), prevail. Lesbians, on the other hand, are under-represented in this new century.

An aspect worth noting is that a number of films, however, challenge or mock the patriarchal ideal that men need to prove themselves to be a 'real man', must 'act like a man', have a 'man's job' and 'dress like a man', among other hegemonic behaviours related to the alpha male that men are expected to follow. Some films also challenge or mock the patriarchal ideal that women have to be housewives, politically passive (as challenged by Rosa in *Black God, White Devil*) and needless to say astonishingly beautiful, but also have a sculptured body while being gentle, a virgin yet *gostosa* (a 'hot mamma'): *Super Woman* is probably the best example that mocks the search for the perfect woman.

To conclude, although mirroring the patriarchal imaginary surrounding gender in Brazil, these films show that such identities are performed. That is, one is a proper man or woman in society's eyes if he or she acts out those traits related to hegemonic genders, which do not necessarily comply with the roles both may adopt away from society's scrutiny. Moreover, even if many of the films portray gender mostly in the traditional ways that are engrained in the social imaginary, various more recent ones have provided patterns that challenge or subvert those conceptions and show new possibilities beyond the binary pair that is seen as the ideal in most of the country's film production. The films therefore touch on notions that 'shape one's sexual experience in contemporary Brazilian life' (Parker 1991: 34).

Antônio Márcio da Silva

References

Butler, J (1990) *Gender Trouble: Feminism and the Subversion of Identity*, New York and London: Routledge.

Cook, P (2005) *Screening the Past: Memory and Nostalgia in Cinema*, London and New York: Routledge.

Moreno, A (2002) *A personagem homossexual no cinema brasileiro*, 2nd edn, Rio de Janeiro: Funarte and EdUFF.

Parker, R G (1991) *Bodies, Pleasures and Passions: Sexual Culture in Contemporary Brazil*. Boston: Beacon Press.

Schaefer, E (2005) 'Dirty little secrets: Scholars, archivists and dirty movies', *The Moving Image*, 2: 2, pp. 79–105.

At Midnight I'll Take Your Soul

À Meia-noite levarei sua alma

Studio/Distributor:

Indústria Cinematográfica Apolo

Director:

José Mojica Marins

Producers:

Geraldo Martins
Ilídio Martins
Arildo Iruam

Screenwriter:

José Mojica Marins

Cinematographers:

Giorgio Attili

Art Director:

José Vedovato

Composer:

Salatiel Coelho
Hermínio Gimenez

Editor:

Luiz Elias

Duration:

81 minutes

Genre:

Horror

Cast:

José Mojica Marins
Valéria Vasquez
Magda Mei
Nivaldo de Lima

Year:

1964

Synopsis

Zé do Caixão or Coffin Joe is a cruel undertaker in a nameless Brazilian village who terrorizes its citizens with extreme violent behaviour. Although obsessed with the supernatural, Zé do Caixão believes that the essence of life lies in the 'immortality of the blood'. His goal is to find the 'perfect woman' – a character with a similar mindset who can bear him the 'perfect son' to continue his bloodline. Having murdered his wife Lenita, whom he considered unsuited to the task of giving him offspring, his sexual desire befalls on his best friend's fiancée, Terezinha. He kills his best friend Antônio, then beats and rapes the latter's fiancée. Terezinha hangs herself after casting a curse on Zé, vowing to return from the dead to take his soul away. On a rampage, Zé gouges out a man's eyes and amputates an adversary's fingers using a broken bottle. He also lashes an opponent with a whip and thrusts a crown of thorns into a man's face. The film climaxes on All Souls' Day with Zé envisioning his own dead body inside a coffin and being chased by a procession of ghosts. He takes refuge in a crypt, where he has to face the decomposing, maggot-infested bodies of the couple he killed. The sight drives him out of his mind and leaves him in a death-like state. The undertaker's trilogy continues in the sequel *Esta Noite encarnarei no teu cadáver/This Night I'll Possess Your Corpse* (1967) and unravels in *Encarnação do demônio/Embodiment of Evil* (2008).

Critique

Although Zé do Caixão's fury is directed at anyone who stands in the way of his plans, the scene of Terezinha's violation could be taken as an example of horror films' gender-specific violence. Shot in black-and-white stock and lit for monochrome, the painfully long battering scene that takes place before the rape is shown almost without any cuts. Zé's *coup de grâce* takes the form of a punch delivered to Terezinha's face. Because of an unexpected change in point of view, the scene becomes a reverse shot and the spectator is the one to receive the blow. Terezinha's lips in extreme close-up are bleeding and half open in a sensual way. Zé now has her on the sofa. He kisses and feels her body, turning his face to the camera with a twisted grin – the scene resembles a vampire attack. The rape takes place off-camera and her deflowering is symbolized by the death of a canary, which Terezinha squeezes in her hand as she is being violated. The sequence concludes with Terezinha on the sofa looking somewhat contented but she then swears supernatural vengeance.

It could be claimed that *At Midnight I'll Take Your Soul* is a female revenge story in which the woman Zé raped comes back in the form of a ghost (real or imaginary). Despite the moralistic conclusion, the sexualized scenes of brutality against women are not less potent because they are vindicated at the end. The problem is the representation of sexual violence in association with eroticism. Sexual violence in horror fiction should not be seen to have a straightforward connection with what would be presumed to be its real-life enactment. The scene in question makes clear that what went on was against the woman's will, illustrates how awful rape is, and effectively shows how it is linked to Zé do Caixão's frustration and desire for dominance. It may galvanize constructive responses to the problem of actual rape in the real world. However, such a scene necessarily involves the possibility of representing violence against women as an act of sexual pleasure. Nevertheless, the lowering of personal anxiety about images of sexual excitement in fiction is not the same as a lowering of moral principles in real life.

The use of reverse-shot reduces the possibility of the audience being able to identify with the aggressor, and may challenge straightforward interpretations of sex-gender association systems. The inevitability of the blow delivered in reverse shot may signify viewers' inability to defend themselves against Zé do Caixão. *At Midnight I'll Take Your Soul* portrayed previously unseen acts of violence for Brazilian audiences in the 1960s – a prelude in certain ways to the Brazilian *coup d'état*, and the perfect introduction to the work of a master director.

Daniel Serravalle de Sá

Black God, White Devil

Deus e o Diabo na terra do sol

Studio/Distributor:

Banco Nacional de Minas Gerais, Copacabana Filmes, Luiz Augusto Mendes Produções Cinematográficas

Director:

Glauber Rocha

Producers:

Luiz Augusto Mendes
Copacabana Filmes

Screenwriters:

Glauber Rocha
Walter Lima Junior

Cinematographer:

Waldemar Lima

Art Director:

Paulo Gil Soares

Composer:

Sérgio Ricardo

Synopsis

Manuel is a cowherd in Coronel Morais's farmland. After being deceived by his boss, Manuel kills the latter in an act of revolt and despair, and flees the farm with his wife Rosa. In their initial escape, the couple encounter Sebastião, who wanders through the backlands promising his followers salvation and prosperity. Manuel blindly devotes himself to Sebastião and abides by his rules, which include burning tax collection papers – believed to be a devilish creation of the newly established republic – and seeking absolution for one's sins through acts of penitence. Unable to bear Sebastião's irrational acts, Rosa kills him. As the couple continue their journey through the backlands, they meet Corisco and his group of *cangaceiros* (rural bandits), who are hiding after the massacre that killed their leader Lampião and most of his group. After being accepted into the group, Manuel joins them in ransacking a powerful landowner's farmstead. The group is soon found by the gunman Antônio das Mortes, who is paid by the landowners and the Catholic Church to kill the bandits, but further events soon ensue.

Critique

Despite its linear narrative, *Black God, White Devil* is a complex film about the decadent rural patriarchal society of the north-east region of Brazil, which is strongly rooted in feudal relations of power. It is not surprising that this is one of the founding films of the *Cinema Novo* movement of the 1960s, which attempted to expose the public to deep-rooted social issues of the rural and urban poor. The film is based on concrete historical facts and characters. Sebastião (Lídio Silva) embodies the religious fanaticism of the messianic leaders of the region, whereas Corisco (Othon Bastos) represents the

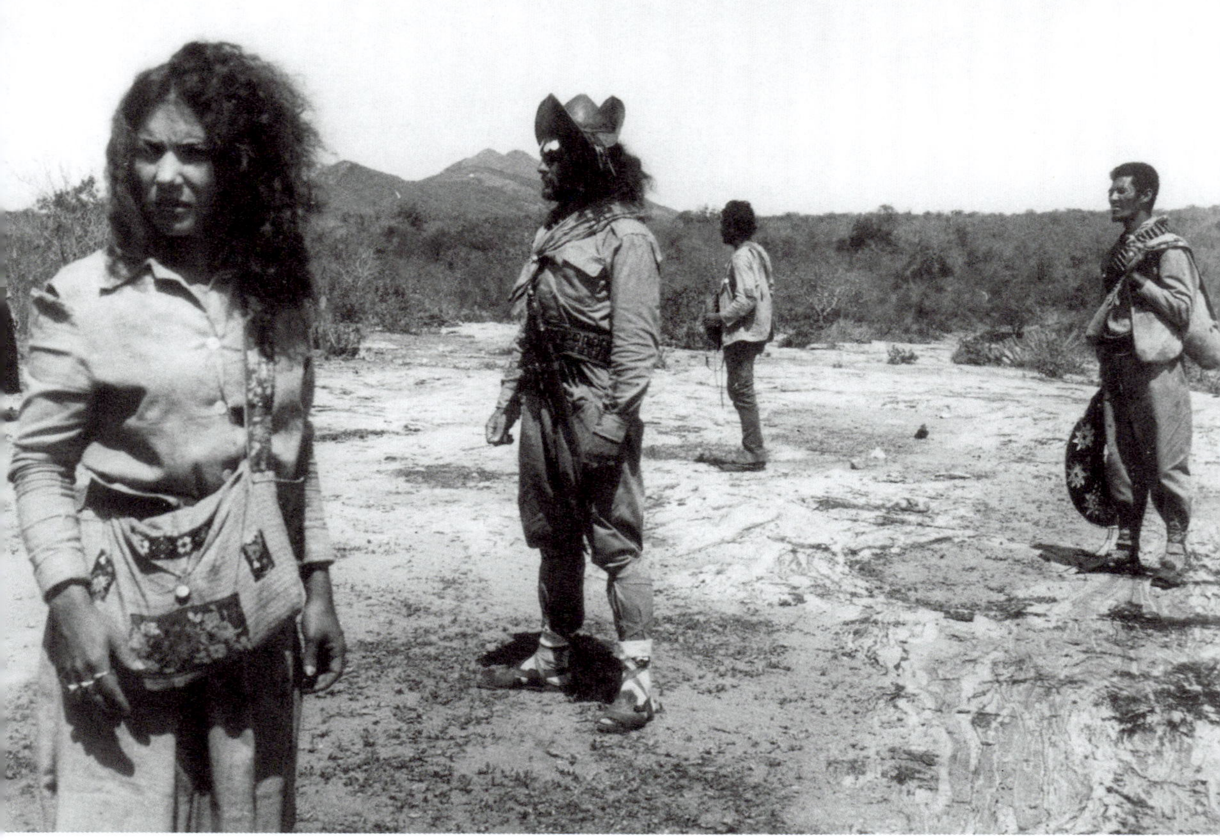

Black God, White Devil

Editors:

Rafael Justo Valverde
Glauber Rocha

Duration:

125 minutes

Genre:

Fiction

Cast:

Geraldo Del Rey
Yoná Magalhães
Maurício do Valle
Othon Bastos
Lídio Silva

Year:

1964

famous character of the *cangaço* movement of rural banditry. The characters take part in a highly allegorical narrative and conjure up the contradictions of good and evil. Beyond this binary opposition, the film also attempts to destabilize the rigid social structure of the traditional rural north-east, particularly evident in the display of gender identities.

In *Black God, White Devil*, the main female character plays a quiet but nonetheless crucial role in the shaping of Manuel's (Geraldo Del Rey) revolutionary consciousness. Rosa's (Yoná Magalhães) visible disbelief in the preacher Sebastião culminates in her stabbing and killing him, saving Manuel from his blind faith. In many ways, Rosa's character represents conflicting aspects of the women of the north-east: she stands by her husband and complies with her traditional household duties on the one hand, yet takes the leading role and uses physical violence to save herself and Manuel on the other. It is in the stunningly composed scene where Rosa and Corisco kiss that Rosa's potentially subversive power emerges, representing the attraction between violence and consciousness.

The leitmotif of the film – the *sertão* will turn into the sea, and the sea into the *sertão* – represents the messianic idea of ultimate freedom. This is played out in the arresting final scene, in which Manuel and Rosa run away from Antônio das Mortes (Maurício do Valle) against the harsh backdrop of the backlands (known as the *sertão*) with its arid climate, dry vegetation and blinding sunlight, which intensify the desolate social environment of violence and poverty throughout the film. Manuel's final run – as Rosa falls down and is left behind – also allegorically represents the fate of thousands of men in the *sertão* who had to flee to large cities in search of work, often leaving behind their wives and families.

The visual aspect of the film is constructed through a complex combination of styles. The choice of camera angles reinforces the film's dichotomy between heaven and earth, as evident in the scenes where Manuel is following Sebastião to the top of Monte Santo, which represent Manuel's ascension to a divine world, depicted through upward and downward-tilted camera angles. When Corisco is introduced in the narrative, a low-angle camera horizontally pans over the arid vegetation, characterizing Corisco's profane qualities. Crucially, however, the cinematography challenges the dialectics between good and evil inasmuch as the narrative emphatically presents Sebastião's and Corisco's contradictions. For instance, Corisco's violent rape of a colonel's wife despite his tenderness towards Rosa, and Sebastião's beating of prostitutes despite his religious devotion reinforce the theme of male violence against women in the *sertão*. Stylistically, the unusual framing, restless handheld camera and frantic editing rhythm are some of the features that preserve *Black God, White Devil*'s originality today.

Mariana AC da Cunha

Giselle

Gisele

Studio/Distributor:

Vidya Produções Cinematográficas

Director:

Victor di Mello

Producers:

Bernardo Goldzzal
Carlo Mossy

Screenwriter:

Vitor di Mello

Cinematographer:

Antônio Gonçalves

Synopsis

After living in Europe, Giselle (Alba Valéria), the daughter of the wealthy farm owner Lucchini, comes back to spend time with her family. Her visit exposes the complexity of the family's ties and relationships, especially those involving Giselle, her stepmother Haydée and the farm worker Ângelo. Haydée, Giselle and Ângelo engage in torrid sexual relations that represent a deviation from the family's hypocritical social status. The trio has many pleasurable sexual encounters and they soon find in Serginho, Haydée's son who is visiting the farm, a suitable partner for both Giselle and Ângelo. Their somehow 'idyllic' sexual encounters arouse the hatred in and spark violence from the small town 'machos'. The four of them are violently raped and this incident slowly disentangles the quartet's intimate relationships. Meanwhile, Giselle meets Ana, a former revolutionary who fought against Brazilian military dictatorship, and has a brief romance with her that triggers Haydée's jealousy.

Composer:

Adolphe Adam

Editor:

Giuseppe Baldacconi

Duration:

90 minutes

Genre:

Pornography (pornochanchada)

Cast:

Alba Valéria
Carlo Mossy
Maria Lúcia Dahl
Nildo Parente
Ricardo Faria
Monique Lafond

Year:

1980

Critique

The time of Giselle's release coincided with the gradual entrance of international porn production in the country. This process drastically changed national cinema, which stemmed from a relationship between the pornographic and other matrices of a 'mass and popular' ('matriz cultural massiva-popular' [Martín Berbero 2003]) cinema. In Giselle, the matrix of *pornochanchada* coalesces with an international porn tradition in the style of *Emmanuelle* (Just Jaeckin, 1974). From the very beginning of the film, there are frequent exchanges of gazes that mobilize desire and pleasure. Although the codes that mark the hardcore tradition (as defined by Linda Williams) are not all present, there is, in the 'sex numbers', an intense choreography of bodies engaged in sexual acts that is structured (in terms of narrative) in a very precise way, emphasizing the political and moral aspects of the film's discourse. In Giselle, sex is both a symptom of socio-political crisis and a form of salvation. Deviance – represented as a symptom – is presented in a rough way, exploring the sounds of violent acts and a '*mise-en-scène* of the camera' that avoids the traditional exploratory movements around the bodies. In these scenes (most notably a rape scene), the camera stays at a distance (in comparison to the very intimate manner that it participates in the other 'sex numbers', particularly those involving the four main characters). As for the potential for salvation from the sexual encounters (which can be related to Pasolini's *Teorema/Theorem* [1968]), especially as represented in the sexual acts of Giselle, Haydée (Maria Lúcia Dahl), Ângelo (Carlo Mossy) and Serginho (Ricardo Faria), the camera seems to act as a participant, inviting us to share the pleasures being exchanged in the group's sexual acts, and the soundtrack marks an intense use of classical music. These narrative elements help to construct a kind of pornotopia where all differences (of gender and class) are overcome by consensual and pleasurable sex that is performed and offered to please the audience's gaze. The way the film presents the homosexual 'sex numbers' between Ângelo and Serginho, as well as between Giselle and Haydée, is particularly striking, especially if we consider the historical context (early 1980s) – when Brazilian society was still living in a conservative and moralist military dictatorship despite beginning its redemocratization process. In these sequences, the choreography stresses the mutual aspect of the sexual acts, the pleasures of giving and receiving, which reinforce the sense of pornotopia. It is the very constraints of the patriarchal society, represented by the hypocritical, moralistic and violent values of the family order, which blow up the pornotopia. At the end of the film, a family ritual conducted by Lucchini (Nildo Parente) – who represents patriarchal society – marks the ultimate dissolution of the family's ties, which makes it possible for everyone to follow their individual paths. The film does not deny its 'mass-popular' roots, presented in the way everything is played out and in the many inserts of 'sex numbers'. These mechanisms invite the audience to engage in a 'passional' and visceral response, in accordance with the so-called body genres such as melodrama, horror and pornography that are structured in an excessive mode. Certainly part of the commercial success of *Giselle* is due to the strategic use of this popular/excessive matrix, but such affiliation does not prevent the film from acting out disturbingly reflexive questions regarding patriarchal traditions.

Mariana Baltar Freire

Reference

Jesús Martín Berbero (2003), *Dos meios às mediações: comunicação, cultura e hegemonia*. Rio de Janeiro: Ed. UFRJ.

If I Were You

Se eu fosse você

Studio/Distributor:

Total Entertainment, Espaço/Z, Fox Filmes do Brasil

Director:

Daniel Filho

Producers:

Walkiria Barbosa
Iafa Britz
Daniel de Castro
Marcos Didonet
Daniel Filho
Vilma Lustosa

Screenwriters:

Rene Belmonte
Iafa Britz
Adriana Falcão
Daniel Filho
Roberto Frota
Carlos Gregório

Cinematographer:

José Roberto Eliezer

Art Director:

Marcos Flaksman

Composer:

Roberto de Carvalho and others

Editor:

Felipe Lacerda

Duration:

108 minutes

Genre:

Synopsis

Cláudio, a successful publicist, and Helena, a music teacher, love each other but struggle to keep their marriage together. One day, they inexplicably wake up having switched bodies: Cláudio's mind has migrated to Helena's body and vice versa. Uncomfortable with this, they agree to maintain a semblance of normalcy until they set about changing the intolerable situation. They decide, therefore, to embrace each other's lives. Professional pressures suffered by Cláudio, family interventions experienced by Helena, and various domestic conflicts and tensions force both characters to deal with the peculiarities of the opposite sex, causing a series of comic situations. By the end, they both reconsider their opinions and behaviour, and unite to try to escape their predicament.

Critique

Films produced by Globo Filmes, since 1998, have performed surprisingly well at the box office, proving fundamental to the enhanced competitiveness of Brazilian cinema. In fact, Brazil's biggest box office successes of the last ten years have all received some form of direct participation or support from the production company. Of course, in terms of marketability, these films have benefited greatly from the promotional vehicles that are part of the Rede Globo media conglomerate, including a number of newspapers, radio stations and television channels across the country.

The success of the 2006 production *If I Were You* is partly because of the closer relations Brazilian production companies (such as Total Entertainment) have forged with national distributors, and partly because of the support received from major North American studios in Brazil (such as Fox Film) – through fiscal incentives under Article 3 of the Audiovisual Law. Other key factors are the casting of TV soap-opera stars (all from the stables of Rede Globo) and the (co) production role of Globo Filmes.

Having TV stars in their cast boosts the competitiveness of Brazilian films in the domestic market because national television productions, especially TV soaps, have been the main wellsprings of fame since the 1970s. Such is the success of Rede Globo's TV soaps that they continue to serve as the audience's most influential benchmark. The presence of TV stars is therefore a huge draw for public attention and tends to facilitate negotiations with channels of distribution.

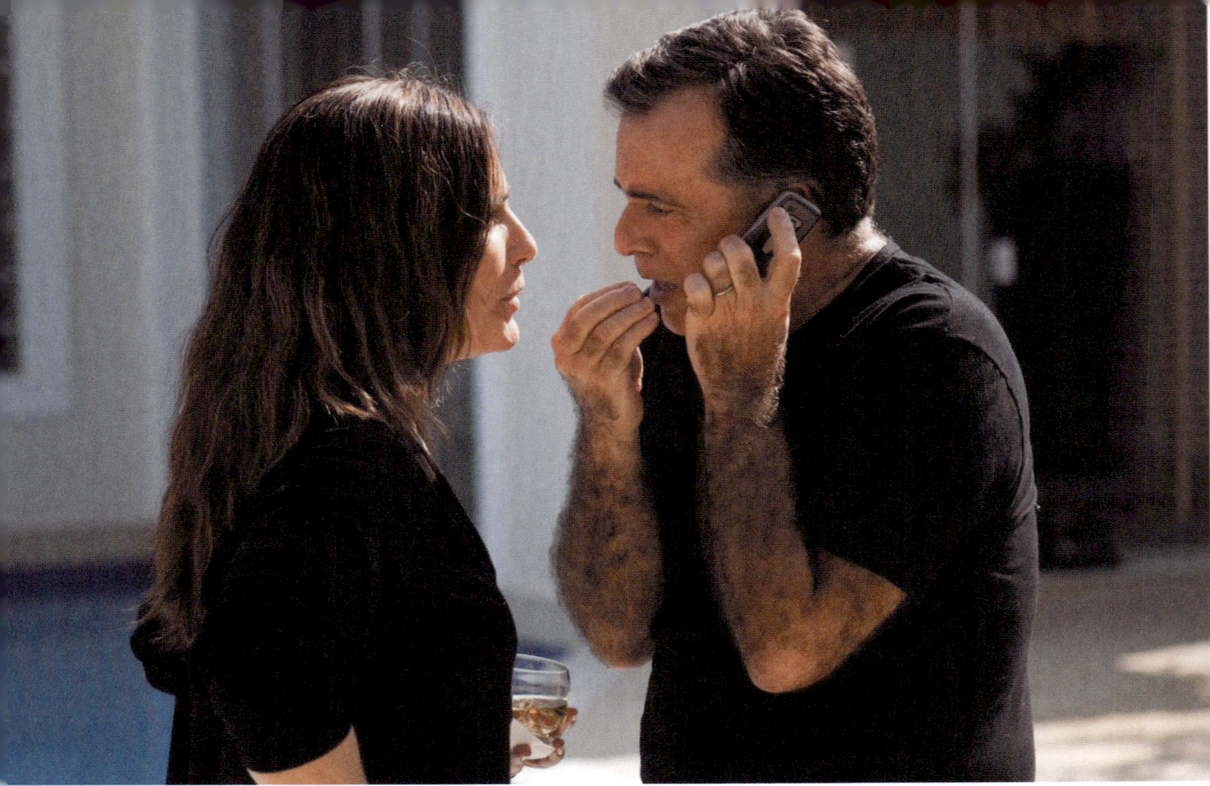

Se eu fosse voce/If I Were You

Comedy

Cast:

Tony Ramos
Glória Pires
Denis Carvalho

Year:

2006

The film *If I Were You* stars Glória Pires and Tony Ramos, two of Globo's longest-standing A-list TV stars. One of the most catching aspects of their performance in the film is that the filmic narrative gave the performers the opportunity to deconstruct their own trademark models of masculinity and femininity, to comic effect. Body-switching as a plot device is by no means new, having been explored in numerous successful comedies such as Tom Hanks's *Big* (Penny Marshall, 1988) and Jim Carrey's *Liar, Liar* (Tom Shadyac, 1997), to name only a few. However, in the Brazilian market, the popular appeal of these TV stars gives this old formula a new lease of life. Another major factor is the well-constructed dialogue, especially as it explores current taboos, mores and notions of alterity. In fact, the dialogue ends up carrying the movie, although, in cinematic terms, it merely revisits clichés and hackneyed formulas.

In 2009, Globo Filmes released *If I Were You 2/Se eu fosse você 2* (Daniel Filho), which set a box office record of six million viewers, and chalked up nearly 40 per cent of total receipts for domestic films that year. Other successful films released by Globo Filmes in 2009, including *Divã/In Therapy* (José Alvarenga Jr.), *A Mulher invisível/The Invisible Woman* (Cláudio Torres) and *Os normais 2 – A noite mais maluca de todas* (José Alvarenga Jr) revealed a clear preference for more commercial, and less authorial comedies leading the Brazilian market.

These observations indicate the need for new strategies to consolidate a wider distribution of Brazilian cinematographic output, and one that can cater for the heterogeneity of the public. It also raises the issue of which model the domestic film industry intends to follow: should it go for the big-budget blockbuster comedy, or should it opt for fewer but better films that struggle to break even? Then again, should not public investment be shared out among low- and middle-budget films in the interests of a genuine democratization of access? The latter is a latent issue when it comes to the still developing Brazilian film industry.

Alessandra Meleiro and Kátia Augusta Maciel

The Lawyer's Daughter

A Filha do advogado

Studio/Distributor:

Aurora Filmes

Director:

Jota Soares

Producer:

João Pedrosa da Fonseca

Screenwriter:

Ary Severo (adapted from the novel of the same name by Costa Monteiro, 1926)

Cinematographer:

Edison Chagas

Duration:

91 minutes

Genre:

Drama

Cast:

Jota Soares
Guiomar Teixeira
Norberto Teixeira
Euclides Jardim

Year:

1926

Synopsis

Paulo Aragão, a respected lawyer, decides to bring his illegitimate daughter, Heloísa, who lives in the countryside, to the city of Recife. Before leaving for a long trip to Europe, he asks his friend Lúcio, a successful journalist, to make the necessary arrangements for the young lady and her mother to come to Recife, stay in a good house and be introduced into the best society. While Lúcio pays court to Heloísa in the most respectful manner, the latter also attracts the interest of a dissolute young man, Helvécio, who insistently attempts to win her. When he gets into her bedroom and tries to rape her, Heloísa shoots him with a gun (conveniently given to her by her father so that she could protect her honour). What Heloísa does not know is that the man she killed was her own brother – the legitimate son of Paulo Aragão. She goes on trial and is defended by a mysterious lawyer who eventually takes off his disguise to reveal his identity: he is the father of both the accused woman and the murdered young man. An unexpected confession salvages her honour.

Critique

During the 1920s, a significant number of films were produced in Recife – the capital of the state of Pernambuco in Brazil's north-east. More than thirty titles, both fiction and non-fiction films, were produced in the second half of the decade. Among them *The Lawyer's Daughter* stands out as one of the most important titles. It was directed by the 20-year-old Jota Soares, who also plays the role of Helvécio. An expensive production by local standards, this urban melodrama attempts to depict Recife's bourgeois milieu while articulating some of melodrama's defining elements: the persecution of innocence, virtue ultimately triumphing over vice, sudden revelations and last-minute rescues. Within the predictable plot, the film celebrates an undisguised fascination with signs of urbanity and modernity, such as streetcars cruising the streets of the city centre, a jazz band enlivening a wild nightclub party, women with bobbed hair and passengers boarding an ocean liner in a crowded, festive city port. Although Recife's production companies did not have proper studios, when it comes to *The Lawyer's Daughter* filming on location is less a limitation than a bonus. Seduced by urban movement, the film often pursues an atmosphere in which the plot and the flow of the city are tightly connected. Yet, this sort of documentary gaze carries a certain amount of idealization. We see not only how Recife was in the twenties but also how it should look on the screen, according to the young director Jota Soares, who was a passionate film fan.

The Lawyer's Daughter seeks to portray the changes in the Recife lifestyle during the 1920s and ends by exhibiting, albeit unintentionally, the contradictions at the very heart of these changes. The film's fascination towards modern practices that begin to transform old habits comes alongside a rejection of the changes that could jeopardize society's moral bases.

The representation of the bourgeoisie is loaded with fascination and condemnation: an attraction to the elite's environment and lifestyle (or, rather, with the film-maker's idealized conception of it) and a moral condemnation regarding the dissipation of traditional values. In respect to women's behaviour and appearance, there is a constant negotiation between modernity and morality. The two main female figures are constructed in terms of polarization, fitting the traditional structure of melodrama. Heloísa is the positive female character in contrast to Antonieta Bergamini, Helvécio's fiancée. The two women are attentive to the changes and latest fashions of their time. Antonieta, however, follows the path of masculinization: she wears men's clothes, short hair and eyeglasses with dark, heavy frames; she has graduated from Law School and pursues a typically male career. While Antonieta is depicted in a scornful way, Heloísa appears as the perfect embodiment of feminine virtue, who knows exactly how to cultivate beauty and fashion in the 'proper' way. When Heloísa moves to Recife, she adopts the latest women's trends, but without falling into anything that could be considered excessive or too bold for a woman. She does not study, has no plans for a professional career and remains devoted to domestic duties.

Although *The Lawyer's Daughter* celebrates modern aspects of urban life, the film ends up reinforcing moral traditions and a conservative understanding concerning gender and class issues. Conceived as a portrait in praise of Recife and its modern urban life *The Lawyer's Daughter* turns out to be an even better translation of the city when it exposes the contradictions that modernity raises.

Luciana Corrêa de Araújo

Neither Samson Nor Delilah

Nem Sansão nem Dalila

Studio/Distributor:

Atlântida Cinematográfica

Director:

Carlos Manga

Producer:

Atlântida Cinematográfica

Screenwriter:

Victor Limo

Cinematographer:

Amleto Daissé

Art Director:

José Cajado Filho

Composer:

Luiz Bonfá and Lyrio Panicalli

Editors:

Carlos Manga
Waldemar Noya

Duration:

90 minutes

Genres:

Comedy
Chanchada

Cast:

Oscarito
Fada Santoro
Eliana Macedo
Cyll Farney
Wilson Viana

Year:

1954

Synopsis

Horácio, an ordinary but comically awkward barber from Rio de Janeiro, finds himself in an extraordinary situation when he and his friends are accidently transported back in time from the 1950s to ancient Gaza. The puzzled denizens of Gaza quickly apprehend some of the time travellers, while Horácio encounters the mighty Samson and his legendary long hair. After gaining Samson's power – which stems not from his hair but from a wig – by trading it for a cigarette lighter, Horácio literally fights his way up the ranks to become a dictatorial king (helped by Dalila's sister, Miriam). However, even Samson's hair cannot keep Horácio from temptation as the beautiful Dalila seduces Horácio into revealing the secret of his strength. Miriam saves the day by retrieving the wig, and justice and harmony are restored in the kingdom, shortly before Horácio wakes up from his dream.

Critique

One of the most important movies of the genre of carnivalesque films that became known as *chanchadas*, *Neither Samson Nor Delilah* is exemplary of the witty creativity of this filmic genre. A parody of Cecil B DeMille's 1949 *Samson and Delilah*, some critics consider *Neither Samson Nor Delilah* to be illustrative of the often-cited underdevelopment of Brazilian cinema. According to this view, the fact that Samson's strength lies in a wig as opposed to real hair would stand as a metaphor for a parodical cinema, in which the film's mockery is understood as self-mockery rather than a critique of foreign cinema.

Although the technical underdevelopment of Brazilian cinema is clear when contrasting the parody with DeMille's *Samson and Delilah* (or with the screwball comedies of the 1940s – the genre to which the *chanchada* is often likened), more recently theorists have emphasized the originality and relevance of the film in its own right. *Neither Samson Nor Delilah* is one of the most interesting Brazilian films of the 1950s, as it contains a series of sophisticated elements: a *mise en abyme* that frames the plot set in ancient Gaza inside the modern Rio de Janeiro story, various cross-references between the two storylines, and references to everyday life in Rio de Janeiro, which at the time was the capital of Brazil. Albeit light-heartedly, social and political criticism permeates the film with clear references to measures employed by the government of the time, including the use of the radio for political propaganda, Horácio/Oscarito's memorable speech parodying one by the then-president (and previously de facto dictator) Getúlio Vargas, and the wave of modernization taking place in the country through metonyms such as the telephone, the radio and the television.

In terms of gender, the mythical figure of Delilah as a femme fatale is effaced in the Brazilian film in which Dalila – played by Eliana Macedo, whose characters tend to be feisty but ultimately vapid – is a weak character who, unlike DeMille's Delilah, poses hardly any threat to the male-dominated status quo. In an inversion that is typical of the carnivalesque (as per Mikhail Bakhtin), Miriam, who is parallel to the character of Semadar in DeMille's film, gains more prominence than her scheming sister. It is the determined and resourceful Miriam who provides a resolution to the story by retrieving the wig – but at no point does she wear it herself. Power (real and symbolic) remains restricted to the male characters in the narrative.

Roberta Gregoli

Possible Loves

Amores possíveis

Studio/Distributor:

Cineluz - Produções Cinematográficas Lda., Consorcio Europa, Labo Cine do Brasil Ltda.

Director:

Sandra Werneck

Producers:

Elisa Tolomelli
Sandra Werneck

Screenwriter:

Paulo Halm

Cinematographer:

Walter Carvalho

Art Director:

Cláudio Amaral Peixoto

Composer:

João Nabuco

Editor:

Isabelle Rathery

Duration:

98 minutes

Genre:

Romantic comedy

Cast:

Beth Goulart
Carolina Ferraz
Irene Ravache
Murilo Benício

Year:

2001

Synopsis

One rainy night in Rio, Carlos is waiting for his date Júlia in the lobby of a cinema. Then the story fast forwards to fifteen years later and shows three possible outcomes of that evening. In the first version, Carlos has become a businessman who is stuck in a marital routine. When he bumps into Júlia at an art exhibition, they start a passionate affair. In the end, however, he returns to his wife. In the second variation, Carlos is gay and lives with his lover Pedro, although he used to be married to Júlia with whom he has a son. When he meets his ex in a club and they spend a day together, he decides to return to her, but discovers he actually loves Pedro. The third possible outcome shows Carlos still living with his mother, who stands between him and his many girlfriends. Then he meets Júlia and they fall in love, but his mother cannot stand his new girlfriend, that is, until she finds a boyfriend of her own. In the last scene, we are back at the cinema and Carlos is once more, or still, waiting for Júlia who eventually shows up.

Critique

In this charming comedy, Sandra Werneck explores the role chance plays in our lives and debunks the myth, looming large over Hollywood, that we are destined for that special someone. When Carlos-the-businessman (Murilo Benício) breaks up with Júlia (Carolina Ferraz), he tells her that things might have turned out differently had she shown up that rainy night at the cinema. But she did not, and he met his wife. There is no telling if he would have been happier had things turned out differently. In the second storyline, Júlia must have shown up and married Carlos, but in the end, he leaves her for a man. In the third version of events, Carlos, who lives with his mother, signs up with a futuristic dating agency and is given a gadget that will beep if he meets his perfect match. The beep, he is told, never fails. However, he only meets Júlia because he misreads the gadget and when he eventually does bump into his soul mate, he dislikes her and throws away the gadget. There is no destiny in love, only happenstance. In all three versions, Carlos ends up reasonably happy with someone else. This does not mean that love and life are without problems. As a businessman in the midst of a midlife crisis, Carlos meets the girl of his dreams, who irrupts into his life like a femme fatale. But he discovers that she is just that: a girl he dreams about, a fantasy. Returning to his wife, he renounces all his 'business

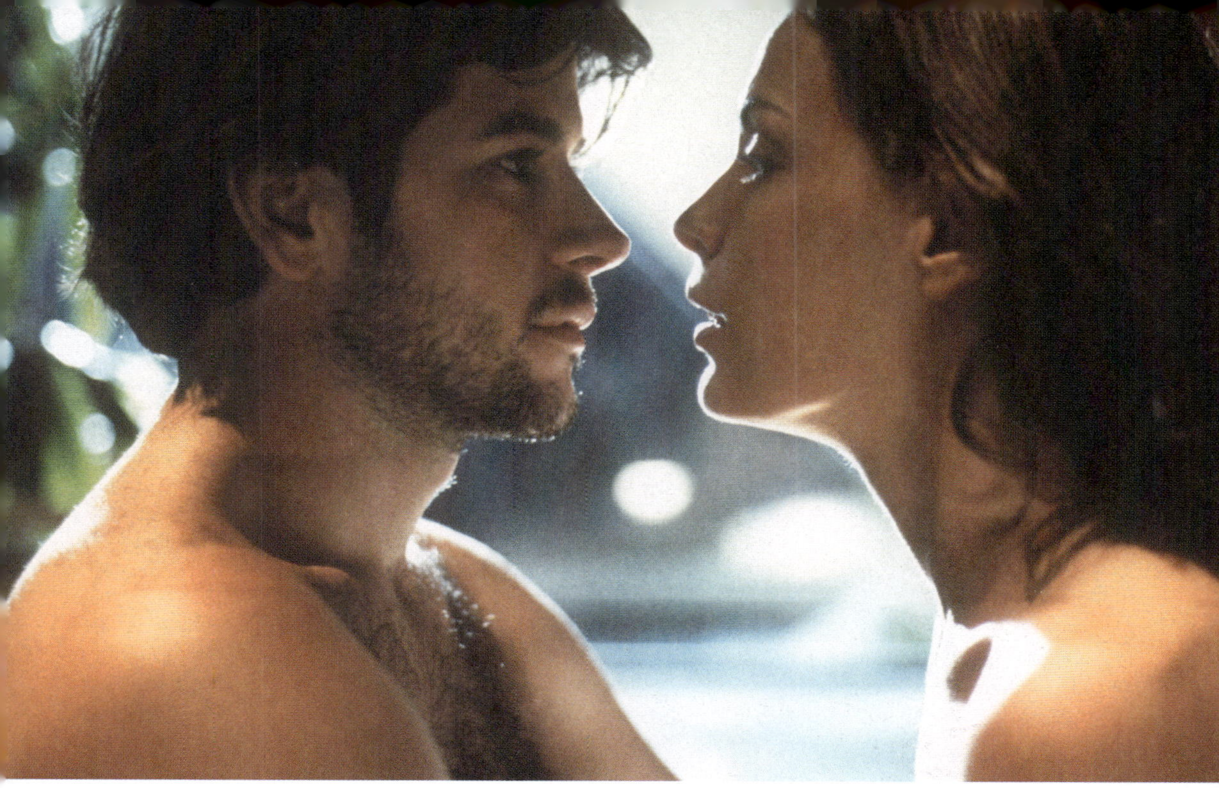

Amores Possiveis/Possible Loves

trips' and accepts married life. As a bachelor, Carlos must overcome his Oedipal relationship with his mother, who embodies the perfect woman for him – except that she does not sleep with him. Having left his wife for a man, Carlos-the-gay-man enters a crisis of doubt about his sexuality. In the event, however, he realizes that he confused his love for the mother of his son with a physically satisfying love for Pedro. One of the refreshing charms of the film is that it shows gay and straight relationships on an equal footing, or, indeed, as perfectly plausible and possible alternatives for the same person.

The film starts and begins at a cinema that announces the very film we are watching. The fact that Carlos is joined by Júlia at the very end suggests that the three stories are fantasies that play through his mind as he is waiting. Her arrival does not alter the fact that he has discovered that whatever happens happens and he will end up happy – gay or straight, married or a bachelor – as long as he is willing to confront life's problems. We may not live, as Candide's master claims, in the *best* of all possible worlds, but simply in one of many where all forms of love are possible.

Sander Berg

Super Woman

A Super fêmea

Studio/Distributor:

Cinedistri

Director:

Aníbal Massaini Neto

Producers:

Osvaldo Massaini
Aníbal Massaini Neto

Screenwriters:

Lauro César Muniz
Adriano Stuart
Aníbal Massaini Neto
Alexandre Pires

Cinematographer:

Lenita Perroy

Composer:

Mário Edson

Editor:

Braun Lúcio

Duration:

100 minutes

Genre:

Erotic comedy

Cast:

Vera Fischer
Perry Salles
Walter Stuart
Georgia Gomide
Libero Ripoli

Year:

1973

Synopsis

In *Super Woman* an ad agency is contracted to promote the newly developed male contraceptive pill to a deeply suspicious Brazilian public. The agency's top creative 'genius', the decidedly eccentric Onan Della Mano is called upon to help. He dreams up the idea of offering in a promotional prize draw a date with a so-called Superwoman (the *super fêmea* of the title), in order to challenge the belief that such a pill would adversely affect men's libido. After much searching, Onan finds the perfect woman: Eva. Eva, a reluctant celebrity who is hounded by men wherever she goes, falls in love with Onan. She is horrified to discover that she is expected to spend the night with the prize draw winner, and flees. Her announcement live on TV that she is pregnant signals the end of both the pharmaceuticals company and ad agency. She goes on to give birth to 100 babies and parades joyously through the streets.

Critique

Film producer Aníbal Massaini Neto's first foray into directing, *Super Woman* is one of the best-known and most popular *pornochanchadas*; the name given to the 'quota-quickie' soft-core comedies that dominated domestic film production and box offices in the 1970s in Brazil. *Pornochanchadas* dealt, in a good-humoured way, with the issue of sex (and how to get some/more of it), using stock characters, many of whom were familiar to audiences from bawdier examples of the Brazilian *teatro de revista* (music-hall). Many *pornochanchadas*, like the early US exploitation films, can be described as movie versions of girlie magazines, and *Super Woman*, starring 1969's Miss Brasil winner Vera Fischer, a blonde-haired, green-eyed model and later successful if troubled TV and film star from southern Brazil, and a host of other (white, and mostly blonde) beauties who are literally paraded in front of the camera in bikinis, is perhaps the best example of this phenomenon. Such literal articulation of voyeurism was a staple of the *pornochanchada*, and in particular, the voyeurism of peering through telescopes, cameras, spy-holes, and so on. Snatched glances, then, are typical of the furtive kind of behaviour displayed by male characters in these films which, through their sustained depiction of sexually incompetent men and promiscuous women, were clearly reflecting on what was perceived at the time to be a national crisis of masculinity.

Since the ultimate goal of the *pornochanchada* was to titillate male viewers, the changing role of women is dealt with only superficially, and only to the extent that it does not interfere with the ultimate goal of female objectification. *Super Woman* notionally deals with the timely issues of contraception and feminism, but merely succeeds in ridiculing both. The film's plot purports to criticize the treatment of women as objects (Onan [Perry Salles] seems more in love with his blow-up version of Eva, at times being incapable of distinguishing between it and the real thing, and the sleazy men who work in advertising are lambasted), while simultaneously endorsing such objectification through the camera's lingering gaze on Vera Fischer's naked body.

Like all good *pornochanchadas*, *Super Woman* appears to revel in its low production values, playfully referencing and thus contrasting itself with blockbusters such as *The Godfather* (Francis Ford Coppola, 1972) and *Barbarella* (Roger Vadim, 1968), and thus confirming Brazil's incapacity to compete with the 'First World', despite the grandiose claims of the right-wing military government to the contrary. The patriotism being vigorously promoted by the dictatorship at that time is mocked in the final scenes of the film: when Eva and her excessive progeny are paraded through the streets to the sound of celebrations the accompanying music is 'Pra frente Brasil' ('Forward Brazil', Miguel Gustavo, 1970), the theme tune to the Brazilian football squad's victorious World Cup campaign in Mexico in 1970.

Stephanie Dennison

Vera

Studio/Distributor:

Embrafilme, Grange, Nexus Cinema e Vídeo

Director:

Sérgio Toledo

Producers:

Sérgio Toledo
Cláudio Kahns
Celso Lofer
Ana María Warchawchik
Ilia Warchawchik

Screenwriter:

Sérgio Toledo

Cinematographer:

Rodolfo Sánchez

Art Directors:

Naum Alves de Sousa
Simone Raskin

Composer:

Arrigo Barnabé

Editor:

Tércio G Mota

Synopsis

Vera has grown up an orphan in a boarding school. Upon her release, she is taken in by a psychologist who offers her a place in his family. However, while in the boarding school and in the same-sex environment with other girls, Vera comes to realize that she does not feel herself to be a woman and that she is really a man trapped in a woman's body. She undertakes to confirm her status as a man publically, adopting an ever-expanding range of the signs of gender identity associated with masculinity. A confirmation of her transgendered experience comes with her frustrated attempts to win the affections of a colleague in the library of a research institute where they both work: it is an undertaking of erotic attachment that is as much a question of the inevitable consequences of her affirmation of sexual identity as it is a decision to confirm the trajectory of her process of female-to-male transgendering, such that a romantic relationship with a woman is the confirmation of the completion of that process.

Critique

It would be a mistake to identify *Vera* as a lesbigay or homosexual film, although it has come to be included in both Brazilian and international registries of such film-making. Since Vera sees herself as a man and wishes, as much as is humanly possible for her, to reconstruct her sexual/gender identity as that of a man, the object of her erotic desire is, quite simply, heterosexual (the anatomy of any actual physical erotics, which never take place in the film, is as here irrelevant as it is in any story driven by the dynamics of courtship rather than fully sexual

Duration:

87 minutes

Genre:

Drama

Cast:

Ana Beatriz Nogueira
Raul Cortez
Aída Leiner
Imara Reis

Year:

1986

lives). The fact that the film title holds on to the subject's feminine name (there is no masculine variant in Portuguese for Vera), rather than substituting a man's name or, perhaps of potentially greater interest, a gender-ambiguous name, is one explanation of how the film is often categorized as lesbigay or homosexual. Vera, however, begins to call herself Paulo. Yet, Clara, who already has a son, complicates matters by seeing Paulo as a woman. She insists on continuing to call Paulo Vera, much to Paulo's consternation.

More properly speaking, *Vera* is a queer film, in the sense that what is at issue is the questioning of the gender binary; the presumed transparency of the interchangeability between gender, sexuality and erotic desire; the assumed redundancy of primary, secondary and tertiary sexual characteristics; and the stability of socio-sexual semiotics. As a queer film, *Vera*, produced barely two years after Brazil's return to constitutional democracy, which brought with it the deconstruction of authoritarian social norms and the exploration of non-hegemonic social identities, is an excellent example of the intersection with this twin process with gender politics in Brazil. A specific feminist agenda (or cluster of such agendas) does not exist in Brazil, where feminism is viewed as a capitalist, Eurocentric ideology. Yet human rights activism in both politics and culture include what elsewhere would be immediately recognizable as feminist and queer agendas.

Brazil's return to constitutional democracy in mid 1985 included a prior transitional period in which there was a gradual return to a cultural production relatively free from censorship (unlike the more abrupt transition in Argentina in 1983). As a consequence, it has been customary to speak of a 'crisis' in Brazilian film-making in the mid 1980s as the result of a certain disarray and shaky criteria in formal government support (through Embrafilme) of the industry; this crisis was exacerbated in the early 1990s by the almost total abandonment of official support for film-making. Yet important films were made during this period. These films, on the one hand, continue a strong line of socio historic commentary associated with the mid-century *Cinema Novo*. On the other hand, films of the late 1980s are an important cultural index of public debate over national issues associated with redemocratization. *Vera* is unquestionably an example of both categories, to the extent that gender identity is crucial to Brazilian social history. At the same time, Toledo's film anticipates the *retomada*, the return to a solid film production of national significance and international importance that has taken place since the 1990s.

The overall artistic quality of Toledo's film, the careful and sensitive way in which Vera's character is handled without any trace of homophobia or sentimentality, and the eschewal of tendentious representation, including the sort of explicit erotic activity that had come to be associated with commercial Brazilian film-making, make *Vera* one of the most important gender-marked films in recent Brazilian film history. Nogueira won a Silver Bear best actress award at the 'Berlin Film Festival' in 1987 for her role.

David William Foster

Women in Fury

Fêmeas em fuga

Studio/Distributor:

R.P.A. Cinematografica, Brasil
Produções Cinematográficas

Director:

Michele Massimo Tarantini

Producers:

Pedro Aurélio Gentil
Rodrigues Chris

Screenwriter:

Michele Massimo Tarantini

Cinematographer:

Lúcia Maria Gutierrez

Art Director:

Lúcia Maria

Composer:

Remo Usai

Editor:

Aida Marques

Duration:

102 minutes

Genre:

Erotic drama
WIP film

Cast:

Suzane Carvalho
Leonardo José
Paulo Guarnieri
Rossana Ghessa

Year:

1984

Synopsis

Women in Fury tells the story of Ângela Duval who receives an 18-year prison sentence for confessing to the murder of a Brazilian drug lord committed by her brother, in the hope that she will receive a shorter sentence than he would. In prison she suffers repeated violent sexual abuse by her fellow inmates. This culminates in a scene in which she is brutally beaten with a water-soaked towel, which leaves her severely wounded and nearly unconscious. As a consequence of this she accepts the sexual advances of the prison warden, an unscrupulous and androgynous woman who offers Ângela protection in return for sex. Her life in prison is also threatened by a group of men who worked for the man Ângela's brother murdered.

Luis, the prison doctor, falls in love with Ângela and risks his career to prove her innocence (in which he ardently believes). In the process he has to face a network of corrupt prison staff who work for captain Bonifácio, a powerful and nefarious prison director who tries to protect his reputation – a secret Ângela holds could compromise it and incriminate him. Meanwhile, Ângela's brother commits suicide and leaves a note in which he confesses his crime. Luis obtains the note and persuades the court of Ângela's innocence; however, the suspension of her sentence arrives too late as Ângela had already seized the opportunity a prison riot gave to attempt an escape.

Critique

Women in Fury is a very violent film in which scenes of unwarranted torture and violent sex occur quite gratuitously throughout, seemingly to support a poor plotline. The plot has the beautiful and innocent upper-class woman, Ângela Duval (Suzanne Carvalho), being forced to do time in prison for a crime that was actually committed by her cowardly brother, but its banality is in no way alleviated by the extremely lengthy scenes of voyeuristic naked exposure of the female body. In this sense it falls aptly into step with the widespread phenomenon of the WIP (Women in Prison) film which took off around the world and in Brazil mostly in the 1970s and 1980s and has enjoyed enduring popularity ever since. Like most WIP films, *Women in Fury* faithfully retains characteristics typical of the genre such as the lesbian prison warden, the queen bee (the dominant prisoner), the new fish (the innocent girl in prison for the first time – Ângela Duval), the exploitation of the strong by the weak in the prison setting, and the disciplining of the female characters through a peculiar and unhealthy mix of eroticized nudity and sadomasochistic sex between women.

Although the lengthy scenes of female nudity and licentious sex appear to be developed and sustained by the plot – Ângela's beating and rape comes as a direct consequence of her imprisonment in the degraded and contaminated environment that prison represents – one cannot help feeling exasperated in the face of the repeated scenes of violent sex which raise pertinent questions as to their purpose in the film, their overwhelming presence not excluding the assumption of their employment for no other purpose than the mere titillation of a supposedly male audience. Reasons for assuming such an audience include, firstly, the conspicuous abundance of phallic objects in the hands of masculinized women such as the truncheon used by the lesbian prison warden, initially to suggest that Ângela's only chance of survival depends on her consent to sex and ultimately to tear her underpants just before she explicitly consents to sex. Even more telling is the hose the same prison warden uses to hose Ângela down, warning her of the consequences of her disobedience and leaving her half-naked and begging for mercy. These are all symbolic manifestations of a patriarchal rule upheld by women in a prison setting that, while working to the disadvantage of women who are depicted in a position of subalternity to men, serve to unmask men's anxieties about their inability to contain the untrammelled female sexuality, which, in *Women in Fury*, can only be satisfied by women.

There is no doubt that such a trivial common plot, compounded by generally poor performances, would fail to awaken the targeted male audience's interest were it not for the erotic display of nudity and much lesbian sex. In this sense *Women in Fury* and other WIP films deserve criticism for portraying women as defenceless and victimized in a society where patriarchy still reigns supreme. However, *Women in Fury* to some extent escapes this categorization by allowing its women to become subversive to patriarchal rule by the end of the film. While at the beginning they are fragmented and divided, each in pursuit of their own individual goal, by the end of the film they are united in their common cause of breaking out of prison – a site of oppression ruled by men which the women escape through intelligent planning and joint cooperation – thereby gaining faith in their own agency. Moreover, they then literally take to arms in the Amazonian jungle and dress in men's clothes to fight for survival against a group of men who tried to rape the women but whom the latter manage to annihilate one by one. Notwithstanding their deliberate visual objectification by a heterosexual audience, it must be highlighted none the less that the women in the film do ultimately attain their freedom and assert their female supremacy over men, thus gaining the film some partial credit for their ultimate portrayal as subversive.

Laura Bojneagu

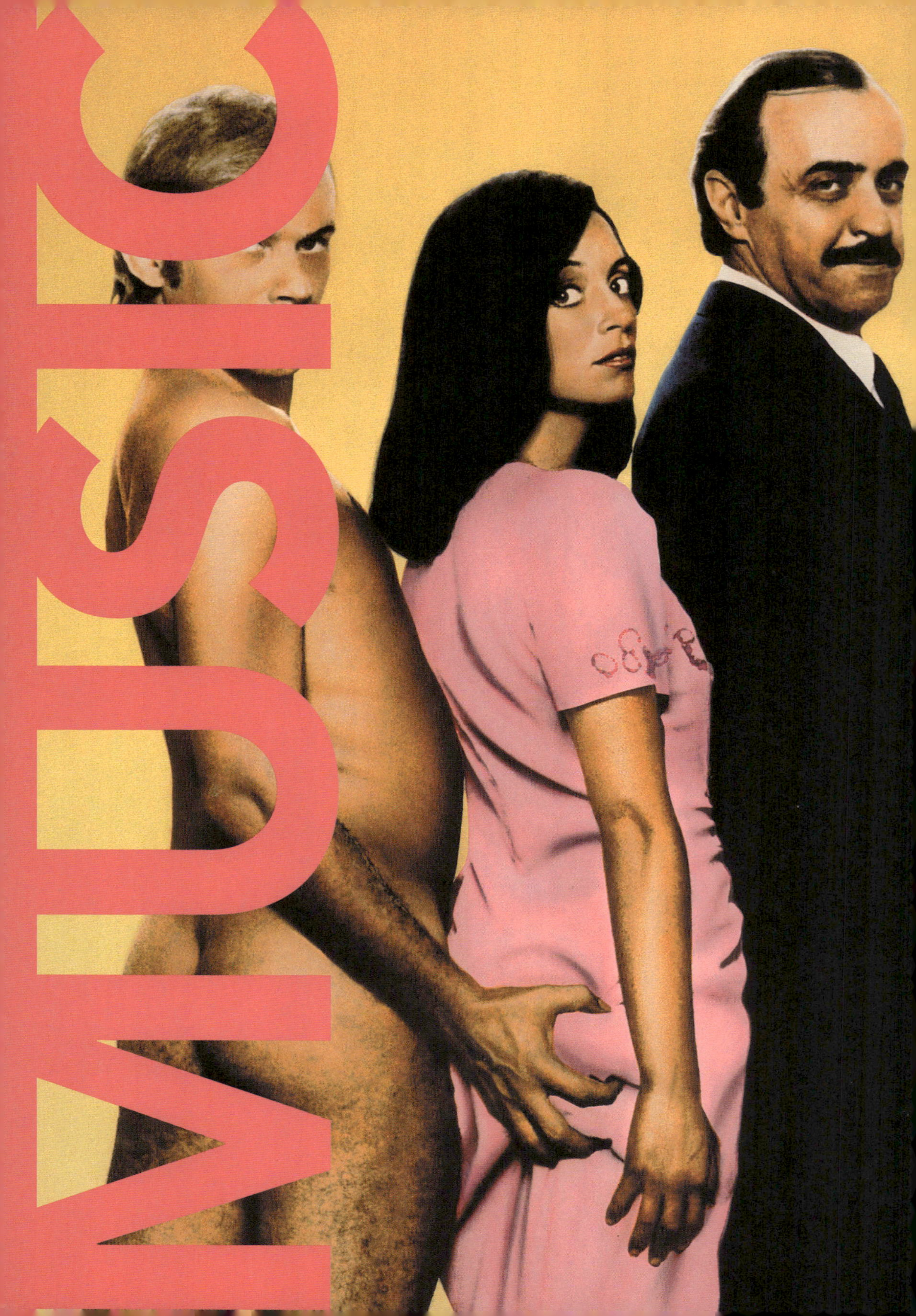

Music, especially popular Brazilian music, has been an essential component of Brazilian cinema since the very beginnings of the sound era. *Chanchadas*, or musical comedies, were Brazil's earliest commercially successful film genre and were closely associated with popular music and festivals, especially samba and carnival. Thus it is no accident that Brazil's first international film star, Carmen Miranda, initially found fame as a samba singer and had her film debut in Adhemar Gonzaga's *Alô, alô, carnaval/Hello, Hello, Carnival!* (1936). This film, one of the few to be preserved from the era, is essentially a vehicle for the famous radio performers of the day to achieve greater exposure on film. The *chanchada* would continue to be the commercially dominant film genre in Brazil until the 1950s and featured performances by Carmen Miranda and many other musical stars, from Francisco Alves to Jackson do Pandeiro.

In the 1950s, the Vera Cruz studio of São Paulo was established in an attempt to develop a native version of the Hollywood drama in Brazil (the studio was funded by money from wealthy industrialists in this economically burgeoning region of the country). Vera Cruz featured some regional music in its films, most famously in Lima Barreto's *O Cangaceiro/The Bandit* (1953), which introduced the north-eastern Brazilian musical genre of *baião* (a kind of country music which in the film is performed by a group of bandits) to an international audience. The film's music received special attention in France, where at Cannes *The Bandit* won the Palme d'Or in the adventure category. However, the music in the film is far more incidental to the plot and structure than had been the case in the *chanchadas*. It was around this period in the 1950s, as the *Cinema Novo* film movement started to coalesce, that music transitioned away from being a central structuring element in Brazilian film. Nelson Pereira dos Santos's *Rio, 40 graus/Rio, 40 Degrees* (1954) is a forerunner of the more modest role music tended to play in *Cinema Novo*. While one of the film's narrative arcs centres around a carnival queen, her ascendance to the musical throne is darkly contrasted with the tragic death of a young boy, a peanut vendor from her *favela*. Santos would give music a greater role in his next film, *Rio, zona norte/Rio, Northern Zone* (1957), only to use it as a vehicle to criticize the music industry and its exploitation of the poor and working-class musicians who largely invented the samba. The central character of this film is played convincingly by Grande Otelo, an actor who had become famous playing comedic roles in the *chanchada* genre. His tragic story in the film contrasts sharply with the musical comedy narratives he had been cast in since the 1930s, and more or less marks the end of that era in Brazilian cinema. The 1950s also saw Brazil's only film to win an Oscar, Marcel Camus's *Orfeu negro/Black Orpheus* (1959), which helped to launch bossa nova as a popular international export through its soundtrack with music composed by Tom Jobim and Luis Bonfá, among other famous songwriters. This film beautifully portrays the Greek myth of Orpheus and Euridice in the modern-day setting of Rio de Janeiro, with Bruno Mello playing an Orpheus who lives in a *favela* and is a master of samba and bossa nova. However, the film was not well received by contemporary Brazilian critics and film-makers, at least partly because its usage of popular culture was deemed by the up-and-coming vanguard of *Cinema Novo* to be aesthetically conservative at best – both romantic and romanticized in its vision of popular culture as the repository of the pure, authentic folklore of the nation – and exoticized cultural tourism at worst.

The works of Nelson Pereira dos Santos and Glauber Rocha typify the *Cinema Novo* approach to soundtrack and score in the 1960s. In Santos's *Vidas secas/Barren Lives* (1963) and *Como era gostoso o meu francês/How Tasty Was My Little Frenchman* (1971), various forms of popular music are utilized diegetically and non-diegetically in innovative ways. For instance, in the earlier film Santos portrays a traditional *bumba-meu-boi* dance with accompanying song and instrumentation in a village square. Yet as the local boss of this rural region is shown enjoying the performance, Santos intercuts this scene with shots of the film's main protagonist (a poor cattleherd who is a victim of police brutality) suffering in jail. In the later film, set in the early colonial era and focusing on the story of one indigenous tribe who capture a French colonist, composers Guilherme Magalhães Vaz and Zé Rodrix frequently utilize wind instruments of indigenous origin to score the film. However, rather than simply reproducing indigenous music these instruments tend to be used to amplify the dramatic tension of the film and even to mock the protagonist's efforts as he seeks to escape the cannibalist ritual of his captors. In the case of Glauber Rocha, Rocha himself had a hand in writing the lyrics of the music that narrates his film *Deus e o Diabo na terra do sol/Black God, White Devil* (1964) in the style of traditional north-eastern Brazilian *cantoria* music. Like Santos, though, Rocha reworks this traditional form to question many of the traditional heroes and anti-heroes of the region and their roles in subjugating the common man and woman. The fruitful partnership with composer Sérgio Ricardo he established in this film would continue in the same vein in *Antônio das Mortes/O Dragão da maldade contra o santo guerreiro* (1969). Overall, *cinemanovistas* tended to feature pared-down soundtracks utilizing some European and Brazilian classical music combined with Brazilian popular music on their scores. This music was often presented through avant-garde techniques that sought to ironize or revolutionize popular culture and its role in the lives of the lower and working classes.

Some of the biggest popular successes of the 1970s, such as Bruno Barreto's *Dona Flor e seus dois maridos/Dona Flor and Her Two Husbands* and Cacá Diegues's *Xica da Silva* (both 1976), were carnivalesque romantic comedies that found a central place for popular music in the soundtrack and score, and at times as structuring elements for plot and character development. One might even argue that carnival music and dancing in excess (combined with alcohol) led to the demise of Vadinho (José Wilker), *Dona Flor*'s male lead. Popular music could also feature the countercultural youth movement and disguise some critical messages about the state of the society under the military regime, as can be heard in some of Chico Buarque's music for the same film. The 1970s and 1980s would also see many films with fairly traditional film scores in the style of Hollywood 'movie music', setting the emotional tone for sundry filmic narratives.

Since the *retomada* or film revival of the 1990s, Brazilian film-makers have not often returned to the avant-garde techniques of *Cinema Novo*, but they do tend to deploy music to support some of the major contemporary narrative trends in Brazilian cinema, including new emphases on regionalism, realism and humanism, as well as biopics of famous Brazilians. All of these contemporary narrative tendencies involve a renewed focus on, at times celebration of, popular culture – and one prime example of this is popular music. In films set in the north-eastern *sertão* (rural backlands), the use of the region's popular music ranges from the minimalist approach to films that are dominated entirely by regional music. Walter Salles and Daniela Thomas rely largely on an orchestral score in *Central do Brasil/Central Station* (1998), but as the characters enter the *sertão*, the lone *rabeca* (traditional fiddle) of north-eastern musician Siba enters the soundtrack to symbolize the homecoming of the young protagonist Josué (Vinícius de Oliveira) to his family and native region. On the other hand, the soundtrack and score of Andrucha Waddington's *Eu, tu, eles/Me, You, Them* (2000) are entirely a celebration of the north-eastern musical genre of *forró* and its most famous musician, Luiz Gonzaga.

The musical choices involved in producing Cacá Diegues's *Orfeu* (1999), a remake of *Black Orpheus*, were justified by composer Caetano Veloso in realist fashion as an attempt to portray the contemporary popular culture of Rio de Janeiro's *favelas* in a more authentic manner than Marcel Camus's original film did. Thus the film's soundtrack and score cite the contemporary funk and rap that are prevalent in the *favelas*, in addition to the ever-popular *samba de enredo* (the 'theme samba' performed in the carnival parades each year) composed in the film by the protagonist, Orpheus.

In terms of the new humanism, we can consider the significance of *capoeira* music and dance in the important documentary *Ônibus 174/Bus 174* (José Padilha and Felipe Lacerda, 2002). A capoeira group focusing on disadvantaged youth is presented briefly but essentially as the one possible salvation or alternative to crime for Sandro Nascimento, a 20-year-old man who ultimately was cornered by the police and killed after taking a city bus hostage. In the fictionalized remake *Última parada 174/Last Stop 174* (Bruno Barreto, 2008), on the other hand, rap is represented as a form of self-expression that Sandro uses to communicate with the media and to criticize his own and his friends' marginal status in society. The North American-directed *Favela Rising* (Matt Mochary and Jeff Zimbalist, 2005) tells a related but more uplifting tale about the inspirational musical activism and entrepreneurship of the musical group, school and community organization called Afro Reggae in Rio's Vigário Geral *favela*.

Finally, biopics of musicians from diverse origins continue to be a popular subject, as evidenced by the great popularity of films like *Cazuza: o tempo não pára/Cazuza: Time Doesn't Stop* (Sandra Werneck and Walter Carvalho, 2004) and *2 Filhos de Francisco/The Two Sons of Francisco* (Breno Silveira, 2005). These films tell the life stories of stars of Brazilian pop-rock and central-southern country music, respectively, and are examples of an important subgenre of the biographical drama in Brazil.

Jack A Draper III

Antônia

Studio/Distributor:

Coração da Selva
Tangerina Entretenimento
O2 Filmes
Globo Filmes
Playarte

Director:

Tata Amaral

Producers:

Geórgia Costa Araújo
Tata Amaral

Screenwriters:

Roberto Moreira
Tata Amaral

Cinematographer:

Jacob Sarmento Solitrenick

Art Director:

Rafael Ronconi

Composers:

Beto Villares
Parteum

Editor:

Idê Lacreta

Duration:

90 minutes

Genres:

Drama
Musical

Cast:

Negra Li
Leilah Moreno
Cindy Mendes
Jacqueline Simão (Quelynah)
Thaíde

Year:

2006

Synopsis

An opportunity to perform as the opening act at a local hip hop event gives four friends from the outskirts of São Paulo – Preta, Barbarah, Lena, and Mayah – the break they have been waiting for: a chance to move beyond singing backup vocals for male rap crews in order to pursue their dream of making it as the all-female hip hop group 'Antônia'. When they catch the eye of charming and ambitious music promoter Marcelo Diamante (played by Brazilian rap legend Thaíde), fulfilment of their singing ambitions finally seems within reach. Yet soon the adversities of daily life in the urban periphery begin to take a toll, as the accumulative demands of family responsibilities, tumultuous relationships and economic uncertainty test the girls' dedication to their music – and their friendship – to the limit. When confronted by unforeseen repercussions of events following a brutal attack on Barbarah's brother, however, the young women find strength to carry on within the bond of friendship – and rediscover that united together, they shine brightest.

Critique

Following four young women's journey within the male-dominated world of hip hop, Tata Amaral's *Antônia* not only gives visibility to one of contemporary Brazil's principal urban subcultures and musical genres (achieving weighted cultural authenticity through the use of active participants in São Paulo's rap scene rather than professional actors), but in doing so, the film simultaneously examines multiple modalities of femininity and diverse societal pressures which shape women's experiences of living in the city's periphery. Four distinct 'archetypal' femininities are assigned to the main characters, each identified through unique personal style and personality traits. These strong female personas combine to depict an empowered and diversified feminine presence acting within the urban environment, and the film attests to the important role of female friendship as a resource of strength and perseverance in overcoming life's challenges.

   Antônia's female-centric approach makes important and refreshing contributions to a typically masculinized cinematic vision of the daily struggle to negotiate urban conditions while fighting to pursue one's dreams in the Brazilian metropolis – as observed in films like *Cidade de Deus/City of God* (Fernando Meirelles and Kátia Lund, 2002), *Cidade dos homens/City of Men* (Paulo Morelli, 2007) and *Linha de passe/Line of Passage* (Walter Salles and Daniela Thomas, 2008). Amaral's film also diverges from customary depictions of urban violence (drug trade, homicide, gun crime, police corruption) often articulated within Brazil's contemporary cinema, instead exposing other facets of violence encountered within Brazilian society such as domestic abuse, homophobia and sustained systemic inequalities. Similarly, *Antônia* adopts a distinct approach towards its spatial visualization of São Paulo. Significant screen time shows the girls in movement – traversing the city on public transport or walking along the winding corridors of auto-constructed neighbourhoods – and the camera frequently follows the actors into cramped interior domestic spaces or up narrow staircases. The sense of proximity achieved by filming in such tight locations is placed in dramatic visual contrast to sweeping panoramic views of the periphery's architectural sprawl, which infiltrates the screen as a textural mass that bursts out from beyond windows or open doorways and frames the ledges of tiny household verandas.

The diversified soundtrack constructs a sonic portrait of São Paulo's periphery, and its mixture of hip hop-inspired tracks and other established genres of Brazilian popular music works to situate hip hop as a genre firmly located within the country's musical lineage – a position symbolically reinforced by the casting of Sandra de Sá and Thobias da Vai-Vai as Preta's parents. The soundtrack selectively surfaces during scenes of live musical performances and impromptu a capella harmonies sung by the film's characters, composing a musical score that fluidly coexists with the ambient noise of the urban soundscape. This diegetic incorporation of music serves multiple functions within the cinematic text, working both to demarcate scenes and also to define specific spaces. Furthermore, music often 'speaks' for sequences in the storyline (with song sometimes substituting dialogue altogether), divulging emotional tone through lyrical and melodic content. Notably, within this context, the girls' increasingly strained friendship is metaphorically expressed through their decreasing harmonization as the quartet steadily dwindles down to Preta's lonesome solo performance – with their ultimate reunion fittingly marked by singing together in vocal harmony.

The 'Making Of' documentary accompanying the film DVD outlines the project's development and collective filming process, which facilitates a fuller appreciation of *Antônia*'s final structure, musical composition and visual aesthetic. While at times one would like to see the film engage slightly more robustly with some of the important social issues it attempts to raise, still Amaral delivers a sincere and uplifting film – a success garnered in part by Solitrenick's cinematography and endearing performances by Li and Moreno – which makes a noteworthy contribution to cinematic portraits of periphery lives, representations of city-space, and depictions of urban culture in Brazil.

Chandra Morrison

Antônio das Mortes

O Dragão da maldade contra o santo guerreiro

Studio/Distributor:

Mapa Filmes

Synopsis

Antônio das Mortes (also in Rocha's *Deus e o Diabo na terra do sol/ Black God, White Devil* [1964]) is a mercenary famous for eliminating all outlaw bands in the backlands of north-east Brazil. He is hired by a landowner, Horácio, to kill Coirana, a new outlaw leader (Ronin) who accompanies a group of mystics (or *beatos*). Coirana also wishes to kill Antônio in revenge for vanquishing the outlaw bands. In a ritualized duel, Coirana is mortally wounded. He is carried to a tree where he dies as if crucified. Witnessing his death, Antônio becomes a holy

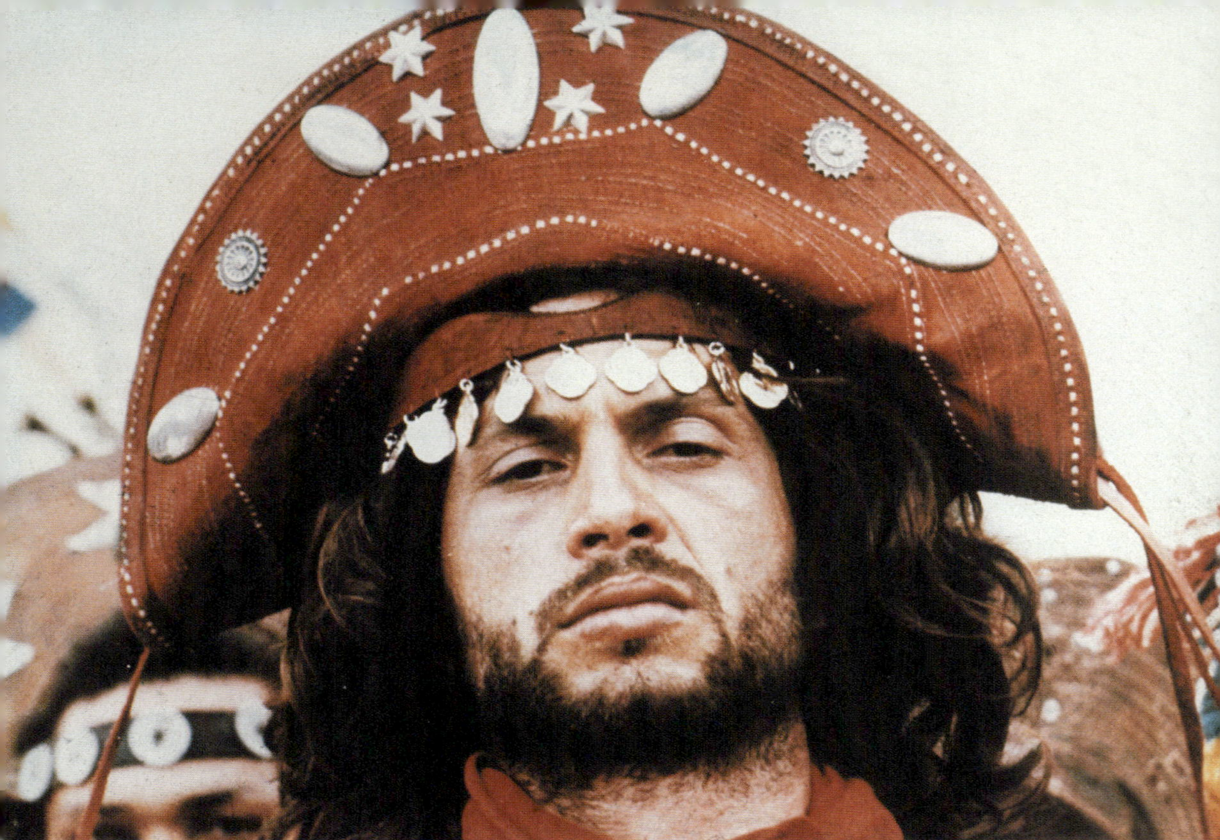

Antonio das Mortes

Director:

Glauber Rocha

Producers:

Glauber Rocha
Zelito Viana
Luís Carlos Barreto
Claude-Antoine

Screenwriter:

Glauber Rocha

Cinematographer:

Afonso Beato

Art Director:

Glauber Rocha

Composers:

Walter Queiros
Glaubér Rocha
Sérgio Ricardo
Marlos Nobre

warrior through the enigmatic power of Santa, the female leader of the mystics. The mystic group is then massacred by another hired gunman, Mata Vaca, who first came to the town to kill Matos (the village's sheriff), himself the lover of Laura (Horácio's wife). Matos is killed by Laura herself, so Mata Vaca receives the task to eliminate the *beatos*. Laura is shot dead. Another mystic leader, an old man named Antão, enters the town riding a white horse and dragging Horácio, who was stabbed by Antão and Santa. Horácio is killed by The Teacher (who loves Laura). There is a bloodbath between the mystics and the landowner's gunslingers. Antônio takes a decisive revenge.

Critique

This is Glauber Rocha's best movie. Rocha uses many theatrical techniques and devices, such as monologues and a stage-like organization of the scenes (e.g. in the duel people sit in a circle while in the centre Antônio and Coirana perform the fight), creating a rich artistic context in which cinema and theatre conflict as dramatic forms each competing for our attention. The fight for justice and enlightenment is represented by a mystical, yet realistic, setting and

Editor:

Eduardo Escorel

Duration:

95 min

Genre:

Drama

Cast:

Maurício do Valle
Odete Lara
Othon Bastos
Hugo Carvana
Jofre Soares
Lorival Pariz
Rosa Maria Penna
Emanuel Cavalcanti
Mário Gusmão
Vinícius Salvatori
Sante Scaldaferri

Year:

1969

plot which challenges the Marxist claim that religion is the opium of the masses, and makes it an ideological motivation for revolutionary action. The movie does so by using, in a profound, intelligent and articulate way, ancient narrative traditions and classical elements of pathos: myth, love and its betrayal, struggle for land rights as a kind of human right, a wicked 'dragon', holy and profane warriors, political ambition, youthful desire for revolution and the escape from the confines of small town life. The movie is exuberant, like *Tropicália* – but, unlike it, it is sublime. The quest for justice is treated as a fight against the universal evil of ignorance which is first personal, than communal. Those who seek such a road, like Santa, Coirana, the Teacher and Antônio have to live in some kind of exile. The dragon to be fought and defeated (and mentioned in the original Portuguese title) is the evil heart of darkness where greed, ambition, desire for and attachment to power dwell. For this reason Coirana must not die at Antônio's hands. The Brazilian title of the movie informs us that it is about a holy warrior hunted by the dragon of wickedness (which Antônio learns is inside himself). The protagonist is named, in Brazilian Portuguese, Antônio of the Deaths, that is, of those who should be delivered to death. The holy warrior is not Coirana, or Santa, or Antão. He is Antônio who is sought first by Oxóssi, the Hunter (Lampião and Coirana), and then Xangô (Santa), The Holder of the Sword of Justice, in order to undertake the just fight. Through Antônio we too are sought to become slayers of dragons – to activate the holy warrior in us to fight the evils of the world.

The complexity, sophistication and beauty of the soundtrack is an attraction in and of itself. A variety of musical forms, many of them north-eastern, appear in the film: secular and religious, vulgar and sublime, profane and sacred, traditional and current, instrumental and a capella, polyphonic and chanted, voiced and whispered, articulated and whistled, lugubrious and manic. There are, for example: *forró* [north-eastern country music], samba, marches, Brazilian pop music (MPB), litanies, and Afro-Brazilian religious music including *cantigas* or *candomblé* chants. A variety of musical instruments ranging from guitar, through conga, *cavaquinho* (a kind of ukulele) and drums to piano are used. In some scenes the music has a life (and a story) of its own, which contrast with the imagery. For example, the *chanson de geste* 'The Arrival of Lampião in Hell', heard when Coirana stands as if 'crucified' on a tree tells the tale of the legendary bandit's arrival in hell, and not of Coirana's deeds which are different to Lampião's. The film's music and narrative are steeped in classical influences, including the overwhelming presence of choruses, together with many allusions to the myth of Dionysus, the god of ecstasy who comes from the outskirts of the town to challenge state power and the status quo. Thus the soundtrack in *Antônio das Mortes* constitutes a commentary on the sophisticated albeit not always appreciated nature of north-eastern culture where traditional forms are put in dialogue with more recent, popular ones.

Sandra SF Erickson

Black Orpheus

Orfeu negro

Studio/Distributor:

Dispat Films
Gemma
Tupan Filmes

Director:

Marcel Camus

Producer:

Sacha Gordine

Screenwriters:

Jacques Viot
Marcel Camus (adapted from
the play Orfeu da Conceição
Tragédia carioca by Vinícius de
Moraes, 1956)

Cinematographer:

Jean Bourgoin

Composers:

Luiz Bonfá
Antonio Carlos Jobim

Editor:

Andrée Feix

Duration:

103 minutes

Genre:

Drama

Cast:

Breno Mello
Marpessa Dawn
Marcel Camus
Fausto Guerzoni
Lourdes de Oliveira
Léa Garcia
Ademar Da Silva
Alexandro Constantino

Year:

1959

Synopsis

Eurydice, a beautiful and naïve girl, arrives in Rio de Janeiro during preparations for the Brazilian carnival. She meets Orpheus, a handsome trolley conductor with talents for singing, samba, guitar-playing and attracting the adoration of local women. He is taken with her, but is already reluctantly on his way to acquire a marriage licence with his fiancée, Mira. During rehearsals for the Babilônia neighbourhood's carnival parade, a man dressed as Death frightens Eurydice but Orpheus protects her. Eurydice and Orpheus spend the night together and Eurydice takes her cousin's place in the following day's festivities, so that she may dance with Orpheus. Mira spots the switch and attacks Eurydice, but is stopped by Death, who chases Eurydice into the trolley station where Orpheus works. Eurydice tries to escape by jumping on to a wire but, in attempting a rescue, Orpheus accidentally electrocutes her. Refusing to accept Eurydice has died, Orpheus begins a frantic search for her.

Critique

A critically acclaimed and award-laden classic (which earned Academy, Golden Globe and Sant Jordi Awards for Best Foreign Language Film, as well as 1959's Palme d'Or), *Black Orpheus* has an international prominence shared by only a handful of other Brazilian films. Its astonishing soundtrack brought bossa nova music worldwide attention and is the most important element of the film, which transposes the Greek legend of Orpheus and Eurydice to a Rio *favela*. Urgent and rhythmic music begins and ends *Black Orpheus*, and plays for much of its running time. When, after Eurydice's tragic death, it stops, its sudden absence conveys Orpheus's desolation better than any line in the script. Seldom has a film that is not explicitly a musical relied so greatly on its score or made such effective use of it.

Beyond its music, *Black Orpheus* is characterized by its vibrancy and colour. Characters are forever in motion – when Eurydice travels to Rio on a ferry, the passengers who swarm around her are all dancing and so, it seems, is everyone on land – and, just as with the quietness that comes after her death, the stillness that follows it announces the emptiness Orpheus feels with remarkable economy. Amplifying the film's visual impact are the colours and costumes of the carnival, which are so exquisitely shot that Jean Bourgoin's cinematography recalls the best of the work of Jack Cardiff. Seldom has a film that was not a hand-drawn animation paid such close attention to the tones deployed in every part of every frame, or created a colour scheme as distinct and evocative.

The images and sounds of *Black Orpheus*, striking as they are, are not in themselves the point of the film. Rather, they are used by Marcel Camus to create an atmosphere of feverish exoticism, which is in turn used to heighten the impact of the plot. There is always a danger in transferring any legend, or classic literary tale, to a modern setting. The broad and familiar strokes of the story can lend the film in question a tiresome inevitability and lack of nuance or the story can, simply, fit poorly with the attitudes and technologies of a different age.

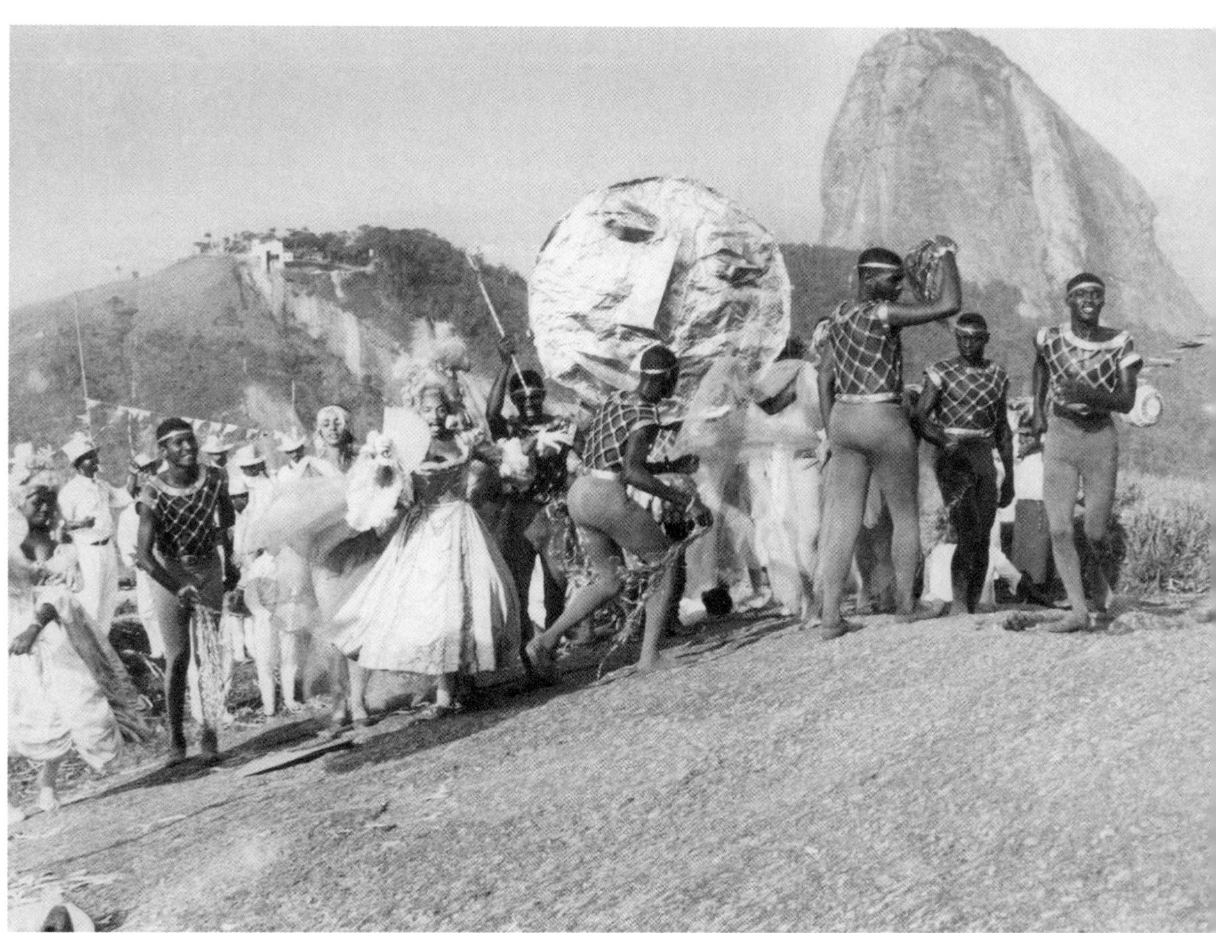

Black Orpheus

Black Orpheus avoids these problems, firstly, by using the unique atmosphere of the carnival to give the film an air of unreality befitting its plot and, secondly, by grounding the story's more outlandish elements in recognizable and realistic events. For Orpheus's descent into hell, for example, we are not shown a literal underworld, but rather Orpheus being led to a ritual of *macumba* (a syncretic Brazilian religion) at which Eurydice does not – as she does in the legend – appear to him, but rather speaks through an old woman apparently possessed by her spirit. This intelligently controlled balance of reality and unreality pervades the film and makes a story that is thousands of years old feel both fresh and relevant, creating a work of rare and unforgettable impact.

It is important to note, however, that while few modern international audiences would doubt *Black Orpheus*'s claim to be one of the great works of Brazilian cinema, on its release Brazilian reaction was less approving. The film was, for example, anathema to the emerging members of the *Cinema Novo* movement, who saw in its exaggerated exoticism and relative lack of class consciousness much that they sought to eschew. Furthermore, the film was technically a French production, and entered for awards as such, which deepened the alienation some Brazilian audiences felt from it. While for many outside Brazil the film provided a beguiling image of the country, for many inside it *Black Orpheus* seemed a flawed and inauthentic representation of their nation.

Scott Jordan Harris

Cazuza: Time Doesn't Stop

Cazuza – o tempo não pára

Studio/Distributor:

Globo Filmes
Cineluz Produções
Lereby Productions

Directors:

Sandra Werneck
Walter Carvalho

Producer:

Daniel Filho

Screenwriters:

Fernando Bonassi
Victor Navas (adapted from the book Cazuza: Só as Mães São Felizes by Lúcia Araújo, 2004)

Cinematographer:

Walter Carvalho

Art Director:

Cláudio Amaral Peixoto

Composers:

Guto Graça Mello
Agenor Miranda Araújo Neto

Editor:

Sérgio Mekler

Duration:

98 minutes

Genres:

Biography
Drama

Synopsis

The film traces the rise to stardom of the emblematic 1980s Brazilian rock musician, Agenor Miranda Araújo Neto, or 'Cazuza'. Picking up the narrative at the beginning of the 1980s, we follow a charismatic and reckless Cazuza from his first encounter with and ensuing membership as lead singer and songwriter of what was to become one of the most influential rock bands of the decade, Barão Vermelho. Backed by big-time music producer Ezequiel Neves, we accompany the group from their early gigs through their escalating success that culminates in a performance during the legendary 1985 'Rock in Rio' concert. With Cazuza's subsequent decision to embark on a solo career comes too the devastating discovery of his contraction of AIDS. Returning home after a period of hospitalization in the United States, he is forced to abandon his bohemian lifestyle and we witness the changing pace that anticipates the final stages of his career before his premature death in 1990 at only 32 years old. Set against the unsettled backdrop of the end of a twenty-year military dictatorship, this portrayal of rebellious youth culture invites broader reflections on attitudes towards liberty of expression and established authority.

Critique

Garnering festival awards and becoming a national box office hit, 'Cazuza' is a household name that clearly continues to resonate with Brazilians today. As co-director and cinematographer Walter Carvalho points out, 'Cazuza was an attitude', and the directorial duo conveys this phenomenon with resounding success. Through the film Cazuza becomes a living, breathing personification of the very spirit of rock and roll, its anti-authoritarian drive and reckless abandon to the pleasures and dangers that life offers. 'Which side?' Cazuza asks his friends as he totters precariously back and forth atop the pedestrian barricade of a highway overpass, contemplating the fatal drop below. Living to excess and fuelled by drugs, alcohol and illicit sex, the film explores its protagonist's outright defiance of socially – and legally – imposed limits. With the sense that only drastic action and radical behaviour can shake wider attitudes of resignation and cynicism, his mindset mirrors the unrest of a younger generation keen to make a stand against authority as they defiantly accompany the nation's first shaky steps toward re-democratization.

Cast:

Daniel de Oliveira
Marieta Severo
Reginaldo Faria
Emílio de Mello

Year:

2004

The film is punctuated with historical and geographical references, and the use of archival footage and 16mm montage sequences achieves a convincing air of authenticity. We are introduced in the opening shot to the notorious 'Circo Voador' ('Flying Circus'), with a tracking motion drawing us into the tantalizing world of performance that is the springboard for Cazuza's musical career. It is his ability with words and his vivacious and imaginative lyrics that establish Cazuza's reputation, leading international superstar of Brazilian music Caetano Veloso to proclaim his status as 'The greatest poet of his generation'. Veloso likely found in Cazuza's non-discriminatory ethos of *mistura* or mixture a clear echo of his own beliefs as a founder of the 1960s *Tropicália* movement – a controversial genre that likewise drew on diverse musical influences (such as international rock) to create its innovative fusions. In Cazuza's case, open-mindedness lies at the core of both his professional and personal life, leading to experimentation with different musical genres and sexual preferences alike. As to be expected, the soundtrack is rich with numerous group and solo hits and the stylistic and thematic progression in his musical production is deftly weaved into the film's chronological narrative, with initially coarse, daring and playful tones giving way to more lyrical and philosophical musings toward the latter stages of his life.

The sound of gently lapping water that precedes the opening scene anticipates a narrative return to the sea at several crucial points during the film, where it also closes. This establishes a cyclical pattern and also emphasizes through the constant crashing of waves the inevitable beat of passing time to which the title of song and film allude. With the discovery of Cazuza's illness it becomes the setting for a change of tempo: a shaky handheld camera chases his mad dash across the beach to the water's edge where he sobs in crumpled despair at the doctor's diagnosis. This marks a clear rupture in the singer's life as he is forced to adopt a more tranquil pace, softening too in his formerly ambivalent attitude to his adoring parents. Where his mother's doting love was suffocating, it is now a source of comfort. Although he was one of the first Brazilian celebrities to publicly acknowledge that he was suffering from AIDS, thereby helping to combat prejudice surrounding the disease, this is surprisingly understated within the film.

Despite being shown to have the obvious flaws of a pampered and over-protected only child, Cazuza is ultimately exhibited in the seductive colours of an undisputed icon. His charm and charisma are adeptly brought to life through the engaging performances of Daniel de Oliveira and the expert eye of one of the nation's leading cinematographers. Though the closing sequence is admittedly somewhat heavy-handed, we might deduce in this a nod to the manner in which Cazuza chose to live, eternally 'Exagerado'.

Alice Allen

Dona Flor and Her Two Husbands

Dona Flor e seus dois maridos

Studio/Distributor:

LC Barreto Ltda.
New Yorker Films

Director:

Bruno Barreto

Producers:

Luiz Carlo Barreto
Newton Rique
Cia Serrador

Screenwriters:

Eduardo Coutinho
Leopoldo Serran (adapted from the homonymous novel by Jorge Amado, 1966)

Cinematographer:

Murilo Salles

Art Director:

Anísio Medeiros

Composer:

Chico Buarque

Editor:

Raimundo Higino

Duration:

118 minutes

Genre:

Romantic comedy

Cast:

Sonia Braga
José Wilker
Mauro Mendonça

Year:

1976

Synopsis

When another long night of *Carnaval* dance and revelry comes close to an end in the streets of Salvador in 1943, clownish Vadinho collapses after a heart attack. Dressed up as a woman, he had been carrying and displaying a large penis made of cloth underneath his skirt. The 33-year-old gambler, gigolo and bohemian is already dead when culinary art instructor Flor, his pious, loyal and timid wife, arrives at the scene. She is devastated, despite the fact that her life with Vadinho was marked by physical abuse, financial irresponsibility and marital infidelity. Barreto's feature, based on the eponymous 1966 novel by acclaimed Brazilian writer Jorge Amado, consists of long and intermittent flashbacks covering the seven years of a marriage in which he is constantly criticized by Flor's neighbours and friends. After one year of mourning, she marries Dr Teodoro, a very kind, polite, honest and financially stable pharmacist; however, she misses the flair, passion and extraordinary sex life she had known with her first husband. She then asks *candomblé* priestesses to utilize their magical powers and bring Vadinho back. He returns as a type of ghost with which only she can communicate, see and touch.

Critique

Dona Flor and Her Two Husbands was made early in Bruno Barreto's successful career. The third of twenty features he has directed or produced, it remained Brazil's greatest box office hit for over four decades. Themes developed in this 1977 work highlight the dichotomy of the popular and erudite domains of culture represented by Dr Teodoro's penchant for classical music and Vadinho's joy in singing and dancing to samba and other *Carnaval* songs. Similar contrasts are also central to Barreto's 1982 adaptation of another novel by Jorge Amado, *Gabriela, Clove and Cinnamon* (with music by Antonio Carlos Jobim): circus art as fascinating entertainment and poetry recital as complete tedium. A wider variety of musical styles appear in *Dona Flor*, however. They include a highly romantic *seresta*, 'Noite cheia de estrelas' (by Cândido das Neves, 1972), offered to Dona Flor in serenade, or 'Somebody Loves Me' (1924), the George and Ira Gershwin title interpreted by actress Betty Faria on Dona Flor's first visit to a casino. The opening scene of the movie displays Vadinho and his cohorts singing *Carnaval marchinhas*, such as 'A jardineira' (by Humberto Porto and Benedito Lacerda, 1939) and 'Marchinha do grande galo' (by Lamartine Babo and Paulo Barbosa, 1936). Three and a half minutes into the film, Vadinho's death scene ends with pop music star Simone's rendition of Chico Buarque's 'O que será' ('What is it?, 1976'), a song which has three different sets of lyrics. The first and shortest version is subtitled 'Abertura' ('Opening'). The poetic voice seems to come from Dona Flor herself and to address her lover, Vadinho, while wondering 'what it is, my love, that which never gives me peace'. She opens her heart about a passion that hurts her and has no limits, and she wonders about his long nocturnal exploits without her. The second version, subtitled 'À flor da pele' ('Emotions on her sleeves'), develops the

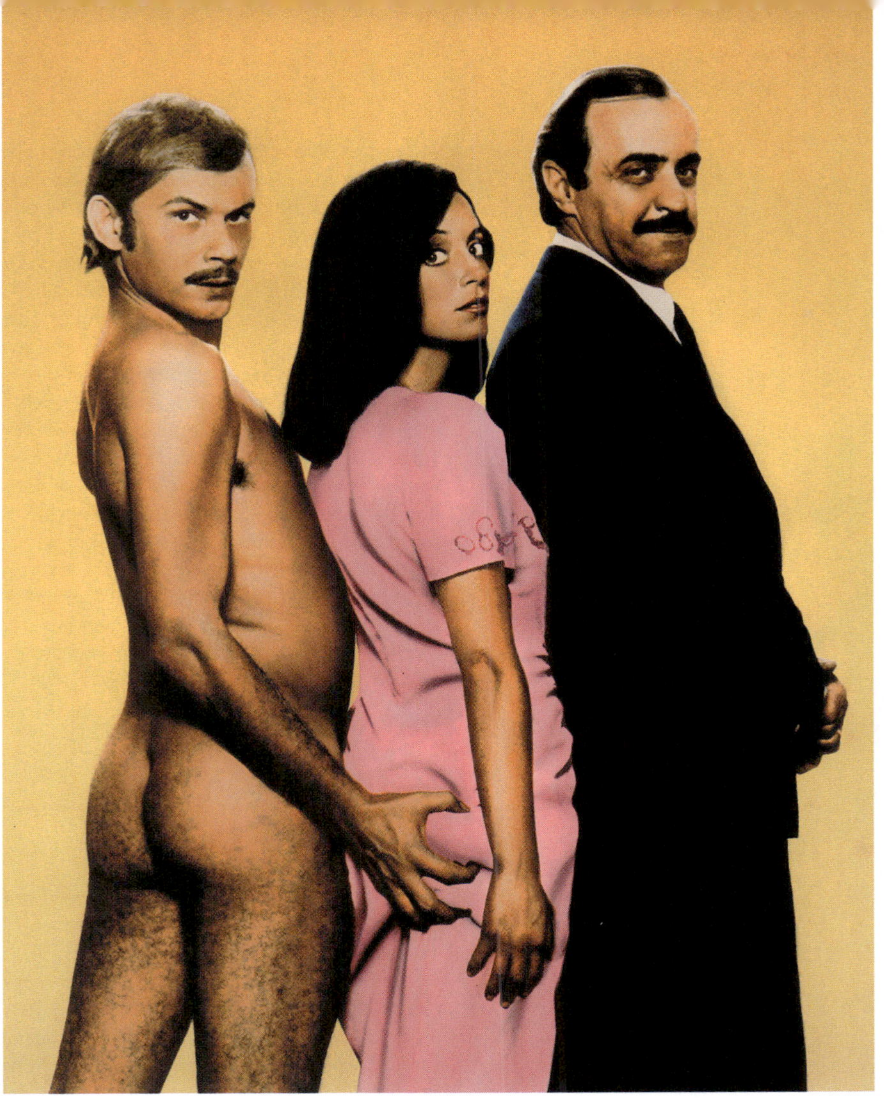

*Dona Flor and
Her Two Husbands*

same theme, with greater emphasis on the enticing, inebriating, painful and spell-binding aspects of passion. 'À flor da Terra' ('On the Edge of the Earth'), the third version, has been considered a major 'protest song' among hundreds of others with similar socio-political concerns written during the most recent years of dictatorship in Brazil (1964–85). Some of the few verses included in all three of these lyrics allude to a society where 'There is no government, and never will be'; 'There is no shame, and never will be'; and 'there is no moral judgement' either. While the first and second versions of the song bear close and clear thematic affinity with *Dona Flor*'s plot, the third version's metaphors and political innuendoes do not relate as directly to the plot. A spirit of revolt and anarchism, as well as frustration and disillusionment, commands a collage of images which are very suggestive of a political climate perceived by those who resisted the military dictatorship's conservative ideology and neglect of human rights. The message, though, resonates less with the characters in the film (despite its mockery of bourgeois values and Catholic mores) than with the Brazilian audience in the 1970s, the real people who joined peaceful or armed organizations, or otherwise expressed their outrage through literature, music and the arts in general. One arguable link between the song's third version and Barreto's screenplay or Amado's novel lies in the theme of escapism through drinking binges which is found in several of the verses. Another connection is the compassion expressed in the song for the lives of those on the margins of society, such as prostitutes and the physically or mentally challenged. Chico Buarque's verses, more than *Dona Flor*'s characters, evoke a faction of Brazilian youth motivated by the ongoing sexual revolution and the appeal of alcohol and drugs, the *desbundados* (wild and alienated); they, likewise, bring to mind the people inspired by Che Guevara's romantic socialism and its paternalistic take on the poor and the proletariat, the *esquerda engajada* (revolutionary left).

Dário Borim Jr

It's Over For You, 1970s

Deu pra ti anos '70

Directors:

Nelson Nadotti
Giba Assis Brasil

Producers:

Nelson Nadotti
Giba Assis Brasil

Screenwriters:

Nelson Nadotti
Giba Assis Brasil
Álvaro Teixeira

Cinematographer:

Nelson Nadotti

Composers:

Augusto Licks
Nei Lisboa

Editor:

Nelson Nadotti

Duration:

103 minutes

Synopsis

It's Over For You tells the story of the coming of age of a loose collection of rock musicians, journalists and sometime university students in Porto Alegre in the 1970s. The action unfolds in the bohemian neighborhood of Bom Fim, where a generation hung out, 'bebendo chopp e fazendo revolução,' drinking draft beer and making revolution, as rocker Nei Lisboa puts it in one of the songs on the soundtrack. In the opening scene, Ceres, an architecture student, boards a city bus and thumbs through a copy of a December, 1979 edition of *IstoÉ* magazine, glancing occasionally out the window at graffiti that warns, 'Deu pra ti, anos '70' – it's over for you, 1970s. The opening credits roll as the soundtrack blares Lisboa's proto-punk, post-psychedelic anthem, 'Delírio 32'. The next scene whisks us back to 1971, introducing us to a typically awkward group of young teenagers, more concerned with finding out where the next party is than with Brazil's military regime. The remainder of the film takes us through the decade in a series of rhapsodic episodes, loosely focusing on the parallel lives of Ceres and her friend Marcelo, an aspiring writer – the two are meant for each other, but circumstances keep them apart until the film's climax in the final days of the 1970s.

Critique

In the late 1970s, Lisboa, Augusto Licks and fellow Porto Alegre rockers channelled the yearning self-discovery of the city's middle-class youth, both in real life and in this charming film, where they play

Genre:

Comedy

Cast:

Pedro Santos
Ceres Victória
Nei Lisboa
Augusto Licks

Year:

1981

themselves as minor characters. They saw out the decade with a show that gave the film its title, and that included many of the songs on its soundtrack.

Lisboa, as well as the film-makers Nadotti and Assis Brasil, was at the forefront of a transition in Brazil, as expressions of youth culture diverged from those of national culture in Brazilian popular music and film. The generation that came to maturity in the mid 1960s, led by composers like Caetano Veloso and directors like Glauber Rocha, had burst on to the scene with youthful exuberance, offering coded messages about national identity. Over the course of the 1970s, those figures had turned from iconoclasts into revered statesmen. By the close of the decade, a younger generation began to chafe at the authority of their elders. In popular music, the youngsters favoured straightforward rock. In cinema, young film-makers rejected a funding system controlled by the military dictatorship in favour of making their own low-budget, independent works. *It's Over For You, 1970s* perfectly synthesizes that transition, delivering the first blast of the fresh air that film-makers from Porto Alegre would bring to the Brazilian scene over the next two decades.

The music in the early scenes is mostly foreign rock, like George Harrison and the Shocking Blue. The Brazilian titans of the 1960s are not absent – Chico Buarque, Caetano Veloso, even rock pioneer Raúl Seixas figure on the soundtrack, but they do so as part of the aural landscape, not revered elders. They are no different in that regard from early Genesis, Marcelo's escapist music of choice (progressive rock exerted an uncanny pull for a certain kind of thoughtful Brazilian teen). Elis Regina's urgent, tender 'Como Nossos Pais'/'Like Our Fathers' (Belchior, 1976) is more pivotal, ushering Marcelo through a key awakening midway through the film.

From this point on, most of the music is from Lisboa, Licks and company, as the movie captures the sound of the Bom Fim bohemians discovering their voice. The music is rough-hewn and unpretentious: its questing, hallucinatory lyrics, leavened with local slang, are matched with unadorned singing and brash electric guitars. This discovery of voice is depicted not as apotheosis but as a sense of incipient change: we see the soundcheck for the rock show, characterized by aimless noodling punctuated by sudden bursts of sincere beauty, and then we see almost nothing of the show itself. Similarly, we see Marcelo and Ceres finally getting together on New Year's Eve, 1979. But the closest we come to a love scene is the final shot of the pair sitting on the floor facing one another, pressing the soles of their feet together. Their heads and hearts are leaning towards adulthood and the wide-open 1980s but their feet are still grounded in the years of their bittersweet adolescence. The soundtrack blares Lisboa's 'Delírio 32', bringing us full circle.

Bryan McCann

Maids, The Film

Domésticas, o filme

Studio/Distributor:

O2 Films

Directors:

Fernando Meirelles
Nando Olival

Producer:

Andréa Barata Ribeiro

Screenwriters:

Cecília Homem de Mello
Fernando Meirelles
Nando Olival

Cinematographer:

Lauro Escorel, ABC

Art Directors:

Frederico Pinto
Tulé Peake

Composer:

André Abujamra

Editor:

Deo Teixeira

Duration:

90 minutes

Genre:

Comedy

Cast:

Cláudia Missura
Graziela Moretto
Lena Roque
Olivia Araújo
Renata Melo
Robson Nunes
Tiago Moraes

Year:

2001

Synopsis

Set amid the tangled streets of São Paulo, with its skyscrapers and endless traffic, the plot revolves around the drama and confusion in the day-to-day life of five domestic maids, with a mixture of reality, humour and romance.

Without any interaction with their employers, who are not even present in the film, the voices of Créo, Roxane, Raimunda, Quitéria and Cida fall on the spectator's ears in a tone of testimony and disillusionment as they share their lives and the dreams they had before coming to the big city, as well as the raw, harsh reality of the search for a better life.

Although the film ends without resolution, the outcome of each individual story reveals the unchanging and conformist nature of the characters, ending with the moving testimony of an anonymous maid of the inevitable destiny of disposable Cinderellas, victims of their own lot.

Critique

Maids, The Film could almost be seen as a tragicomedy were it not for the permeating humour of its soundtrack. Based on Renata Melo's play of the same name, this first full-length film by Fernando Meirelles, in partnership with Nando Olival, would be his training ground in terms of lighting, tone, colours and editing for the production of his great success, *Cidade de Deus/City of God* in 2002. Meirelles makes his debut with a journalistic satire, in which the humour of the situations reveals a realism in which the audience plays the role of accomplice to and confidant in the secrets that the five protagonists take turns telling, told in scenes that reveal their origins, personal anguish, relationships, and the unavoidable problems of class, race and social inequality.

The popular and critical success of the film is due in large part to the music that accompanies the frenzied scenes of cars, buses and people. However, when the storyline calls for an intimate moment, the music is suddenly silenced or faded and the film switches to black and white to capture the personal drama of each maid. Using close-ups and strategic angles, the camera focuses on each character's direct monologue to the audience.

This silence sharply contrasts with the soundtrack designed to be merely entertaining, allowing characters to demonstrate a certain consciousness of their social problems from basic but striking perspectives. No interference is allowed, particularly from the employers who are physically absent from the film; only the voices of the protagonists are heard, thus humanizing the maids. These brief moments of reflection directed towards the spectators, whether they be employers or employees, are soon interrupted and accompanied by incidental music, most of which are songs from the *brega* [tacky] genre, revealing the levity of the film's unpretentious, carnivalesque tone.

Brega music arose in Brazil in the 1960s, and along with the *Jovem Guarda* movement was criticized for its lack of awareness of the political climate of the times. Although popular, *brega* was seen as a genre in bad taste with pretentions to elegance, as demonstrated by Roxane in her appearance, attitude and desire to quit her job as a maid. *Brega* presents a certain simplicity and naivety which could be said to belong also to its fans, particularly in its romantic exaggeration and touch of spontaneous and care-free gaiety. Unlike the political overtones found in the music of Chico Buarque and Milton Nascimento, the *brega* style attracted artists who targeted the masses, including Lindomar Castilho, Waldick Soriano and Sidney Magal, all of whom appear on the soundtrack of *Maids*. This musical contrast establishes the distinction between the upper-middle and lower classes within the film itself: since the employers are not allowed in the film, neither is their music.

The movement and noise of the city are constantly present in the story, but they are interspersed with silences, following which the music returns to ease the tension and envelop the spectator in easily-recognizable lyrics and rhythms. Cida offers an example of this: Sidney Magal's music accompanies her in her new relationship with Jailto, marking the importance of the change in her romantic life despite the fact that her social situation continues unchanged.

As part of the original soundtrack, the film reserves a brief space for the rap that breaks through the rhythm and comfort of the otherwise romantic music, jolting and awakening the entranced audience to a way of denouncing reality.

In the final scenes, the camera uses a sequence to depict the monotonous routine to which each maid is enslaved. As each scene transitions, so does the music, creating the illusion of a transistor radio changing stations. In the midst of the series, we see a young man Gilvan becoming alienated and resorting to crime just as a radio would find static between stations. In the end, the camera settles on Créo and her daughter, Kelli, who becomes the first not to transition but rather transform out of the domestic sphere, breaking out of the vicious circle.

Although *Maids* never reached the level of success of other works by Fernando Meirelles, the film transcends banality by humanizing, in a vivid and carnivalesque manner, the lives of otherwise invisible and voiceless people.

Vanessa C Fitzgibbon

Me, You, Them

Eu, tu, eles

Studio/Distributor:
Conspiração Filmes
Director:
Andrucha Waddington

Synopsis

The film begins with Darlene, the central character, abandoned by her fiancé on the steps of a village church somewhere in north-eastern Brazil. Quickly we realize her path in life will not be the traditional, ideal romance and marriage. Even though she is clearly pregnant, the father of the child seems to have deserted her and his future son. After leaving the area for several years in search of work in the capital, Darlene returns to find that her mother is on her deathbed. After her mother's funeral, a considerably older man named Osias proposes to her despite being practically a stranger. Darlene chooses to marry

Producers:

Flávio R Tambellini
Andrucha Waddington
Leonardo Monteiro de Barros
Pedro Buarque de Hollanda

Screenwriters:

Elena Soarez
Andrucha Waddington

Cinematographer:

Breno Silveira

Art Director:

Toni Vanzolini

Composers:

Gilberto Gil
Luiz Gonzaga

Editor:

Vicente Kubrusly

him out of desperation, but from this point on, the viewer begins to realize that she is not one to give up on fulfilling her desires. Even as she endures the drudgery of housework and labour in the sugar cane fields while living with a man who clearly sees her as little more than a domestic slave, she pursues other loves that are more emotionally fulfilling. Osias's cousin Zezinho and Darlene's co-worker Ciro end up moving into the house, and Darlene develops extramarital relationships with both of them that suit her various emotional and sexual needs.

Critique

The character of Darlene (Regina Casé) is loosely based on a real woman named Marlene Sabóia from the state of Ceará in north-eastern Brazil. Director Andrucha Waddington's decision to fictionalize this woman's life and make it the centrepiece of his film set in the north-eastern interior reflects the new realism of the *retomada*, or Brazilian film revival of the 1990s. A kind of populism based in the everyday lives of the common folk and their popular culture is typical of films in this era based in the same region. This is a new vision of the *sertão* (north-eastern backlands), breaking from the 1960s *Cinema Novo*

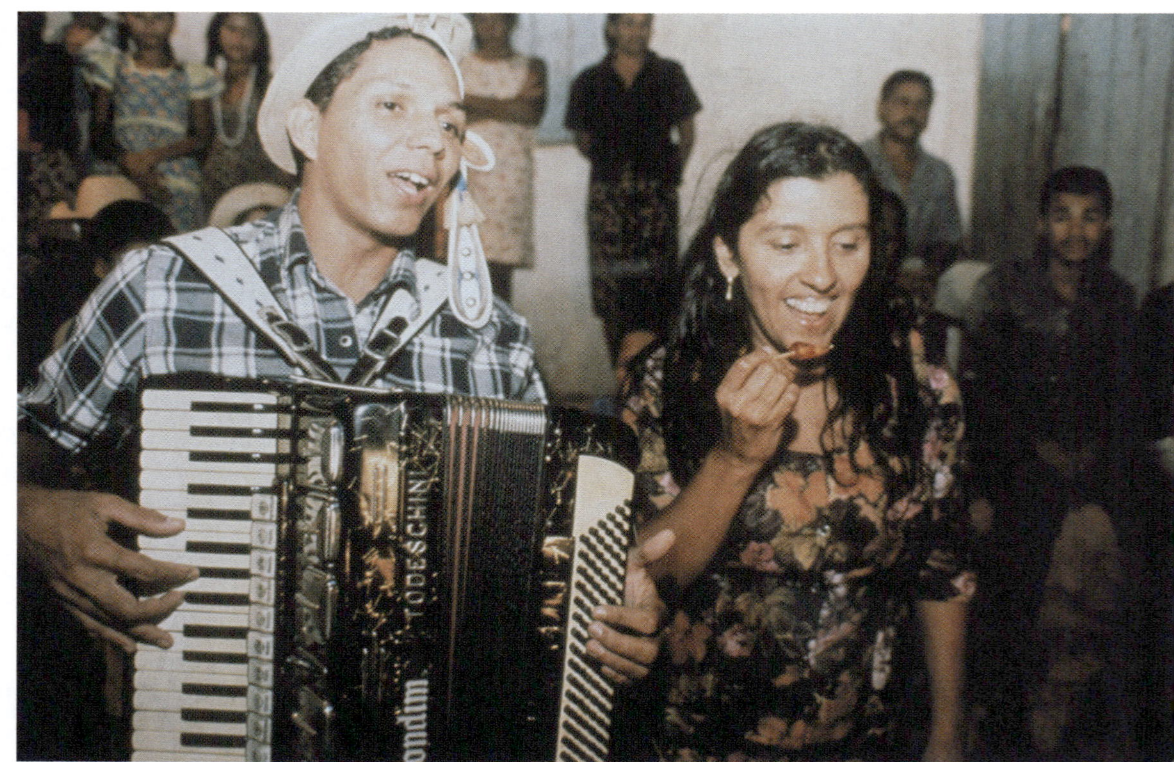

Eu tu eles/Me, You, Them

Duration:

104 minutes

Genre:

Drama/Comedy/Romance

Cast:

Regina Casé
Lima Duarte
Stênio Garcia
Luis Carlos Vasconcelos

Year:

2000

movement which tended to emphasize class conflict and popular revolt in the region. The new *retomada* focus on popular culture explains the great importance of *forró* (north-eastern country music featuring voice, accordion and percussion) to the soundtrack, including the score selected/composed by musical director Gilberto Gil, as well as the diegetic, recorded or performed music heard in local bars, at festivals and on the radio in various scenes. *Forró* and related dancing are also a central part of how Darlene expresses her individuality and passion. The music of the film is the clearest sign of the rise of regionalisms in Brazil's era of economic liberalization and then redemocratization since the 1970s and 1980s. Since that time, regional musical genres like *forró* have risen to popularity with some regularity on the national level. Waddington's own characteristic contribution to *retomada* regionalism is the close focus on a few characters and the emotional/ psychological dance between them in a relatively isolated setting (this kind of character focus, especially on strong female leads, becomes even clearer in his next film, *Casa de areia/House of Sand* (2005). The characters developed by Waddington and his co-screenwriter Elena Soarez give a subtle portrayal of the relational nature of gender in a setting where one might expect gender roles to be all the more firmly fixed by traditional norms. However, as they attempted to solve the mystery of how the real woman Marlene was able to manage a polyandric relationship in this environment, Waddington and Soares clearly realized that a certain degree of malleability in gender roles would be essential to achieve a modus vivendi in a household of one woman and three men (not to mention four children all biologically related to different fathers). Thus the film reveals that each member of the family's conformity to a more active/passive or traditional male/ female gender role depends largely on the context in which we see them in any given scene. For example, while we often see Darlene slaving away in her house, she becomes much more empowered and active outside the home, enjoying *forró* and dancing with whomever she pleases at the local bar. Osias (Lima Duarte) himself becomes more passive in the same context; in the scenes at the bar he never dances and only watches his wife dance with other men. Inside the household, Zezinho (Stênio Garcia) quickly becomes the homemaker after moving in, and Osias's sister Raquel (Nilda Spencer) thereafter mockingly observes that Osias now has 'two wives'. Yet when Ciro (Luis Carlos Vasconcelos) arrives on the doorstep a bit later, we see a marvellous scene which begins with Zezinho attempting to appear as the head of the household. At this point Zezinho has fathered a child with Darlene, and indicates this to Ciro. However, as soon as Zezinho sees Osias come out of the house, he fades into the background looking sullen and Osias takes the lead, acting the part of magnanimous head of the family who invites Ciro in as guest and orders his wife to make them all dinner. This amusing scene is but one example of the innovative look at gender relations in the Brazilian backlands this film establishes.

Jack A Draper III

Rio, Northern Zone

Rio, zona norte

Studio/Distributor:

Nelson Pereira dos Santos
Produções Cinematográficas

Director:

Nelson Pereira dos Santos

Producers:

Nelson Pereira dos Santos
Ciro Freire Cúri
Roberto Santos

Screenwriter:

Nelson Pereira dos Santos

Cinematographer:

Hélio Silva

Art Director:

Lito Cavalcante

Composers:

Alexandre Gnatalli
Radamés Gnatalli
Zé Kéti, et al.

Editor:

Mario del Río

Duration:

86 minutes

Genres:

Drama
Musical

Cast:

Grande Otelo
Jece Valadão
Paulo Goulart
Mária Petar
Malú
Haroldo de Oliveira
Vargas Júnior
Ângela Maria
Zé Kéti

Year:

1957

Synopsis

The black samba composer Espírito da Luz Soares falls from a suburban train. While he is rescued and brought to a hospital he remembers scenes of hope and sadness: two white middle-class contacts, the ruthless businessman Maurício and the composer and violinist Moacir promise him radio broadcastings and recordings of his original samba music. Espírito starts dreaming of a better life in one of Rio de Janeiro's Northern Zone *favelas*. He plans to build a home for his fiancée Adelaide and his son Norival. But then Maurício steals one of his songs and a gang of thieves robs him of his beggarly compensation for an unfair transfer of rights; Norival is killed in front of his eyes and Adelaide terminates their relationship. Nevertheless Espírito keeps his spirits up. The famous singer Ângela Maria (appearing as herself) agrees to record his music, but Espírito, who is not able to write musical scores, depends on Moacir. In the last moments before his accident in an overcrowded train, Espírito joyfully composes new class-conscious lyrics: 'My samba, that is Brazil's too, larará, they try to make you a nobody.'

Critique

Rio, Northern Zone is one of the most important films of the first of three phases of the *Cinema Novo* movement that lasted from 1954 to about 1972. Coming after *Rio, 40 graus/Rio, 40 Degrees* (1955) it is the second part of Nelson Pereira dos Santos's unfinished '*Carioca* Trilogy' devoted to Rio de Janeiro's distinct social spheres. The project won the admiration of Glauber Rocha because of its examination of the poor citizen's life, through which dos Santos developed the setting for an original new Brazilian cinema. In the transition between city centre and periphery, *Rio, Northern Zone* links characteristics of diverse forms like neo-realism, melodrama and the musical and the typical Brazilian musical comedy the *chanchada*. But by staging the dramatic downfall of *chanchada* star Grande Otelo, in the role of Espírito da Luz Soares, and simultaneously featuring the radio star Ângela Maria as part of an exploitative system, it can be seen as a critical reflection on genre or an 'anti-*chanchada*' (Ivana Bentes, 2003: 131).

With its sad plot and its likeable but naïve protagonist, the film confronts a problem that is still present in Brazilian cinema: the exploitation of the culture of the poor and especially of the *favela*'s samba composers by an opportunistic cultural industry. On the one hand, in *Rio, Northern Zone* this problem has to be understood in its historical context. The samba, a musical genre which is almost a synonym for 'Brazil', has not always been widely accepted as high culture. Previously it was stigmatized through association with marginality and crime, like the *favela* as a whole, and mainly became popular through radio and film stars like Ângela Maria and Carmen Miranda in the 1930s and 1940s. So the film can be seen as a reminiscence on the time of the genre's initial period of popularization and acceptance. On the other hand, it emphasizes the media's hierarchichal commodification of music, the marginalized territories the cultural industry exploits and agents it utilizes to record and market popular music in such a way as to reproduce class and power relations. Rio de Janeiro does not just differ in social or architectural aspects, but Rio consists of different musical zones.

The samba of the *favela* is presented as an authentic way of being. Whenever Espírito sings one of his songs there is percussion or a guitar in the background; or a box of matches or a rail track serve as accompanying rhythm. Samba is everywhere, played at school or at home with the family. It is the samba that serves as true expression for the self-taught composer, singing about love or daily sorrows. Longing, romance or social aspirations are the font without which there would be no samba; which in turn makes life's harshness bearable. But in the end it is careless composing that throws Espírito off-track. His samba tunes are transitory and mostly not written down, but rather passed on through listening and playing by ear as part of the *favela's* cultural memory.

Radio can save lives. That is one characteristic the film makes clear when showing Espírito's rescue procedure. For the composer radio broadcasting and recording offer the chance for his work to be ubiquitous, but the radio is also a threat. Radio can kill unknown samba stars.

It is film that can put in discussion the differences between live, broadcasted and recorded samba and the functioning of the radio and the industry that surrounds it. However samba and radio also interact with film: when Espírito sings whole songs and repeats them several times, it becomes obvious that film and its soundtrack are made for rotation – and so *Rio, Northern Zone* is, fittingly, told in flashbacks, as if it is somehow the record of a composer's musical memory.

Mariana Baltar Freire

Reference
Bentes, I (2003) 'The Sertão and the Favela in Contemporary Brazilian Film' in Lúcia Nagib (ed.) *The New Brazilian Cinema* London: I.B. Tauris 121-139.

The Two Sons of Francisco

2 Filhos de Francisco

Studio/Distributor:

Conspiração Filmes
ZCL Produções
Columbia Tristar Filmes do Brasil
Globo Filmes

Synopsis

This movie tells the true story of the ultra-successful Brazilian 'country' music duo Zezé di Camargo and Luciano (Mirosmar and Welson Camargo). It begins deep in the interior, in the state of Goiás, where Francisco, the boys' father, dreams of turning his two sons Mirosmar and Emival into a star duo in the 'country' genre of *música sertaneja*. When they are ejected from their land, the brothers start singing in bus stations in the state's capital, Goiânia, but their local success is suddenly cut short by an accident which kills Emival. Mirosmar is grief-stricken, but continues writing songs. He obtains some recognition, marries his first love, and moves to São Paulo, but his album does not sell well. About to give up, he is joined by his much younger

Director:

Breno Silveira

Producers:

Lucian Camargo
Leonardo Monteiro de Barros
Emanoel Camargo
Luiz Noronha
Pedro Buarque de Holonda
Pedro Guimarães
Rommel Marques

Screenwriters:

Patrícia Andrade
Carolina Kotscho

Cinematographers:

André Horta
Paulo Souza

Art Director:

Kiti Duarte

brother Welson (Luciano), and with a little help from their determined father, their first album together goes on to become a tremendous success. The rest, as they say, is history – with the duo selling more than twenty million records by 2005. The film ends with documentary scenes of the actual brothers returning to the house where they were born for some tearful remembrances.

Critique

This film is very much like a central-southern Brazilian 'country' song. *Música sertaneja*, or 'country' music, is one of the most popular genres in Brazil. The simple material is most frequently sung by pairs of brothers, and is often highly produced, with electric guitars, keyboards and strings. Its lyrics recount love and loss, leading some to accuse it of mawkishness. And like a country song, the unadorned rags-to-riches tale of this film unfolds in a straightforward way, impelled by the dreams of a father and the determination and talent of the three boys. Obstacles get in the way: the greed of those wishing to profit from the brothers' gift; poverty; lack of education; Emival's death; and an indifferent music industry.

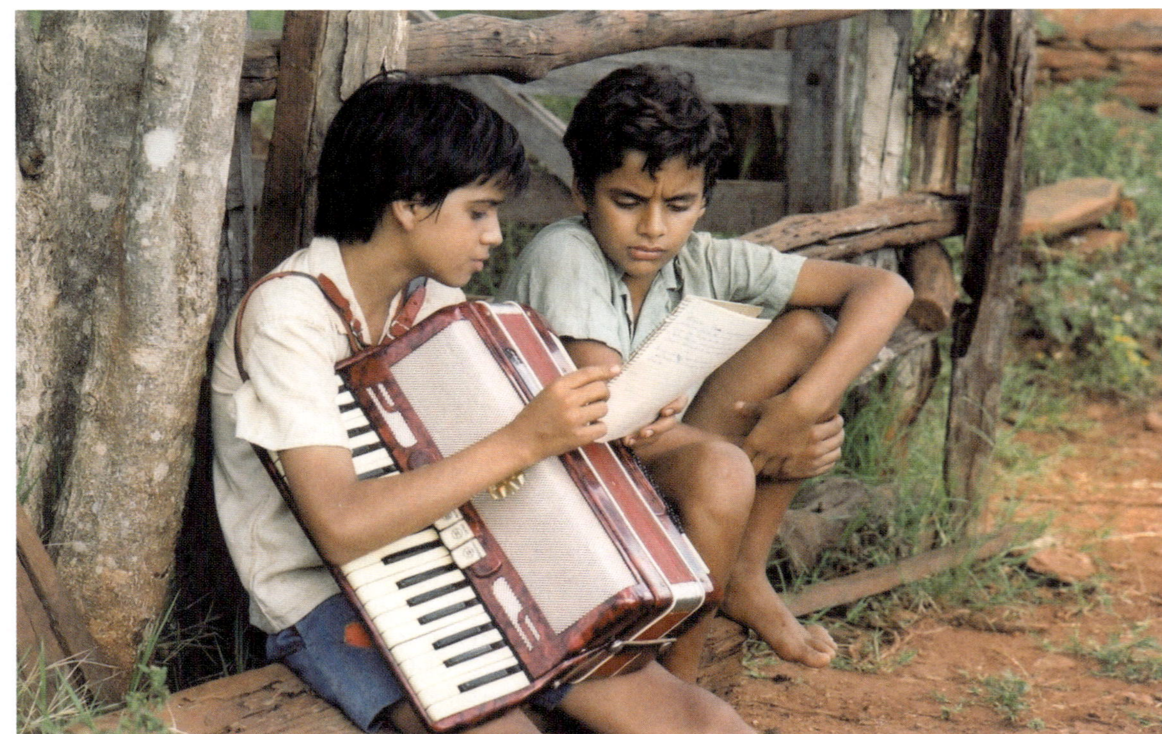

The Two Sons of Francisco

Composer:

Caetano Veloso

Editor:

Vicente Kubrusly

Duration:

132 minutes

Genre:

Drama

Cast:

Ângelo Antônio
Dira Paes
Marcio Kieling
Thiago Mendonça
Paloma Duarte
José Dumont
Lima Duarte

Year:

2005

The director chose to shoot in many of the actual locations where the boys grew up, and these sequences are strong in that they not only communicate a sense of the culture and landscape, but of the period as well. For instance, we get an honest portrayal of the simplicity of country folk when the father unwittingly composes an anti-military song during the heat of the dictatorship, and his sons are subsequently ejected from a radio station where they are supposed to sing. We also get to see the rapid transformation of the central-southern region from a primarily agricultural zone into a highly urbanized one.

The film runs into some trouble near its middle. The urgency of the denouement we all know is coming makes for a rushed feel. Welson's character must be established, along with the writing of the duo's first hit 'It's Love' ('É o amor') 1991. Here, the pastoral qualities of the earlier story-telling give way to more forced performances as we hurry to arrive at mega-stardom. The documentary sequences at the end of the film detract slightly from the narrative's power.

Overall, however, the film is an important departure from the samba-carnival-soccer-*favela* nexus that customarily prevails in successful Brazilian cinema. Here, we have the central-southern region in all its hickishness, a kind of unlikely mixture of Texas and Alabama with New York City as its capital. Furthermore, it is an easy film to watch, not only because of the good taste with which much of this age-old story is told, but because of the affection it displays for central-southern rural music; the soundtrack contains a number of country classics such as 'The Sadness of Armadillo Joe' ('Tristeza do Jeca', Angelino de Oliveira, 1918) and 'Backcountry Moonlight' ('Luar do Sertão', Catulo da Paixão Cearense and João Pernambuco, 1914). Indeed, central-southern rural music is treated with reverence throughout, as Brazilian stars from the high-brow and decidedly urban MPB (popular Brazilian music) are brought in for performances (Maria Bethânia) and even to craft the soundtrack itself (Caetano Veloso). The film also contains a heartfelt dose of solo Brazilian ten-string guitar (known as the *viola*).

The film is therefore strongly recommended. It represents a significant shift in the field of cultural production from a moment in which Brazilian rural genres are thought to be little more than lower-class moaning about lost love, to one in which a film like this can break box office records and feature a soundtrack from MPB stars like Veloso and Bethânia. In other words, the reception of the film suggests that country is all grown up, and for anyone attempting to understand contemporary Brazil, this realization is an important corrective to the often Rio-centric view promulgated at home and abroad.

Alexander Dent

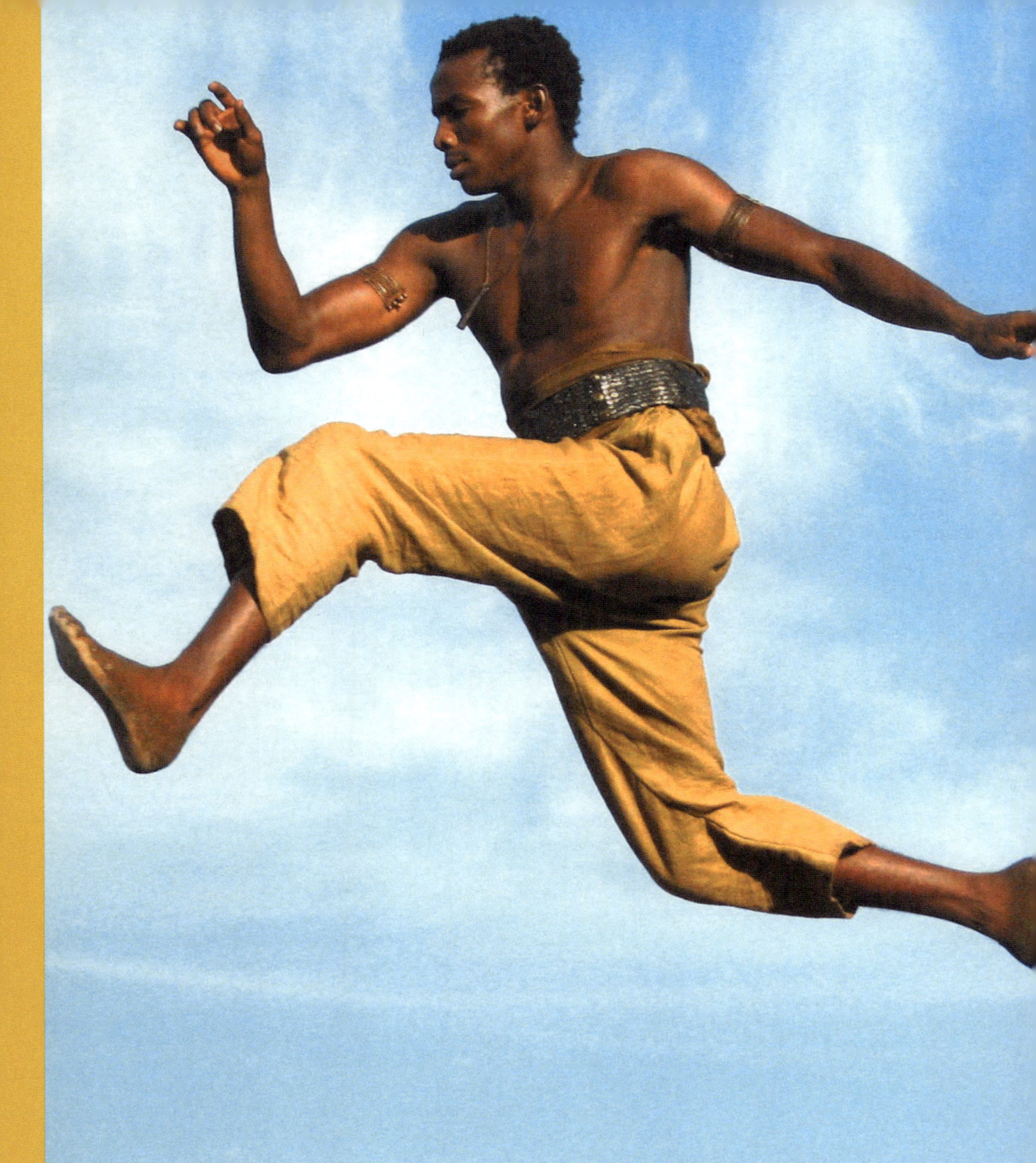
AFRO-BRAZILIAN
IDENTITY

Almost two hundred years after the establishment of Brazil as a nation, Afro-Brazilians are still treated paradoxically as the victims and perpetrators of the main social challenges the country faces today. Violence, poverty and illiteracy, are a few of many challenges Brazil continues to grapple with as a nation, oft-times predominantly within the Afro-Brazilian community. An attempt has become necessary for an open, honest, and egalitarian dialogue between marginalized communities and dominant society, largely represented by the same elites from the colonial times, but this attempt embodies a challenge that in many ways could be seen as impossible. The central question has become 'How will Brazil overcome the social and racial discrimination that has marked its history?' The answer is complex, and only through cooperation between government, elites and low income communities can a solution which includes the different elements that form Brazilian identity be possible.

In recent years, the world has witnessed a significant advance in quantity and quality in the Brazilian film industry, as a result of the many financial incentives, as well as a general awareness of the role and power of cinema in representing the country's social ills. The four Academy Awards nominations for Fernando Meirelles's *Cidade de Deus/City of God* (2002) contributed to the debate on the racial and social issues that have for centuries trapped millions of Afro-Brazilians who are stigmatized by the colour of their skin. Brazilian cinema developed traits that promoted common ground where language, image, art and idealism portrayed the main struggles faced by both society and the state. This new cinema became a powerful tool for social and cultural transformation, and was keen to reveal much more than the many *Brazils* of the *Cinema Novo*, but instead the many *Brazilians* of the twenty-first century. This cinema can also be seen as an ally with which to observe and evaluate the dynamics of a globalized world, evolving side by side with the sociopolitical demands of art. A distinctive trait of this new tendency is the increased presence and appreciation of Afro-Brazilian traditions, music and religious syncretism. Above all, the importance of the characters' lives takes on a greater pertinence, being more than secondary characters telling the country's collective story, with the focus primarily on new perspectives, psychological depth and distinctiveness.

Looking over Afro-Brazilian participation in history, we can observe that despite their active presence in Brazilian society and the economy since the sixteenth century, Afro-Brazilians became visible in the national media only in the 1850s when the Anti-Slavery campaign began, following the European tendency. While the model in European literature was of a humanistic portrait of blacks as noble, pitiful and faithful, Brazilian literature, and later media, first accepted the European model but then created their own depiction of Afro-Brazilians invariably as sensual and violent creatures, threatening the white families who became victims of the slaves' defensiveness and hostility. The elites became obsessed with abolishing the African *slave*, but not necessarily *slavery*. Lamarckian eugenic theories were embraced later in the nineteenth century in order to accommodate the country's reality, in particular miscegenation. A great part of the Brazilian intelligentsia from that time, headed principally by Sílvio Romero, believed the inferior races that tainted Brazil's image could disappear within four generations through another miscegenation process, only this time with *superior* races. New immigration incentives were created to attract

European workers in search of better opportunities. African traditions were banished from the country's identity, and were seen as undesirable and treacherous.

It was not until Gilberto Freyre's 1933 *The Masters and the Slaves* that African influence gained noteworthy consideration. Two years later, in 1935, Humberto Mauro directed *Favela dos meus amores/Favela of my Lovers* which may be considered the first production to 'really look to the life and music of the *favelas*' (Stam 1997: 82), and as Jorge Amado would comment, it managed 'to show the atmosphere of the *favela*, its misery and at the same time its tremendous beauty' (cited in Stam 1997: 82). Getúlio Vargas's nationalism and efforts to reinvent Brazilian identity once again embraced African traditions and rhythms with an exoticism aimed not just at attracting international attention, but also at increasing his popularity as the 'Father of the poor'. Carmen Miranda, the white *baiana* 'lady with the tutti-frutti hat', mixing samba with other Latino rhythms, became Brazil's successful image in the international media, an image appropriated by Vargas's powerful regime as a symbol of the country's prosperity. The image of Carmen Miranda, which was meant to export Brazilian culture, was accused of being 'too Americanized' in the context of the good neighbour policy. Thus the glorification of Brazil was not only in the Estado Novo's interest but also that of the United States government who wanted to pay a compliment to their allies. Although the image of Carmen Miranda is often considered a stereotypical one which worked as a tool for the political interests of the time, she is also recognized as having embraced Afro-Brazilian culture, and thus having paved the way for a different perception of Brazil as a modern country.

The first full-length film produced by Atlântida Studios in 1943, *Moleque tião*, also brought for the first time in Brazilian cinema a black actor, Grande Otelo, in the leading role. Otelo was already well-known by the national critics and public since the 1930s, and through the carnivalesque *chanchadas* and his comic partnership with Oscarito, he later became known as one of the most creative and notorious actors in Brazilian history. He participated in more than 100 films, remaining active in Brazilian cinema and television until his death in 1993. Regardless of Grande Otelo's pioneering spirit, talent and determination in opening an unprecedented space for black actors, his efforts were still not enough to overcome prejudice towards the Afro-Brazilian community in the media.

In the late 1950s, with the decline of the *chanchadas*, Vargas's suicide and its political consequences prior to the military *coup d'état*, Brazilian cinema began a new phase and the pre-*Cinema Novo* directors embraced the influence of Italian neo-realism to portray the country's history and social reality, using the slums and their dwellers, invariably black and poor, as shocking representations of the Brazilian reality. However, such representations empirically brought up the social consequences of the abandonment and invisibility of Afro-Brazilians to a public that was not ready to accept or face this reality. The productions of the 1960s intertwined metaphors with a political agenda, keeping the lives and dramas of the black characters in the background, emphasizing universal motifs and the political turmoil the country was facing. Black actors serving as shadows in secondary roles were still denied their own views and voice as racial discrimination remained unresolved and unspoken.

One can consider whether Afro-Brazilians really did want to have their lives and racial struggles interpreted and portrayed by a predominantly white media. In a country where Afro-Brazilian identity received an ambiguous treatment, being both celebrated and marginalized, Afro-Brazilians acknowledged that their colour was frequently racially stigmatized. Brazilians struggled to identify themselves as black, since the simple acknowledgement of their colour would bring upon them the stigma of their race and their so-called indisputable unfitness to take part in Brazilian society. The presence of racial issues in films would not just upset the public, but would also admit the social and racial inequality that the government and society in general had been trying to deny and hide for centuries under the country's fallacy of racial democracy. Afro-Brazilian issues were not always addressed in the revolutionary film-making of the 1960s and 1970s given its focus on class struggle and collective ideals over race. Storylines and representations were focused on problems that often were not even experienced by the majority of the black characters. On other occasions, the partial, incomplete or allegorical representations perpetrated images of subservient Afro-Brazilians in the hands of the elites, partly to avoid confrontation with directors' own intellectual and political interests. It will not be until the advent of the *cinema da retomada* that Brazilian cinema will allow Afro-Brazilians actors and characters a more significant representation of their traditions, social situation, racial struggles and above all, identity.

The films selected for this chapter represent a small part of Afro-Brazilian identity as perceived and portrayed in history and fiction, drawing in particular on literature, for instance in the adaptations of *The Plantation Owner's Daughter* (1953) by Maria Dezonne Pacheco Fernandes (*Sinhá Moça* – film version directed by Tom Payne and Osvaldo Sampaio, released in 1953), and the best-sellers *Jubiabá* by Jorge Amado (1935, film version dir. Nelson Pereira dos Santos, 1986), *Carandiru* by Drauzio Varella (1999, film version dir. Hector Babenco, 2003), and the remake of *Orfeu* by Vinícius de Moraes (1956, film version directed by Cacá Diegues, released in 1999), who used to proclaim himself as the 'blackest white_man in Brazil'. As mentioned before, the adaptation of Paulo Lins's *City of God* (1997) brought taboo issues including violence, drug-trafficking and the lost childhood of the forgotten Afro-Brazilians to national and international audiences, opening up discussion on social and historical issues, and provoking an unprecedented reaction to the social and racial tragedy that had never been seen before in the cinema. As a result, spectators today are more willing to accept films like *Quilombo* (Cacá Diegues, 1984), *Quase dois irmãos/Almost Brothers* (Lúcia Murat, 2004) and *Besouro* (João Daniel Tikhomiroff, 2009) which portray questions of Afro-Brazilians' resistance, as well as issues of gender and power found in the stories of *Xica da Silva* (Cacá Diegues, 1976) and *Madame Satã/Madame Satan* (Karim Aïnouz, 2002). Through the social role in which Brazilian cinema has been invested, Afro-Brazilian representations have become accepted as part of the national identity, not as a state project as embarked upon by Vargas, but as self-identification by Afro-Brazilians themselves, who became proud of their heritage and their skin colour; directors in cinema and television have transformed and placed value on black characters using different techniques in filming and editing to retell Afro-Brazilian history. However, many critics, led in part by Ivana Bentes's criticism to *City of God*, have suggested that the aestheticized way in which race is portrayed by recent directors have made palatable, consumed, commodifying markers of racial difference rather than denouncing prejudice. Hence, centuries of participation and the constant presence of Afro-Brazilians in Brazil's society and economy have undeniably helped to construct the powerful country Brazil has become, placing them as an unquestionable part of the country's national identity that can no longer be silenced or ignored.

Vanessa C Fitzgibbon

Reference

Stam, R (1997) *Tropical Multiculturalism: A Comparative History of Race in Brazilian Cinema & Culture*, Durham and London: Duke University Press.

Almost Brothers

Quase dois irmãos

Studio/Distributor:

Taiga Filmes e Vídeo

Director:

Lúcia Murat

Producers:

Ailton Franco Jr
Branca Murat

Screenwriters:

Lúcia Murat
Paulo Lins

Cinematographer:

Jacob Sarmento Solitrenick

Art Director:

Luiz Henrique Pinto

Composer:

Nana Vasconcelos

Editor:

Mair Tavares

Duration:

102 minutes

Genre:

Drama

Cast:

Caco Ciocler
Flavio Bauraqui
Marieta Severo
Werner Schünemann
Antônio Pompêo
Maria Flor
Luiz Melodia

Year:

2004

Synopsis

The two principal protagonists spring from two separate families in this film. *Almost Brothers* depicts the life and circumstances that bring together two boys: Miguel, a middle-class white boy, and Jorginho, a black boy and son of the family's maid. The storyline takes place over three different decades in Rio de Janeiro, and concludes with the establishment of the two boys' adulthood identities. The first moment, in 1957, alternates between Miguel's apartment and Jorginho's *favela*, Santa Marta, at a time when their fathers' passions for samba result in the boys' friendship. The second one, in the 1970s, takes place in the prison of Ilha Grande, where Jorginho, arrested as a bank robber, again meets Miguel, a political prisoner who has taken a stand against the military dictatorship. Finally, in 2004, the two friends face each other one last time in Bangu, a maximum security prison. This time, however, Jorginho is portrayed as an intransigent drug lord who commands his army from prison, while Miguel, a prominent senator, tries to establish peace between their two worlds. The drama is intertwined with Miguel's daughter who represents the reality of many young people from the upper-middle class in Rio de Janeiro, attracted to the guns and funk music of the hills, proposing a new form of revolution and ethics as a panacea for the society of a hegemonic upper class.

Critique

Lucia Murat and Paulo Lins combine their own experiences during the years of the military dictatorship, the former as the wife of a political prisoner and the latter as a *favela* dweller, to fictionalize Brazil's sociopolitical history as experienced by two different marginalized communities: the so-called terrorists and the *favela* dwellers. The film can be seen as a sequel to *Cidade de Deus/City of God* (Fernando Meirelles and Kátia Lund, 2002) in the manner it narrates the establishment of the *Falange vermelha* (Red Phalanx) as the merging of political prisoners' strategies with the violence of the apolitical prisoners. The narrative moves forward through alternate flashbacks, and linearity is kept within three different spheres, making a patchwork of sequences, differentiated by light, colour and music styles.

The story begins with Jorge's and Miguel's fathers' utopic friendship trying to diminish their social and racial differences through music, specifically samba, at the time considered to be an Afro-Brazilian style associated with the *favelas* and which ought to stay there. Lins's outlook throughout the film, as in *City of God*, is one which sees any attempt to create an egalitarian society without any social or racial prejudice or discrimination as inevitably obstructed by different levels of intolerance.

The same pessimism and irreconcilable differences are found again in the 1970s: Miguel is labelled a terrorist by the military government while Jorginho remains the stigmatized black *favelado* alienated from the country's political turmoil. The paradigm of the white intellectual revolutionary vs the ignorant black bank robber is underscored when

Miguel and the left-wing political prisoners try to impose themselves upon the apolitical and *favelado* prisoners, to foment a political movement through education and the adoption of new rules in prison. The result is the establishment of an unbridgeable abyss between the two groups, founded on racial and social differences. The political prisoners' 'egalitarian' discourse transfers their superiority over the majority black ordinary criminals. However, the unexpected resistance to the proposed alliance ironically reveals a defiance based on the awareness and tools learned by the *favelados* from the political prisoners. The outcome will be an uncontainable social violence which will transcend the prison walls to reach the outside world.

The two main characters' destinies culminate in their last confrontation at Bangu maximum security prison. Beyond the recollection of the establishment of the resistance and violence of the marginalized, Murat and Lins lead the audience to a parallel drama this time in the lives of the marginalized communities from the *morros* (hills) fighting in the drug war against the rich white girls from the *asphalt*, represented by the rebellious Juliana. Her fearless desire to transgress social norms, represented by her father's social and racial status, embodies another form of reciprocal intolerance. Moreover, this attempt to break the socioeconomic and cultural barriers between the two worlds proves to be unacceptable to both sides and, once again, risky and devastating.

The juxtaposition of Murat's and Lins's personal stories is a poignant reminder that violence has deep roots in Brazil's sociopolitical and racial conflict. In a country whose rulers ignored racial and social inequalities for centuries, *Almost Brothers* uses fiction and history to demystify the imaginary Brazil of racial democracy and paradise. The film denounces a society that at the same time condemns and supports the use of violence in marginal realms as long as it does not trespass the geographical and social borders that could promote reconciliation between these similar but distinct worlds.

Vanessa C Fitzgibbon

Besouro

Studio/Distributor:

Mixer

Director:

João Daniel Tikhomiroff

Producer:

Vicente Amorim

Screenwriters:

Patrícia Andrade
João Daniel Tikhomiroff

Cinematographer:

Enrique Chediak

Synopsis

Set in the post-abolition Brazil of the 1920s, where the majority of Afro-Brazilians continue to suffer in slavery-like conditions, a poor Afro-Brazilian boy named Manoel aspires to learn the art of *capoeira*. Rooted in martial arts, Afro-Brazilian mysticism and dance, and also outlawed at the time, *capoeira* represents precisely what the government strives to suppress – Afro-Brazilian culture and a violent uprising from the nation's poor. Despite the ban, Manoel becomes one of the great masters of *capoeira*, and he takes on the name Besouro (beetle), alluding to his ability to fly and surprise his opponents. Upon the death of his master, whom Besouro failed to protect from local whites seeking to quell the Pro-Afro-Brazilian movement, it falls upon his shoulders to continue the fight. While Besouro seeks refuge in the backlands bordering his town, his childhood friend becomes enraged upon finding Besouro with his ex-

Art Director:

Claudio Amaral Peixoto

Composers:

Pupillo
Tejo Damasceno
Rica Amabis

Editor:

Gustavo Giani

Duration:

94 minutes

Genre:

Drama

lover, Dinorá, and betrays his location. Though Dinorá warns Besouro of the impending battle with the plantation owner, he remains and fights.

Critique

Besouro effectively ties together significant aspects of Afro-Brazilian and north-eastern culture along with *capoeira* in a visually compelling film. The cinematography shifts at various points in the film to the perspective of a beetle, and at times a frog, serving as a reference both to Besouro as well as the commonplace practice of theriomorphism in north-eastern culture. Theriomorphism is predominantly used to signify the harsh existence of people in the north-east. Found not only in the name of Besouro, but also

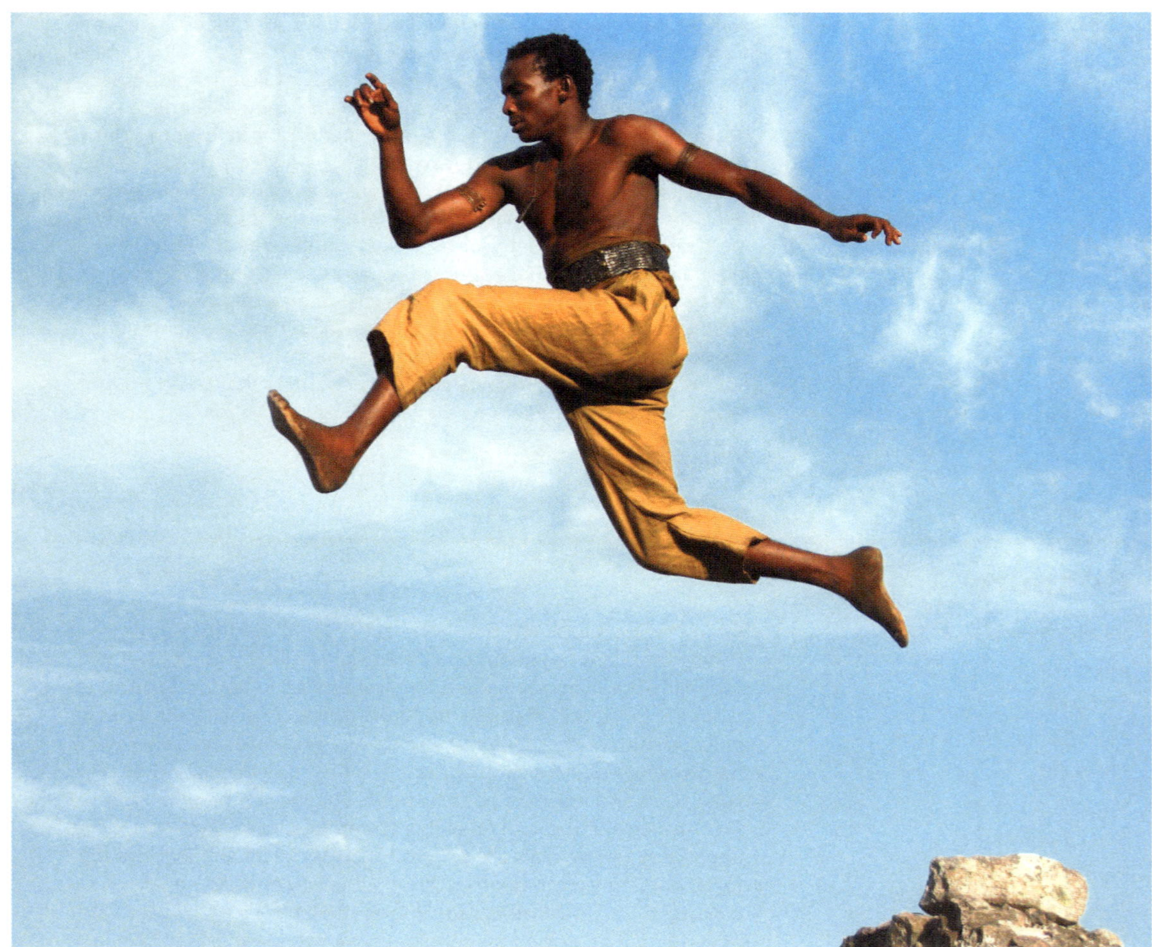

Besouro

Cast:

Ailton Carmo
Jessica Barbosa
Anderson Santos de Jesus
Flavio Rocha

Year:

2009

his childhood friend, Quero-Quero, named after a bird that eats beetles, these men take on the characteristics of these animals during the course of the film. The names also serve as a subtle use of foreshadowing, alluding to who will be responsible for the demise of Besouro in the final struggle against the plantation owner. The use of theriomorphism throughout the film also nods to the roots of *capoeira*, which heavily incorporates the use of animal movements and names in the chants and moves of this martial art form. By making theriomorphism a central theme of the film, many aspects of north-eastern and Afro-Brazilian culture are both implicitly and explicitly displayed in a striking and interesting manner.

Director João Daniel Tikhomiroff also creates a third dimension of being in the film, where characters are neither alive nor dead; they simply exist as spirits. This belief harks back to Afro-Brazilian mysticism, *candomblé*, which is largely based on communing with spirits and gods who are human in form but manifested in spirit. As the film continues, it exemplifies this dimension, specifically during the scenes of the apparition of the gods who help prepare Besouro to carry on his master's purpose, as well as the master's appearing to Besouro to guide and give him council. This third dimension softens the reality of Besouro's passing for the viewer, as he becomes a spirit who can then inhabit the bodies of those in need of help, and continue his efforts to bring down the plantation owner and the oppressive whites. Closely tied with this idea of a third dimension is the cyclical nature of some aspects of the plot. While some cycles are brutal in the film, such as those of poverty and severe discrimination against the Afro-Brazilians, there are also cycles that afford the viewer a sense of hope. The ultimate example is found at the end of the film, when Besouro's only child chooses the same name as his father – suggesting that the fight against discrimination and the plantation owner begins again with the younger generation, and that it will be carried out until there is social and economic equality for the Afro-Brazilian community.

Kristin Brown

Carandiru

Studio/Distributor:

Globo Filmes
HB Filmes
Columbia Tristar

Director:

Hector Babenco

Producer:

Hector Babenco

Screenwriters:

Victor Navas
Fernando Bonassi

Synopsis

A doctor lands in the labyrinthine halls of Carandiru, the largest prison of Latin America, responsible for the new program aimed to curb the spread of AIDS and other illnesses among the detainees. His arrival coincides with the resolution of a clash between inmates. The infirmary has become a narrative anchor, a place where the prisoners can relate the secrets of their crimes, where both solidarity and conflict are fostered. A series of flashbacks arranges the multiple histories of the prisoners: an unexpected murder resulting from a Christmas Eve assault; the eccentric romances of Highness, torn between two women; the tenacious friendship between Zico and Deusdete, who ends up in Carandiru for killing the man who raped his sister; stories of tragic misunderstandings and trickery. The tension grows in prison. Zico slips into drug addiction, and one night, in a

Hector Babenco (adapted from
the book Estação Carandiru by
Drauzio Varella, 1999)

Cinematographer:

Walter Carvalho

Art Director:

Clóvis Bueno

Composer:

André Abujamra

Editor:

Mauro Alice

Duration:

145 minutes

Genre:

Drama

Cast:

Ivan de Almeida
Caio Blat
Milhem Cortaz
Milton Gonçalves
Aílton Graça
Maria Luíza Mendonça
Wagner Moura
Rodrigo Santoro
Luiz Carlos Vasconcelos

Year:

2003

rage, he pours a pot of boiling water over Deusdete. This provokes the reprisal of the other inmates who stab him to death. A riot breaks out and the prisoners set Carandiru on fire. When the police break in, the resulting onslaught leaves 111 of the detainees dead.

Critique

After *O Beijo da mulher aranha*/*Kiss of the Spider Woman* (1985), Hector Babenco returns to jail, renouncing this time the poetic evocations of the cell despite political struggle and focusing, rather, on squalid and miserable scenarios, cramped corridors, gloomy staircases and the outbreak of violence. The prison is the main character of *Carandiru*. Through its faded bars, leaks and cracked walls, Babenco builds an architecture of aggression. The opening sequence, however, peeks through these gaps, casting light upon the dreariness of prison through the coloured frames of outside: the somehow trite vignettes that show how the inmates ended up in prison and the discreet gaze of the camera, reflected by the confidence the doctor (Luiz Carlos Vasconcelos) inspires little by little in his patients.

Are they ill or are they prisoners? The movie constantly works with this fusion of terms, disarticulating its underlying assumption. Lady Di (Rodrigo Santoro), for example, is a transvestite inmate who has had over 2,000 partners, and yet is still HIV-negative. Her queer romance with the midget No Way (Gero Camilo) is perhaps the most delightful fragment, just a weak light before the macabre finale, a half-hour-long display of raw brutality. This long closing sequence reduces these prisoners once again to mere bodies that shudder, twist and lifelessly scrub the floor. It is the dog that the camera follows amidst the shapeless mass of blood-covered flesh that highlights this display of 'bare life' – life stripped of the marks that make it legible, in which the body emerges as mere residue. In the end, the gallery of rogues that is *Carandiru*, which is based on a memoir by Drauzio Varella (the doctor who treated Babenco's own lymphatic cancer), arouses sympathy and humanity more than resentment or repudiation in the viewer. It renders visible the margins of citizenry and, while the film refuses to betray or belittle their tragedies, the abject figures, those expelled from society, return in the form of gripping shots.

Luigi Patruno

City of God

Cidade de Deus

Studio/Distributor:

02 Filmes
Globo Filmes
Studio Canal
Wild Brunch

Directors:

Fernando Meirelles
Kátia Lund

Synopsis

The film opens with a sequence of close-ups – a knife being sharpened, music playing, people barbequing and a dead chicken – that culminates in a follow-shot where a gang of young people frantically chase a chicken. Next, a wide-shot reveals the end of the pursuit where the armed youths confront the runaway chicken and a young man named Rocket, the narrator of the film. Accompanied by Rocket's voice-over narration, the action flashes back to the 1960s and eventually returns to this opening scene in the 1970s near the end of the movie. City of God is a government public housing project built in the 1960s in Rio de Janeiro. By the 1970s, it had become the most dangerous part of the city, ruled by two warring drug-trafficking gangs. The first outlaws of the community in the 1960s were three

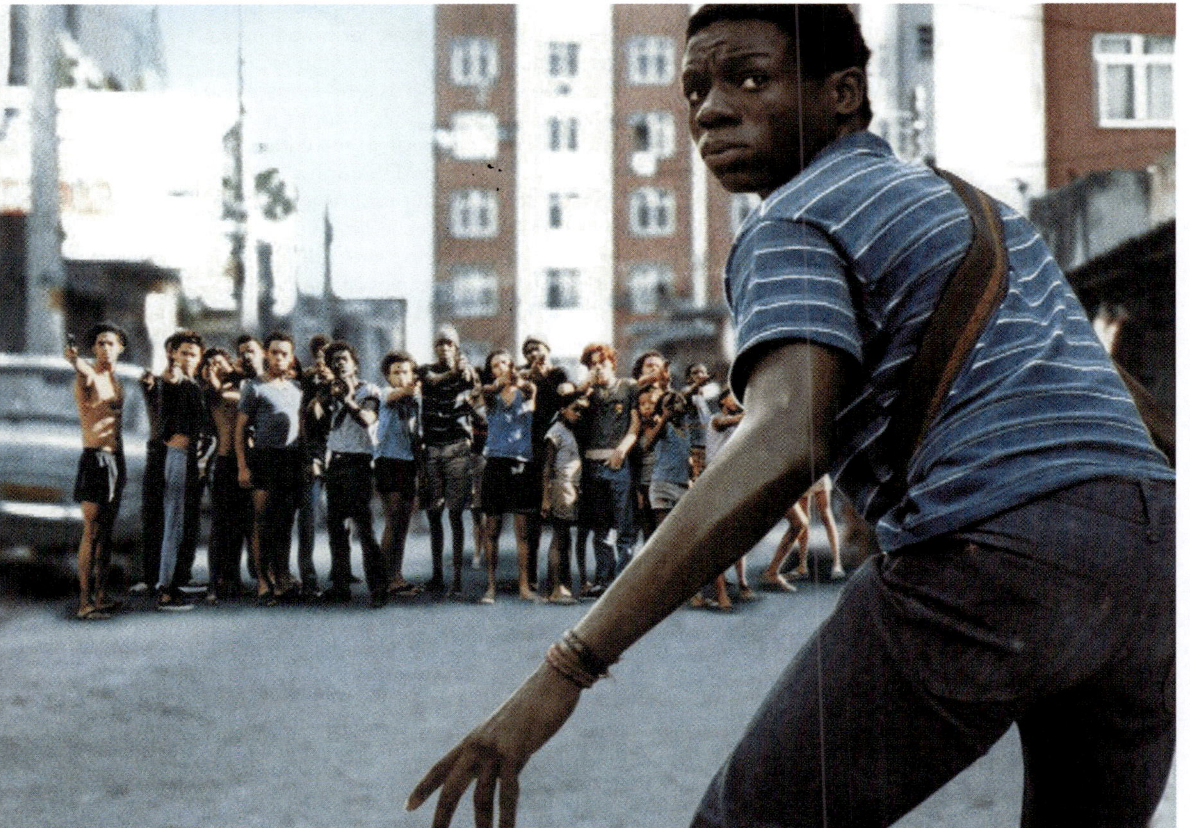

City of God

Producers:

Andrea Barata Ribeiro
Mauricio Andrade Ramos
Walter Salles

Screenwriter:

Bráulio Montovani (adapted
from the novel by Paulo Lins,
1997)

Cinematographer:

César Charlone

Art Director:

Tulé Peak

Composers:

Ed Côrtes
Antonio Pinto

Editor:

Daniel Rezende

Duration:

130 minutes

Genre:

Drama

Cast:

Alexandre Rodrigues
Alice Braga
Leandro Firmino
Phellipe Haagensen
Douglas Silva
Honathan Haagensen
Matheus Nachtergaele
Seu Jorge
Roberta Rodrigues
Graziella Moretto

Year:

2002

adolescents called the Tender Trio who began as petty thieves. After
witnessing the violence that shapes the lives of people in the City of
God, Rocket refuses to follow that life. Another young resident named
Lil' Dice, on the other hand, becomes Rocket's antagonist. While
helping the Tender Trio in what was supposed to be just a burglary,
Lil' Dice secretly murders all the victims of the theft. The lives of
Rocket and Lil' Dice take different paths after this critical juncture.

Critique

City of God is based on a novel written by Paulo Lins comprising
550 pages and 250 characters. Making it into a film and deciding
what to include in the picture was most likely a challenging task for
the director and the screenwriter. Furthermore, it is intriguing that,
although the film is not a representation of the country's daily life
but rather a somewhat romanticized representation of the lives of
the criminals who lived in the City of God, the success of the film
was contingent upon a social conviction that the picture is indeed
not overly romanticized. That is, in *City of God*, the fine line that
separates fiction and the reality of the *favelas* (mainly as portrayed by
the media) is almost as invisible as its depiction of the city of Rio de
Janeiro; nonetheless, the viewers are led to believe it is a faithful and
complex representation of that metropolitan area.

City of God can be understood as a *Bildungsroman* in which
Rocket and Lil' Dice (who as an adult changes his name to Lil' Z), who
are both exposed from an early age to the criminality of the *favela*,
grow from childhood to adulthood through a quest for identity that
leads them to very different maturities. As a child, Rocket always
wanted to be a photographer. As he grows and succumbs to peer-
pressure, he smokes marijuana and flirts with crime. Nevertheless,
by registering the subaltern identities of the *favelas* as well as the
criminality related to drug-trafficking, Rocket becomes a promising
professional photographer in a newspaper outside the City of God.
On the other hand, Lil' Dice is an example of a tragic *Bildungsroman*,
a life somehow pre-destined, a product of his environment. Lil' Dice's
early voracity for crime is revealed in the episode of the hotel burglary
in which the child manages to execute several people without being
noticed. As the adult Lil' Z, he enjoys the unlawful reputation he has
built, and his desire for power is unstoppable: he strives to control all
the drug-trafficking businesses in the City of God, which ultimately
helps split the community into two antagonistic gangs whose violent
wars get out of control, finally forcing the police to intervene. To a
great extent, the characters of Rocket and Lil' Z are depicted as the
embodiment of good and evil and as the confrontation between this
two-way spectrum of ethics and morality.

Among the many aspects of *City of God*, it is worth mentioning
the use of the camera in developing a visual aesthetic whose graphic
images not only grab the audience's attention from the beginning of
the film to the end but also condense and present a narrative filled
with extensive and diverse characters and situations. The use of the
camera changes dramatically from the 1960s to the 1970s, from a
linear narrative with static shots in the 1960s to postmodern nervous
shots in the 1970s. And this filming rupture continues frenetically to

the end of the film, as if aiming to create a hallucinogenic state of mind in the viewer. Shocking scenes of children shooting people may pass almost unnoticed while the viewer follows the fate of Lil' Z and Rocket. In pioneering this aesthetic, *City of God* became a precursor of a new film genre in Brazil that has helped the success of other similar Brazilian films.

Anita DeMelo

Jubiabá

Studio/Distributor:

Embrafilme

Director:

Nelson Pereira dos Santos

Producers:

Regina Filmes
Societé Française de Production

Screenwriters:

Jorge Amado
Nelson Pereira dos Santos
Henri Raillard
Ney Sant'anna (adapted from the 1935 novel by Jorge Amado)

Cinematographer:

José Medeiros

Art Director:

Juarez Paraíso

Composer:

Gilberto Gil

Editors:

Yvon Lemiére
Yves Cheroy
Catherine Gabrielidis
Sylvie Lhermenier
Alain Fresnot

Duration:

100 minutes

Genre:

Drama

Cast:

Charles Baiano
Françoise Goussard
Catherine Rouvel
Grande Otelo

Synopsis

Antonio Balduíno, or 'Baldo,' is a black boy living in early twentieth-century Bahia. After his aunt dies, he is taken to live with a wealthy white family, where he forms a childhood relationship with the daughter of the family, Lindinalva. As the two mature, they continue in their relationship until their budding romance is cut short by Amelia, the family's jealous servant. She accuses Baldo of peeping on Lindinalva, after which the family sends him to the street. The movie follows the two would-be lovers: Baldo, from his life on the streets through his various occupations, and Lindinalva, who has become pregnant from her former fiancé, through her family's destitution after her father squanders the family's wealth, to her desperation in having to earn a living as a prostitute. In the end, Amelia brings Baldo back to help Lindinalva, who has fallen ill, but there is no hope for them; Lindinalva is about to die. Even though her child is not his, Baldo agrees to care for him as his own, the only fulfillment of his longstanding devotion to her.

Critique

Jubiabá presents a story of contrasts and instability. For example, the film haphazardly follows Baldo (Charles Baiano) through his various occupations – we briefly see him making a living on the streets, when he quickly takes on a career as a professional boxer. After going undefeated for several matches, Baldo is finally beaten (in a scene in which we see the defeat brilliantly put before our own eyes). He decides to run away and finds work on a tobacco plantation. The sudden change in setting and story after the knock-out does not seem logical, and once we finally understand what is happening, we see Baldo as a fugitive on the verge of death, who then joins the circus, only to end up back in Salvador on the docks as a worker promoting a strike. As we try to keep up with Baldo as he moves from one thing to the next, we realize that nothing in his life is constant – a theme that Nelson Pereira dos Santos transmits very strongly, borrowing from Amado's novel.

We see that other things that had been constant in Baldo's life are also continually changing. Relationships with friends or women which had once been important are largely brushed off. Of particular note is Baldo's relationship with Jubiabá, the *candomblé* magician, who had been a sort of mentor when Baldo was a boy. As an adult, however, Baldo rarely visits Jubiabá. On his final return, as he speaks to Jubiabá's

Year:

1986

congregation (in another brilliant blending of images, in which Baldo speaks to the assembled workers simultaneously), Baldo criticizes the old religion, which had once been a source of strength to him.

Contrasted to this ever-changing lifestyle is the fantastic romance between Baldo and Lindinalva (Françoise Goussard). At every stage, Baldo daydreams of her, and each woman that he makes love to becomes her – quite literally, as the women onscreen transform into Lindinalva. We understand that no matter who they are, to Baldo, they are all the same woman. This fantasy is the same for Lindinalva, as her fiancé, and later on, a client, suddenly change into the boy from her childhood. Amidst all of the changes in their lives – Lindinalva's life changes nearly as much as Baldo's – the only constant is their unfulfilled feelings for each other. However, even this cannot continue, as Lindinalva dies, taking with her any fantasy that Baldo may have held.

In *Jubiabá*, Nelson Pereira dos Santos presents a faithful adaptation of Jorge Amado's celebrated novel of the same title. Dos Santos does not copy every line and detail from the written work – in fact, he largely ignores much of the detail and saves only the most basic parts of the plot. However, the faithfulness of his portrayal lies in the style of presentation, rather than the particulars of the presentation itself. He relies on the balance and contrast of continuous change versus constancy to bring Amado's work to the screen.

Robert M Jeffrey

Madame Satan

Madame Satã

Studio/Distributor:

Videofilmes
Wild Bunch
Lumière

Director:

Karim Aïnouz

Producers:

Isabel Diegues
Maurício Andrade Ramos
Walter Salles

Screenwriter:

Karim Aïnouz

Cinematographer:

Walter Carvalho

Art Director:

Marcos Pedroso

Synopsis

A biographical portrait of the life of João Francisco dos Santos (also known as Madame Satan), a notorious *malandro*, or street-tough who lived in Lapa, a bohemian neighbourhood of Rio de Janeiro in the 1930s and 1940s. Dos Santos also became something of a local celebrity for his transvestite cabaret acts and his spirited participation in carnival costume competitions. The film chronicles the daily injustices confronted by Dos Santos, who is of African descent, on account of his race and sexuality. The narrative begins with Dos Santos in police custody, and works backward to reveal the events that put him there. As part of the film's concern to explore his personality beyond the delinquent we see in the first frames, simultaneous plotlines follow his desire to find fame on the stage and to discover romantic and familial love. The film follows him through the cobbled streets of Lapa, an area that has resisted repeated and destructive waves of urbanization of the city centre, and in whose bars subcultures flourish that are more tolerant of nonconforming individuals. Here he carves out a space for his exuberant drag performances, which allow free rein to his fantasies of self-invention.

Critique

Karim Aïnouz's film is remarkable for its direct yet nuanced treatment of 'race', combined with a finely crafted dissection of

Composers:

Sacha Amback
Marcos Suzano

Editor:

Isabela Monteiro de Castro

Duration:

105 minutes

Genre:

Drama

Cast:

Lázaro Ramos
Marcélia Cartaxo
Flávio Bauraqui
Felippe Marques

Year:

2002

gendered identities. The film has a dual impulse: on the one hand it contemplates the construction of a black queer body as a spectacle mediated by racist discourses and images. On the other hand, it explores the experiential politics of race and gender of a subaltern subject like Dos Santos. In other words, his life story is narrated in terms of his negotiation of ideologies of race and gender that seek to exclude someone like him from the patriarchal national narrative. This national imaginary is based heavily on the samba-dancing *mulata* as a symbol of an idealized, mixed-race Brazilian community. The film invokes colonial and neocolonial male fantasies of sexual consumption in its referencing of the *mulata*. However, the viewer is denied fulfillment of such fantasies, and is bombarded instead by close-ups of the body of Lázaro Ramos, the actor playing Dos Santos, revealed in minute detail thanks to the use of bleach bypass in the processing of the film that gives a grainy, tactile quality to his dark skin. This is one of the ways in which the film meditates on the question of (in)visibility for subjects excluded from the national project. His stage performances and the centrality they are accorded in the film's action counter his negation in the public sphere. These performances are ambivalent self-representations that partly replicate mainstream racial discourses and images (such as the scene in which dos Santos dresses and sambas in the guise of a sensual *mulata*). Simultaneously, however, his unique re-articulations of such racialized and gendered icons also destabilize normativity. Perhaps the film's most significant contribution to thinking through intersections of race, gender and identity lies in its exploration of how subaltern subjects negotiate dominant culture to achieve their own desires.

Lorraine Leu

Orfeu

Studio/Distributor:

Rio Vermelho Filmes
Globo Filmes

Director:

Cacá Diegues

Producers:

Paula Lavinge
Renata Almeida Magalhães

Screenwriters:

João Emanuel Carreiro
Cacá Diegues
Paulo Lins
Hamílton Vaz Pereira
Hermano Vianna (adapted from the 1956 play by Vinícius de Moraes, Orfeu da Conceição Tragédia carioca)

Synopsis

Orfeu, a musician and composer, puts his womanizing days to an end when he meets his Eurídice, a young woman from rural Acre who arrives in the *favela* of Rio de Janeiro. Her arrival coincides with the final preparations for Carnival, where Orfeu leads a samba school. But life is not all celebration: the *favela* is under the rule of the drug lord Lucinho, Orfeu's childhood friend. Tension increases after Lucinho and his gang take the law into their own hands by killing a man and, in an effort to impress Eurídice, Orfeu demands that Lucinho leaves the *favela*. Lucinho refuses and instead orders his gang to kill Orfeu during the carnival parade, only to reverse his decision and let him live. However, death overshadows the lovers, since Lucinho kills the girl from Acre instead. Orfeu returns from carnival, ready to leave with Eurídice and upon learning of her death, Orfeu kills Lucinho and descends down the *morro* – or Hades – to retrieve the body of his lover. As the bard carries Eurídice in his arms, his ex-girlfriend kills him in a jealous rapture. In death, Orfeu and Eurídice ultimately leave the *favela* fulfilling their dream of being together.

Cinematographer:

Affonso Beato

Art Director:

Clóvis Bueno

Composer:

Caetano Veloso

Editor:

Sérgio Mekler

Duration:

110 minutes

Genre:

Drama

Cast:

Toni Garrido
Patrícia França
Murilo Benício
Zezé Motta
Milton Gonçalves

Year:

1999

Critique

Directed by Brazilian film-maker Cacá Diegues, one of the inaugurators of *Cinema Novo*, *Orfeu* is an adaptation of Brazilian composer and poet Vinícius de Morães's 1956 play *Orfeu da Conceição: Tragédia carioca*. Unlike the original play or its first film adaptation, the 1959 French production *Orfeu negro/Black Orpheus* directed by Marcel Camus, Diegues weaves the conflict of violence and drug trafficking in contemporary Rio de Janeiro into the story. Although the movie makes use of pervasive images of the *favela* – stereotypes of race, crime, carnival, sexism and poverty are all present in the film – the story of Lucinho and Orfeu, the criminal and the poet, adds a new dimension to the tragic love story of Orfeu and Eurídice. Beyond portraying the Manichaean struggle between good and evil, Lucinho and Orfeu's story underscores Orfeu's powerful nature: he not only seduces all the women in the *favela*, but also enthralls Lucinho with his mesmerizing personality. This is evident in the triangular relationship between Orfeu, Eurídice and Lucinho, which ends with Lucinho killing Eurídice and, consequently, Orfeu avenging his lover and killing his boyhood friend. In a way, Orfeu's act rewrites the myth of Cain and Abel and the first fratricide, and also brings to the fore the homoerotic bond underlying the relationship between Lucinho and Orfeu. For Lucinho, possessing Eurídice through death is the equivalent of possessing Orfeu, as evident in the drug trafficker's confrontation of Orfeu, telling him that he cannot abandon the *favela* nor belong to only one person. The drug lord and killer Lucinho embodies Death, a figure central to the classical Orpheus story, but by adding this bond between the two male characters, the movie also explores complex forms of love, desire and sociability, creating intriguing characters like Lucinho.

Despite the stunning images of Rio de Janeiro's glorious natural landscape and the impressive sequence depicting the carnival parade, *Orfeu* fails to depart from a romanticized portrayal of the *favela*. This becomes evident in the scenery, special effects and, to a degree, the music in the movie. The *favela* is portrayed as a gigantic, organic, and at times magical element, a place where hills, alleyways and corners tell a different story, communicated by the musical rhythms of samba, bossa nova, rap and funk. In the first adaptation of the movie, the musical score of samba bossa nova emerges as the sound of national identity, representative of an authentic Brazilian sentiment. However, under Caetano Veloso's musical direction, the soundtrack for *Orfeu* gains a new dimension by including rhythms like funk – a type of music that originated in the *favelas* of Rio de Janeiro. In this sense, the movie aims for a contemporary representation of life in the *favela* and the cultural productions that constantly emerge from these vibrant communities.

In other versions of the story, the tragic love story of Orfeu and Eurídice might have been the axis, but in Diegues's version it becomes less compelling than other aspects of the movie, such as the depiction of violence and the codes of law established by organized crime. Once the movie focuses on this aspect of the story, it becomes a far more relevant film, one invested in the social problems affecting Rio de Janeiro and, in this sense, earns a solid place alongside other films by Diegues that also explore key aspects of Brazilian history and society like *Xica da Silva* (1976), *Bye bye Brasil/Bye Bye Brazil* (1980) and *Quilombo* (1984).

Talía Guzmán-González

The Plantation Owner's Daughter

Sinhá Moça

Studio/Distributor:
Vera Cruz Studios
Directors:
Tom Payne
Osvaldo Sampaio
Producer:
Edgard Batista Pereira

Synopsis

During a time when Brazil was divided on the question of slavery, a young abolitionist and daughter of a slave owner, Sinhá Moça meets the self-professed proslavery Rodolfo on a train headed for São Paulo. Despite her initial attraction to Rodolfo, Sinhá Moça's determination to see slavery abolished keeps her at a reasonable distance from him during most of the film. Meanwhile, among the slaves owned by Sinhá Moça's father are a husband and wife, Fulgêncio and Sabina. After raping Sabina, the slave driver (Benedito) wants to punish Fulgêncio for his attempted escape, but in a climactic confrontation Fulgêncio breaks Benedito's whip, an action for which he is publicly whipped and killed. In a subsequent slave escape, the leader of the revolt, Justino, wounds Rodolfo. Later in court, Rodolfo surprises the crowd by exposing himself as a pro-abolitionist and actually defending Justino's actions just as an important announcement arrives.

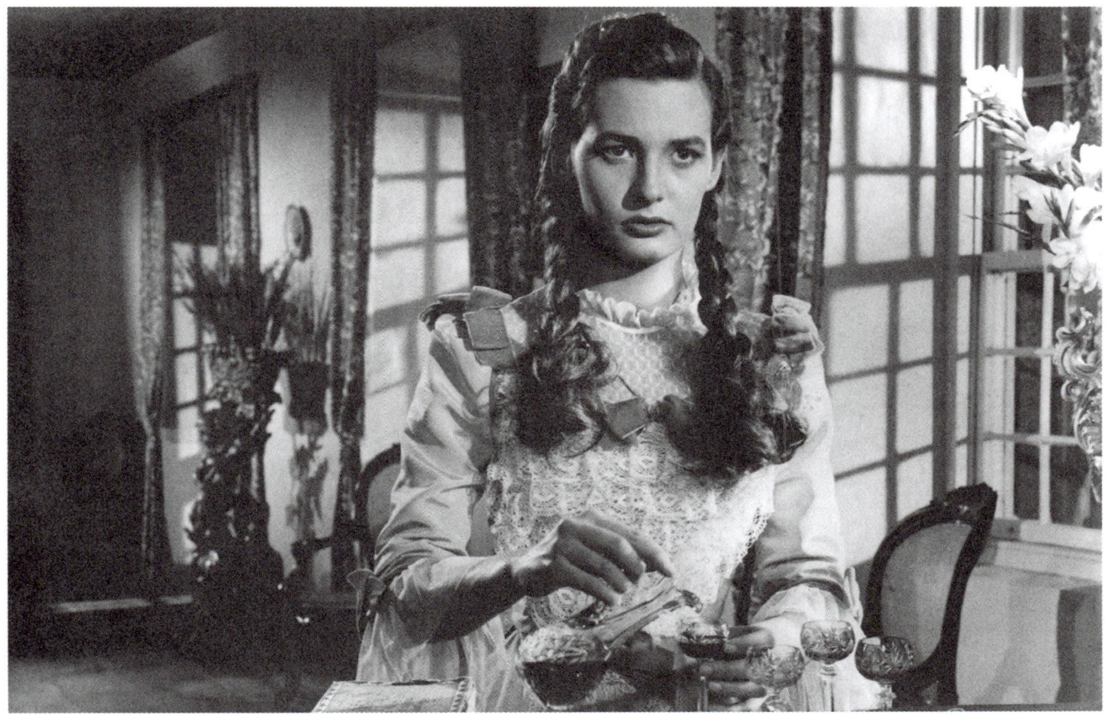

Sinhá Moça

Screenwriters:

Fabio Carpi
Guilherme de Almeida

Cinematographer:

Ray Sturgess

Art Director:

João Maria dos Santos

Composer:

Francisco Mignone

Editors:

Edith Hafenrichter
Oswald Harenrichter

Duration:

120 minutes

Genre:

Drama

Cast:

Anselmo Duarte
Eliane Lage
Ricardo Campos
José Policena
Ruth de Souza

Year:

1953

Critique

The Plantation Owner's Daughter represents an important step in the portrayal of black characters in Brazilian film. Many realities about the lives of slaves are set before the spectators to be considered and to hopefully evoke their sympathy. The importance of the institution of slavery in Brazilian society is clearly demonstrated in the scene in which Fulgêncio is punished and killed in the town square. The location of the whipping (in the centre of town) represents the central position that slavery held in economic and social terms in the country. In direct contrast with the mass ceremony taking place in a nearby church, this climactic scene creates a distinction between Fulgêncio's murder and a mere death, thus emphasizing the injustice of this important part of Brazilian society at the time.

This film includes several references to the abolition of slavery in the United States (for example, Rodolfo [Anselmo Duarte] and Sinhá Moça [Eliane Lage] are reading *Uncle Tom's Cabin* (Harriet Beecher Stowe, 1852) on the train to São Paulo), which link Vera Cruz's objectives with Hollywood portrayals of abolition. Even though this film shows a more realistic view of slave life than other films created around the same time, it still shows traces of romanticism in its depiction of the institution of slavery. For example, although the slaves are shown doing hard physical labour and being punished and tortured, the film is still based on the white protagonist, as suggested by the title of the movie. Even before the film begins, the spectators' attention is turned to this pro-abolitionist woman, even though some could argue that the black actors are actually the more talented members of the cast.

Romanticism is also seen in several other aspects of the film, for example in Rodolfo's character as he turns into a type of mystery hero who poses as a supporter of slavery by day and goes about freeing slaves by night. His secret pro-abolitionist identity makes for a 'happily ever after' ending typical of Hollywood, especially in the courtroom scene in which his legal success in Justino's case is amplified by the announcement of emancipation only moments later. In the final moments of the film, suffering is almost forgotten as Rodolfo and Sinhá Moça finally unite in their common love for each other and for freedom, and even the plantation owner himself sees the error of his ways, repents, and reconciles himself to his daughter. This fairy tale ending is sharply contrasted with the actual history of abolition in Brazil, in which life continued to be very difficult for the ex-slaves.

While also dealing with the position of women in general in society, whether in or out of slavery, this film is based in large part on the question of the treatment of slaves in Brazil. Although less idealized than other films about slavery of the time, it still contains many threads of romanticism tying it back to the Hollywood style, and gives the most prominent positions to the white characters in the film, enforcing their domination and superiority.

Berkeley Kershisnik

Quilombo

Studio/Distributor:

CDK

Director:

Cacá Diegues

Producer:

Cacá Diegues

Screenwriters:

Cacá Diegues
João Felicio dos Santos
Décio Freitas

Cinematographer:

Lauro Escorel Filho

Art Director:

Luiz Carlos Ripper

Composers:

Gilberto Gil
Waly Salomão

Editor:

Mair Tavares

Duration:

119 minutes

Genre:

Drama

Cast:

Zezé Motta
Antônio Pompêo
Tony Tornado
Grande Otelo
Daniel Filho
Maurício do Valle
Vera Fischer

Year:

1984

Synopsis

In 1650, after killing a group of Portuguese soldiers, several slaves flee to Palmares, a *quilombo*, or community of escaped slaves. Along the way, Gongoba, a former house slave, gives birth. Upon their arrival, Palmares's spiritual leader divines that one of the new arrivals will become leader of the *quilombo*, Ganga Zumba. Five years later, a group of children and elders is ambushed by slave hunters, who kill Gongoba and capture her son. Having defeated the Dutch for control of what is now north-eastern Brazil, the Portuguese have turned their attention to capturing escaped slaves and destroying the *quilombos*. Ganga Zumba leads Palmares to victory over the whites and prophesies that Gongoba's child will return. Fifteen years later, that boy, now fully grown and serving as a priest, escapes to Palmares. As he reintegrates himself into the community, he gradually becomes the legendary leader Zumbi, who wreaks vengeance on the whites, freeing slaves and allowing the *quilombo* to grow ever larger and richer, eventually comprising several villages surrounding Palmares. The stronger the *quilombo* gets, the more it has to protect itself from an increasingly irritated Portuguese community, leading eventually to all-out war between the former slaves and the Crown.

Critique

Directed by one of the most well-known names in Brazilian cinema of the era, *Quilombo* relates historical events while also linking its plot to contemporary concerns, most notably race relations and democracy. The film, released in the last full year of the Brazilian military dictatorship, valorizes the voice of the people above all, demonstrating in several crucial scenes how dictatorial decisions or leadership that ignores the voices and opinions of the people can lead to disaster. An official selection at Cannes in 1984, this historical drama also includes other contemporary moral messages, while still clearly situating itself in a specific seventeenth-century context.

Director Diegues does not hide his sympathies, clearly laying out the good Africans against the evil Portuguese. A few poor whites do join the *quilombo*, but they are rare exceptions to the portrayal of the majority of the Portuguese colonizers, who are almost single-mindedly motivated only by greed and personal enrichment. Meanwhile, nearly all of the *quilombo* residents are pure of heart, in touch with both nature and the spirit world, and focused on the greater good of their entire community. Scenes in the *quilombo* are filmed in rich colours and frequently include singing, dancing and playing, while scenes outside the escaped-slave community are generally cast in a gritty tone full of browns and greys. The residents of Palmares are surrounded by the bounty of nature, copious amounts of fruits and other foods, and speak openly to each other in spirited democratic discussions. Conversely, the most noticeable elements of the Portuguese world are dark buildings and constricting clothing. This contrast, while frequently bordering on absurd exaggeration, makes sense in the context of a film that is one of the few voices of its time trying to counter an official discourse that vilified the escaped slaves as rebels and lauded the Portuguese as the bringers of civilization and modernity.

Music is integral to this film, and song lyrics frequently propel the story forward or convey a moral message. One of the most famous songs from the film, summarizing the history of Palmares, refers to the *quilombo* as a black El Dorado. The soundtrack by Gilberto Gil, one of the biggest names in Brazilian popular music, is openly contemporary to the time of filming. Songs and background music are heavily influenced by the *Tropicália* movement and replete with both musical and lyrical references to samba, *capoeira*, and other cultural tropes, further evidence that Diegues was clearly trying to recast the then-dominant discourse of national identity. Moreover, this questioning and reshaping of Brazilian identity is explicitly militant, a point of view perhaps most clearly expressed in the music. The lilting melody of a song that appears several times in the film, especially during battle scenes, cannot hide its revolutionary message, which asserts that the happiness of the blacks is a warrior's happiness. Borrowing heavily from other patriotic, identity-based songs that every Brazilian would know, the song concludes by equating this warrior sentiment not only with a 'Brazilian Brazil' but also with freedom and emancipation.

Steven K Smith

Xica da Silva

Studio/Distributor:

Distrifilmes
Embrafilme and Terra Filme

Director:

Cacá Diegues

Producer:

Jarbas Barbosa

Screenwriters:

Cacá Diegues
João Felício dos Santos

Cinematographer:

José Medeiros

Art Director:

Luiz Carlos Ripper

Composers:

Jorge Ben
Roberto Menescal

Editor:

Mair Tavares

Duration:

117 minutes

Synopsis

Xica da Silva fictionally recreates the events that transpired after the arrival of João Fernandes de Oliveira, the most successful diamond extractor of colonial Brazil, to Vila Rica and his return to Lisbon in 1773. Francisca (Xica) da Silva, a slave woman, met João Fernandes de Oliveira and seduced him into taking her as his slave. He freed her and made her his lover. During the years that João de Oliveira dominated the region, Xica enjoyed the economic and political power that came from the social position she came to occupy. However, all of this came to an end when the Portuguese Crown ordered João Fernandez de Oliveira's return to Lisbon for the threat that his increasing wealth and Xica's behaviour and power posed to the Crown and to the social order. Xica loses all the social favour she enjoyed and returns to her position as a slave.

Critique

Xica da Silva is the sixth film by Cacá Diegues, one of the original participants of the *Cinema Novo* movement that envisioned the creation of a national film industry. Originating in the period of the Brazilian military regime effects the narrative definitively, since the film not only had to wrestle with North American influences but also evade censorship. A simple look at Xica's characterization will suffice to show the caricatured portrayal of the black female Brazilian slave. From the beginning of the movie, Xica is the centre of all sexual desires which she uses in order to gain freedom, power and favours.

Genre:

Drama

Cast:

Zezé Motta
Walmor Chagas
Altair Lima
Elke Maravilha
Stepan Nergessian
Rodolfo Arena
José Wilker

Year:

1976

Her depiction, however, does not escape the traditional reduction of women to the corporal and animal impulses that drive them to the satisfaction of immediate desires. She neither appears to be a liberating agent nor furthers the cause for the abolition of slavery since she adopts and exaggerates the behaviour of the oppressors: exploits others, abuses power and lives surrounded by luxury at the cost of others' suffering. Not only this, but her only attempt to save what could be thought of as an incipient nation fails terribly and ends her reign and Fernandez de Oliveira's. Nevertheless, the exploitation of sex as the only tool to level with the oppressor could be read as a message to Brazilians to use whatever tools at their disposal to fight back during the military regime. It is precisely the caricaturization that enables one to hypothesize that the film uses humour as a means to criticize not only the eroticization of black women slaves, but also the different power struggles in which both Xica, in the film, and the Brazilian spectators, are immersed: struggles which are racial, political and based in gender. The exaggeration of her mistakes and her faulty logic alert the audience to how easy are the traps of power and discrimination which eventually lead to the defeat of those who side with the oppressors.

Jara M Ríos Rodríguez

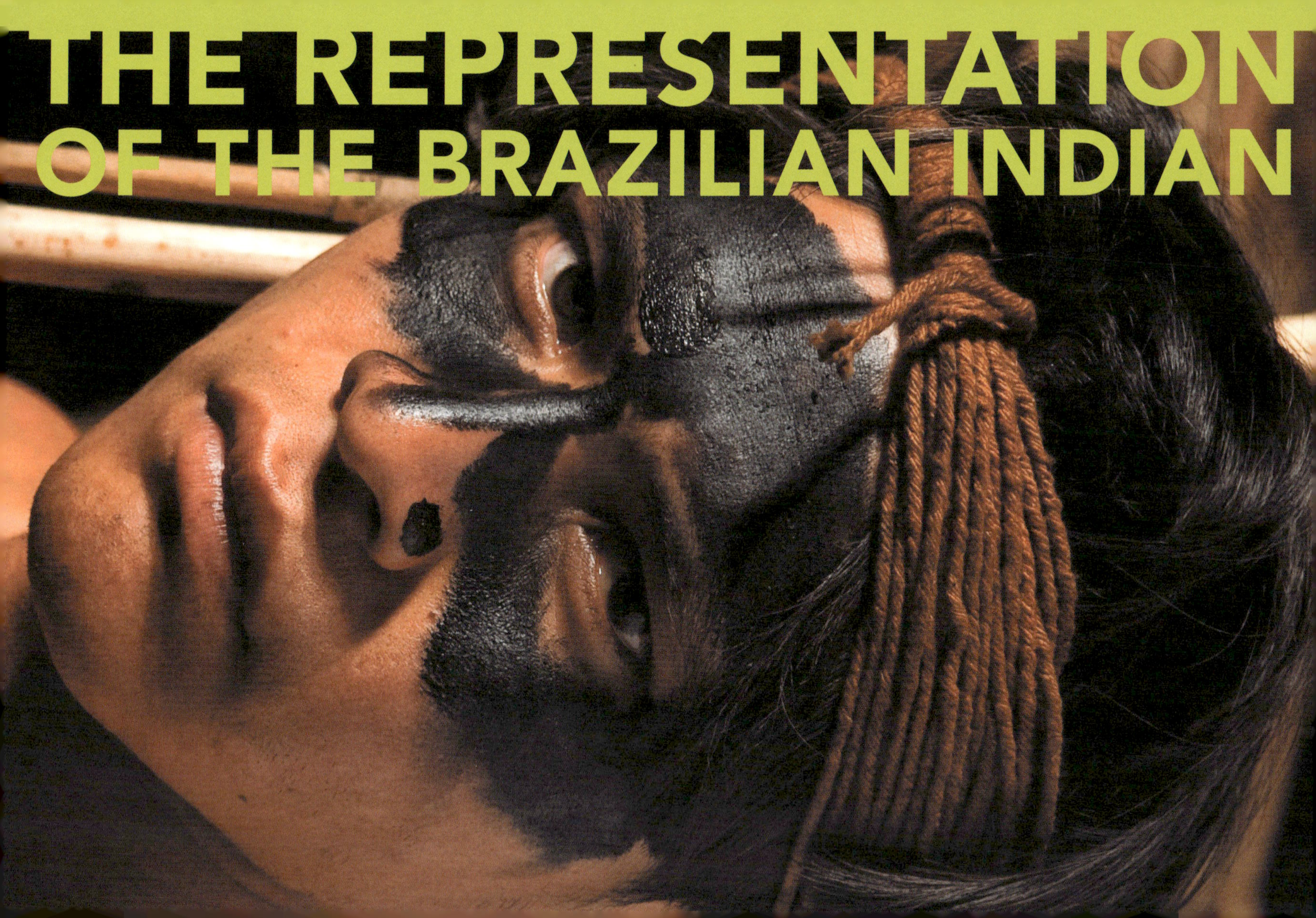

THE REPRESENTATION
OF THE BRAZILIAN INDIAN

The representation of the original inhabitants of Brazil is often discussed in relation to the encounter between European and indigenous people and their subsequent resistance to domination, which was installed by the colonizers and perpetuated by Brazilian society. Of course, the discussion of how some filmic representations of indigenous people are shaped by the continued existence of modes of representation common to colonialism goes far beyond Brazilian cinema to engage with issues pertaining to postcolonial theory. The colonial legacy, including Eurocentric approaches of Brazilian history, is embedded in understandings of the nation that are sometimes disseminated in school education. The earliest film of this chapter *O Descobrimento do Brasil/The Discovery of Brazil* (Humberto Mauro, 1936) not only testifies to the assumption that history is European, but idealizes the conquest, by giving it a transcendental aura. In the film, linguistic, cultural and religious domination is treated as an 'inevitable path'.

Another recurring characteristic of films portraying the 'Indian'[1] set during the colonial period is the male European protagonist, which perpetuates the association between colonized land and the female body. Amongst the films centring on male Europeans who get involved with female indigenous characters are *Como era gostoso o meu francês/How Tasty Was My Little Frenchman* (Nelson Pereira dos Santos, 1971), *Caramuru – a invenção do Brasil* (Guel Arraes, 2001) and *Hans Staden* (Luis Alberto Pereira, 1999). Although *How Tasty Was My Little Frenchman* and *Hans Staden* were based on diaries written by Europeans during the discovery, their approaches and cinematic contexts differ greatly. *Hans Staden*, a film of the *retomada*, allows an identification with the European protagonist and an association of the natives with savagery and cannibalism, the two 'horrors' of the colonial discourses. Released two years after *Hans Staden*, *Caramuru* offers a more playful approach to colonization, but still reminiscent of colonialist discourses particularly present in the eroticization of the encounter between European and indigene. Made nearly thirty years before these two films, precisely during the *tropicalista* phase of *Cinema Novo*, *How Tasty Was My Little Frenchman* adopts an 'anthropophagic'[2] approach to criticize European colonialism. The representation of the European in captivity, waiting to be eaten by cannibals, does not evoke concern about the 'civilized' person amongst the natives. Instead, the allegorical representation of cannibalism suggests that digesting European domination within a 'native' Brazilian body is a way to subvert through appropriation. Another key *tropicalista* film that provides an 'anthropophagic' critique of both the military dictatorship and the capitalist practices is *Macunaíma* (Joaquim Pedro de Andrade, 1969), reviewed in the *Cinema Novo* chapter.

Predatory capitalism and social exploitation of indigenous people in Brazil have emerged as global matters when combined with environmental issues, as intergovernmental organizations and a number of NGOs have emphasized the role of indigenous culture in safeguarding the environment and biodiversity. This preoccupation with indigenous and environmental issues comes into play in the films *Iracema: uma transa amazônica/Iracema* (Jorge Bodansky and Orlando Senna, 1976), *Brincando nos campos do Senhor/At Play in the Fields of the Lord* (Hector Brabenco, 1991) and, more recently *Serras da desordem/The Hills of Disorder* (Andrea Tonacci, 2006). *Iracema*, a reference to José de Alencar's classic Indianist romance *Iracema* (1865), is another film that evokes the relationship of a European, in this case a white lorry driver, and an indigene. The film, however, updates the figure of both the colonizer and colonized to the twentieth century so as to explore the perpetuation of colonial structures that keep the indigenous as subservient, an approach also adopted by *Ajuricaba: o rebelde da Amazônia/Ajuricaba* (Oswaldo Caldeira, 1977). The traditional romance between European and indigene that uses miscegenation as metaphor for the foundation of Brazil is subverted in *Brava gente brasileira/Brave New Land* (Lúcia Murat, 2000). The film shows seduction by the indigene, who has some agency in the film, as a weapon to be used against the European colonizer.

One striking legacy of colonial discourses and their perpetuation is the internalization of a set of values established by the colonizer that leads a subject to regard themselves as the inferior 'other', engendering a sense of low self-esteem,[3] which can have serious consequences including suicide, a topic addressed in *La Terra degli uomini rossi/Birdwatchers* (Marco Bechis, 2008), the most recent film of this chapter. Unfortunately, the best known filmic representations of indigenous characters in Brazilian cinema remain by and large a construct by non-indigenous film-makers. It is hoped that initiatives that promote media literacy amongst indigenous people will encourage a more significant emergence of their voices in films, which will prompt a wider debate on issues relating to the self-perception of the colonial subjects.

Natália Pinazza

References
Berkhofer, RF (1978) *The White Man's Indian*, New York: Vintage.
McLeod, J (2000) *Beginning Postcolonialism*, Vancouver: University of British Columbia.

Notes
1.   It is worth noting that in this volume the original inhabitants of Brazil will be referred to either as 'indigenous', 'Indians' or, in some cases, 'natives'. Although the term 'índio' translated as 'Indian' in English has been highly contested for its colonial roots (Berkhofer 1978), its use remains widespread in Brazilian society and culture. Moreover, the term 'Indian' is also employed as to refer to objectified and stereotyped images of indigenous people, which are recurrent in the films present in the chapter.
2.   Oswald de Andrade's use of the concept of 'anthropophagy', the cannibalistic rituals of Tupinambás, as an anti-colonialist metaphor and its famous slogan 'Tupi or not Tupi that is the question', suggested that Brazilian intellectuals should symbolically digest European culture in a Brazilian native's body in order to create a distinct national culture.
3.   A process that can be called 'colonising the mind', which 'operates by persuading people to internalise its logic and speak its language; to perpetuate the values and assumptions of the colonisers as regards the ways they perceive and represent the world' (Mcleod 2000: 18).

Ajuricaba

Ajuricaba: o rebelde da Amazônia

Studio/Distributor:

Embrafilme
Fundação Cultural do Estado
do Amazonas

Director:

Oswaldo Caldeira

Producer:

Oswaldo Caldeira

Screenwriters:

Oswaldo Caldeira
Almir Muniz

Cinematographer:

Edison Santos

Art Director:

Anísio Medeiros

Composer:

Airton Barbosa

Editor:

Carlos Brajsblat

Duration:

115 minutes

Genre:

Drama

Cast:

Rinaldo Genes
Paulo Villaça
Nildo Parente
Emmanuel Cavalcanti
Sura Berditchewsky.

Year:

1977

Synopsis

A canoe carries the corpse of a smuggler to the banks of the Amazon. His name is Ajuricaba. The sequence is brief and set in the present. The narrative moves back to the eighteenth century, depicting the capture of an Indian by a Portuguese man in the jungle. After the foundation of Manaus, the Indians, headed by Ajuricaba, had sparked off resistance to the colonizers. Ajuricaba, who can turn himself into a bird, a fish or a snake, is seized by the captain of the Portuguese forces, Belchior Mendes de Morais, and taken through the forest. During the crossing, Pedro, one of the followers of Belchior, registers in his diary the chronicle of the expedition. The captain shoots a bird; the former begins to bleed. The troops arrive to an estuary, waiting for the galleons that will lead them to Manaus, but Ajuricaba jumps into the river and escapes. The narrative returns to the present with scenes of a folk concert, an airplane-landing and a police shootout. In the police encounter, Ajuricaba (whom we find dead in the first sequence) is killed. Ajuricaba comes back to life in the morgue. The film closes with a shot of an unknown worker raising a pickaxe.

Critique

A metonymic chain structures Cladeira's movie: Ajuricaba (Rinaldo Genes) manifests in different forms as a bird, as an Indian, and as the oppressed man of the people. The action takes place in the balance of these signs, shuttling back and forth between the social sidewalks of the 1970s and their formation in Portuguese colonization. The opening chase of the Indian in the jungle repeats a theme initiated in José de Alencar's *Iracema, uma transa amazônica/ Iracema* (1865), where an arrow shot by the titular protagonist anticipates a hybrid community. In *Ajuricaba*, the execution by a carbine marks the failure of the conciliatory project. Here, zoom-ins function in a similar manner to the telescopic lens, compressing the entire image into a thumbnail-like miniature. Through this visual technique, the Indian 'shot' in close-up represents Brazil as a whole. A close-up spanning an even shorter period in the film's composition (and interrupting its dominant Indian discourse) is the image of a crouched black servant in the background of an aristocratic banquet. The shot goes beyond the totality of Brazilian history, to encompass the global history of slavery. This moment is problematic because it constructs a false equivalence between unequal processes of domination, the annihilation of the Indians and the slave trade.

There is an ethnographic aspect to *Ajuricaba*, an element that the movie shares with other contemporary works on the Amazon: the Manaus grate tapioca, grill fish, mesh leaves, etc. The main action, the expedition of an old and tired captain in a state of perpetual agony, is often interrupted by stereotypical activities performed by the Indians. It would not be a stretch to classify *Ajuricaba* as a romanticized piece: the emotional sunsets in the jungle, the violent contrasts of light and shadow, the anachronisms and the tenebrism of certain compositions, convert the movie into a dark canvas through which to characterize civilization more generally.

Luigi Patruno

At Play in the Fields of the Lord

Brincando nos campos do Senhor

Studio/Distributor:

The Saul Zaentz Company

Director:

Hector Babenco

Producer:

Saul Zaentz

Screenwriters:

Jean-Claude Carrière
Hector Babenco (adapted from
the novel At Play in the Fields
of the Lord [Peter Matthiessen,
1965])

Cinematographer:

Lauro Escorel

Art Director:

Clovis Bueno

Composer:

Robert Randles

Editor:

William Anderson

Duration:

187 minutes

Genre:

Drama

Cast:

Tom Berenger
John Lithgow
Daryl Hannah
Aidan Quinn
Tom Waits
Kathy Bates

Synopsis

Based on the 1965 novel of the same title by American writer Peter Matthiessen, *At Play in the Fields of the Lord* describes the encounter between a family of evangelical missionaries and the Niaruna in the Amazonian jungle, a fictional indigenous tribe inspired by the Yanomami of Brazil. The idealistic Martin Quarrier is pushed by his fundamentalist boss Leslie Huben to rapidly convert the Niaruna so they can outdo their Catholic counterparts. Eager to befriend the tribe, Quarrier's own empathetic and curious nature soon clashes with his wife's cultural prejudices and with Huben's selfish ambition. Meanwhile, half-Cheyenne mercenary pilot Lewis Moon and his partner Wolf are stranded in a nearby jungle outpost and accept Comandante Guzman's proposal to bomb the Niaruna, who live on gold-rich land, in exchange for some gasoline and a passport. Conversations with Quarrier and Padre Xantes, together with a drug-induced trance, make Moon realize the ontological contradiction he is about to engage in. Transformed, he decides to go native and join the Niaruna instead, where he is taken for a god. A kiss exchanged with Huben's flu-stricken wife Andy will make the infected Moon responsible for a fateful epidemic that ultimately brings tragic destruction to the tribe.

Critique

Despite its rhythmic unevenness and length, Babenco's adaptation offers an interesting reflection on cultural identities and a strong indigenous screen presence. *At Play in the Fields of the Lord* features compelling native communities that are realistic and not exoticized, as Babenco heavily relied on suggestions made by indigenous non-professional actors themselves in workshops held during the shoot (Okrent 1992). Although generally avoiding a romanticized portrayal of the Niaruna, the opening credits scene, with its languid music and shreds of smoke that fade away in the air, immediately call to mind the Hollywood stereotype of the vanishing Indian, exploited in coetaneous films such as *Dances with Wolves* (Kevin Costner, 1990) or *Last of the Mohicans* (Michael Mann, 1992). Mixed-blood Lewis Moon is a character also plagued with contradictions. He first plays the archetype of the proud, resentful, and inscrutable Indian soon to be transformed (under the effects of the hallucinatory *nipi*) into the wild loose-haired warrior howling under the influence of the moon and the drug. Parachuting himself over the Niaruna and stripped of all his clothes, the Niaruna mistake him for Kisu, the messenger of their spirit of Thunder, an influential title that empowers him within the tribe. Throughout his stay in the village, Moon unlearns western habits and embraces Niaruna traditions, progressively constructing

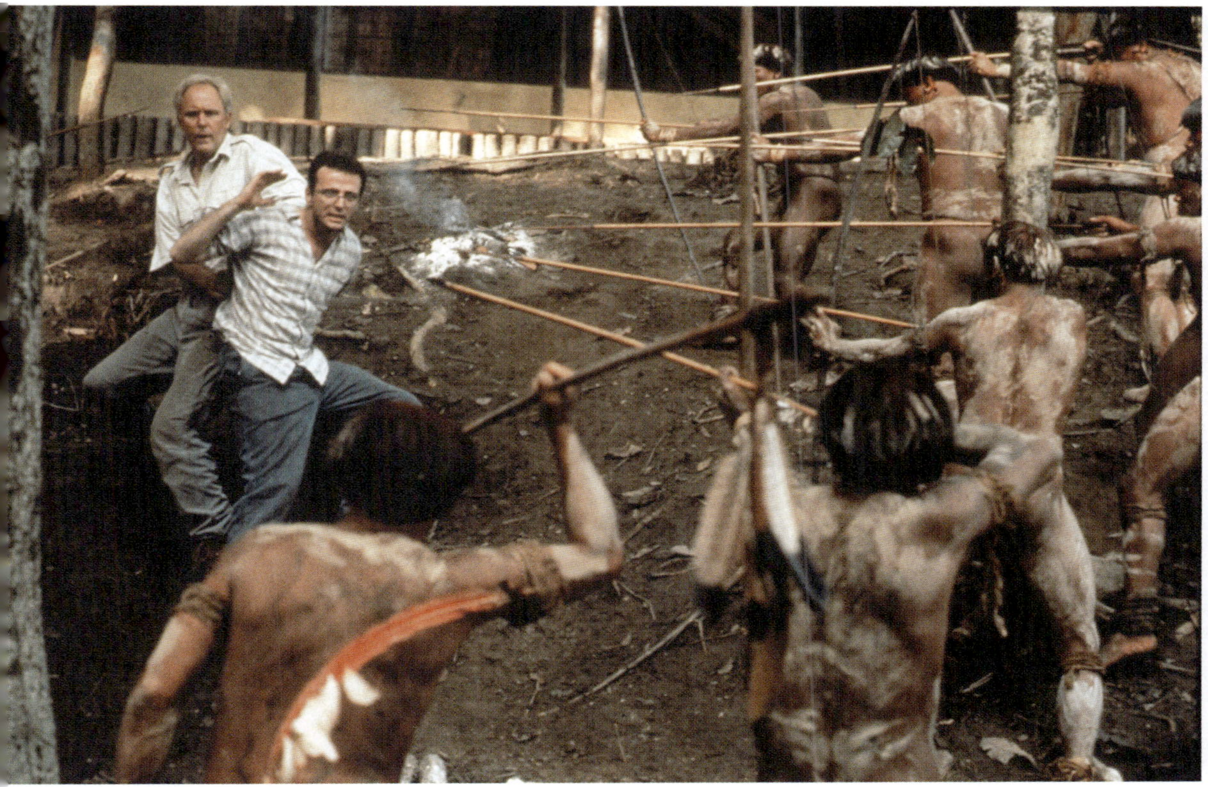

At Play in the Fields of the Lord

Year:

1991

himself as a 'true native'. Proof of the fragility of his transformation is the fact that one libidinous glance at the naked white body of Andy Huben swimming in the river suffices to make him forget his new responsibilities. Moon's cruel rape of his Niaruna 'wife' Pindi brings about a flu epidemic that will ironically accomplish Guzman's genocidal mission over the natives. Soon after leaving the bombed village, and accused by Aeore of being a white man, Moon further realizes that cutting his hair and painting his face does not make him a native. Feeling utterly guilty, he abandons himself in the middle of the jungle in what is a dubious end, but one that underscores the contradictions and dangers of romanticizing and homogenizing the 'other'. Unlike Matthiessen's novel, Babenco criticizes Moon's irresponsibly individualistic search of identity, a cliché in North American fiction. Guzmán and Huben are portrayed as cartoon villains who demonize and animalize the natives in their greedy campaigns that justify land theft and cultural destruction. Martin Quarrier moves from the romantic missionary to the committed ethnographer when he strives to document, by means of photographs, tapes and writing, what he believes to be a disappearing culture. His is still an idealistic construction of the Indian and, despite his genuine admiration of the Niaruna, both his preaching and his material presents bring further conflict into the tribe. Against these classic portrayals of whites in the American frontier, the Niaruna themselves and also the Tiro, an acculturated indigenous tribe that lives around the outpost, defy stereotypes and appear as complex and savvy political agents able to defend their traditions and way of life through rhetoric, trickster poses and violence, thus undermining clichéd images of passive victimhood. Ultimately, and despite its strong criticism of the military, religious and multinational mining agents responsible for the destruction of Amazonian cultures, Babenco's film remains a pessimistic depiction of a vanishing world. It describes a system in which the natives are fighting for a cause that has been lost from the beginning, lyrically symbolized by the arrows flying against a bomb-filled sky.

Anna M Brígido-Corachán

Reference

Okrent, N (1992) 'At Play in the Fields of the Lord: An Interview with Hector Babenco', *Cineáste: America's Leading Magazine of Art and Politics of Cinema*, 19: 1, pp. 44–47.

Brave New Land

Brava gente brasileira

Studio/Distributor:

Riofilme
Tanga Filmes e Vídeo

Director:

Lúcia Murat

Producer:

Renê Bittencourt

Screenwriter:

Lúcia Murat

Cinematographer:

Antônio Luís Mendes

Art Directors:

José Joaquim Salles
Shell Júnior
Inês Salgado

Composers:

Heron Alencar
Lívio Tragtenberg

Synopsis

The first Brazilian film of the new millennium to portray indigenous people turns to the XVIII century, when Brazil was still a largely unknown territory to Portugal with many mysteries and strange inhabitants. The Crown already has an idea of the country's geography but still needs to map it. In 1778, a ship is sent to do a topographical study of Pantanal, a land disputed by the Portuguese and the Spanish. The man responsible for this study is Diogo, an astronomer, naturalist and cartographer. The ship is en route to the Coimbra Fort, but is approached constantly by a group of indigenous knights called the *Guaicurus* with whom Portugal has a peace agreement. The crew is formed by Portuguese, *mestizos* and Antônio (who has a map indicating the possible existence of silver mines), and is commanded by Pedro. The group's journey will be marked by all sorts of violence and barbarism, primarily against beautiful indigenous women, whom they meet along the way. In fact, Diago kidnaps a *Guaicuru* woman. The film also cast members of the indigenous community Kadiwéu to play the role of the *Guaicurus*, a tribe which had already been made extinct by the colonizers.

Critique

In *Brave New Land*, the indigenous female characters are represented as the procreators of the conquistadores' offspring. Submissive and fascinated by the foreigner, they are seen as trophies, as savages whose subjugation symbolizes the 'victory' of one culture over another. The male Indian continues to be seen as the enemy, that is

Editors:

Simone Petrillo
Carlos Fox

Duration:

104 minutes

Genre:

Adventure

Cast:

Diogo Infante
Luciana Rigueira
Floriano Peixoto

Year:

2000

the eternal savage that needs to be pacified. The female *Guaicurus* are portrayed as moved by the principles of pleasure. This becomes clear the moment in which Dom Diogo returns to the Coimbra Fort with Anote, an indigenous woman. In this sequence, they are very happy and he has his face painted with indigenous graphisms, as had Anote. However, she is also ridiculed by the Commander of the Fort. It is true that this representation can be taken to its extreme opposite: a configuration of a quasi-idealization of the indigenous as good, pure and incorrupt savage, in perfect harmony with nature, who lacks European 'evilness' and is a hero simply for existing. Moments before Anote had made a comparison between Diogo and the monkeys, situating them at the same level as both inhuman. This is also a consequence of the fact that both monkeys and Diogo had hair (the male *Guaicurus* are hairless). This makes evident an ethnocentrism in opposition to the colonizer's eurocentrism. This idea is reiterated when the *Guaicuru* trip decides to adopt a white child after saving him from the abandonment to which he was imperilled in the narrative.

In *Brave New Land* the white man, ultimately characterized by the character Antônio, seems to be moved by the incessant search for richness and colonial resources. In his position as the captain's assistant, Antônio systematically moves towards ways that will enable him to search for hidden treasure. If this idea is placed in a wider context of discovery, it echoes the descriptions of the 'New World', including in 'The Letter of Pero Vaz de Caminha', in which everything means possible material gain. The role of the church in legitimizing the genocide and barbaric killing of the 'soulless' heathen acquires an absurd and comic representation in the grotesque figure of the greedy preacher. The obese preacher is only seen eating and does not even try to legitimate his evangelization.

Anote, the *Guaicuru* princess who gets pregnant after a rape perpetuated by Diogo, witnesses her captor/husband's fantasy of founding a new race and defending its positive impact on the world. Anote's answer to the whole situation concretizes when, after delivering their child, she commits infanticide to set the children free from living as slaves. The war against the Indians is represented through the point of view of the indigenous resistance, where the indigenous population, faced with extermination, achieves 'national' identity when their heroes receive names. *Brave New Land* determines and exposes the acts of heroism performed by the *Guaicuru* women during this period of resistance, foregrounding a neglected aspect of the construction of the female indigenous character, that of female participation in the struggle. In this way, the indigenous women pretend to seduce the soldiers and the occupants of the Fort in a moment of festivity made to deceive them and win the war over the invaders. In a narrative turn-around, the women open the gate of the Fort for the indigenous warriors, who come inside and defeat the conquistadores. *Therefore, Brave Women!* (An allusion to the original title 'Brava gente brasileira', which literally translates as Brave Brazilian People.)

Juliano Gonçalves da Silva (trans. Natália Pinazza)

Birdwatchers

La Terra degli uomini rossi

Studio/Distributor:

Classic
Rai Cinema
Karta Film-Gullane

Director:

Marco Bechis

Producers:

Amedo Pagani
Marco Bechis
Fabiano Gullane
Caio Gullane

Screenwriters:

Marco Bechis
Luiz Bolognesi (in collaboration
with Lara Fremder)

Cinematographer:

Hélcio Alemão Nagamine

Art Directors:

Clóvis Bueno
Caterina Giargia

Composer:

Andrea Guerra

Editor:

Jacopo Quadri

Duration:

104 minutes

Genre:

Drama

Cast:

Abrísio da Silva Pedro
Alicélia Batista Cabreira
Ademilson Concianza Verga
(Kiki)
Ambrósio Vilhalva
Nelson Concianza
Chiara Caselli
Leonardo Medeiros

Year:

2008

Synopsis

Birdwatching tourists glide along a rainforest river in Mato Grosso do Sul; hostile-looking natives – naked, with loincloths, traditional jewellery, face painting and weapons – stand by the shore and watch the tourists. In the second scene, we see the *indígenas* put on modern clothes and receive scant payment for their playacting, which will help them to survive in a society where they are dispossessed of their land and cooped up in small reserves. After two girls commit suicide, a Guarani-Kaiowá group decides to relocate to their traditional land since they cannot be a healthy community apart from their *tekohà*. They establish a make-shift camp right outside a farmer's field and cross it regularly in order to haul water from the river and go hunting in the adjacent rain forest. More and more people arrive and support the movement to reclaim their traditional land. The movement is weakened by the influences of alcohol, internal struggles, the intransigence of the *cacique*, and another youth suicide, and events continue to worsen.

Critique

With this extraordinary film Chilean-Italian director Marco Bechis takes issue with the unacknowledged injustice of the colonization of indigenous peoples in Brazil and with their continuing dehumanization, impoverishment and paternalistic treatment by mainstream culture, which are intensified by the increasing clear-cutting of the rainforest, the interests of multinational companies, and the world's hunger for beef, sugar, soy, wood and biofuels. Guarani-Kaiowá, who are mostly film novices, enact indigenous experiences and the growing land reclamation movement – *retomadas*.

Very beautifully, the film opens and closes with aerial shots of the dense green forest and adjacent clear-cut lands, which visually supports the antagonism between Brazilian landowners and indigenous people. At eye-level the camera moves through the reserve and shows the squalid living conditions of the people. Osvaldo and Irineu go hunting with traditional weapons; a mother angrily rants about her daughter's yielding to the lures of modernity; Nádio purchases flour, rice and tea at the local store and succumbs to alcohol; the people harvest sugar cane on big plantations for little money; Irineu buys sneakers out of his wages instead of food; the shaman teaches Osvaldo his art and must witness both his promise and his distressing blunders – the film thus ingeniously creates a complex picture of contemporary indigenous people who, often painfully, negotiate the traditional and the modern.

The battle over land is played out in well-arranged oppositions: the poor reserve and camp are juxtaposed with the luxurious farmer's mansion; while the people work getting water and food, the farmer's daughter Maria and her friend kill time sunbathing and smoking pot. The hunters are scared off the land they cross to reach the rainforest; a guard is installed to observe the peaceful occupants; an airplane sprays pesticides on to the camp; Nádio is shot. The powerful moments when the people slowly move on to their former

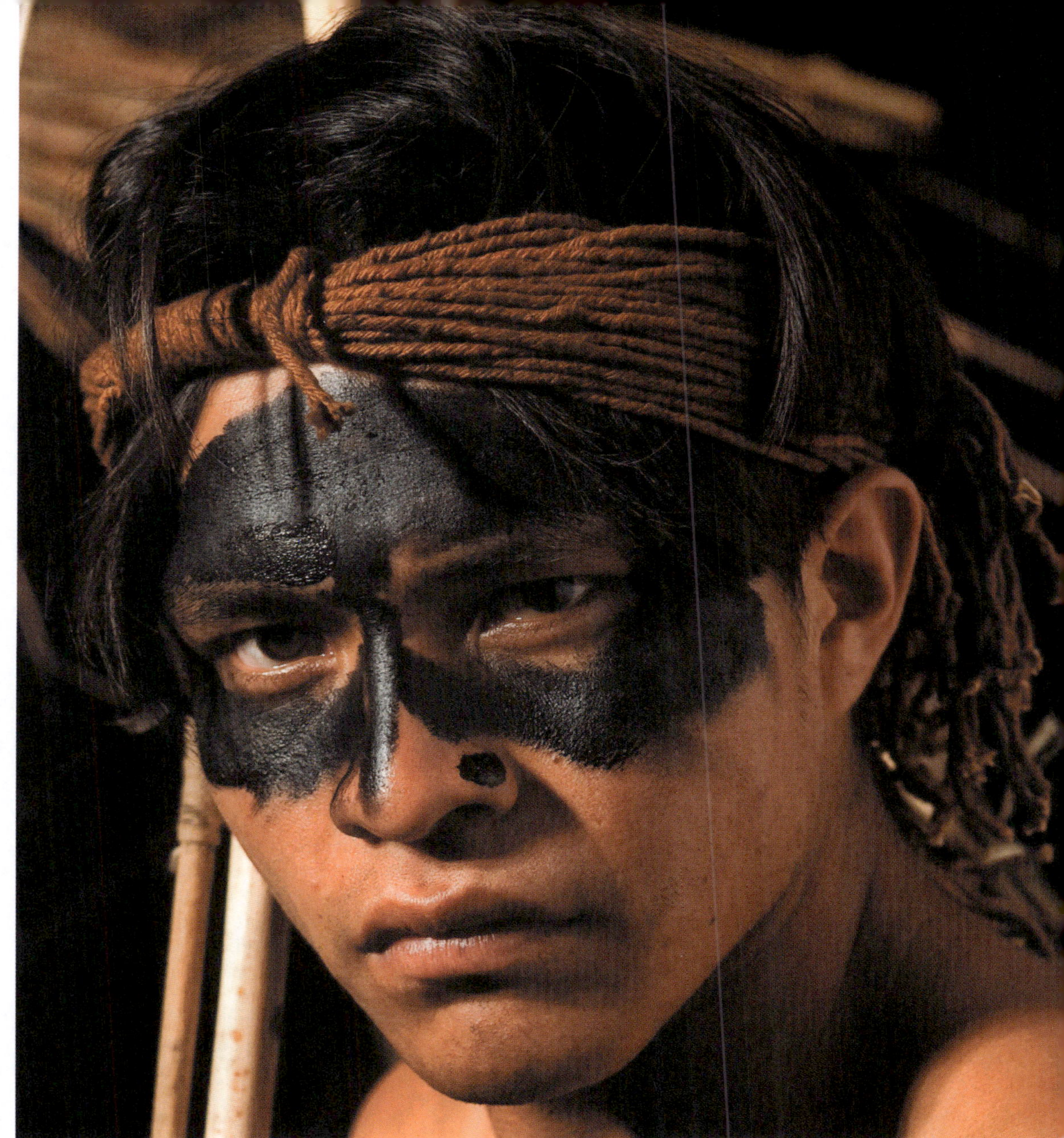

Birdwatchers

land seem like visualizations of Leslie Silko's vision of indigenous land reclamation in *Almanac of the Dead* (1991). Here the camera highlights the land in low angle-shots and compellingly films the defiant faces of the *indígenas*. Bechis says he avoided a mobile camera and preferred stable shots like those found in westerns. The 'shoot-out' does not involve guns but the soil: while the farmer takes red soil into his hand claiming he owns the land, Nádio eats some of it – he is of the land that nourishes him. Similarly symbolic is the first scene: the intruding tourists are watched by natives while watching – a masterful repetition of colonial contact situations. Recurring Italian baroque music also reminds viewers of European colonization. The antagonism is visually supported by a careful colour composition. The rich green, brown, red and ochre tones of the forest, river, earth, the people's skin and their face paint are offset by the artificial blue and green of the farmhouse pool, the blue dresses and bikinis of the girls, the garish colours in a mall, the blue tractor ploughing the field, and Maria's red motorbike in the forest.

But Bechis is wise enough not to reduce a complex conflict to a black-and-white picture: a cautious love develops between Osvaldo and Maria; the *indígena* Lia seduces the guard; a paid *indígena* man betrays Nádio; the land conflict will be settled in court. The end neither moralizes nor gives a solution: Osvaldo screams out his anger and desperation against the farmer's family and confronts *Anguè*.

This film is a rewarding complement to the indigenous films *Dueños del agua/Owners of the Water* (Laura Graham et al., 2008), which documents the fight of the Brazilian Xavante against deforestation and pesticide poisoning of their rivers, and *El Grito de la selva/ The Cry of the Forest* (Nicolás Ipamo et al., 2008), the first Bolivian indigenous feature film, which narrates the indigenous struggle against similar exploitation of natural resources.

Kerstin Knopf

Caramuru – a invenção do Brasil

Studio/Distributor:

Globo Filmes, Rede Globo de Televisão

Director:

Guel Arraes

Producers:

Eduardo Figueira
Daniel Filho

Screenwriter:

Guel Arraes, Jorge Furtado

Cinematographer:

Felix Monti

Art Director:

Lia Renha

Composer:

Lenine

Synopsis

The history of Caramuru and the invention of the country named Brazil begins in Portugal, where the talented painter Diogo Álvares Correa creates an art that embellishes reality and causes many problems with the powerful Portuguese court. Contracted to illustrate the maps to be used in the journey of de Pedro Álvares Cabral, Diogo has an affair with the seductive Isabelle, a French woman who frequents the court in search for gold. The courtesan then steals the map from Diogo, who is punished and deported to the Brazilian coast, where people call him 'Caramuru'. He then meets the beautiful Indian Paraguaçu and her sister, Moema, living out the first love triangle of Brazilian history.

Critique

This film by Guel Arrares and Jorge Furtado is based on a television mini-series and is a loose adaptation of a true story which has gone down in legend in Brazil. Narrated as a fable, but supported by historical research, the film tells the story of Caramuru and the Indian sisters Paraguaçu (Camila Pitanga) and Moema (Deborah Secco). It focuses, in particular, on the story of Caramuru and Paraguaçu, who the Portuguese man marries. Being a comedy and a loose adaptation, the film's mixture of history and fiction informs both its cinematography and plot, which is shaped by the historical inventions from the popular imagination of Caramuru, Paraguaçu and Moema

Editor:

Paulo H Farias

Duration:

88 minutes

Genre:

Comedy

Cast:

Selton Mello
Camila Pitanga
Deborah Secco
Tonico Pereira
Deborah Bloch

Year:

2001

that are added to the fiction created by the film's screenwriters. It is this very mixture between historical and fictional events, emerging from creative freedom, that makes *Caramuru – a invenção do Brasil* an interesting film. To start with the title: Brazil was an invention of the Portuguese from the era of maritime exploration and colonial expansion. The exploration of the countries' resources and natural wealth, the extermination of the native population, and disputes between European nations for control of the Pindorama territory (Brazil) are each well-known matters of historical record. However, the film's first surprise lies in the encounter between Diogo (Selton Mello) and Paraguaçu. The Indian speaks Portuguese fluently. Therefore, the first barrier, the linguistic one, is broken since communication is immediate. Like communication, love and sex also occur straight away.

After an intense conversation, Paraguaçu's sister Moema also falls in love with Caramuru, who reciprocates. The second surprise of the film is that Moema speaks with a Bahia accent. The film-makers are making a joke out of the historical facts here, as Diogo's shipwreck happened in 1509 off the coast of Bahia de Todos os Santos next to the Rio Vermellho, to which the Tupinambás referred as Mairyqui (place of the French). Another game played with history is the image of the Tupinambás as worriers and practictioners of anthropophagy (again, a matter of historical record). In the film, however, not only does the chief Taparica (Tonico Pereira), father of Paraguaçu and Moema, decide not to eat Diogo, he also offers him his daughters and negotiates with the French. Nevertheless, this negotiation involves advertising the natural beauty of the place in an attempt to sell it and its Pau-Brasil wood.

Diogo Álvares was, according to history, a trader of products that were smuggled by the French. In the filmic deconstruction and recreation of history, another relevant element is the portrayal of the 'oca', the form of housing that the Indians used. In contrast to a real 'oca', where up to fifty families could live together, in the film the chief's house is only inhabited by him and his daughters. The house is also clean and decorated, incongruously for such habitation in the middle of the forest. In fact, there are very few moments in the film when we see other members of the tribe, only the sequence of the shipwreck and that of commerce. As if in an open-air theatre performance, the carefully designed *mise-en-scène* is the setting to Caramuru's romance with the Indians, who in turn wear well-made and nicely designed costumes. In order not to clash too much with actual history, the film has Paraguaçu leave for France and marry Caramuru. If in Brazil's official history the country was created by the Portuguese, in Guel Arrares and Jorge Furtado's film, deliberate invention makes no compromise in telling the real history of the Indians. Nevertheless, one element must be noted: it is Paraguaçu who writes the history of the lovers after learning how to read. Therefore, in the film, the narration comes from the point of view of an Indian who became a legend in Brazil.

Rogério Ferraraz and Maria Ignês Carlos Magno (trans. Natália Pinazza)

The Discovery of Brazil

O Descobrimento do Brasil

Studio/Distributor:

Instituto do Cacau da Bahia

Director:

Humberto Mauro

Producer:

Alberto Campiglia

Screenwriters:

Humberto Mauro
Bandeira Duarte (adapted from
'The Letter of Pero Vaz de
Caminha' [1500])

Cinematographers:

Manoel Ribeiro
Alberto Botelho
Alberto Campiglia
Humberto Mauro

Art Director:

Bernardino José de Souza

Composer:

Heitor Villa Lobos

Editor:

Alberto Botelho

Duration:

135 minutes

Genre:

Historical

Cast:

Álvaro Costa
Manoel Rocha
Alfredo Silva
Reginaldo Calmon
João de Deus
João Silva

Year:

1936

Synopsis

This is the first and only filmic reconstruction of the discovery of Brazil, based on 'The Letter of Pero Vaz de Caminha', the writer on board Pedro Álvares Cabral's fleet in 1500. The film was directed by Humberto Mauro in collaboration with the National Institute of Educational Cinema. Initially set on the ship, the film shows the events of the journey as well as daily life, emphasizing the work of cartographers and navigators, sailors, and the commanders of the mission including Cabral and its preacher Dom Henrique de Coimbra. In the new land, the conquistadores encounter the indigenous people, in which the moving semi-naked bodies of the indigenous characters stand out in contrast to those of the Portuguese. The contrast between different habits and activities makes the indigenous people curious, in particular in relation to the Portuguese conquistadores' interest in transforming the land into an object of scientific discovery with tools such as the astrolabe or more general tools like the axe which cuts down big trees. In the end, during the First Mass, the conversion of the indigenous people to Christianity and their loyalty to their colonizers seems assured. The film is practically silent, creating a strange effect for audiences who were already used to talking films. The absent dialogue is replaced by music, in particular the choral music of Heitor Villa Lobos.

Critique

The Discovery of Brazil, produced in 1936 and considered the first Brazilian 'superproduction' – the most expensive film made in Brazil up to that point – narrates the epic of the Portuguese people in their discovery of the new world. It is based on the descriptions found in 'The Letter of Pero Vaz de Caminha', a document written in 1500, which marks the foundation of Brazil. In approaching the journey of discovery and the contact between colonizers and the indigenous people, what stands out are the major technical–scientific endeavours of the Portuguese, who are organized hierarchically and are obedient to their wise chief commanders.

In regard to the indigenous people, they are all played by actors or extras of either Afro-Brazilian or white descent, and are made up and in wigs. The film's images characterize the indigenous as naïve and carefree creatures, lacking malice and sin, like children needing to be led and taken care of. They are constantly in movement, dance and talk a lot. However, they do not work and, like children, they do not know shame, as they walk around semi-naked. Moreover, the film continually shows the indigenous people scratching themselves a lot, including when they are inside the ship or dressed, while the whites seem to be left alone by the insects and are heavily dressed for the tropical heat. The indigenous people also jump around, frequently bare-footed, in contrast to the assertive march of the heavy-booted colonizers.

The fact that the film represents the indigenous people as being ill-adapted to their environment removes the entitlement that they have to the land and everything to be utilized therein. As they treat nature sustainably without exploiting it, they do not realize the benefits which the colonizers bring. In the film, the indigenous people are inhabitants of the land but they do not have the right to be so. In this representation, the role of the foreigner seems to be turned on its head, as they do not appear as conquistadores arriving in those lands for the first time. Instead, the colonizer is the inhabitant most suited to the environment.

The productive appropriation of the land, therefore, is justified by the fact that it appears to rightfully belong to the Portuguese colonizer. Such a notion is made evident through the religious perspective which the original text takes on the story (that of the colonizing mission as a legitimate 'salvation'). In contrast, the film makes this idea evident at the level of culture. The indigenous people – poor and uneducated – call for direction and guidance from those who know what is best for them.

The climax of the film is the long sequence of the reconstitution of the First Mass, which draws on Victor Meirelles's painting of 1860. In the painting, Meirelles offers an observation of two different worlds in an encounter between savage and civilized. In the film, the evangelical nature of the conversion is made evident in images which are accompanied by the music and choir of Villa Lobos, creating effects that suggest an epic and spiritual realm. The Mass and the fact that the indigenous people adhere to Christianity constitute the capstone of the voyage of discovery, testifying to the transcendence explored by Caminha when religious narratives impact upon everyone during this ritual. It is in this moment that the Portuguese conquest is signified as the salvation of a land and its natives.

If Caminha emphasizes the religious faith of the natives, the film expands and further foregrounds this process. In Humberto Mauro's film, the indigenous people are baptized, given the sacrament and converted. Therefore, the director's view of indigenous people in *Discovery* is the dominant one of the 1930s. On the one hand is acknowledgement of the indigenous ancestry of the Brazilian land, which acts to dignify the nation's history. On the other, however, portrayed as barbarian and primitive, the indigenous people need protection and guidance (this idea, when placed in the context of the 1930s, is also connected to the notion that Brazilian people as a whole need guidance from an elite). If the representation of the indigenous people constructed by Humberto Mauro reproduces this perspective, it also mirrors the director's individual vision: it is not the figure of the good savage of romanticism nor Cândido Rondon's peaceful savage, but one that is pure and permeable and, at the same time, curious.

Sheila Schvarzman (trans. Natália Pinazza)

Hans Staden

Studio/Distributor:

IPACA, Jorge Neves Produção
Audiovisual, Lapfilme

Director:

Luis Alberto Pereira

Producers:

Jorge Neves
Luis Alberto Pereira

Screenwriter:

Luis Alberto Pereira

Cinematographer:

Uli Burtin

Art Director:

Chico de Andrade

Composers:

Marlui Miranda
Lelo Nazano

Editor:

Verônica Kovensky

Duration:

92 minutes

Genre:

Drama

Cast:

Carlos Evelyn
Ariana Messias
Darci Figueiredo

Year:

1999

Synopsis

The film tells the story of Hans Staden, a German who embarked
on two voyages to Brazil in the middle of the sixteenth century. The
first one was as an artilleryman in a Portuguese ship, which went to
Pernambuco in 1547, whilst his second journey was with the Spanish
armada commanded by Diogo de Sanábria in 1550, which sank off
the Santa Catarina coast. In 1553, he was nominated 'commander
of the Bertioga Fortress' by Tomé de Sousa. Worried about the
disappearance of his slave, a Carijó Indian, Staden decides to search
for him. During his search, however, he is captured by the Tupinambás,
who are enemies of the Portuguese. Hans Staden remains imprisoned
in the Cunhambebe settlement for nine years. Threatened with
cannibalism in an anthropophagic ritual, Hans Staden manages to
postpone his death and is rescued by a French ship, which takes him
to his homeland. In Hesse, he writes and publishes the testimony of his
trips to the Americas between the years 1547 and 1549.

Critique

Luis Alberto Pereira's film follows almost the whole narrative
of Staden. The film is spoken in Tupi Guarani as well as in the
languages of the European invaders: Portuguese, Spanish and
French. The filmic narrative limits itself to Staden's testimony, an
option that gained the film both awards and criticism. Nevertheless,
although the focus of the film is on Staden's story of survival,
particularly on his escape from the cannibal Tupinambás and his
return to Germany, the film does present an important indigenous
protagonist, which is an important one in Brazilian cinema.
Considering the many analyses of this film, I will highlight some
important interpretations that this film allows. Because the plot
centring on Hans Standen's adventure is already well-known, the film
enables us to turn our eyes from the main, European protagonist
to the indigenous characters while simultaneously awakening in the
spectator a curiosity in the testimony provided in his book *Duas
viagens ao Brasil* (1557).

Working on this testimony, the director not only shows how
foreigners regarded Brazil and its original inhabitants, but also how
the indigenous people discuss their invaders. From Hans Staden's
foreign perspective, Brazil is described as a country inhabited by
naked and ferocious savages who perform cannibalistic rituals.
However, even though the film does not show the meaning of the
war amongst the Tupis or of the anthropophagy practised by the
Tupinambás, what the director's gaze shows is the representation of
the indigenous as people who speak, argue, debate and question
as well as demonstrate their beliefs. If the survival of Hans Staden
is understood by some as a consequence of the fact that he could
speak and argue in the language spoken by the Tupinambás, it
is also through this language that Staden's testimony – and Luis
Alberto Pereira's film – brings in an Indian who has a voice, a sense of
humour and feelings. It is impossible to consider the film as a neutral
representation of Staden's journey, just as it would be difficult to

watch the film without wanting to know the meaning of the melody which is magnificently registered by the voice of Marlui Miranda.

Rogério Ferraraz and Maria Ignês Carlos Magno (trans. Natália Pinazza)

The Hills of Disorder

Serras da desordem

Studio/Distributor:

Extrema Produção Artística

Director:

Andrea Tonacci

Producers:

Sérgio Pinto de Oliveira
Wellington Gomes Figueiredo

Screenwriters:

Andrea Tonacci
Sydney Ferreira Possuelo
Wellington Gomes Figueiredo

Cinematographers:

Aloysio Raulino
Alziro Barbosa
Fernando Coster

Art Director:

Arnaldo Zidan

Editor:

Cristina Amaral

Duration:

135 minutes

Genre:

Biopic

Cast:

Sydney Possuedo
Karapiru

Year:

2006

Synopsis

Andrea Tonacci's film narrates the story of a Karapiru Indian from the *Awá-Guajá* tribe who has escaped the farmers and miners' massacre that his group experienced in the state of Maranhão in 1977. Karapiru wandered alone on the lands of central Brazil for ten years until he was found in November 1988 2,000 kilometres away from where he escaped. Taken to Brasília by *sertão* (rural backlands) explorer Sydney Ferreira Possuelo, he became a news item across Brazil and the subject of discussion amongst anthropologists and linguists, who debated his origins and identity. In an attempt to identify his origins, he re-encounters his son with whom he returns to Maranhão.

Critique

The Hills of Disorder by Andrea Tonacci cannot be understood or analysed just as a representation of indigenous people in Brazilian cinema, for it goes beyond that. Analysed and discussed by many theorists from cinematic and anthropologic aspects, the film can be seen as the result of two different perspectives: that of the protagonist, Karapiru, a member of the *Awá-Guajá* tribe, and that of the director. The history of the *Awá-Guajám* (*Awá* means 'man' or 'people') has always been obscure. Research indicates that they originated in Baixo Tocantins and belong to the linguistic family Tupi-Guarani. Initially they were sedentary cultivators. However, upon the arrival of the colonizers, they started to migrate to Maranhão, where they settled. Their lives were uncertain and required adaptation. The only thing they could be sure of across their history has been the internal and external invasions and subsequent extinction of their customs, culture, religious structure and social relations.

The story of Karapiru also recounts a journey marked by ruptures, uncertainty and adaptation: from life in a tribe, through which the lands are explored, the experience of the massacre that killed his whole family, to the subsequent displacement of the protagonist, who after ten years of wandering is found and taken back to his tribe. On his return, after a period of feeling like a stranger, there ends up being continuity to life. In his wanderings are encounters, friendships and discoveries. This film is based on a true story, and, transformed by its director and screenplay, we see the re-enactment of the story of an Indian as imagined by Andrea Tonacci. However, it is not only the story of an Indian, narrated by the director and played by Karapiru himself. The spectator experiences an estrangement which raises the following questions: why does Karapiru not narrate his story? Why did he accept to play the role of himself? And why are there so many melancholic and long, silent scenes?

All the actors play the role of themselves, including the Indians and Sydney Possuedo. Significantly, the media had already made Karapiru a famous character prior to Tonacci's documentary re-enactment, as he was featured in the news from the moment he was found to the moment he returned to his tribe. Vis-à-vis the film's juxtaposition of archive images, historical and journalistic research, fictionalized re-enactment and interviews, the only thing the spectator can be sure of is of having changed through watching the film and the representation of the Karapiru Indian. We also know that the film achieves its aims by leaving us indignant and thoughtful: indignant about the history of the Indians in Brazil and by the way in which they are represented, thoughtful about the stories that cinema narrates and, especially, by what it omits. The parallel stories that we do not see include the process of film-making, the many discoveries that occur in making such a film, and the relationship established between film-makers and characters. One of these relationships is that between Tonacci and Karapiru, a journey that is not featured in the film.

Maria Ignês Carlos Magno (trans. Natália Pinazza)

How Tasty Was My Little Frenchman

Como era gostoso o meu francês

Studio/Distributor:

RioFilme
Sagres Video

Director:

Nelson Pereira dos Santos

Producers:

Nelso Pereira dos Santos
Luiz Carlos Barreto
Condor Filmes

Screenwriters:

Humberto Mauro (Tupi dialogue)
Nelson Pereira dos Santos

Cinematographer:

Dib Luft

Art Director:

Régis Monteiro

Synopsis

A French mutineer who worked as a mercenary in the Villegagnon army escapes from execution. After fleeing by sea and through a wild forest he is imprisoned by the Tamoio Indians whose chief Cunhambebe has acquired canons for the purposes of overcoming the Portuguese. The chief treats the Frenchman like a slave and as he has no goods to offer, condemns him to death. The Tamoio give him as companion a beautiful woman, possibly because of his artillery skills although this remains unstated. The protagonist learns how to speak the indigenous language and how to survive in the paradisiacal forest. Together with an older French trader he discovers treasure, but, overcome with greed, kills the merchant and tries to escape. He tries to convince his indigenous wife to go with him, but fails. Instead she prepares him for the death ritual, teaching him how to challenge the enemy according to Tupínamba custom and introducing him to the patio where the Indians perform his dance of death. Cunhambebe gives no chance for negotiation, and threatens him in his anthropophagic ceremony. The Frenchman jinxes the chief, anticipating the future massacre of the Tamoios.

Critique

Nelson Pereira dos Santos brings the use of intertitles (a common technique in silent movies and ethnographic film) to narrative sound cinema to quote from the sixteenth-century travel writer Cunhambebe. Although his message is quite contemporary, it reflects ironically on the awkward strategies of dominated peoples to beat their stronger adversaries, showing Cunhambebe´s aim to appropriate French artillery and canons in order to defeat the

Composer:

Zé Rodrix

Editor:

Carlos Alberto Camuyrano

Duration:

91 minutes

Genre:

Historical drama

Cast:

Arduíno Colassanti
Ana Maria Magalhães
Eduardo Imbassahy Filho

Year:

1971

Portuguese forces. He places his Frenchman in a fictional indigenous culture, mixing historical characters such as Hans Staden, Villegagnon and Tupinanbá Indians with fictional characters who speak in French and the native Tupy language, which are subtitled. The echo of the Brazilian modernist movement can be felt in the work of the *Cinema Novo* film-maker, in particular Oswald de Andrade's claim that his Anthropophagic Manifesto (1928) was a genuine response to European Dadaist Cannibalism whose main idea was based on the exaltation of native unconscious language. He pictures the Frenchman's astonishment at the fear of his execution, showing him as an estranged object of desire in disputes between Tamoios (a Tupínamba subgroup) and Portuguese, Tupinanbás and Tupiniquins, and even between tribal fellows. He depicts an exotic nakedness as an allegory of native life in an exuberant forest together with the foreigner's melancholic weakness in the face of indigenous customs: at first the Frenchman refuses Sebiopebe when she tries to bite him in his hammock. After reinforcing the chief's conviction that the Frenchman deserves slavery, the French trader warns him that he has to enjoy his last moments with Sebiopebe. Emerging from a heavenly lake, the protagonist moves up close to the fair woman's belly seeing a golden bead lodged in her navel and wonders where she found it. Then the protagonist joins the merchant on his journey for treasure. When they find the buried treasure the Frenchman reveals his savage side by killing his older patron, dismembering his body and quickly burying him. Sebiopebe refuses to go with him when he invites her to leave her homeland. Then the chief threatens to kill him, asking him if he will sweep at the ceremony, then offers his neck to Sebiopebe who, painted for ritual war, continues to threaten him until death. The film reinforces the left-wing modernist Anthropophagic Manifesto against the oppressive, clothed social reality – 'reality without complexes, without madness, without prostitution, and without the penitentiaries of the matriarchy of Pindorama' (1994: 44), re-elaborated by Oswald de Andrade in his thesis as a metaphor for class struggle as motor of history.

The cinematographic savage life is an allegory for violence in dark times of military government. Launched in 1971 the film was at first censored for alleged pornography but the argument that indigenous nakedness was a legitimate expression of Brazilian cultural heritage enabled authorization of the film's public exhibition, anticipating the political democratization that began in the late 1970s. Extrapolating from the claim against censure, the film was an allegory for democratic freedom. Shortly afterwards this sort of cultural liberalism was easily appropriated by commercial media. The film was also accepted by national elites as an expression of Brazilian originality.

Priscila Faulhaber

References

de Andrade, O and Barry, L (1991) 'Anthropophagic Manifesto' *Latin American Literary Review*, Vol. 19, No. 38 (Jul. - Dec., 1991), 38-47.

Iracema

Iracema, uma transa amazônica

Studio/Distributor:

Stopfim

Directors:

Jorge Bodansky
Orlando Senna

Producer:

Wolf Gauer

Screenwriters:

Orlando Senna
Jorge Bodansky
Hermano Penna

Cinematographer:

Jorge Bodansky

Art Director:

Orlando Senna

Composer:

Jorge Bodanzky, Achim Tappen

Editors:

Eva Grundmann
Jorge Bodansky

Duration:

90 minutes

Genre:

Drama

Cast:

Edna de Cássia
Paulo César Pereio
Conceição Senna
Rose Rodrigues

Year:

1976

Synopsis

Tião Brasil Grande (translated as 'Big Brazil Tião'), a truck driver from the south, is stuck on the Trans-Amazonian highway. In Belém do Pará, during a large religious celebration named 'Círio de Nazaré', he meets Iracema, an indigenous adolescent who came to Belém but who got lost from her family amidst the chaos of the festivities. She joins him for part of his journey, but he leaves her in a small village in the middle of the highway and then continues on his route. Tião's journey serves as a pretext to show the problems of the Amazon region including uncontrolled deforestation and poor conditions of work and health, therefore showing a reality characterized by misery which does not correspond to official propaganda. Filmed in 16mm, with direct sound and without a pre-determined script, Iracema only features two professional actors.

Critique

Co-produced with a German television channel, the film was initially prohibited in Brazil, but received international appraisal in film festivals. The film was 'rediscovered' when it was awarded in Brasília, and *Iracema* still has an impact more than 37 years after its making because of its unique expressive style. It is without a doubt one of the best Brazilian films produced in the 1970s, and offers an intriguing, unexpected and even revolutionary experience. *Iracema* widens and reshapes the legacy of *Cinema Novo*. The film starts with the image of a boat reflecting on the river and the noise of its engine, which is slowly replaced by the sound of the radio. Following the opening sequence are other shots that draw our attention to details. This is the moment we see a boat named 'Graçasdeus', written all as one word,[1] as well as the poverty and simplicity of the people. In the Amazon, boats have many functions: means of transportation, means of livelihood, places of commerce and even home. Then emerges what is not there: the isolation of the people, the long distances between riverbank settlements, and difficulties in interpersonal communication.

The main protagonist is first introduced when she tells a friend that she wants to travel to São Paulo. From the moment Iracema leaves her community by the banks of the Amazon River to go to Belém, the trans-Amazon route becomes a site of her transformation from woman into commodity, as she leaves her adolescence behind. In the journey, she is driven by Tião, a truck driver, characterized as 'European' by being played by a southern actor. Tião feels superior to Iracema and he ignores and then makes fun of her innocence. To him, she is nothing but a casual distraction and if she causes any inconvenience to him he can abandon her. He represents the national discourse of progress which justifies and obscures poverty. He is the new conquistador, who defends the plans to expand Brazil and to make economic interventions in politics. The negative images that *Iracema* provides contradicts government rhetoric about expansion and development which the country was supposedly experiencing.

Iracema opens up to a variety of possible meanings as a consequence of the director's stylistic choices: the film is an

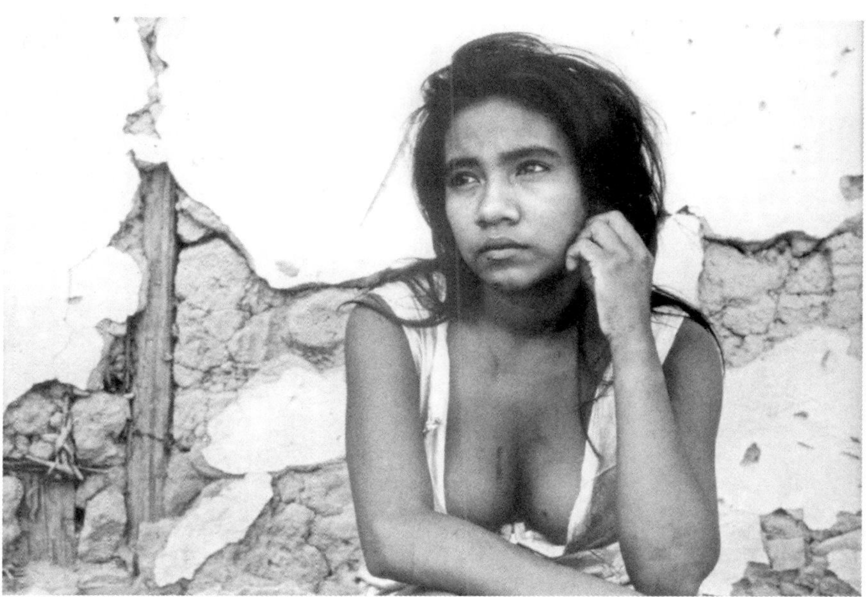

Iracema

adaptation (although it is far from faithful to the literary text, namely *Iracema*, a famous indigenist novel by José de Alencar published in 1965), that mixes elements of fiction with documentary. The fiction attempts to represent reality at its most expressive points, thereby constructing a very particular style of realism. The reality which lies behind the fictional narrative of power relations in the Trans-Amazon highway emerges as a registration of Iracema's abandonment in a 'backwater' to 'make a living' and 'sort herself out', in Tião's words. This involves a break from her previous world to be plunged into chaos, where existence is about survival, specifically, as a prostitute. She testifies to key problems in Brazilian life in which lack of hope, torpor and alcohol are the norm.

Examples of this occur when we see Iracema with another woman in search of a razor to defend themselves, or lost in a forest with the farm workers, serving coffee on a construction site, carrying gallons of water, fighting with the other woman over a client, arrested by policemen, or in the last sequence of the film, in which she is as toothless and dirty as the other prostitutes on the road. In the sequence in question the narrative no longer appears to the spectator as fictional. This approach adopted by Bodansky structures his aesthetics, giving it unique characteristics.

Iracema exists in a 'free market for all', characterized by vast and cheap manpower which reduces human beings into what their bodies can offer. If for a man, this means his physical power, for a woman it means sexual commodification. This terrible situation, which intends to substitute the jungle for 'development', reveals the colonizing impulse behind discourses of progress and development: illegal trade of woods and occupation of untitled lands, and slave labour, apparent and hidden.

Juliano Gonçalves da Silva (trans. Natália Pinazza)

Note
1.   'Graçasdeus' (in Portuguese, these words written separately become 'Graças a Deus', which translates as 'Thank God').

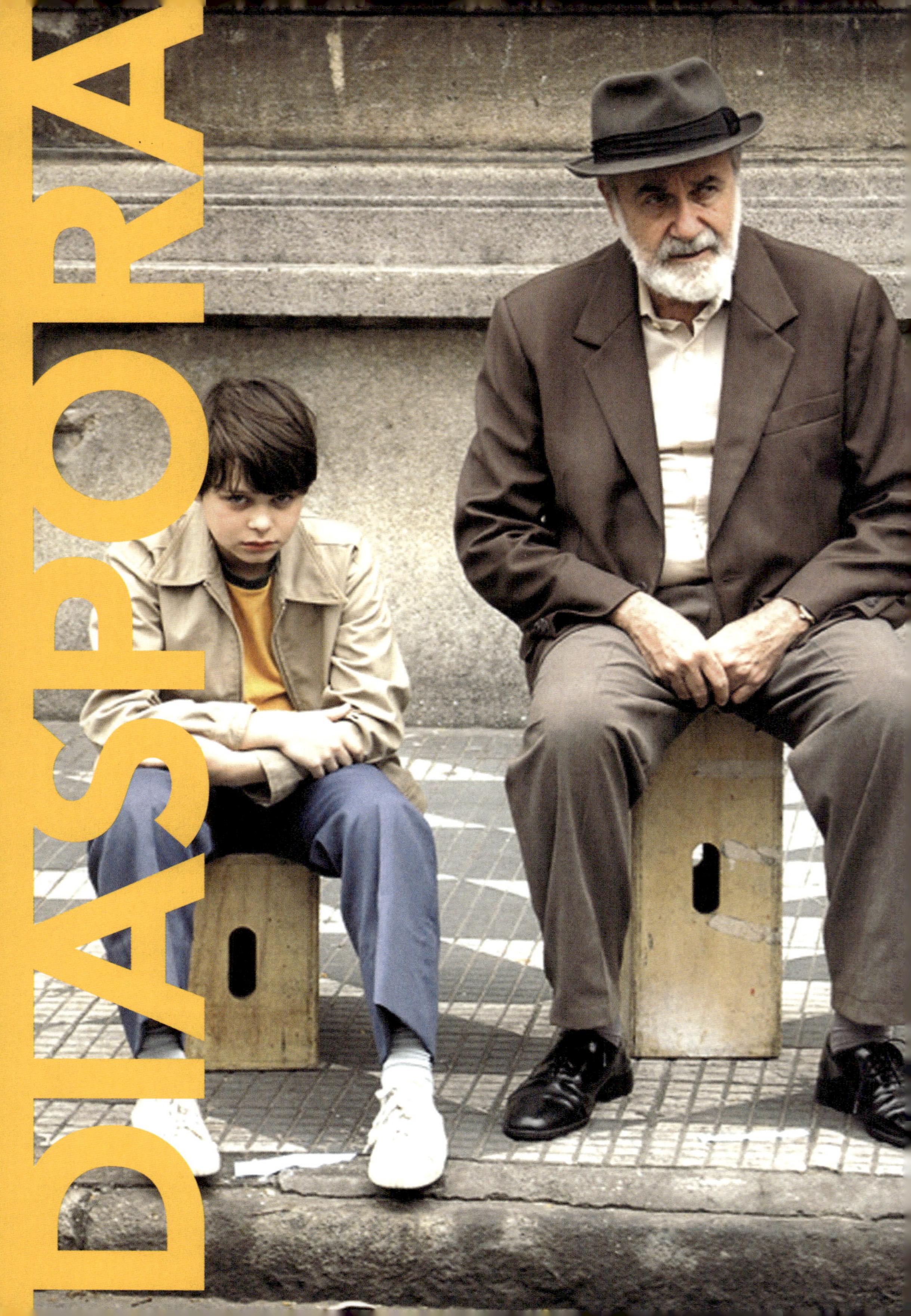
DIASPORA

Soon after their arrival in Brazil in 1500, the Portuguese began a massive importation of enslaved Africans to work in large sugar and coffee plantations in the new colony. Running parallel to the importation of slaves was the migration of the Portuguese. In the 1600s and 1700s, the Portuguese started to settle in Brazil in significant numbers. Contrary to the British settlers in North America of the same era, Portuguese males were not allowed to take their families with them to Brazil. As a consequence, they had common-law marriages with native Indians and Africans. A significant minority of the newcomers competed for the European-born women who were sent by the Portuguese Crown to Brazil as a means to boost the 'white race', as Portuguese authorities feared Brazil's black population would grow far more than other groups.

Although it is difficult to document given the dearth of information on the subject, the sense of loneliness and isolation of the European women upon arriving in Brazil, as *Desmundo* (Alain Fresnot, 2002) portrays, must have been profound. With *Desmundo*, Fresnot taps into Brazil's colonial past to critically treat an important, yet usually 'forgotten' facet of this historical period: the oppression, violence and subjugation under which these women lived. Although films set in the colonial period abound, until *Desmundo*, women in colonial Brazil were conspicuously absent from films that treated this historical period. Brazilian cinema's inclination has been to focus on the indigenous and African enslaved populations and on their strategies of resistance and struggles for independence or freedom, rather than on the oppression (and resistance) of white women in colonial Brazil. *Desmundo*, which consolidated the reputation of Fresnot as one of Brazil's leading contemporary directors, fills this critical gap.

With the end of the traffic of enslaved Africans to Brazil in 1850 and the abolition of slavery in 1888, the labour force changed from predominantly African to European. A number of German, Spanish, Portuguese and in particular Italian immigrants arrived in Brazil in the late nineteenth century and early twentieth century, becoming over time the largest immigrant communities in the country's south, and in particular São Paulo. As a number of Brazilian film historians have pointed out, these first European (notably Italian) immigrants were, from the very start, engaged in all aspects of Brazilian cinema: acting, direction, production, exhibition and distribution. Stigmatized as 'manual labourers' and further barred from access to the hegemonic culture due to language, religion and cultural traditions, Brazil's newly constituted international labour force immersed themselves in cultural activities produced within their communities, associations and trade unions, and film, in particular, provided comfort and familiarity as emblems of national homeland culture. Directed by Fábio Barreto, *O Quatrilho* (1995), which was nominated for the Academy Award for best foreign language film, provides a glimpse into this facet of Brazilian history as it follows the story of two Italian couples living in the state of Rio Grande do Sul in the early twentieth century.

Moreover, after Brazil and Japan signed a treaty allowing Japanese migration to Brazil in 1907, many Japanese – the majority of whom hailed from poverty-stricken rural regions – also began to emigrate to Brazil in search of better living conditions. The vast majority of them intended to work a few years in Brazil, make some money, and return to their homeland. The first of these Japanese immigrants arrived in Brazil (São Paulo) in 1908. But upon reaching São Paulo, where they joined European immigrants in large coffee plantations under exploitive working conditions, a harsh life and a bleak future quickly became apparent. Relying heavily on director Tisuka Yamasaki's 'melodramatic imagination', *Gaijin: os caminhos da liberdade/Gaijin: A Brazilian Odyssey* (1980) features the violent and oppressive working conditions that the country's newly arrived immigrants endured during these years. As the film shows, they often resorted to suicide, *yonige* (escape at night), or labour strikes to escape and resist the extremely harsh living conditions in the coffee plantations.

In addition to Europeans and Japanese, migrants from the poorest regions of Brazil, especially from the drought-stricken north-eastern *sertão* (backlands), also started arriving in São Paulo in the late nineteenth century and early twentieth century. Lured by the dream of a better life as workers in the factories that were emerging, this Hegira rapidly changed the urban landscape. This internal migration was further boosted in the 1930s by the south's rapid industrialization and modernization, and continued to grow in the next decades.

Accompanied by the north-eastern rhythmic melodies and emphasizing street musicians, the documentary *Saudade do futuro/Saudate for the Future* (Marie Clémence and César Paes, 2000) provides an unflinching portrait of the lives of assorted *Nordestinos* (north-easterners) in São Paulo. In a more fictional tone, *O Homem que virou suco* (João Batista de Andrade, 1980) shows how the newly arrived north-eastern immigrants negotiate their identity and cultural (as well as physical and symbolic) space in the city of São Paulo, where they suffer daily discrimination as undesirable outsiders.

Notwithstanding the fact that Brazil has become a haven for huge waves of immigrants throughout its history, especially during the modern period, Brazilian society has not always being exactly the happy, unprejudiced melting pot that some would like to believe. This is exemplified in the famous case of Olga Benário, the German-Jewish political activist who participated in a plot against Getúlio Vargas (1930–45) that was led by her husband, the leader of Brazil's Communist Party, Luís Carlos Prestes. Seven months pregnant, Olga was imprisoned and later deported to Hitler's Germany, where she died in a concentration camp gas chamber. Directed by Jayme Monjardim, the film *Olga* (2004) tells her life story until her imprisonment and deportation to Germany. While it may be disputed whether it is a film on the German-Jewish diaspora, *Olga* certainly allows for discussion about nation, history, memory, belonging and exclusion, and the retelling of a historical moment in which immigrants were looked upon with suspicion and prejudice.

Although Brazilians have either travelled or moved to other countries since at least the nineteenth century, the Brazilian diaspora is a fairly recent phenomenon driven mainly by the economic crisis afflicting the country since the end of the military dictatorship in the 1980s, and which was aggravated in the 1990s. Additionally, during the 1964–81 period, many Brazilians were either forced into exile or left the country in self-proclaimed exile. Having lived in exile with his parents (both immigrants to Brazil) in the 1970s, Cao Hamburger directed *O Ano em que meus pais sairam de ferias/The Year my Parents Went on Vacation* (2006), a film that is partly based on his childhood memories. Set in 1970, the film takes place in São Paulo's Bom Retiro, where people of different ethnicities (and religions) mix with each other, producing a multi-ethnic neighbourhood. Against the backdrop of the World Soccer Cup, the film depicts the story of a 12-year-old boy whose parents are involved in political conflict and forced to hide and ultimately leave the country.

In spite of the fact that emigration from Brazil has slowed down in recent years due to the country's economic stability and sustained growth, Brazilians continue to pack their bags to seek better work opportunities elsewhere in the hope of returning home after saving enough money to ensure a comfortable lifestyle.

The Brazilian diaspora has been treated in contemporary Brazilian film, such as *Dois perdidos numa noite suja/Two Lost in a Dirty Night* (José Joffily, 2002) which explores the relationship between Tonho and Paco (actually a girl whose real name is Rita), two of the many illegal immigrants barely holding on to the fringes of New York City. While Tonho is naïve and determined to overcome his adversities through hard work and return home a success, Paco is an artist with a devil-may-care attitude and a strong belief in her talents as a musician but without a place to return to. The volatile yet tender feelings between these two very different people mirror the conditions of the city where, like many other illegal immigrants, they try to survive. In its turn, *Jean Charles* (Henrique Goldman, 2009) tells the tragic true story of Jean Charles de Menezes, shot dead by British police in 2005 at the height of the London terrorist alerts.

Capturing the dissatisfaction with everyday life that motivates many Brazilians to leave the country, *Embarque imediato/Now Boarding* (Alan Fiterman, 2009) tells the story of Wager, a young Brazilian man who works at Rio de Janeiro's International Airport and yearns for a better life in New York. Through a failed attempt to stow away on an airplane bound to the United States, he meets Justina, an airport employee who, disenchanted with New York, where she had lived illegally until being deported to Brazil just a few years before, with dreams of a better life of her own.

Undoubtedly, these and many other Brazilian films have had an important role in promoting awareness of Brazilian history and in rendering visible the plight of Euro- and Afro-Brazilians and other immigrants who have made Brazil their home. While many of the films with diaspora themes depict historical events, more recently Brazilian films have also portrayed the Brazilian diaspora, a product of the economic crisis that made the country quaver in the 1980s and 1990s. It remains to be seen whether this will be an enduring genre or will fade from the Brazilian screen as Brazilians continue to return to their homeland in its current economic boom.

Cacilda Rêgo

Desmundo

Studio/Distributor:

AF Cinema & Video

Director:

Alain Fresnot

Producer:

Alain Fresnot

Screenwriters:

Alain Fresnots
Sabina Anzuategui
Anna Muylaert (adapted from
the homonymous novel by Ana
Miranda, 1996)

Cinematographer:

Pedro Farkas

Art Directors:

Adrian Cooper
Francisco Andrade

Composer:

John Neschling

Editors:

Junior Carone
Alain Fresnot
Mayalu Oliveira

Duration:

101 minutes

Genre:

Historical drama

Cast:

Simone Spoladore
Osmar Prado
Caco Ciocler
Beatriz Segall
Berta Zemel
Débora Oliveira

Year:

2002

Synopsis

Directed by French-born Brazilian film-maker Alain Fresnot,
Desmundo is a historical drama based on the homonymous novel by
Brazilian writer Ana Miranda. Set in Brazil circa 1570, the film tells the
story of a group of orphans sent to the New World by the Queen of
Portugal to marry the first European settlers and bear their children.
Among them is the young and religious Oribela, who reluctantly
marries Francisco de Albuquerque, a crude sugar-cane plantation
owner who is much older than she is. Oribela endures numerous
hardships after trying to escape from the plantation house where
she lives with Francisco and his family. She ultimately enlists the help
of slave trader Ximenes in order to sail back to Portugal. Spoken in
archaic Portuguese with subtitles, *Desmundo* captures the incestuous
family life of the Albuquerqueses and the cruelty shown by the
colonizers towards the indigenous people of that time.

Critique

Desmundo is a sensitive story of the plight of an orphaned, young
immigrant woman who is destroyed in and by a heartless, nightmarish
patriarchal environment. Sent to Brazil by royal decree to marry a
European colonist, upon her arrival in Brazil Oribela (Simone Spoladore)
reluctantly agrees to marry Francisco de Albuquerque (Osmar Prado),
a slovenly, repugnant man who has an incestuous relationship with his
domineering mother. After one frustrated escape from the plantation
house in which she is confined, Oribela enlists Ximenes (Caio Ciocler),
a slave trader, to help her return to Portugal. However, Francisco learns
of the plot, captures her, and brings her back to the plantation where,
alone and devastated, she spends the rest of her life.

In the context of Brazilian cinema, *Desmundo* is one of the many
films covering historical themes produced in recent years. Centred
on the themes of colonization and migration, the film works as a
metaphor for much of Brazil's social reality. While the film primarily
chronicles the victimization of women within a system that grossly
overvalues masculine subjectivity, included in the tableau are
the brutal conditions of African slaves and indigenous peoples.
Desmundo is a vivid portrayal of one woman caught in a 'damned if
you do and damned if you don't' system of masculine bias, a system
that only supported and maintained the colonial experience, but
whose legacy still informs much of contemporary Brazilian culture and
society. What makes the film stand out is the fact that it stands less
as a retelling of the history of Brazil under Portuguese rule and more
as a telling of the previously untold, 'forgotten' history of European
women's experience in the New World, thus revealing a side of
colonial life little, if at all, discussed in academic books, and until
Desmundo largely ignored by Brazilian film.

Without any feminist pretensions, the film treats the question
of feminine agency and (oppressed) desire in a very conservative
manner. In spite of Oribela's attempts to break free from her
predicament, her actions do not represent any threat of subversion
to the dominant patriarchal order. In fact, the film implies that

she will never escape the 'prison' imposed on her by the white patriarchal order. Ultimately, Oribela has no hope, given that the only alternative available to her is to return to Portugal and take lifelong vows in a convent. But it is this very lack of optimism that makes the film so powerful a vehicle for critical commentary of women's oppression (and resistance) experienced under a patriarchal system and supported by the Catholic Church in the context of the sixteenth century. Having won several awards at film festivals across Brazil, the film establishes Fresnot as one of the leading directors of Brazil's cinema since its renaissance in the mid 1990s.

Cacilda Rêgo

Gaijin: A Brazilian Odyssey

Gaijin: os caminhos da liberdade

Studio/Distributor:

Centro de Produção e Comunicação (CPC)
Embrafilme

Director:

Tisuka Yamasaki

Producer:

Carlos Alberto Diniz

Screenwriters:

Tisuka Yamasaki
Jorge Durán

Cinematographer:

Edgar Moura

Art Director:

Yurika Yamasaki

Composer:

John Neschling

Editors:

Lael Alves Rodrigues
Vera Freire

Duration:

105 minutes

Genre:

Drama

Synopsis

Considered Tisuka Yamasaki's masterpiece, *Gaijin* (Japanese for foreigner) is a personal tribute to her Japanese grandmother who as a young woman, in 1908, left her homeland with the first wave of Japanese immigrants to Brazil to find fortune, but found instead discrimination, oppression, exploitation and loneliness. Bearing the distinction of being the first Brazilian film to take up the theme of Japanese immigrants, *Gaijin* focuses on a small community that includes a young woman named Titoe and her husband-of-convenience Ryuyi Yamada, whom she gradually comes to love and respect. Narrated in flashback by Titoe, the film traces the protagonist's emotional and political awakening during her stay at a coffee plantation in the state of São Paulo, where the Japanese workers are ostensibly isolated as much by their culture as by the nearly insurmountable language barrier. The last shots of the film intimate that after her husband's death, Titoe moves to the city of São Paulo, where she works in a factory, and develops a relationship with Tonho, a former foreman at the coffee plantation who had become a labour leader.

Critique

Having assisted prominent *Cinema Novo* directors Nelson Pereira dos Santos on *O Amuleto de Ogum* (1974) and *Tenda dos milagres/Tent of Miracles* (1977), and Glauber Rocha on his last film, *A Idade da terra/The Age of the Earth* (1980), in 1979 Tisuka Yamasaki embarked on a solo directing venture with *Gaijin*. Shot in 1979 and released in 1980, *Gaijin* is a work about discovery – a discovery of identity, history and memory, at both the individual and national levels, where the juxtaposition of Japanese and Brazilian cultures serve as a backdrop while being explored at a personal level in the foreground. The film follows the director's grandmother's journey from Japan – a country which at the time was facing high unemployment and a serious shortage of housing – to São Paulo, where waves of European and Asian immigrants were lured to coffee plantations to replace the African manpower which began to sharply decline after the end of slave traffic to the country in 1850. Soon after their arrival in São

Cast:

Kyoko Tsukamoto
Antonio Fagundes
Jiro Kawarasaki
Gianfrancesco Guarnieri
Alvaro Freire
José Dumont

Year:

1980

Paulo, however, the hope of earning enough to return to Japan starts to fade, and the newly arrived immigrants have no choice but to adapt to the new life in Brazil, while tenaciously clinging to their Asian roots.

Gaijin won several awards, including Best Film at the 1980 'Gramado Film Festival'. Recognized as one of the most prominent Brazilian women directors, Yamasaki has established an impressive body of work in a number of different media. In 2003, she completed a sequel to *Gaijin*. Titled *Gaijin, ama-me como sou* (*Gaijin 2*), the sequel tells the story of Japanese-Brazilians who immigrate to Japan, a country they were brought up to think as their 'true' homeland. In a supreme irony, once they arrive in Japan, they are treated as foreigners – *gaijin* – and many then realize just how Brazilian they are.

A meaningful discussion of *Gaijin* requires a look at its sequel, *Gaijin 2*, which finishes the story and lends potency to the plight of *Gaijin*'s protagonists. A few years – and generations – later, Japan itself faced a shortage of manpower, a situation that prompted it to open its doors to immigrants of Japanese ancestry. Japanese-Brazilians, or *kikkei*, began then to immigrate in waves to Japan, where they were treated as foreigners. Shot both in Japan and Brazil, *Gaijin 2* portrays this diasporic population, showing not only how the newly arrived 'guest worker' participate in the formation of a transmigrant working class in contemporary Japanese society, but the many cultural challenges and daily obstacles they face. *Gaijin 2* ultimately conveys this group's poignant estrangement as foreigners in a land they 'imagined' (in Arjun Appadurai's term) as their own.

In the final analysis, both films are one story about the settlement of migrants (or 'guest workers') in different social and cultural contexts, and the eventual – and certainly inevitable – ruptures of the umbilical cord that link the homeland (be it Japan or Brazil) to their respective diasporas.

Cacilda Rêgo

O Homem que virou suco

Studio/Distributor:

Dinafilme
Embrafilme and CDI

Director:

João Batista de Andrade

Producer:

Raiz Produções

Screenwriter:

João Batista de Andrade

Cinematographer:

Aloysio Raulino

Synopsis

O Homem que virou suco portrays Deraldo, the popular poet from the north-east region of Brazil, during his migration and subsequent adjustment to São Paulo. In search of a better life, he initially tries to make a living selling his poems on the streets until the public authorities force him to stop. To complicate his life even more, Deraldo is confused with another north-eastern immigrant, Severino, who killed his boss during a ceremony to honour him (Severino) as the employee of the year. It is because of this accusation that Deraldo spends most of his time trying to flee police prosecution and to find any kind of job to support himself. His journey becomes a desperate attempt to survive in a very oppressive environment and, at the same time, to keep some sense of cultural identity in a very fragmented urban space.

Art Director:

Marisa Rebolo

Composer:

Vital Farias

Editor:

Alain Fresnot

Duration:

90 minutes

Genre:

Drama

Cast:

José Dumont
Aldo Bueno
Rafael de Carvalho
Ruthinéa de Moraes
Denoy de Oliveira

Year:

1980

Critique

Released during the military dictatorship (1964–85) in Brazil, *O Homem que virou suco* is a strong witness to the ethical and aesthetic stand of its director, João Batista de Andrade. Batista's cinematic achievements are prolific and distinguished. Beginning in 1967 with his documentary *Liberdade de imprensa*, a film that was censured by the authoritarian government of the time, João Batista de Andrade is defined as a director who assumes explicitly the political dimension of his cinematic activity. *O Homem que virou suco* is part of the legacy. The film is highly charged with a Marxist conception of social relations and cultural production. The treatment of the issue of immigration in this film is an opportunity to reflect on the structure of inequality that has historically characterized Brazilian society.

Deraldo (José Dumont), the main character, is an immigrant who leaves his native state of Paraíba, in the north-east region of Brazil, in search of better opportunities in his life. In the megalopolis of São Paulo he faces discrimination and very adverse living and working conditions. It is in São Paulo, the economic engine of Brazil, that Deraldo comes to understand that the modernization process that some regions of Brazil experience leaves a great part of its population out of the economic benefits. The film represents in three dimensions the challenges that subjects like Deraldo face in the migratory process: lack of material/emotional support; loss of 'cultural identity'; and racial/cultural discrimination. The depiction of Deraldo is constructed with a sympathetic attitude towards the main character's journey. As such, Deraldo is the antithesis of Severino (José Dumont), the politically disengaged worker. What saves Deraldo from the same tragic destiny that afflicts Severino at the end of the film is his political awareness and his ability to convey in writing his rage against the system of oppression under which he lives.

The film ends with a panoramic view of São Paulo's industrial districts shown in stark contrast with the poor shantytowns that surround them. With this contrast, the director leaves the audience with an almost visceral reaction to the dichotomy of class structure of the capitalist system: the main source of suffering and tragedy that defines the lives of millions of immigrants in Brazil's urban centres. Films like *O Homem que virou suco* converse with a significant movement in the Brazilian cinematic tradition, *Cinema Novo*, which seeks to represent the reality of Brazil with a language that challenges the political and economic status quo. The film aligns itself with the political and aesthetic values of other *Cinema Novo* directors such as Nelson Pereira dos Santos, Glauber Rocha, Cacá Diegues, Joquim Pedro de Andrade, Leon Hirszman, Roberto Santos, Rogério Sganzerla and Ruy Guerra. *O Homem que virou suco*, therefore, inserts itself into a longstanding debate about the inequalities of Brazilian society and, in a utopian language, suggests that it is only the political awareness and solidarity of workers that can create the conditions of a just and equal society.

Marcus Brasileiro

Jean Charles

Studio/Distributor:

Mango Films
Já Filmes

Director:

Henrique Goldman

Producers:

Carlos Nader
Henrique Goldman
Luke Schiller

Screenwriters:

Henrique Goldman
Marcelo Starobinas

Cinematographer:

Guillermo Escalón

Art Director:

Martina O'Loughlin

Composer:

Nitin Sawhney

Editor:

Kerry Kohler

Duration:

90 minutes

Genre:

Drama

Cast:

Selton Mello
Vanessa Giácomo
Luís Miranda
Patrícia Armani
Maurício Varlotta
Daniel de Oliveira
Marcelo Soares
Rogério Dionísio

Year:

2009

Synopsis

Jean Charles tells the story of Jean Charles de Menezes, a Brazilian immigrant killed in 2005 by London police who confused him with a suspected terrorist. The film starts with the arrival of Vivian, Jean Charles's cousin, who moved to London to live with him in a very small apartment, as is typical of Brazilian immigrants to the United Kingdom. Jean Charles's life is like the lives of the majority of uneducated Brazilians in London: he works at low-paying construction jobs while dreaming of becoming self-employed and creating enough prosperity to help other immigrants in his same situation. Because he has lived in London for more than three years, Jean Charles is able to overcome some of the difficulties that most unskilled immigrants encounter with the language. He, therefore, takes on the role of mediator between new Brazilian immigrants and the world around them. It isn't until the second half of the movie that the audience learns of Jean Charles's tragic death. Jean Charles's closest friends begin a campaign to bring justice to the event, opening a debate about the forms of prejudice that immigrant groups face today, especially in a post-9/11 world.

Critique

As a film based on a real life event but portrayed by actors, *Jean Charles* exists in the borderland between fiction and documentary. This is the second feature film of the director Henrique Goldman. Together with Marcelo Starobinas, Goldman wrote a masterful screenplay that not only recasts the life of Jean Charles (Selton Mello), but in the process, sheds light on the experience of immigration itself. The film functions as a graphic depiction of the poverty, and the challenges and struggles, of low-income Brazilians who have immigrated to London.

It is within a montage of the lives of several characters facing an immigrant's reality, including lack of language skills, underpaid jobs, homesickness, issues of illegality, and more, that the film constructs the complex character who is Jean Charles. It would be simplistic to silence some of his personality traits in order to construct a victimized hero, a protagonist who battles against the antagonistic evils of state repression. At the beginning of the movie, we are confronted with an image of Jean Charles lying to airport authorities to facilitate the entrance of his cousin into England. The audience is immediately aware that the intention of the movie is not to idealize Jean Charles, but to give an honest account.

The film uses this tragic plot to explore other issues related to immigration, in particular the prejudice many immigrants face in a post-9/11 world. Indeed, this is a key point of the movie. The film works best when, during the second half of the plot, the audience is transported to an environment fuelled with paranoia and revolt. After the tragic event of the killing of Jean Charles, the film assumes a completely different tone. Until that point, the film describes the life of hardworking people, both its merits and pitfalls. With Jean Charles's

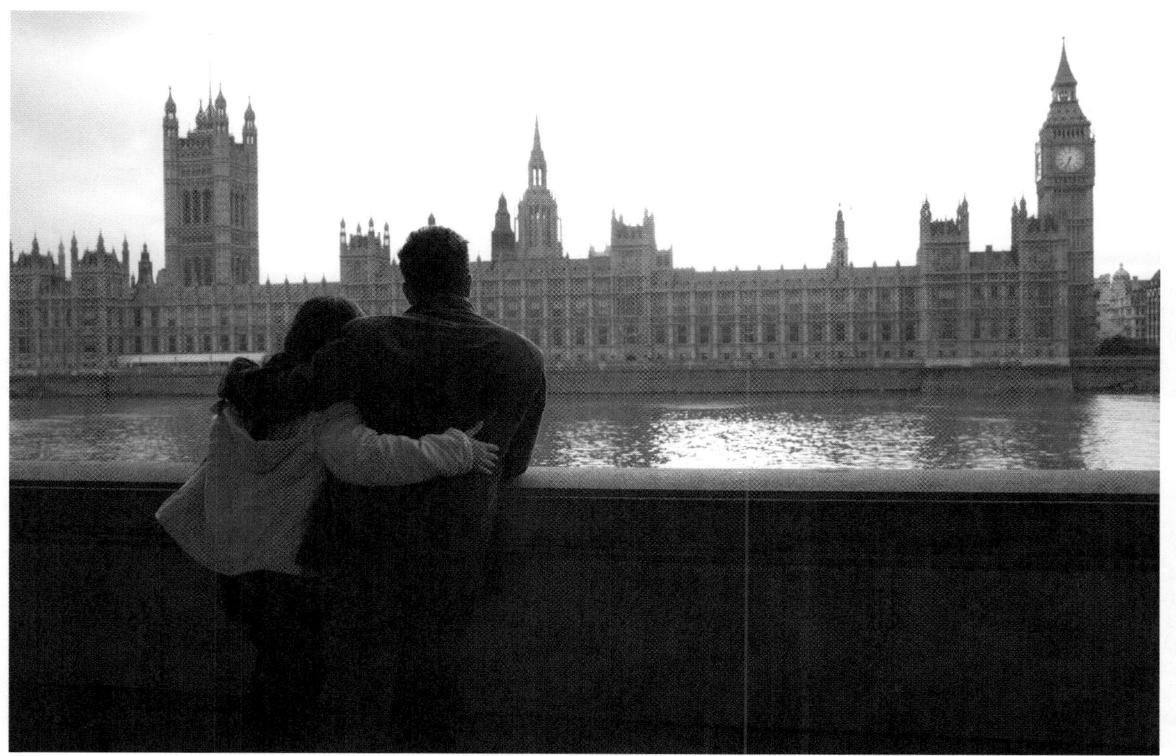

Jean Charles

death, the film considers the paranoia and xenophobia that inform transcultural relations at the beginning of the twenty-first century. Indirectly, the film also points to the socio-economic conditions of Brazil. Despite its position as an emerging economy in the global scene, Brazil still must deal with issues of inequality and distribution of income. The cause-and-effect relationship of poverty within and immigration out of Brazil is an important subtext. Another subtext, which is more subjective and is a legacy of colonialism, is related to the mystifying aura that Europe still has on the Brazilian imagination. For the Jean Charles constructed in this movie, Europe represents the possibility of being in a mythical space that defines culture and civilization. The tragedy embedded in this narrative is the fact that this idealized place also becomes the symbol of a brutal reality.

Marcus Brasileiro

Now Boarding

Embarque imediato

Studio/Distributor:

Bang Filmes/Fera Filmes

Director:

Allan Fiterman

Producers:

Juliana de Carvalho
Marcelo Florião

Screenwriters:

Marcelo Florião
Laura Malin
Aloísio de Abreu (adapted from
a story by Marcelo Florião)

Cinematographer:

Allan Fiterman

Art Directors:

Beli Araújo
Zilda Moschkovich

Composer:

Daniel Tauszig

Duration:

90 minutes

Genre:

Comedy

Cast:

Marília Pêra
Jonathan Haagensen
José Wilker
Clara Choveaux
Marta Nieto
Sandra Pêra
Caio Graco
Fred Assis
Edi Oliveira
Rafael Martins

Year:

2009

Synopsis

Now Boarding is the story of Wagner, a young man trying to improve his life in Rio de Janeiro. His ultimate dream is to move to New York, and despite all the difficulties he encounters in Rio, he doggedly sticks to his goal. During one of his attempts to immigrate illegally to New York, Wagner is intercepted by Justina, an airport employee who develops a sense of responsibility for Wagner's destiny. Justina has lived in New York, and because the experience was a traumatic one, she is skeptical about the possibility of a positive transformation of one's own life through change of location. Throughout the film, Wagner and Justina both complement and challenge each other's perspectives on real life and dreams.

Critique

At its heart, *Now Boarding* is a light and humorous look at the diasporic experience. As such, this film treats dislocation without great emphasis on the political implications of the process of moving from one culture to another. However, important questions dealing with this experience come to the forefront of the narrative: the symbolic and material conditions that define the experience of immigration and its implications. The film's narrative is the relationship between Justina (Marília Pêra), an airport employee who was deported from the United States a few years earlier, and Wagner (Jonathan Haagensen), a young man who lives with financial difficulties in Rio de Janeiro and dreams of immigrating to New York. It is through this relationship that we learn about the traumatic experience that immigration has had for Justina. This character expresses the disillusionment that frequently comes with living abroad. The traumatic event of Justina's deportation became the turning point of her life, reflected in the silencing of the only passion that she has ever had: singing. Justina represents the dark side of the diasporic experience: the potential for success and the construction of a new life become a nightmare, full of regret and bitterness. Justina's failed migratory experience silenced her real self, the one defined by desire and passion. It is through the naïve and passionate desire that Wagner has for a life in New York that Justina is able to release herself from her traumatic past. She ends up helping him realize his dream, thereby allowing him to live his own experience and not be informed by her perspective on what it means to live outside Brazil.

Now Boarding provides its audience with the context and motivation to immigrate that many young Brazilians have, a context that is merely insinuated in *Jean Charles* (Henrique Goldman, 2009), another film that deals with the same issue. In *Now Boarding* as in many other accounts of the same experience in Brazilian cinema, the reasons for immigration are mainly economic. As in *Jean Charles*, *Now Boarding* also touches on the issues of idealizing the experience abroad. The difference between both films is found in the fact that Wagner is constructed as a character not yet infected with cynicism. In Wagner, the film portrays the experience of an everyman young Brazilian from the lower-income classes. The financial difficulties that define his life in Rio de Janeiro reverberate with the audience's own experience and frustration, and constitute an imaginary future outside Brazil that seems promising when compared to the reality Wagner – and by extension the audience – lives in. New York appears in the movie only through the distorted images of Justina's traumatic memories or Wagner's naïve expectations and projections.

The film also plays with the Brazilian popular imaginary of waiting passively for the resolution of one's conflicts. Wagner constitutes a counter-discourse in relation to this commonsensical attitude toward life. His proactive and adventurous personality redefines the passive attitude, and replaces it with the modern attitude of constructing his own narrative in life. This attitude, sometimes naïve and romantic and sometimes modern and courageous, is the fuel that drives Wagner to take charge of his diasporic experience.

Marcus Brasileiro

Olga

Studio/Distributor:

Globo Filmes

Director:

Jayme Monjardim

Producers:

Rita Buzzar

Screenwriters:

Rita Buzzar
Fernando Morais

Cinematographer:

Ricardo Della Rosa

Art Director:

Tizia de Oliveira

Composer:

Marcus Viana

Editor:

Pedro Amorim

Duration:

141 minutes

Genres:

Drama
Biopic

Cast:

Camila Morgado
Caco Ciocler
Edgar Amorim
Gustavo Berriel

Synopsis

A historical drama, *Olga* is the first feature-length film of seasoned TV director, Jayme Monjardim. The film is based on Fernando Morais's biography *Olga* (1994) about the life of Olga Benário, a German Jew and communist militant who was assigned by the Communist Party to 'pass' as Luís Carlos Prestes's wife and to help spread communism in Brazil in the 1930s. The film begins the night before Olga is set to be sent to the gas chamber in a German concentration camp. Through the use of flashbacks, she remembers her life as a young, daring girl. The film next moves to her youth as an equally courageous militant in Nazi Germany who resorts to violence to free her boyfriend Otto Braun with whom she runs away to the USRR. Once there, she decides to undergo military training. Her commitment to the Communist Party and endurance lead to her being selected to accompany Prestes to Brazil. *Olga* narrates the romantic involvement between Benário and Prestes and their work together in Brazil until their arrest in 1936. This marks the beginning of the end for Olga who, even though pregnant, is deported to Germany where she gives birth to her daughter, Ana Leocádia, and later dies in a concentration camp in Bernburg in 1942.

Critique

Director Jayme Monjardim (one of Globo TV's directors) insisted on casting Camila Morgado as Olga Benário, given the actress's expressive eyes and her physical resemblance to Benário. While some critics disagree with the film's reliance on enlarged close-ups, music used to heighten the emotional impact, and other televisual techniques, *Olga* successfully recreates the overall look and feel of a concentration camp. Shot in Rio de Janeiro, the film achieves the cold, damp, darkness of northern Europe by minimizing long, exterior shots. Consequently, *Olga*'s technical achievements, made possible by Globo's investment in this production, have shaped the film as a well-finished cinematic product that aimed to attract numerous viewers.

Leona Cavalli
Maria Clara Fernandes
Year:
2004

The film was immensely popular in Brazil with over three million viewers and received several film awards. It was also Brazil's entry for the Best Foreign Language Film for the Academy Awards and was thought to have a chance of winning given its use of a historical character and successful recreation of the pre-World War II years both in Europe and Brazil. However, given that the love story between Benário and Prestes (Caco Ciocler) is highlighted, the representation of history is simplified and used as a background.

The film's release took place during the presidency of Luiz Inácio Lula da Silva, a founding member of the Partido dos Trabalhadores who, during the military dictatorship, was also persecuted and sent to prison. Thus, a parallel could be made between Olga's persecution and other left-wing victims of the military government. Nonetheless, the film is also part of a recent trend in Brazilian arts regarding the consumption of biographies of important people.

Worldwide, *Olga*'s premiere coincided with a growing interest in rescuing the historical figure of Benário who was also the subject of a documentary released in Germany in 2004 and of several acts commemorating her as a victim of Nazism.

The film also presents a nuanced representation of Olga's gender as she is successively masculinized and repressed as a militant, softens and falls in love with Prestes, and is eventually depicted as a martyred mother. Her depiction as a woman in love and a caring mother allows the audience to empathize with the character, but critics have also pointed out that this portrayal constitutes a patriarchal view of women's role. Finally, Olga subtly debunks the myth of Brazil as a welcoming land where all immigrants are well-received.

Carolina Rocha

O Quatrilho

Studio/Distributor:

Filmes do Equador
Luiz Carlos Barreto Produções
Cinematográficas Ltda.

Director:

Fábio Barreto

Producers:

Luiz Carlos Barreto
Lucy Barreto

Screenwriters:

Antônio Calmon
Leopoldo Serran

Cinematographer:

Felix Monti

Art Directors:

Paulo Flaksman

Synopsis

O Quatrilho tells the story of two couples (Angelo and Teresa; Massimo and Pierina) who live in an Italian immigrant settlement in the southern region of Brazil at the beginning of the twentieth century. Angelo and Massimo become partners in a business venture and, as a consequence, their families decide to live together under the same roof. The friendship that bound these two couples is complicated when different love interests start to develop among them, leading to the ultimate dissolution of the group. Massimo and Teresa realize that they have more in common with each other than with their respective partners. Thus, they decide to leave the farm where they reside, leaving Angelo and Pierina with the dilemma of having to confront their personal humiliation and the prejudice of the small and conservative community that surrounds them.

Critique

O Quatrilho is a film adaptation of the homonymous novel by José Clemente Pozenato published in 1985. The film had a great critical reception and was nominated for an Oscar in the Best Foreign Film

Sérgio Silveira

Composer:

Jaques Morelenbaum
Caetano Veloso

Editor:

Karen Harley
Mair Tavares

Duration:

80 minutes

Genre:

Drama

Cast:

Patrícia Pillar
Glória Pires
Alexandre Paternost
Bruno Campos

Year:

1995

category. As an important piece in the very active career of the director Fábio Barreto, since his beginning as a film-maker with his short film *A História de José e Maria/The Story of Joseph and Mary* (1977), *O Quatrilho* depicts a slice of life in the diasporic experience of Italian immigrants in southern Brazil: woven into the background of this story of love and betrayal are economic difficulties and strategies for overcoming them; attempts to maintain cultural identities and customs in a new environment; and the difference in moral and political mentalities among the members of an immigrant community. This last aspect, in particular, defines the widely different actions among the main characters and signals their different attachments to European values, especially in relation to the religiosity and political/economic systems of the early twentieth century.

Angelo (Alexandre Paternsot) and Pierina (Glória Pires) (the abandoned couple) represent the more conservative side of the European mentality that European immigrants of their era brought with them. They build their identities around the importance of religious values, alongside a pragmatic mindset that reinforces the modus operandi of the capitalist system. It is this subjective constitution that defines their economic success at the end of the film. Angelo and Pierina perceive the diasporic experience as a way to change one's economic condition and prosper through hard work, intelligence and utilizing capitalist strategies, all culminating in a disciplined focus on becoming rich.

The director contrasts the system of values embodied in Angelo and Pierina with those of Massimo (Bruno Campos) and Teresa (Patrícia Pillar). These two characters represent a subjectivity intellectually committed to a romantic vision of life. They constitute themselves in an open attitude towards an understanding of desire as a fundamental part of the human condition. In this sense, their identification with urban values signals their lack of attachment to conservative values. Consequently, their search is for an environment that is diverse and open to the construction of a future not defined by reified traditions and costumes. The migratory experience for Massimo and Teresa means a process not just of economic success but of searching for opportunities to realize their potential as human beings. In the film, they decide to migrate again, this time to Porto Alegre and São Paulo, urban centres with a completely different set of values to the small village they were living in. *O Quatrilho* suggests that the configuration of values and social institutions, such as marriage, family, religion, love, etc., is a historical process; thus, they cannot be taken as rigid and inflexible entities. Resistance, and at times disobedience, is represented in this film as attitudes which are fundamental to the process of reconfiguring not just individual journeys but also the historical movement of communities. With its poetic depiction of the migratory process, *O Quatrilho* reveals the values of its very diverse characters. Through this portrayal, the audience comes to understand the protagonists' inner desires that prompt them to assimilation and adaptation, or to movement and change.

Marcus Brasileiro

Saudate for the Future

Saudade do futuro

Studio/Distributor:

Laterit Productions in
association with Cobra Films
and others

Directors:

Marie-Clémence Paes
César Paes

Producer:

Marie-Clémence Paes

Screenwriter:

Marie-Clémence Paes
César Paes

Cinematographers:

César Paes
Michel Berck

Composers:

Fábio Freire
Thomas Rohrer

Editor:

Agnès Contensou

Duration:

94 minutes

Genre:

Musical documentary

Persons:

Luiza Erundina
Fábio Freire, Ezequias Lira

Year:

2000

Synopsis

Saudade for the Future is a musical tribute to the bustling city of
São Paulo, and to the *Nordestinos* (north-easterners) who stream
to the city from the country's drought-stricken north-east's *sertão*
(backlands) for the hope of a better future. The sounds of the
Nordestinos of this documentary are its focus, and the musical genre
Repente is the rhythmic heartbeat of the film. Like North American
rap or hip hop music, *Repente* consists of an improvised rhythmic and
rhyming speech that is chanted by a duo in the form of a lyrical duel.
Often accompanied by a guitar and a tambourine, the *Repentistas*
(street music performers) can be found on popular plazas of the city,
where they hawk their lyrical wares to appreciative passersby. When
not spotlighting a particular musician or musical group, the camera
wanders the different neighbourhoods of São Paulo, juxtaposing
images of the São Paulo Stock Exchange, the Municipal Market,
the Estação da Luz (a historical railway station), the subway, and the
Paulista Avenue – one of the most important thoroughfares of the
city and the site of many cultural centres, museums and a multitude
of skyscrapers. Without any narration, the documentary shows
individuals and emblematic representatives of *Nordestinos* from all
walks of life who have made São Paulo their home.

Critique

Saudate for the Future is the fifth in a series of ethnic documentaries
produced and directed by Marie-Clémence Paes and César Paes,
founders of Laterit Productions (France), which include *Angano …
Angano, Tales from Madagascar* (1989), *Songs of Tears and Nature*
(1992), *Haiti: Un temps en conserve* (1993) and *Awara Soup* (1995).
Accompanied by north-eastern rhythmic melodies, the film provides
an unflinching portrait of the lives of assorted *Nordestinos*, with an
emphasis on the city's street musicians. Through carefully chosen
cinematic techniques, the directors seek to highlight the humanity
of the characters and draw connections between those that inhabit
entirely different and distinct social worlds. Thus, despite the separate
spaces that social groups inhabit, fast-paced editing, the juxtaposition
of scenes, and thematic links between stories serve to create a sense
of commonality among street performers, shantytown dwellers,
and middle- and upper-class characters. Besides the musical duo
Sonhador and Peneira, and Zé Honório, a dance-hall accordionist,
and the Banda de Pífanos de Caruaru, a family ensemble from the
state of Pernambuco, the film also profiles several other *Nordestinos*
who live in São Paulo, including a famous sculptor, a former city
mayor, a disc jokey, a housekeeper, a cab driver, and several couples
dancing at a night club.

The combined talents of the Brazilian, César Paes, and the
Malagasy, Marie-Clémence, directors have produced a fine work
that is both a celebration of São Paulo and an affirmation of Brazilian
popular culture. Without narration, translation or subtitles, the film
projects São Paulo through the eyes of the *Nordestinos*. Their songs
sing the city, often humorously and usually improvised. Through their

everyday life and their lively performances, they 'long for the future' (a rough translation of the film's paradoxical title) and for a better life in one of the world's largest cities. Despite the focus on the personal rather than the political, this is a film that ultimately reflects on the lot of the *Nordestinos* in São Paulo, where they suffer discrimination as undesirable outsiders. And yet, the film poses a number of unanswered but provocative questions regarding what exactly are the socio-historical, political, cultural and economic forces driving São Paulo into the future: a future the *Nordestinos* long for.

Cacilda Rêgo

Two Lost in a Dirty Night

Dois perdidos numa noite suja

Studio/Distributor:

Riofilme

Director:

José Joffily

Producer:

Alvarina Souza Silva

Screenwriter:

Paulo Halm (adapted from Plínio Marcos's homonymous play, 1966)

Cinematographer:

Nonato Estrela

Art Director:

Claudio Amaral Peixoto

Composer:

David Tygel

Editor:

Eduardo Escorel

Duration:

100 minutes

Genre:

Drama

Cast:

Roberto Bomtempo
Débora Falabella
David Herman

Synopsis

This film chronicles the lives of Tonho and Paco, two Brazilians trying to adapt to New York. Tonho is a naïve and hardworking immigrant from the state of Minas Gerais. The difficulty of his immigrant experience in New York reinforces his nostalgic feelings about Brazil and his desire to go back home. On the other hand, Paco – in reality a girl called Rita – is living a very dangerous life involving drugs and prostitution. Their lives come together when Tonho invites Paco to share his apartment with him. What seems a supportive relationship takes a different route when the reality of marginal immigrant life becomes more visible. The feelings of desperation, frustration and resentment that constitute their lives become the source of irreconcilable differences that define the opposite paths that they choose at the end of the movie. The explosive and ambiguous relationship between Tonho and Paco reach a point where it becomes impossible for them to recognize love and friendship in a violent and indifferent environment.

Critique

Two Lost in a Dirty Night is the film adaptation of Plínio Marcos's homonymous play. Although the screenwriter Paulo Halm kept many original elements, unlike the film, Plínio Marcos's play does not focus on issues of immigration. In José Joffily's film, the characters Tonho (Roberto Bomtempo) and Paco (Débora Falabella) struggle to make a living as immigrants in New York, but they use very different strategies to achieve their goals of prosperity and success.

Two Lost in a Dirty Night is a film that treats the issue of immigration without any concession to a romantic vision of the diasporic experience. The construction of space in this film represents a New York City that, instead of the idyllic image of the land of opportunity that informs the dreams of many immigrants like Tonho, reveals itself as the symbol of an environment that can also be oppressive, violent and dirty. In this sense, the film keeps the original spirit of Plínio Marcos's aesthetic and ethic perspective and functions as a way to deconstruct the *naïveté* of the hopes and dreams of many poor immigrants who are completely oblivious to the political implication of the diasporic experience. Tonho is constructed as the embodiment of

Guy Camilleri
Year:
2002

the hardworking, honest, but also naïve immigrant that idealizes New York, only to realize afterwards that the poor and unskilled immigrant's reality is riddled with humiliation and discrimination.

Paco/Rita represents the opposite of Tonho, vis-à-vis their understandings of the political reality of the immigrant's life. S/he is a character that is more aware of the socio-economic conditions that inform the immigrant's reality. His/her subjectivity is defined in opposition to the idea of a passive surrender to a social system that undermines women and poor people. At the same time, s/he also desires to become successful and financially secure, but on his/her own terms. The fact that Paco/Rita's dream is to become a famous rap musician functions as a way to constitute him/herself as a rebellious artist, who attempts to 'tell truth to power' with politically informed lyrics.

Unfortunately, the film leaves us with the impression that this project is as naïve as Tonho's dreams of overcoming his adversity through hard work. The harsh truth of frustrations and disappointments comes between the two characters, making it impossible for them to develop their relationship into a romance. One of the sources of the conflict between the two characters is Tonho's refusal to assume the same political and existential positions that define Paco/Rita. Doing so would mean that he would have to abandon his attachment to values of empathy and solidarity that he is struggling to keep alive. In this sense, *Two Lost in a Dirty Night* represents the dilemma of subjects who are lost in an environment that denies the possibility to realize their desires. This impossibility affects not only the material conditions of their lives, but also destroys their capacity to reconfigure their emotional structure so as to redefine their own object of desire.

In the case of Tonho, his choice to go back to Brazil at the end of the film is his last attempt to recover a part of his self that could provide some form of emotional comfort: relationships with his family and friends. For Paco/Rita, the film defies any attempt to project his/her future, because s/he does not have a place to return to. For him/her, the concept of homeland – and for that matter, the nostalgia for home – is a memory that is as oppressive as the reality of his/her present.

Marcus Brasileiro

The Year My Parents Went on Vacation

O Ano em que meus pais saíam de férias

Studio/Distributor:

Gullane Filmes, Caos Produções Cinematográficas, Miravista

Synopsis

Set in 1970, *The Year My Parents Went on Vacation* tells the story of Mauro, a 12-year-old boy from Minas Gerais, whose parents are young left-wing militants. The parents leave Mauro with his grandfather Mólte, who lives in São Paulo, as they go underground. The timing to their arrival in São Paulo coincides with the death of the grandfather, and hence, young Mauro is left by himself in an unfamiliar environment. The grandfather's neighbour, Shlomo, a Jewish immigrant like Mólte, reluctantly accepts responsibility for the boy while 'his parents are on vacation'. Left to explore on his own, Mauro quickly familiarizes himself with the Jewish rites which are part and parcel of his ancestry, and he joins the local children, guided

Director:

Cao Hamburger

Producers:

Fabio Gullane
Cao Hamburger

Screenwriters:

Adriana Falcão
Claudio Galperin
Cao Hamburger
Bráulio Mantovani
Anna Muylaert

Cinematographer:

Adriano Goldman

Art Director:

Cássio Amarante

Composer:

Beto Villares

Editor:

Daniel Rezende

Duration:

105 minutes

Genre:

Drama

Cast:

Michel Joelsas
Germano Haiut

Year:

2006

by precocious Hanna. Thus, Mauro discovers the heterogeneity and camaraderie of the immigrants of the neighbourhood of Bom Retiro amid the repression taking place in São Paulo during July 1970 when Brazil was a prominent participant in the World Cup.

Critique

The Year My Parents Went on Vacation is loosely based on the life of director Cao Hamburger, whose inspiration for the film grew while he was in England. In the 1970s, Hamburger's parents went underground to avoid imprisonment by the military dictatorship. *The Year My Parents Went on Vacation* was well-received in Brazil and garnered

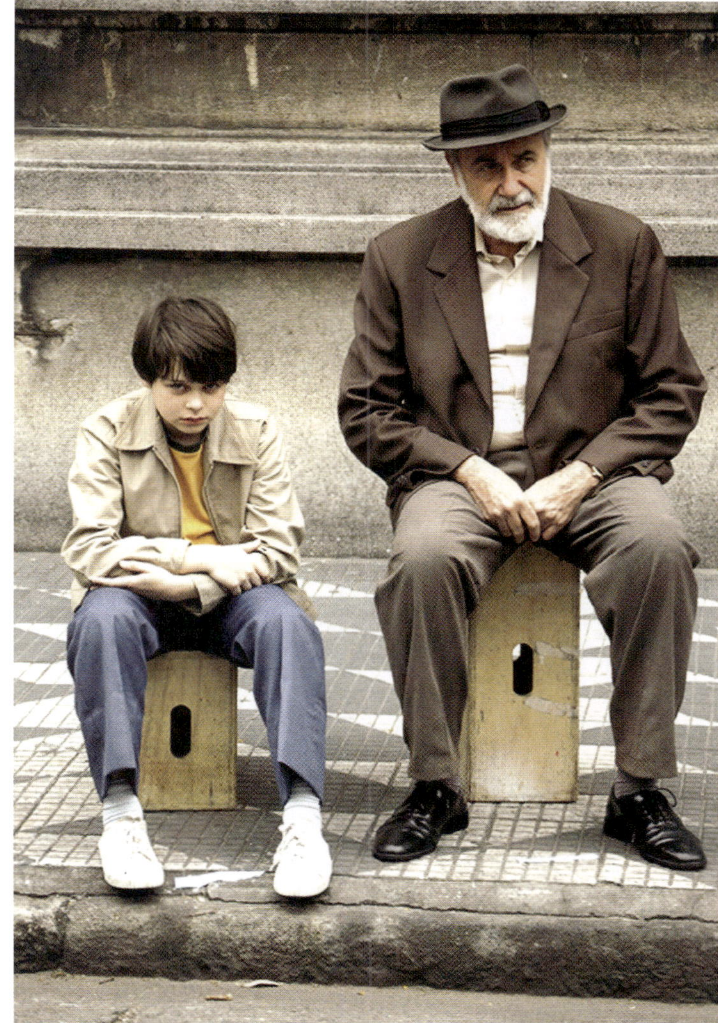

The Year My Parents Went on Vacation/
O ano em que meus pais sairam de férias

several awards. It has been compared with Roberto Benigni's *La Vita è bella/Life is Beautiful* (1997) which centres on a young boy's survival amid the violence and intolerance of occupied Italy during War World II. Indeed, the topic of political violence has divided critics: for some it is a central feature of the film, while for others it never gains prominence as Mauro's interests and feelings are central for the narrative development. Whether one agrees with either side, it is important to highlight the participation of Miravista as one of the film's producers, a fact that may have helped in the uncontroversial tone of the film. This entertaining and light tone is achieved through scenes that focus on Brazil's participation in the soccer cup championship.

As a film directed at a broad audience, the topic of political violence is represented in politically correct terms. Even at the film's end, the young protagonist still repeats the euphemism 'my parents are on vacation' even though his father has disappeared and he is forced to leave Brazil with his mother. Nonetheless, the performances of the young actors – Michel Joelsas as Mauro and Daniela Piepszik as Hanna – have been consistently praised.

The Year My Parents Went on Vacation evokes the sepia tone of old photographs as it recreates the subjectivity of a young boy who sorts what he is told from what he experiences and sees. Of particular importance is the depiction of the Bom Retiro neighbourhood as a place of communal bondings and ethnic harmony. The cohesion of the Jewish immigrants is evident when, after the death of Mauro's grandfather (Paulo Autran), they 'adopt' the young non-Jewish boy as one of their own. The friendship between Shlomo (Germano Haizut), a neighbour of Mauro's grandfather, and Mauro helps him understand and come to terms with his 'Jewishness'. Therefore, the depiction of Bom Retiro is made vivid through immigrant characters from different European countries, thus complementing the vision of Brazil as a melting pot of ethnic and racial differences.

Carolina Rocha

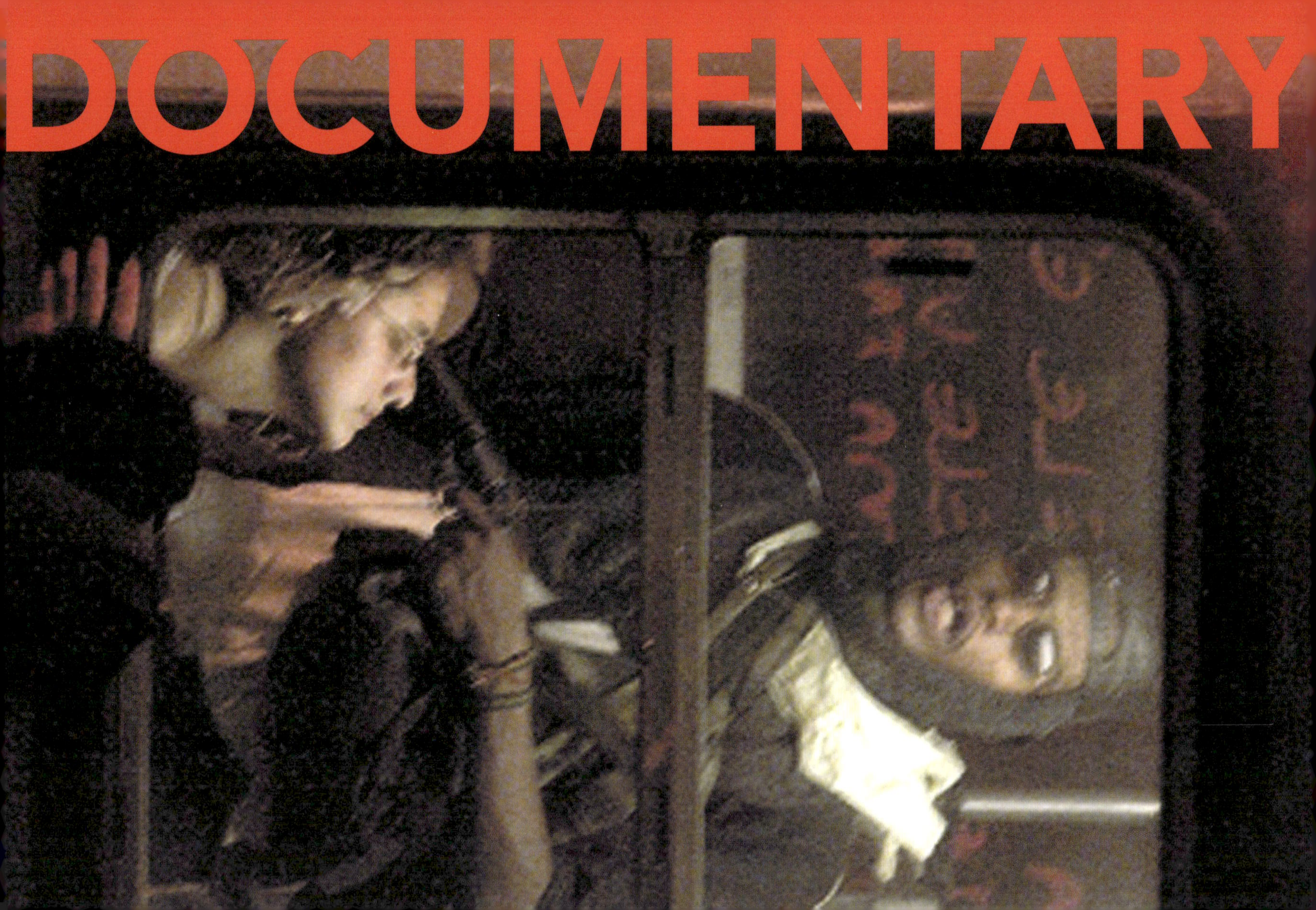
DOCUMENTARY

Often seen as the foster child of Brazilian cinema, documentary has recently enjoyed a comeback in critical and box office success. National entries in the São Paulo-based 'É tudo verdade' ('It's All True') festival have steadily risen from 45 titles in 1996 to over 400 in 2007. DocTV, a cable channel specializing in the documentary idiom, has broadcast over 120 films shot in 27 different states. And although the vast majority of releases still struggle to break through the ceiling of 20,000 viewers, features such as Miguel Farias Jr's *Vinícius* (2005), Walter Carvalho and João Jardim's *Janela da alma/Window of the Soul*, 2002) and Lírio Ferreira's and Hilton Lacerda's *Cartola: música para os olhos/Cartola: Music for the Eyes* (2007) have played to audiences of between two and three hundred thousand. In fact, documentary has always been a staple of Brazilian cinematic modernity, and its most acclaimed directors – Nelson Pereira dos Santos, Glauber Rocha, Ruy Guerra, Leon Hirszman, Arnaldo Jabor – have alternated between documentary and fiction throughout their careers, in the process also blurring the boundaries between them. Being less dependent on the commercial circuit, documentary film-making could maintain some degree of autonomy both with respect to mainstream cinema and to television, sometimes antagonizing and sometimes allying itself with these.

From the very beginnings of national cinema, a pattern established itself of, on the one hand, films exploring the social or ethnic 'other' and, on the other hand, those looking behind society's everyday routines to cast new light on the close and familiar. In the 1920s, Portuguese immigrant Silvino Santos made a number of documentary travelogues, foremost *No país das amazonas/In the Land of the Amazons* (Agesilau de Araújo and Silvino Santos, 1922), which starts with images of indigenous villages and goes on to narrate the encroachment of 'civilization' on the Amazon region: steamboats on the river, the sapping of rubber trees, a factory producing mattresses from the raw material. A year later, Santos released *Terra encantada/Enchanted Land* (1923), Brazil's first feature-length urban documentary, chronicling his visit to Rio de Janeiro during the celebrations of the independence centenary. Humberto Mauro, another early pioneer, made numerous documentary shorts for the Ministry of Education between the 1930s and the 1970s, most notably the series 'Brasiliana' (on popular feasts, inspiring Leon Hirszman's 'Cantos de Trabalho' trilogy in the 1970s) but also social and urban-themed films such as *Engenhos e usinas/Plantations and Factories* (1955), chronicling the decadence of the once-opulent sugar industry.

It was in the 1950s and 1960s, however, paralleling the advent of *Cinema Novo*, when documentary film-making truly took off: the convergence of political radicalization and new technical possibilities such as light camera equipment and direct sound recording – pioneered by Joaquim Pedro de Andrade in *Garrincha, a alegria do povo/Garrincha, Joy of the People* (1963) – focused interest on the vast urban and rural underclass to whose demands cinema would 'give voice'. Nelson Pereira dos Santos's *Rio, 40 graus/Rio, 40 Degrees* (1954) and *Rio, zona norte/ Rio, Northern Zone* (1957) chronicled the life of Rio's urban poor, introducing a fictional narrative structure (influenced by Italian neo-realism) to hold together its documentary sequences of life in the city and its *favelas*. This hybrid model would be revisited by films such as Orlando Senna's and Jorge Bodanzky's *Iracema, uma transa amazônica/Iracema* (1976) – where the documentary register of the Trans-Amazonian highway's construction is triggered by the performances of 'real' and vocational actors – or Arthur Omar's *Triste trópico* (1974) and Sérgio Bianchi's *Mato eles?/ Shall I Kill Them?* (1983), which employ found footage to narrate a fictional hero's journey to the centres of European modernity and back into the Brazilian rainforest, or to expose the underlying complicity of documentary humanism with the very production of the 'otherness' it purports to decry.

Linduarte Noronha's *Aruanda* (1960), a short film on the descendants of runaway slaves still living an isolated, 'primitive' life in the *quilombo* (slave community) of Olho d'Água in backland Paraíba, was an early forerunner of *Cinema Novo*'s infatuation with the rural north-east. In a number of films shot just before the coup of 1964 – Leon Hirszman's *Maioria absoluta/Absolute Majority* (1964), Paulo César Saraceni's *Integração racial/Racial Integration* (1964) or Sérgio Muniz's *O Povo do Velho Pedro/ The People of Old Pedro* (1964) – the director's interest, just as in fiction drama, is not merely to reveal the living conditions of the poor under the regime of the rural *latifundio* but also to understand, and thus begin to transform, the consciousness of the oppressed. Although it absorbs many of the technical elements and stylistic features of contemporary *vérité* and Direct Cinema, the documentary of *Cinema Novo* remains overall confined to the expository mode in which the film-maker provides the spectator with an explanation of the footage seen, and the relation between the 'voice of the other' and the film-maker-intellectual's voice-over is still the vertical one between documentary evidence backing up the analytical truth of the argument.

Viramundo (Geraldo Sarno, 1964), part of the quartet of medium-length documentaries produced and released by Thomas Farkas as *Brasil verdade/True Brazil* (1964), closes the cycle by following north-eastern migrants to the city of São Paulo. At the same time, it inaugurates a period characterized, on the one hand, by a growing interest in areas of society beyond *Cinema Novo*'s imaginary geography of *sertão* (backlands) and *favela*: Luis Sérgio Person's *São Paulo S/A/São Paulo Inc.* (1965) and Arnaldo Jabor's *A Opinião pública/A Public Opinion* (1967) both dissect the conservatism of the urban middle class in an attempt to understand the popular support for the military coup. On the other hand, the frustration of *Cinema Novo*'s revolutionary hopes leads to a questioning of the 'sociological paradigm' of pedagogical truth-production, most notably in Arthur Omar's *Congo* (1972) and his *Antidocumentário* manifesto of the same year, which challenge the exteriority of the camera and voice speaking 'on behalf of' its subjects: 'The documentary only records that in which it does not participate'. In *Jardim Nova Bahia* (1971) and *Tarumã* (1975), Aloysio Raulino radicalizes the gesture of 'giving voice to the other' by handing the camera over to the 'subject' itself – a peasant woman – whereas Glauber Rocha, in *Di/Glauber* (1977) pioneers the 'subjective documentary' by focusing less on the funeral of the painter Di Cavalcanti than on his own emotional responses.

In the early 1980s, already during the period of 'democratic opening', Eduardo Coutinho – who had worked on TV's *Globo Repórter* programme over the previous decade, a platform for Direct Cinema-influenced documentaries with a markedly auteurist profile – releases his seminal *Cabra marcado para morrer/Twenty Years Later* (1984). This documentary incorporates footage from an earlier project on peasant resistance against latifundist violence cut short by the military coup, revisiting its locations and protagonists who only re-encounter one another in the process of shooting after years of persecutions and clandestinity. Thus, *Twenty Years Later* is at once a verdict and epitaph on cinema's relation with 'the people' since the 1960s and foreshadows a new, different model of documentary reality as negotiated and produced in the intersubjective encounter between the film-makers and their subjects. This model is centred on the interview as a moment of truth-performance that Coutinho radicalizes in his subsequent films *Santo forte/The Mighty Spirit* (1999) – one of a number of documentaries investigating popular faiths, also including Wolney de Oliveira's *Milagre em Juazeiro/Miracle in Juazeiro* (1999) and Ricardo Dias's *Fé/Faith* (1999), *Babilônia 2000* (Eduardo Coutinho, 1999) and *Edifício Máster* (2002).

If Coutinho's interview-based documentaries are arguably the dominant paradigm of the last decade – forced to its very limits and beyond in his own most recent *Jogo de cena/Playing* (2007) and *Moscou/Moscow* (2009) – other trends include the return of the documentary biopic – no longer focusing, as in Sílvio Tendler's political sagas of the late 1970s and early 1980s, on political leaders such as Juscelino Kubitschek and Jânio Quadros but, rather, on popular musicians: *Nelson sargento* (Estevão Pantoja, 1997), *Laurindo de Almeida, muito prazer* (Leonardo Dourado, 1999) or *Um certo Dorival Caymmi* (Aloísio Didier, 1999). A new, militant and testimonial cinema had already emerged in previous decades, connected with the resurgent trade unions in São Paulo's industrial belt but also other social movements: examples include João Batista de Andrade's *Trabalhadores, presente/Workers Unite* (1979), Renato Tapajós's *Linha de montagem/Factory Belt* (1982) and Leon Hirszman's *ABC da greve/ABC of Strike* (shot in 1979 but only released in 1990). Following the lead of Andrea Tonacci's work with indigenous communities (culminating in his brilliant *Serras da desordem/The Hills of Disorder* [2006]), community projects such as 'Vídeo nas Aldéias' encourage indigenous film-makers to use the medium for their own communal and political purposes: *Pirinop, meu primeiro contato* (Mari Corrêa and Karané Ikpeng, 2007) narrates the community's title-giving 'first contact' with white 'civilization' from their own viewpoint, radically inverting the ethnographic gaze. A host of recent releases, finally, work in the idiom of Direct Cinema-influenced observation of singular lives, including Roberto Berliner's *A Pessoa é para o que nasce/Born to Be Blind* (2003) or the work of João Moreira Salles who, in *Santiago/Santiago (Uma reflexão sobre o material bruto)* (2007), also experiments with autobiographical and self-reflexive elements, as do Sandra Kogut in *Um Passaporte húngaro/A Hungarian Passport* (2001) or Kiko Goifman in *33* (2003). Here the subject behind the camera turns itself into the object of investigation, in films that straddle (and in the process question) the boundaries between documentary, fiction and even theatre.

Jens Andermann

ABC of Strike

ABC da greve

Studio/Distributor:

Taba Filmes

Director:

Leon Hirszman

Producer:

Carlos Calil

Screenwriter:

Leon Hirszman

Cinematographer:

Leon Hirszman

Art Director:

Adrian Cooper

Editor:

Leon Hirszman

Duration:

75 minutes

Genre:

Documentary

Persons:

Vinícius de Moraes
Ferreira Gullar
Lula

Year:

1979/90

Synopsis

The documentary *ABC of Strike* follows the long strike, in 1979, of 150,000 steelworkers of São Paulo's industrial belt (also known as ABC) in an attempt to improve wages and living conditions. It exposes the complex relationship between workers and trade unions, employers and officials of the military dictatorship, shaped by class antagonisms. Luis Inácio Lula da Silva played an important role during the strike, as one of the leaders of a trade union that suffered government intervention. As a consequence, workers lost their remaining spaces of expression, including factory occupations and public demonstrations, depending instead on the support of politicized sectors of the church. The film accompanies the workers' emergent class awareness as they invent new forms of organization, and other forms of struggle, which the strike both accompanies and vindicates. After 45 days an agreement is reached over wages, but not everyone is happy with it. Whatever its results, however, the events of 1979 forever changed the role of the Brazilian labour movement.

Critique

With his documentary *ABC of Strike* Leon Hirszman put into filmic practice his unionist and political sympathies. Hirszman, under the influence of his father, had joined the Communist Party at age fourteen and had maintained an active engagement with Marxist philosophy and its internal divisions and revisions ever since. Two ideas in particular are dear to this film-maker: firstly, the notion of a philosophy of praxis, and secondly, the commitment of the intellectual. Philosophy of praxis refers to Marx's reply to those *Philosophes* who believed that change in the world could effectively come about as a result of changes of thought. Against this idea he directed the well-known eleventh aphorism of the Feuerbach theses: 'Philosophers have hitherto only interpreted the world in various ways, the point is to change it.' From this perspective, the intellectual could only enter praxis by means of empathy, by putting himself in place of the victim, thus acquiring the objective intelligence of the latter. This 'objective intelligence' would be developed further in Gramsci's concept of the organic intellectual, whose knowledge does not stand apart from history but represents a scientific, philosophical knowledge and a political action at the same time. This is also, in general terms, the theoretical background of the *ABC of Strike*, the protagonist of which is not Luis Inácio Lula da Silva but the strike as such.

In comparison with his previous film *Eles não usam black-tie/They Do not Wear Black-Tie* (1981), Hirszman no longer holds a naïve or romantic view about workers, not necessarily seeing them as a political force. The battle in *ABC of Strike* is between the worker and the large multinational corporations, but it is also a battle waged against the union apparatuses, against the government, and against one's own body in front of the machines and the alarming working conditions these impose. The strike gains different proportions at any moment, becoming increasingly large in scope until it targets the military government itself. Yet all the time there is a tension between the workers and the military forces. The film also acquires a poetic dimension when it pans, in slow motion, over the sea of cars built by the workers, the gigantic queues for job openings and, above all, the factories themselves – appearing in all their overwhelming might, huge machinery dwarfing the frail bodies, the gases and chemicals inhaled by workers clearly visible. The documentary shows how industrial labour physically affects the body. However, it also demonstrates how class consciousness and peaceful self-organization can achieve at least some of the workers' aims.

Hirszman's professed Marxism was fully in line with his film. He had been among the strikers throughout the strike period, thus having not only the vision of the outsider but also that of the participant. A reason for making the film, in fact, was to give workers the opportunity to watch their own practices, and thus to see themselves as agents. The importance of the strike, from this point of view, lay in the struggle for rights as such. At the time of shooting, the film was banned from public release and was only completed and released after the director's death in 1990. Even then, the film started to circulate first in small niches such as film clubs and on the Internet. Seen today, the film takes on a different shape, even as regards the charismatic figure of Lula who never lost his political force and charisma. The idea of political empathy may seem outmoded today but, the film shows, remains necessary in all human relationships.

Rafael Leopoldo AS Ferreira

Bus 174

Ônibus 174

Studio/Distributor:

Zazen Produções

Directors:

José Padilha
Felipe Lacerda

Producers:

José Padilha
Marcos Prado

Screenwriter:

Braúlio Mantovani

Cinematographers:

Cezar Moraes
Marcelo Guru

Composers:

Sacha Amback
João Nabuco

Synopsis

Bus 174 revisits one of Brazil's most-watched media events of 2000 – a bus hijacking in a middle-class neighbourhood of Rio de Janeiro. What was meant to be a 'routine' holdup turned into a protracted stalemate when the hijacker found himself trapped inside the bus, surrounded by police who appeared unequal to the challenge presented by the situation. By chance, the hijacking occurred close to the headquarters of the media giant TV Globo, and was broadcast live to millions of viewers around the country. The film is structured around two parallel stories – an account of the hijacking, and the carefully reconstructed story of the hijacker Sandro's difficult and tragic life. Padilha's film gradually reveals narrative information for both of these stories, so that we come to understand and rationalize the hold-up in the context of the institutionalized abuse suffered by Sandro and others like him. Underlining the narrative is an urban landscape constituted of violent streets, and the usually invisible spaces of prison cells and youth detention centres.

Critique

Until the bungled bus hijacking, Sandro existed socially only as a case number within the legal system. Through interviews with those who knew him, the film reconstructs Sandro's life as a former street kid and

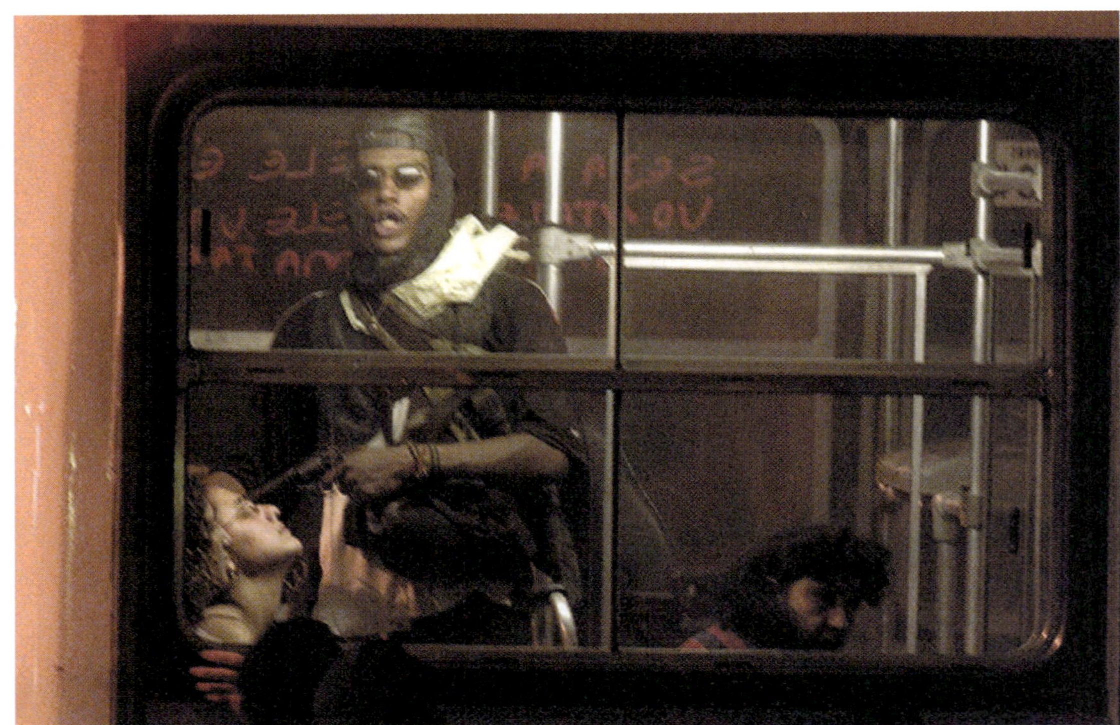

Bus 174

Editor:

Felipe Lacerda

Duration:

122 minutes

Genre:

Documentary

Persons:

Sandro do Nascimento, Rodrigo Pimentel and Luiz Eduardo Soares

Year:

2002

a petty thief. By doing so, the film engages in a public memorializing of his life, thereby acknowledging him as a valid actor in the city's recent history. The film links its creation of Sandro as a social subject with the creation of a media subject. It engages in a running meta-commentary on the representational politics of documentary films and other forms of the media. For example, once Sandro realizes the opportunities offered by the cameras for social visibility, he engages in an ambivalent process of subjectification. Activating a symbolic repertoire based on popular perceptions of dangerous criminals disseminated by the media, he plays the role for the sake of the cameras.

The hijacking itself therefore becomes a subaltern speech act – his performance in the precarious space of empowerment offered by the bus attempts to redress his negation and invalidation as a speaking subject. It finally affords him the possibility of bearing witness to and denouncing the injustices he has suffered.

The film also challenges the silences and absences of the dominant narrative and iconography of Rio de Janeiro. It constructs a subaltern geography in which the disenfranchised fear for their lives. A former street child, for example, recalls the danger of being attacked by pedestrians in the streets of the commercial hub of downtown Rio. The city's memory-scape is thus reconfigured around sites of civilian and institutionalized violence, instead of the celebratory landscape of social cordiality and racial democracy that has traditionally imaged Rio. The film also engages in a work of mourning for the lives lost to the human rights abuses of the 1990s – lives that were not considered socially valid, and that have not been publicly grieved. For example, through testimony and film footage it recreates the murder of eight street children outside the Candelária Church in the city centre in 1993 – an attack which Sandro survived. Given the lack of official commemoration of those lives, the film attempts to insert them into a collective memory of the city. In a parallel move, it seeks to transform the trauma story that Sandro tries to articulate during the hijack into a narrative language that resists the will to forget.

Lorraine Leu

Di/Glauber

Alternative titles: Di Cavalcanti Di Glauber; Ninguém Assistiu ao Formidável Enterro de Sua Última Quimera; Somente a Ingratidão, Essa Pantera, Foi Sua Companheira Inseparável

Studio/Distributor:

Embrafilme

Director:

Glauber Rocha

Producer:

Ricardo Moreira

Screenwriter:

Glauber Rocha

Cinematographers:

Mário Carneiro
Nonato Estrela

Composers:

Pixiguinha
Heitor Villa-Lobos
Paulinho da Viola
Lamartine Babo
Jorge Ben

Synopsis

The material in Glauber Rocha's documentary-meditation on the life, work and death of Brazilian painter Emiliano Di Cavalcanti is not organized in any linear or previously decided pattern. Rather, in accordance with Glauber's own dismissal of 'scripted movies', it represents an improvised discourse. The film starts with a travelling shot from a car moving through Rio's streets set to a voice-over from Glauber himself, to then give itself over to a celebration of the painter's life that contrasts with the exhibition of his remains during Di Cavalcanti's funeral and with his friends and family in mourning. Occasionally, image and sound converge as when the song 'O velório de Heitor' ('Heitor's Funeral') by Paulinho da Viola accompanies the funerary procession. At other times the two are violently opposed, as when the image of the coffin is set to a carnival *marchinha*, 'O teu cabelo não nega' ('Your hair can't deny it') by Lamartine Babo (1932). This contrast is taken to an extreme when the flowers thrown on to the coffin as it is lowered into the grave are combined with the frenetic rhythms of Jorge Ben's 'Umbabarauma, Homem Gol' (1976). The reason for such juxtapositions may be found in one of the argumentative strands running through the documentary: the notion of Di Cavalcanti as a painter of Rio de Janeiro's mixed-race, *mestiça* and *mulata*, beauty. As Glauber says in the film, the painter's great achievement was 'the Madonnization of the mulatta'.

Critique

Emiliano Augusto Cavalcanti de Albuquerque e Melo, better known as Di Cavalcanti, died on 26 October 1976, in Rio de Janeiro. A visual artist who had taken part in the Modern Arts Week of 1922, Di Cavalcanti was, along with Candido Portinari, the most important painter of Brazilian modernism. His remains were invigilated at Rio's Museum of Modern Art and then buried at the city's João Batista

Editor:

Roberto Pires

Duration:

18 minutes

Genre:

Documentary

Persons:

Joel Barcellos, Marini Montini, Glauber Rocha

Year:

1977

cemetery. According to Glauber Rocha, '*Di Cavalcanti* was made from an impulse. I'd woken up at seven thirty in the morning, read that Di Cavalcanti had died, and by nine I started shooting' (2006: 332). Glauber thus went to the vigil and subsequently to the cemetery, where he recorded the event with a 35 mm-camera. Despite the family's protests, Glauber managed to get a close-up of Di Cavalcanti in his coffin on take. During the funerary procession he also shot extensive close-ups of Marina Montini, an Afro-Brazilian model and one of the painter's muses. Glauber then combined these with images of Di Cavalcanti's work: shots of paintings and catalogues, and of Antonio Pitanga, a black actor, dancing in front of the paintings. These sequences are set to popular music (Pixiguinha, Lamartine Babo, Martinho da Vila, Jorge Ben), as well as a Villa-Lobos score and Glauber's voice from off-screen reciting texts by Vinícius de Moraes, Augusto dos Anjos, press coverage and his own personal impressions.

After a prolific decade in which he had directed several classics of Latin American and indeed global cinema (*Deus e o Diabo na terra do sol/Black God, White Devil* [1964], *Terra em transe/Entranced Earth* [1967], *O Dragão da maldade contra o santo guerreiro/Antônio das Mortes* [1969]), followed by two polemic and explosive films (*Der Leone Have Sept Cabeças* [1970] and *Cabeças cortadas/Cutting Heads* [1970]), Glauber Rocha experienced a difficult and erratic period during the 1970s. He lived in Cuba and various European countries, then returned to Brazil. Leaving a number of projects unfinished, he directed two feature-length films: *Claro* (shot in Italy in 1975) and *A Idade da terra/The Age of the Earth*, his last work, in 1980. A third feature, *Câncer*, had been started at Rio de Janeiro in 1968 and completed in Cuba in the early 1970s, but it would only reach the screens after Glauber's death in 1982. Exile, a 'weariness of classical cinema' as well as economic and political difficulties, are some reasons for Glauber's ambulant life, which ends with his return to Brazil on 23 June 1976, after five years abroad.

His return was polemical. Having voiced his support for the president Ernesto Geisel, Glauber became involved with Embrafilme and embarked on several projects, even conducting a TV programme. *Di* must be read in the context of the gradual opening-up of the dictatorial regime and of the ambivalent and tense position Glauber maintained towards Brazilian modernism: a reckoning to which he submitted not only visual artists but also writers (*Jorjamado no Cinema*, on the Bahian writer Jorge Amado, is from 1977) and above all himself and the 'New Cinema' he had led during the 1960s. Among his memories of Di Cavalcanti invoked in the film, Glauber especially highlights the fact that it was the painter who had introduced him to Roberto Rossellini during the latter's trip to Bahia in 1958. Glauber had witnessed how Rossellini filmed 'with an idea in his head and a camera in his hands', an idea that remains valid when Glauber himself decides to go and film the funeral. In *Di* and *Jorjamado no Cinema*, then, Glauber pays homage to the 'modernist Olympus' of 'national glories' (the inclusions of Vinícius and Villa-Lobos have to be read in the same key) at the same time as he destroys the monument and ceremonial solemnity, allowing for vitality to manifest itself. *Di* is a profanation in the purest sense of the term: following Oswald de Andrade's teachings, the film transforms taboo into totem. As Oswald sustained, one must not convert the Orpheic feeling of transcendence into a promise beyond terrestrial life but rather into inclusive and earthbound happiness.

At the time the documentary was made, modernism's canonization (which included the *Cinema Novo* proper) was already in full course – the Di Cavalcanti retrospective at the São Paulo Museum of Art had taken place in 1971. In order to carry out his ritual destruction, which is at the same time a celebration of life, Glauber applied his 'anarcho-constructivist, or trans-realist' vision through a 'nuclear montage', in which the association between successive images emerges from a compositional core which does not follow a linear order of progression. Indeed, for *The Age of the Earth*, made according to the same principle, Glauber suggested that projectionists should exhibit the rolls in the order of their choosing. Through synthetic montage, Glauber Rocha proposed to reveal the potential for modernism's survival in popular music, dance, in bodies, poetry, images and even in death itself.

A 'baroque-epic' film, in the words of its author, *Di* is a funerary feast, the banquet of an anthropophagic cinema, affirming life as a gobbling-up of experiences, even in the face of the taboo of death. Due to judicial action initiated in 1979 by Elizabeth Cavalcanti, the painter's adopted daughter, the film cannot be publicly exhibited.

Gonzalo Aguilar (trans. Jens Andermann)

Reference
Rocha, G (2006) *O século do cinema*, São Paulo: Cosac Naif.

Garrincha, Joy of the People

Garrincha, alegria do povo

Studio/Distributor:

LC Barreto
Herbert Richers SA

Director:

Joaquim Pedro de Andrade

Producers:

Armando Nogueira
Luiz Carlos Barreto

Screenwriters:

Joaquim Pedro de Andrade
Luiz Carlos Barreto
Armando Nogueira

Synopsis

In the opening sequence, there is a succession of photographs – shots of matches, legs, faces of players and supporters – set to the dry and enthralling rhythm of an Afro-Brazilian percussion. On Copacabana beach, a group of poor kids play football. In the changing rooms of Maracanã stadium, Garrincha's Botafogo team prepares for the final of the Rio championship. Dribblings around powerless opponents carry the trademark of the o-shaped legs of Brazilian football history's most gifted dribbler. The film embarks on a search for Garrincha's origins. In the small town where he was born, we get to know his house, his wife and seven children, the textile factory where he used to work, his old workmates, now drinking companions on bar crawls. The joy of hanging out contrasts with the discipline and boredom of professional football training sessions. Throughout the film, the attitudes and expressions of the supporters rival the players' feats on the field. The retrospective of the two world championships of 1958 and 1962 leads on to the anticlimax of the 'traumatic' defeat to Uruguay in 1950. The Maracanã – the world's largest football stadium at the time – empties only to fill up again, every single weekend.

Mário Carneiro
David Neves
Cinematographer:
Mário Carneiro
Composers:
Carlos Lyra
Severino Silva
Editors:
Nello Melli
Joaquim Pedro de Andrade
Duration:
58 minutes
Genre:
Documentary
Persons:
Herron Domingues, Garrincha
Year:
1963

Critique

In 1962, Brazil won the Football World Cup for the second time in a row. This documentary is dedicated to one of the 'heroes' of this feat, Garrincha, the right-winger of the Brazilian team. Joaquim Pedro de Andrade, an active member of the first generation of *Cinema Novo*, just back from a period of study in Europe and the United States, wanted to make a film inspired by French *cinéma-vérité*. Due to numerous problems, in particular the deficiency of direct sound recording, the project acquired a more hybrid character and became fundamentally a work of montage. In *Garrincha*, Joaquim Pedro invents a new way of filming football in Brazil, with several cameras shooting the game from various angles at field level, emphasizing details, facial expressions, gestures and dribblings rather than the overall story of the match. Alternating moving images with photographic stills, the editing is more interested in the passion of football, in moments of luminescence and explosion, than in drama and narrative.

The conventional voice-over contrasts with the complexity of the editing and the film generates spaces for irony: an orthopaedist, looking at X-rays of Garrincha's legs, declares them unfit for sports (the film opposes this medical knowledge to the practices of faith healers and the superstitions proper to football culture); the narrator discusses several hypotheses for the passion of the supporters (for one of them, the ball represents the mother's breast; for another, an escape from everyday frustrations). Included among the curiosities of a film that attempts a variety of approaches to its main character, is the first explicit case of 'merchandizing' in Brazilian documentary (when Garrincha visits the local agency of a bank sponsoring the production).

Just as twisted, in many ways, as the legs of its hero, *Garrincha* eventually rewards the director with the discovery of the character that would become fundamental for his entire work. In the disconcerting movements of this entirely improbable football player and in the various portraits of supporters on the stands – poor, black, toothless faces the camera keeps looking out for – a first sketch of *Macunaíma* (Joaquim Pedro de Andrade, 1969) already takes shape: the Brazilian anti-hero, lazy and inventive, unconscious of his powers. A hero present in multiple incarnations throughout the film-maker's oeuvre, a baroque figure just like Garrincha himself, always willing to risk one turn too many, an unnecessary excess, for the sake of pure, irresponsible fun. The quote from playwright and journalist Nelson Rodrigues which opens the film ('If we were seventy-five million Garrinchas, what a country this would be, greater than Russia, greater than the United States') promised a glorious panegyric. To the deception of the sponsors and, to a large extent, the viewers, *Joy of the People* begins with the thrill of victory only to end with the disappointment of defeat, taking leave from the hero to inquire about the human landscape that should have been just a backdrop for the former. Structured as an anti-epic, the film finally inverts the meaning of the opening quote: maybe the Brazilians really are 'seventy-five million Garrinchas'. For the young *cinemanovistas*, at the start of the 1960s, this suspicion encapsulated both the tragedy and the strength of Brazil.

Maurício Lissovsky (trans. Jens Andermann)

Playing

Jogo de cena

Studio/Distributor:

Videofilmes
Matizar

Director:

Eduardo Coutinho

Producers:

Bia Almeida
Raquel Freire Zangrandi

Cinematographer:

Jacques Cheuiche

Editor:

Jordana Berg

Duration:

105 minutes

Genre:

Documentary

Persons:

Aleta Gomes Vieira
Andréa Beltrão
Claudiléa Cerqueira de Lemos
Débora Almeida
Fernanda Torres
Gisele Alves Moura
Jeckie Brown
Lana Guelero
Maria de Fátima Barbosa
Marília Pêra
Marina D´Elia Mary Sheyla
Sarita Houli Brumer

Year:

2007

Synopsis

Playing evolves around women who responded to an advert in the classified section of a Rio de Janeiro newspaper asking for volunteers wishing to take part in a documentary. Their conversations with the director take place on a theatre stage. They talk about work, everyday life, emotional relations and especially about their children. The stories that emerge are about love, troubles and difficulties, loss, pain and suffering, but also about conflicts and moral recovery. At the same time, Coutinho invited actresses to re-enact these same stories, confusing in the process the distinction between the staged and the real. This procedure results in the establishment of a relation between *Playing* and the audience that alternates between belief and disbelief, putting into question not only the 'authenticity' of the film itself but also that of Coutinho's previous documentaries.

Critique

At the start of *Playing*, it is still possible to suspect that we are about to undergo an experience similar to the ones offered by previous documentaries directed by Eduardo Coutinho. Essentially, it seems, little has changed in his work. The film once again puts us face to face with individuals telling stories of their lives, in the minimalist style which had characterized Coutinho's work since *Santo forte/The Mighty Spirit* (1999): an absolute focus on the characters' speech, restricting the soundtrack to recordings on location, an editing structure based on the succession of characters rather than by topic, and the use of light equipment. The restriction of the shooting to a single location is likewise maintained, however, this time the speeches take place on a theatre stage rather than a real location – such as a *favela* or an apartment building, for example.

This is the film's first layer of meaning. But the title *Jogo de cena* (literally 'stage-play') and the shooting in a theatre suggest yet another. Fragments of already-told stories begin to re-appear in some speeches, gradually leading viewers to doubt what they see on-screen: whether a real person relating their stories or an unknown actress representing them. Among the actresses invited by Coutinho, three are famous in Brazil. The viewer can immediately identify them but even here, in many moments, a kind of short-circuit occurs between the actress and the real person. Moreover, *Playing* exhibits the variations between ways of acting and makes the viewer understand the art of acting as something unstable and exposed to risks – very close to the documentary as understood by Eduardo Coutinho. With the actresses who are not widely known, the short-circuit is total: the anonymous women narrating intimate moments of their lives to Coutinho's camera acquire a force of truth, which immediately re-affirms the viewers' belief in the documentary image.

'Authentic', 'truthful', 'spontaneous' – adjectives that have always set the tone for the reception of Coutinho's work, even in spite of his own objections (he always emphasized the dimensions of fabulation and 'self-staging' necessarily contained in real characters' statements) – are shattered one by one. The uncertainty spreads out across the entire film, and in the end we do not know whose are the hesitations, the silences, the tears, the emotions; whether the actresses' or the characters'. We lose control over what is or is not staged, and even the indications that the film may be playing tricks on us, paradoxically, make us surrender to its game even more. We let ourselves be moved twice by the same story, without caring which of the women is the 'real' bearer of the story. And there can be no absolute guarantee: both may be 'false', actresses playing the part of a third woman entirely absent from the film. What Eduardo Coutinho's film stages, then, is something practically unprecedented in contemporary Brazilian production: the capacity to trouble the viewers' belief in what they are watching, to raise doubts over the documentary image and to bring about such a perception less from intellectual comprehension and more from sensible experience provoked by film form itself.

Playing was an immediate success with audiences and critics alike at several film festivals. It succeeded in living up to that other great documentary film of post-dictatorship Brazil, Coutinho's own classic *Cabra marcado para morrer/Twenty Years Later* (1964/84). Both are films that must certainly be included among the most forceful in the history of Brazilian cinema.

Consuelo Lins (trans. Jens Andermann)

Prisoner of the Iron Bars

O Prisioneiro da grade de ferro (auto-retratos)

Studio/Distributor:

Olhos de Cão Produções Cinematográficas

Director:

Paulo Sacramento

Producers:

Paulo Sacramento
Gustavo Steinberg

Screenwriter:

Paulo Sacramento

Cinematographer:

Aloysio Raulino

Editors:

Idê Lacreta
Paulo Sacramento

Synopsis

In 2002, in the final months before the demolition of São Paulo's Carandiru penitentiary complex – South America's largest prison, with around 9,000 detainees, which made international headlines in 1992 when military police killed 111 prisoners during an uprising – Sacramento and his team organized a series of video workshops with inmates of Carandiru's nine pavilions. *Prisoner* combines their 'self-portraits' with footage shot by the professional crew, resulting in an audiovisual conversation about everyday life inside Carandiru: from the 'reception speech' new prisoners receive on arrival to activities of work, prayer, music and sports, the various legal and illegal transactions between prisoners – including arms and drug trafficking, prostitution, a tattoo studio or a clandestine distillery – family visits and medical appointments. Shot in digital video, in an observational, direct-cinema-influenced style and edited without any narrative voice-over save for the workshop participants' occasional commentaries from behind camera, *Prisoner* constantly moves in and out of the prison's cells and pavilions, without for the most part attributing its point of view unambiguously to either 'professional' or 'amateur' film-makers.

Critique

Starting with footage of the prison's demolition played backwards, followed by a long travelling shot down a crowded and dilapidated corridor, *Prisoner of the Iron Bars* proposes from the outset to engage

Duration:

123 minutes

Genre:

Documentary

Year:

2004

in a peculiar kind of memory-work. Although the 1992 massacre is only mentioned twice – in the opening credits and in the photographs of lacerated bodies taken in the prison morgue by a fellow detainee (who normally makes his living, as the film shows, by offering visual memories on days of family visits) – the threat of violence from guards as well as fellow inmates to which prisoners were constantly exposed and which ultimately led to Carandiru's closure, lingers constantly in the background of the image. This dimension of latent violence is most evident in the hand-held shots, probably taken by the prisoners without their film-maker-tutors present, of clandestine crack dens and knifemaking workshops, where the faces of the interviewees remain cautiously out-of-frame. But it is also thematized, without actual scenes of violence ever appearing on camera, in many of the interview sequences and in the rap lyrics composed by prisoners, who perform their songs in front of the film apprentices' camera panning around them in a way that demonstrates their literacy in the genre of the rap video.

Rather than narrate the prison's history, the film's cinematic dialogue revolves around two questions: firstly, what are the conditions under which violence flourishes? But also, just as importantly, how do prisoners resist being reduced to victims and perpetrators and instead re-affirm their subjectivity even under conditions of extreme abandonment and lack of protection? Music, faith, martial arts, communication with loved ones, all reveal themselves as forms of 'care of the self', which the film not just registers but in which it actively partakes. The very process of learning the documentary idiom and applying it to their own reality is turned by the prisoners into yet another of the techniques of self-affirmation which Sacramento's film records. Thus, the relation between the film's two questions (which is also one between an external observer's desire to know and the inmates' attempt to become subjects of their own representation) provides a structuring rhythm, expressed in the dialogue between long shots of the prison buildings during different times of day and hand-held shots taken from inside – most notably during the final sequence where the inmates use the tele-zoom to film the city in the distance. The great majority of shots, however, are located somewhere in-between these clearly attributed points of view. Often there are two cameras present during the same sequence, one operated by an inmate, the other by a professional, each recording not only the action itself but also the other camera's recording of it. Yet as soon as the other camera is out-of-frame, the image's authorship (and thus its value as an 'impartial' document or a self-performance) becomes impossible to ascribe.

Prisoner's director of photography Aloysio Raulino had pioneered the 'testimonial' use of a camera operated by the very subject of the narrative in the early 1970s. Just like Raulino's, Sacramento's film is ultimately about the production of its own 'co-authors' – a process that is marked in the opening and closing credits, where the workshop participants are introduced, first, through their voice-over reading out their civil names, police records and cell number over a mugshot image, whereas at the end their everyday nicknames appear superimposed over the same images.

Jens Andermann

Rio, 40 Degrees

Rio, 40 graus

Studio/Distributor:

Moacyr Fenelon

Director:

Nelson Pereira dos Santos

Producer:

Nelson Pereira dos Santos

Screenwriter:

Nelson Pereira dos Santos

Cinematographer:

Hélio Silva

Art Directors:

Júlio Romiti
Adrian Samoiloff

Composers:

Radamés Gnatalli, Alexandre
Gnatalli, Cláudio Santoro

Editor:

Rafael Valverde

Duration:

91 minutes

Genre:

Drama

Cast:

Modesto de Souza
Roberto Batalin
Jeca Valadão
Ana Beatriz
Glauce Rocha

Year:

1954

Synopsis

It is Sunday morning in Cabuçú, one of Rio de Janeiro's hillside *favelas*. Maria Helena, a fifty-something housewife scolds her husband Joaquim, for lying and drinking. Her daughter Alice goes to run errands with a friend at an open-air market down below while five *favela* boys set out to sell peanut cones. One of these cares for his sick mother, another is so young that he still has chubby cheeks. From there, we follow these characters' amblings throughout Rio. Alice and Rosa meet their respective boyfriends while the boys go to various key sites of the city, including Copacabana beach, the Maracanã stadium, Corcovado with its emblematic statue of Christ the Redeemer, Sugarloaf Mountain and a nearby zoo. There, tourists and *cariocas* carry on at a leisurely pace while the boys each try to sell a few cones. While men bet on the upcoming soccer game, the bourgeoisie's young men and women lounge on the beach, and an up-and-coming politician sets his daughter up with an older north-eastern landowner. The boys are rather unlucky: they have run-ins with local hustlers, one of them is kicked out of the zoo and left to watch well-dressed children walk by, another loses consciousness after being hit by an oncoming car. While the soccer game and other goings-on across Rio culminate and wind down, the *favela* also partakes in the changes the day has brought, as Alice becomes engaged to her suitor. When all have returned to the *favela*, the day ends with the performance of Portela, a famous samba school, while Alice, crowned queen of the samba, sings.

Critique

Rio, 40 Degrees is Nelson Pereira dos Santos' first full-length film. While its style, its almost exclusive use of outside locations, its focus on everyday life and political position register the influence of Italian neo-realism, it is also considered a key precursor of the *Cinema Novo* movement. The film was intended to be part of a trilogy, yet, possibly due to its focus on a multiplicity of characters, it has had more of a lasting influence than the second part, *Rio, zona norte/Rio, Northern Zone* (1957). The city of Rio de Janeiro, with its hills, beaches, belvederes, gathering places, as well the cultural rituals of samba and *futebol*, are just as much protagonists as the characters. These typical activities create a documentary-like tone, as they pace a day that otherwise does not fit into the mechanisms of a classical plot structure, encouraging the spectator to pay attention to routine and repetition instead of dramatic climax. While the plotlines also involve a host of secondary characters, the repetition of sequences featuring individual *favela* boys humanizes these characters, sometimes highlighting the lack of principles or hypocrisy of the middle class, bourgeoisie and political establishment. The north-eastern landowner-cum-politician speaks of Brazil's progress, but he also refers to his 'lands' and insinuatingly hires the young woman as his 'secretary', despite her father's attempts to marry the two off. By featuring a cross-section of Brazilian society in the city that was then the national capital, *Rio, 40 Degrees* frequently evokes the systemic violence exercised upon these boys, as well as the conflicts within the *favela*. In that sense, it goes against previous simplistic portrayals of the poor by focusing on the hardships inherent to life in the *favela*, and the injustices that became more glaring as Brazil experienced a new wave of modernization during the 1950s.

With the inclusion of non-professional actors, its focus on a community, and on key aspects of popular culture in a way that did not emphasize their staging but presented them rather as shared experiences and practices, *Rio, 40 Degrees* opened new possibilities for Brazilian cinema. If breathtaking bird's-eye views of Rio de Janeiro highlighted the city's modernization, this film innovated in its constant movement up and down the hills where it was shot. While it is not as aesthetically experimental as the *Cinema Novo*'s films – starting with Pereira dos Santos's *Vidas secas/Barren Lives* (1963) – it is an ideal introduction to the movement.

Isis Sadek

Santiago

Santiago (Uma reflexão sobre o material bruto)

Studio/Distributor:

Videofilmes

Director:

João Moreira Salles

Producers:

Mauricio Andrade Ramos
Beto Bruno

Screenwriter:

João Moreira Salles

Cinematographer:

Walter Carvalho ABC

Art Director:

Marlise Storchi

Editors:

Eduardo Escoral
Lívia Serpa

Duration:

80 minutes

Genre:

Documentary

Persons:

Santiago Badariotti Merlo
João Moreira Salles

Year:

2007

Synopsis

Thirteen years before making *Santiago*, João Moreira Salles had started a documentary project he never completed. That film was to be about Santiago Badariotti Merlo, the butler of Moreira Salles's own family, part of Rio's wealthy and influential upper class. *Santiago*, then, is a film about that earlier, failed film. Even if its theme is based on the prior footage and maintains its focus on the butler's life, it is much more ambiguous and ambitious. It is still a film about Santiago: an Argentine who served the Moreira Salles family for 30 years and who spent most of his free time researching and writing about European royal dynasties. However, the 2007 movie is also a brilliant reflexive, melancholic and autobiographical work that dwells on the director's childhood home and memories and on the hierarchical relationships between a servant and the boss's son, and between an object of documentation and a film director.

Critique

Santiago begins with a self-critique. A first-person narrator (voiced by Moreira Salles's brother Fernando) impersonating the director tells the spectator how he wanted the original film to open. The film we watch starts the same way he intended the original, failed film to start. However, the ironic distance of the narrator's comments highlights the impossibility of adopting a simple, linear narrative when taking on personal memories, or of assuming an objective point of view when making a documentary. The butler's perspective is – in this sense – privileged. Internal enough to the director's family, but without being completely part of it, Santiago has an ambiguous status as a member of the household. João Moreira Salles assumes this displaced position to talk about his childhood and about his family. In this move, he creates a tension between his earlier, more naïve stance as a film-maker and the current – reflexive and critical – one.

In the course of the film, we repeatedly watch sequences from the old movie in which we hear the director's voice giving orders to Santiago. Towards the end of *Santiago*, the critique of the director's

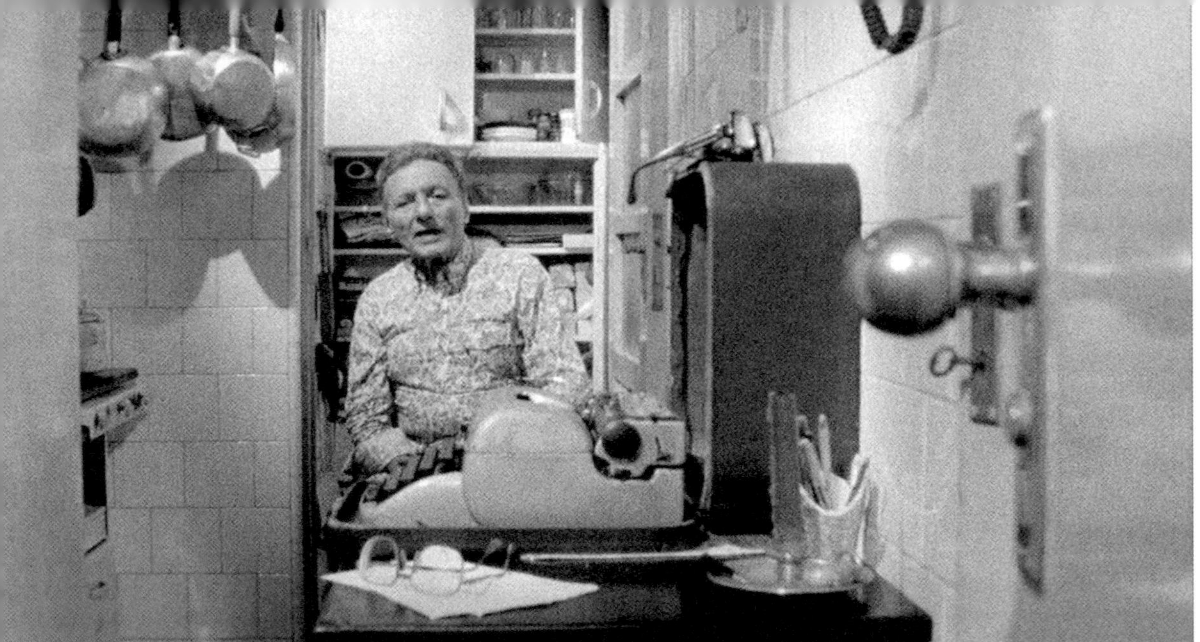

Santiago

position is made explicit: the narrator suggests that the absence of close-ups of Santiago's face, the distance he maintained towards the person behind the butler and the way he conducted the interviews were due to the fact that he never ceased to be the boss's son, and Santiago the servant. In this sense, *Santiago* is a film about power, about the hierarchy conveyed in being the 'master', but also in being the director of the film, revealing the documentarist's position as hierarchical. However, in this gesture the film inverts the problem. The director could have chosen to talk about a family such as his from a magnificent angle, highlighting the opulence and the famous names of Brazilian political and cultural life that passed through their lives, but he chooses instead the servant's perspective: a domestic, behind-the-scenes point of view.

Santiago talks about his favourite members of the royal European dynasties and about the parties at the Moreira Salles's house, longing for a world that no longer exists. This melancholic tone is highlighted in the film by the beautiful black-and-white images of the Moreira Salles's huge and empty modernist mansion in Rio de Janeiro's Gâvea district, inviting us to imagine a bygone past: children playing inside the house; elegant dinners and parties; servants walking around eminent personalities such as Christina Onassis, Jucelino Kubitschek or João Goulart. But the detailed perspective Santiago adopts to talk about his favourite characters adds a minor viewpoint that is taken up by the director to regain an intimacy with his own personal past. Towards the end of the movie, we watch close-ups of Santiago's writings while the director reads aloud some passages in which the lives of famous people are rescued through seemingly insignificant and gratuitous anecdotes, showing that these tiny details are also part of history. In this way, we end up with the sensation that even public families such as the Moreira Salles's have intimate lives and minor stories to tell. It is just a question of finding the right – critical, reflexive, displaced – angle for unveiling them.

Luz Horne

Twenty Years Later

Cabra marcado para morrer

Studio/Distributor:

Eduardo Coutinho Produções Cinematográficas, Mapa Filmes

Director:

Eduardo Coutinho

Producers:

Eduardo Coutinho

Screenwriter:

Eduardo Coutinho

Cinematographers:

Edgard Moura (1981)
Fernando Duarte (1964)

Composer:

Rogério Rossini

Editor:

Eduardo Escorel

Duration:

119 minutes

Genre:

Documentary

Persons:

Elizabeth Teixeira
Eduardo Coutinho

Year:

1984

Synopsis

Twenty Years Later is, on one level, a film about a film, recounting the failed production of a fictional movie about the assassination of a real-life peasant leader. In 1962 Eduardo Coutinho travelled to the north-east of Brazil where he learned about the recent murder of João Pedro Teixeira, leader of Sapé's peasant league in the state of Paraíba. This event inspired the director to return to Sapé in 1964 to shoot a fictional film that would re-enact the political life and death of Teixeira. Local peasants would be the actors together with Elizabeth Teixeira, the leader's widow, who would play herself. But with the military *coup-d'*état, on 1 April 1964 the film was interrupted and nearly half of the material shot was confiscated under the suspicion of subversive activities. In 1981, without a script, Coutinho returned to the north-east in an attempt to find and interview Elizabeth and the peasants involved in the 1964 production. The documentary combines footage from the 1964 film and interviews with Elizabeth and some of the other actors from 1981, thereby recounting the story of João Pedro Teixeira and reconstructing a collective memory of the peasants' struggle in the rural north-east in the 1960s.

Critique

The first scene of *Twenty Years Later* shows a film projector being prepared for the 1981 screening of footage shot in 1964 for the fictional film about the life of João Pedro Teixeira. Eduardo Coutinho gathered some of the peasants who acted in the 1964 production to watch what had been rescued of the film after its interruption. Like the method used by Jean Rouch and Edgar Morin in *Chronique d'un été/Chronicle of a Summer* (1960), the images of the peasants watching themselves reveal the documentary's subjective dimension. *Twenty Years Later*'s importance in Brazilian film history lies in its inauguration of a new way of documentary-making, one that breaks with the model of the 1960s and 1970s, which usually provided an exterior interpretation of historical events narrated by an omniscient voice. At the same time, the film breaks with the leftist militant tradition of speaking on behalf of the underprivileged to defend an ideological stance.

Twenty Years Later is the reconstruction of central events from the 1964 film: the peasant league's activities and struggle, Teixeira's life and the events that led to his assassination. However, these are just the starting point for a poignant rescue of personal and collective histories, which connect past events and the present of the interviews. The gap of seventeen years between the 1964 and the 1981 productions was also the period during which many of the peasants were jailed and tortured by the army, or lived in hiding, as was the case for Elizabeth Teixeira, who escaped to another state in 1964 and lived under the name of Marta Maria da Costa, out of touch even with several of her children.

Besides interviews with the participants, *Twenty Years Later* is composed of images of the rural north-east from Coutinho's first trip in 1962, unedited footage and eight production stills of the film shot in 1964, and newspaper articles from that period, which are juxtaposed to reveal the trajectories of the actors of the unfinished film. The fragmented editing mirrors the characters' lives and their varied discourses, often revealing a common story but sometimes contradicting each other. This heterogeneity is also felt in the interweaving of various styles, which overturns the traditional documentary method of representing historical events. Hence the film's subjective approach: Coutinho and his crew are visible in the frame, which constantly reminds the spectator of the production process. The director ceases to be an external interpreter and participates in the events unfolding before and because of the camera. A crucial illustration of this is Elizabeth's decision to abandon her cover during the production of the 1981 documentary and look for her children after seventeen years in clandestinity. *Twenty Years Later* becomes an examination of the events leading to João Pedro's death and its consequences, including the interrupted film project, through the oral testimonies of the surviving peasants. In this process, the impact of documentary-making itself is unveiled, thus establishing an aesthetic and ethical posture that would transform *Twenty Years Later* into a landmark in Brazilian cinema.

Mariana AC da Cunha

Viramundo

Director:

Geraldo Sarno

Producer:

Thomas Farkas

Screenwriter:

Geraldo Sarno

Cinematographers:

Thomas Farkas
Armando Barreto

Composer:

Caetano Veloso

Editor:

Sylvio Renoldi

Duration:

40 minutes

Genre:

Documentary

Year:

1964

Synopsis

Viramundo begins with the arrival of a train bringing migrant workers from the north-east of Brazil to São Paulo in search of work. Some of them tell their stories outside the station, we then meet more of them in construction work, a foundry and sometimes their homes. A company boss comments on the nature of the labour market, and we learn about the difference between holding down a job and the precarious life of an unskilled casual labourer. To support the unemployed there is charity; charity is linked to religion, both Pentecostal Christianity and Umbanda, whose roots are African, have devoted followers and claim to perform miracle cures in a long sequence that serves as a guided tour of the maladies of the urban poor, before returning us to the railway station, where some of the unlucky ones have opted to return from whence they came, but only to be replaced by the next train arriving from the north-east.

Critique

Viramundo is one of the paradigmatic documentaries of the first years of the continent-wide movement that emerged in Latin America in the 1960s, known as the *Nuevo Cine Latinoamericano* (New Latin American Cinema), and of its Brazilian wing, *Cinema Novo*. The timing of Geraldo Sarno's first film – it was made immediately after the military coup of 1964 – may well explain the choice of style: its adoption, instead of political denunciation, of the classic discourse of sober objectivity, following the agenda of a sociological investigation of urban poverty and religion in collaboration with social scientists at the University of São Paulo. It is nevertheless politically incisive, although dated in its social construction of the fatalism of naïve religious belief as contributing to the state of oppression. Looking back on it twenty years later, Jean-Claude Bernadet called it a landmark film for introducing the subject of the urban proletariat, speaking as themselves, in their own voices, of their conditions, for the first time on Brazilian screens (the subject of *Cinema Novo* previously being focused on the rural poor). Indeed *Viramundo* exemplifies the importance of the new documentary of the 1960s – be it *cinéma-vérité* in France, Direct Cinema in North America or *Cinema Novo* in Brazil – not only of mobile 16 mm shooting but the use of direct sound, the film's impact deriving from the combination of the two. Bernadet also remarks how *Viramundo* came to be discussed in terms of multiple voices and different levels of discourse: the hesitant, fractured speech of the ill-educated migrants contrasted with the smooth utterance of the boss, for example, or the fluency of the commentary. The film is framed, however, by a musical commentary, a song about the character in the folk literature of north-eastern Brazil who lends his name to the film's title. Viramundo's fate, as the word suggests (*virar* = to turn, *mundo* = world), is to roam the world in an unsettled state. The song was written for the film by José Carlos Capinam, set to music by Caetano Veloso, and sung by Gilberto Gil, all of which are further reasons for the emblematic status of this film. Bernadet is astute about the significance of this song:

This is not sociology. The singer belongs to the sphere of popular poetics; he hails from the same cultural universe as the migrants being interviewed. The song is composed in the first person, like the interviews, and provides a contrast to the commentary. The origin of Viramundo and the first-person lyrics draw us closer to the migrants; their effect is empathetic.

The film gives priority to the voices of those who have not been heard in the public sphere, but without hiding their inevitable differences of situation and opinion – on the contrary it works with them. A skilled worker reveals that he enjoys a certain minimal level of comfort, while one of the unskilled is homeless and unemployed; there are differences of opinion about the value of trade unions. About religion, however, the film does not equivocate. Religious trance and miracle cures are seen as a kind of hysterical despair on the part of people who see no way out, and resort to the saints as a last resort. If everything else in the film still rings true, it would not be long before Brazilian documentarists working in the tradition that Sarno pioneered, would be making films about the theology of liberation, and indeed Sarno would subsequently criticize himself for his narrow view in this first film of his.

Michael Chanan

Reference
Bernadet, JC (1989) 'The Sociological Model, or His Master's Voice: Ideological Form in *Viramundo*', in Julianne Burton (ed.), *The Social Documentary in Latin America*, Pittsburgh: University of Pittsburgh Press.

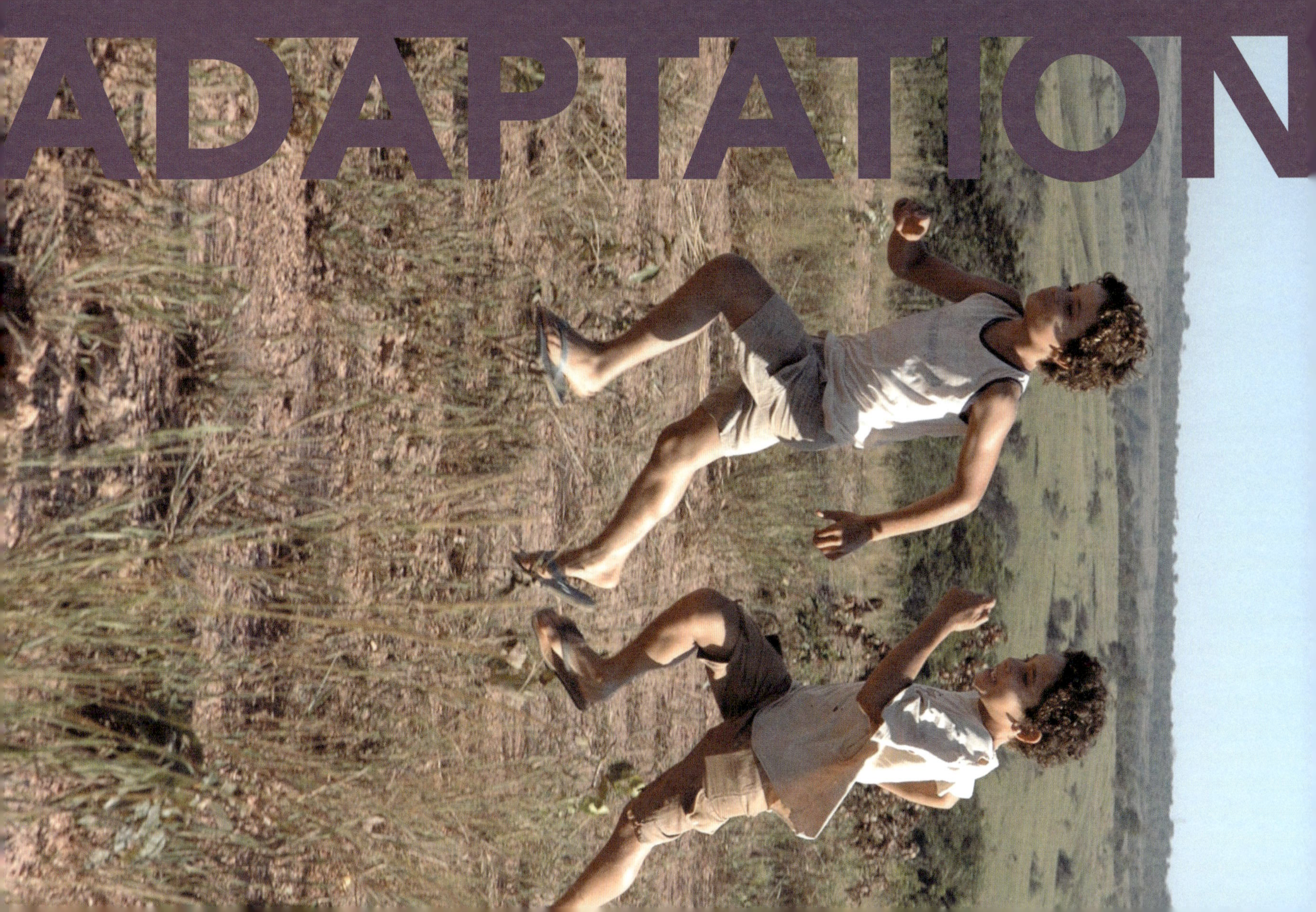
ADAPTATION

Literary adaptations are central to all national cinemas. Since early cinema, they have been a potent tool to establish cinema's respectability and its recognition as an art form. Canonical novels or pulp fiction have been major sources for stories, besides their important role in negotiating cultural identity. Since there is no limit to the type of texts or to their origin, comics, poems, short stories, novels from the most divers cultural and national backgrounds have inspired commercial successes, box office flops, cult movies and masterworks.

Brazil is no exception. One of the country's first adaptations was Humberto Mauro's feature *O Descobrimento do Brasil/ The Discovery of Brazil* (1936), based on the famous letter by Pero Vaz de Caminha that describes the journey and landing of Pedro Alvarez Cabral's fleet on the shores of 'Vera Cruz'. The choice of the first literary text ever to be produced on Brazilian soil, authored by a representative of the Portuguese colonizers and adapted without critical reflection, marks one of the points that define the wide spectrum of possibilities that spans from slavish fidelity to critically rereading the source text in the audio-visual media. While Mauro's early film expresses submission to the point of view of the colonial power, Brazil's film history is full of famous examples that read against the grain. In fact, *Como era gostoso o meu francês / How Tasty Was My Little Frenchman* (1971) by Nelson Pereira dos Santos is certainly the Brazilian adaption on which the greatest number of scholarly articles and papers has been produced.[1]

However, much work remains to be done in this field of comparative studies, in order to further map the complex relationship between literature, the silver screen and cultural history. Ismail Xavier's (2003) study on Nelson Rodrigues's adaptations produced between 1952 and 1999 might serve as a rare and significant contribution. It reveals the relationship between a country's cinema and its process of transformation during the twentieth century by showing that the films echo or try to break bourgeois morals and outmoded ideas on sexuality, a central issue of this major playwright. More studies of this kind would help to improve the understanding of the role of other canonical authors within Brazil's cinema history, such as Jorge Amado, Machado de Assis, Clarice Lispector, Graciliano Ramos and Guimarães Rosa, to name but the most prominent and most often adapted authors or those responsible for the most legendary filmic adaptations.

Beyond these key figures and their texts, which have already been established as national treasures, are many popular writers with commercial or literary interests whose contemporary cultural significance has attracted the interest of a wide range of film-makers. There is a set of films based on crime novels that depict urban violence, written by Marçal de Aquino, Fernando Bonassi, Paulo Lins, Patrícia Melo, Tonio Belloto or Luiz Alfredo Garcia-Roza, as well as historical novels by Ana Miranda, Antônio de Assis Brasil or by bestselling Jô Soares. Moreover, there has been a trend to discuss key historic or social issues, such as the dictatorship, or events based either on autobiographies or biographies that make remaining authoritarian structures or other social problems perceptible.

Accounts of people who have achieved some sort of fame in the public sphere by means of their political involvement, their extreme experiences with drugs or sex, or due to their outstanding achievements in the arts, sports or politics have provided source material for many recent productions. Authors such as the politician Fernando Gabeira, but also the call-girl Raquel Pacheco, the physician Drauzio Varella, the drug dealer João Guilherme Estrella or Austregésilo Carrano Bueno, a victim of old-fashioned ideas on drug use and psychiatry, can be mentioned in this context, as well as life stories of the famous soccer players Garrincha, described by Ruy Castro, and Heleno, depicted by Marcos Eduardo Neves.

Since film is an industry and a business, commercially successful or critically acclaimed books or plays are bound to be adapted for the screen. This can happen to respected authors such as playwright Ariano Suassuna, new talents such as Renata Melo, or professional profit-oriented writers such as the already mentioned Jô Soares.

Last but not least, as a former colony but also as a country in which literature and literary criticism has played a central role in the formation of cultural identity, perhaps more than any other art form, it is worthy of note that directors with commercial or authorial interests have turned towards writers who are part of the lusophone heritage: Eça de Queirós and his renowned ironic view of Portugal has often served as a possibility to bridge the cultural divide between Brazil and its colonizer. And figures such as António José da Silva and Manuel Maria du Bocage, respectively the major playwright and the major poet of the eighteenth century, as well as Nobel-prize winner José Saramago, have inspired films of note in this regard.

Since literary adaptation is not a genre and most film movements throughout film history have used it in one way or another, many eminent or remarkable literary adaptations can be found in other chapters of this book. This chapter nonetheless tries to bring together descriptions of films that show the political potential of adaptations, from the canonical Machado de Assis to contemporary Raduan Nassar and Marçal de Aquino. Focusing mainly on national authors, prominent figures such as Graciliano Ramos, Nelson Rodrigues, Jorge Armado and Clarice Lispector are not missing, as well as the irreverent Bocage. But even though this introduction has focused on the names of the original authors and not of the film-makers, it is their capacity to create independent works of art that has been responsible for their selection: Leon Hirszman, Nelson Pereira dos Santos (twice), Suzana Amaral, Djalma Limongi Batista, Ruy Guerra, Luiz Fernando Carvalho, Beto Brant, Sérgio Bianchi and Sandra Kogut demonstrate through their films that the art of adaption consists in the dialectic of fidelity and appropriation.

Carolin Overhoff Ferreira

Reference
Xavier, I (2003) *O Olhar e a Cena*, São Paulo: Cosac & Naify.

Note
1.   Some of the reasons for which are discussed in the entry on the film that appears in this volume in the section 'The Representation of the Brazilian Indian'.

Bocage – The Triumph of Love

Bocage – O triunfo do amor

Studio/Distributor:

Cinema do Século XXI,
Prefeitura Rio Filme

Director:

Djalma Limongi Batista

Producers:

Edith Limongi Batista
António da Cunha Telles

Screenwriters:

Djalma Limongi Batista
Gualtar Limongi Batista

Cinematographers:

Djalma Limongi Batista
Zeca Abdall

Art Director:

Bruno Testore Schmidt

Composer:

Livio Tragtenberg

Editor:

José Carvalho Motta

Duration:

85 minutes

Genre:

Drama

Cast:

Víctor Wagner
Francisco Farinelli
Viéta Rocha
Majô de Castro
Linneu Dias

Year:

1998

Synopsis

Loosely based on the life and poetry of one of the most famous and controversial Portuguese poets of the eighteenth century, Manuel Maria Barbosa du Bocage, the film does not have a plot which proceeds according to cause and effect but, according to its subject, a conceptual structure divided into a prologue, three *cantos* and an epilogue. To build its story it uses themes and characters from Bocage's erotic, satirical and love poems, as well as allusions to real events (his journeys as second-lieutenant to Brazil, Mozambique and Goa from where he deserted and travelled to India, China and Macau, his bohemian life in Lisbon and his early death at the age of 40), in addition to biographical elements from people of his time (representatives of the Portuguese monarchy that condemned him for *lèse-majesté*, the lower clergy that gave him shelter or his different lovers). While not following a coherent or chronological scheme, *Bocage – The Triumph of Love* is a tale about the poet's coming of age: from a scandalous, emotionally reckless yet recognized poet, Bocage learns through experiences in his public and private life that it is not by celebrating and practising sexual liberation that one is set free and becomes an author of uncontested standing; rather, it is necessary to praise love as an analogy of political freedom.

Critique

Bocage is one of the first films of the so-called *retomada*, the revival of Brazilian film production, which resulted from the new Audio-visual Law launched in 1993. It is also one of the first co-productions that ensued from the Luso-Brazilian Agreement on Cinematographic co-productions, dating from 1994. Among transnational literary adaptations it is outstanding, since it actually establishes a dialogue with the ancient colonizer by offering a new perspective on myths of transnational cultural identity. The film is transgressive in all its aspects: linguistically, visually and in relation to the (sexual) politics of its famous protagonist.

Linguistically, the film discloses the richness and variations of the Portuguese languages, instead of implying the neocolonialist notion that a shared language corresponds to a shared culture. The dialogue consists mainly of Bocage's poems, but Asian, African, Arabian, Brazilian and Portuguese characters speak them with multiple accents and inflections. The existing bonds between these people from the different places explored and colonized by Portugal are expressed visually in all their complexity. Indeed, the editing establishes the most unimaginable spatial connections, cutting, for example, in the same sequence from a hut in the Amazon to a church in Portugal – the famous Igreja Bom Jesus do Monte outside Braga – and then to the statues of the Twelve Prophets of Aleijadinho – the famous Brazilian Baroque sculptures that stand in front of the Sanctuary of Bom Jesus de Matosinhos in Minas Gerais. Shot in cinemascope, the film consequently not only suspends linear time but also the coherence of space, establishing an imaginary geography that is both testimony to (post)-colonial distance and proximity.

Accordingly, the lusophone world appears to be intertwined not by its language, but by the crossing of borders. This is initially related to the individuals' passions and sexual relationships (Bocage's adventures with Mantegui, a concubine from the Persian Gulf in the first canto; the *ménage à trois* between Bocage, Olinda and Alzira in the second canto; and the liaison between Bocage and Jocindo in the third canto), but becomes allegorical and political in the end. The third canto brings the political bonds to the foreground: on the one hand, regarding the colonial and imperial past and, on the other, concerning the long awaited end of the authoritarian regimes that characterized the twentieth century in both Portugal and Brazil. This is when the protagonist begins to comprehend a number of restraints: first of his erotic poetry and his desire to become an immortal poet, and then of his country's imperial splendour. Only when he comes to recognize art as being political, in the sense that love is a metaphor of both individual and collective freedom (in a sequence that alludes to the Carnation Revolution of 1974 and the recent end of Brazil's dictatorship), does he qualify for immortality and is crowned in the epilogue with an olive branch.

Aesthetically stunning and politically daring, Djalma Limongi Batista's film is a vital contribution to the art of literary adaptation. In the context of postcolonial cinema, his questioning of the prevailing myths of lusotropicalism and lusophony by proposing the existence of both identity and difference is outstanding: he actually redefines the transnational bonds between former colonizer and ancient colony.

Carolin Overhoff Ferreira

The Deceased

A Falecida

Studio/Distributor:

Herbert Richers Produções Cinematográficas, Produções Cinematográficas Meta

Director:

Leon Hirszman

Producers:

Joffre Rodrigues
Aluisio Leite Garcia

Screenwriters:

Leon Hirszman
Eduardo Coutinho (adapted from the eponymous play by Nelson Rodrigues, 1953)

Synopsis

The Deceased, directed by Leon Hirszman in 1965, is based on the eponymous 1953 play by Brazil's most important playwright, Nelson Rodrigues (b.1912–d.1980). It tells the story of Zulmira, a suburban housewife in Rio de Janeiro who suffers from tuberculosis and becomes obsessed with her own death. She lives in a house with her unemployed husband Tuninho and her mother, who remain for the most part oblivious to her deteriorating physical and mental health. Zulmira dreams of having a luxurious and expensive funeral as a way of showing off to her neighbours and especially to her cousin Glorinha, whom she considers snobbish and moralistic. She visits the local undertakers and browses their catalogue for the most expensive coffin and hearse. In the meantime, her husband spends his time playing pool and worrying about the football derby Vasco X Fluminense, scheduled for the following Sunday. On Saturday, however, Zulmira's health takes a turn for the worse. On her deathbed, she begs Tuninho to go see a man called Pimentel, a rich and shady character who she guarantees will pay for her dream funeral.

Cinematographer:

José Medeiros

Art Director:

Régis Monteiro

Composer:

Radamés Gnattali

Editor:

Nello Melli

Duration:

85 minutes

Genre:

Drama

Cast:

Fernanda Montenegro
Ivan Candido
Paulo Gracindo
Nelson Xavier

Year:

1965

Critique

From the 1950s onwards, Brazilian cinema 'discovered' Nelson Rodrigues. A controversial figure, hated by the conservative right for his domestic dramas filled with sex, incest, prostitution, abjection and dirty hidden secrets, and by the left for his supposed political conservatism and support for the military regime (1964–85), Rodrigues was a revolutionary playwright, whose influence spanned decades and reached beyond the stage. Film producers gradually realized that Rodrigues's colourful stories, built around Rio de Janeiro's middle and lower-middle classes, had strong cinematographic potential. After a series of tame adaptations in the 1950s, and with the relaxation of censorship in the early 1960s, films such as *Boca de ouro/The Golden Mouth* (Nelson Pereira dos Santos, 1963) and *Bonitinha, mas ordinária* (Billy Davis, 1963) got closer to the spirit of the plays, and the wave of Rodrigues adaptations lasted up until the early 1990s.

The Deceased, however, appeared at the height of the *Cinema Novo* movement (see the chapter on *Cinema Novo* in this volume). Leon Hirszman himself had made his directorial debut with an episode in *Cinco vezes favela/Five Times Favela* (1962), one of the first *Cinema Novo* films, followed by a series of documentaries that set him out as a politically committed director. Therefore, his move towards a Rodrigues adaptation did not seem like a natural choice for him, especially in the aftermath of the 1964 military coup. Yet, and as the film itself shows, Hirszman's take on Rodrigues, despite being faithful with regards to the fable, distances itself in many ways from the original play. Structurally, the film does away with the three-act dramatic punctuation of the original text and consequently has events flow rather than spring up at the end of each act. Small but important changes to the story also help smooth out the narrative drive or attenuate the ironies of the original play. One example is the crucial scene of Zulmira's death, consummated as a serious event in the film while in the play the audience hears about it from Tuninho's friends, at the end of the second act. Rodrigues thus trivializes her death – there is even comment on her bad timing by 'choosing to die' on the eve of the football derby, whereas Hirszman treats it as a tragic event. But it is perhaps the cinematographic style, much in tune with the *Cinema Novo* in its use of natural lighting and hand-held cameras, which most clearly removes the film from Rodrigues's world. Shot on location in the suburbs of Rio de Janeiro and in black-and-white stock, *The Deceased* unfolds in and out of ugly, drab houses, through grey and rainy streets. Dialogue is for the most part restrained and grave, much in contrast with the play's nimbleness and excesses. Technical awkwardness, especially in the editing and sound, helps to dampen the mood. It is thus significant that Tuninho's desire to go to the beach at some point in the film is met with a resounding 'no' by Zulmira, for the beach does not fit into the bleak and gloom that impregnate not only her life but also the film's style.

The Deceased collected the odd award in Brazil but was ultimately a commercial fiasco, which left Nelson Rodrigues and his son Joffre, one of the producers, dismayed and in great debt. Today, it stands out especially for Fernanda Montenegro's cinematographic debut as Zulmira. Already a well-established stage actor, whose credits included some of Rodrigues's plays, Montenegro's anti-naturalist performance of a suburban Bovary from Rio de Janeiro is testament to why she came to be one of the country's most accomplished actors to date.

Cecília Mello

Hour of the Star

A Hora da estrela

Studio/Distributor:

Raíz Produções
Cinematográficas

Director:

Suzana Amaral

Producer:

Assunção Hernandes

Screenwriters:

Suzana Amaral
Alfredo Oroz

Cinematographer:

Edgar Moura

Art Director:

Clovis Bueno

Composer:

Marcus Vinícius

Editor:

Idê Lacreta

Duration:

96 minutes

Genre:

Drama

Cast:

Marcélia Cartaxo
José Dumont
Tamara Taxman
Fernanda Montenegro

Year:

1986

Synopsis

Based on Clarice Lispector's homonymous novel, Suzana Amaral's first film was an Oscar nominee for best foreign picture in 1986. It features an extraordinary character, Macabea, an immigrant from the poor north-east region of Brazil, who leads a humble and dreary life in São Paulo, where she works, even though almost illiterate, as a typist. Macabea captures our sympathy with her attempts to fill her dull and solitary existence in the consumer society of the huge city with extravagances such as drinking Coca-Cola, listening to unrelated facts on a radio show and by falling in love with an equally uncultured man from the same background. Olímpico de Jesus lacks, however, her daring for knowledge and romance: his aim is to become a politician, and probably a corrupt one. He treats Macabea with disdain and finally replaces her with her co-worker Gloria, an experienced and socially more appealing woman who charms him following the advice of a Tarot-card reader. After having taken her boyfriend away, Gloria sends Macabea to the same fortune-teller who promises her that she will meet a rich foreigner. The encounter actually occurs, but with an ironic twist.

Critique

The film was an international success that won a number of national and international awards and gained its starring actress the Silver Bear in Berlin. The intriguing character is deeply convincing in her desire for a better life, and also moving, since she is so obviously trapped in her marginal existence and highly limited cultural horizons. *Hour of the Star* raises issues related to feminism (especially with regard to the macho boyfriend), and concerns the culture industry and commodity fetishism (the intent to assemble knowledge from mass media and the fascination with advertisements), as well as labour exploitation and the general lack of education in Brazil.

While based on Lispector's novella, which is set in the more flamboyant Rio de Janeiro, *Hour of the Star* focuses on the depiction of the lower classes in the country's biggest city, São Paulo, with great detail. In the book, this portrayal is foregrounded by means of a male narrator from the upper class who constantly ponders self-reflexively on how to write a story on the disadvantaged. Given its interest in reality and its dismissal of melodrama, the original text came to be considered a revision of neo-realism and a step away from the writer's famous introspection. In her cinematographic take on the story, the director discards the reflexive dimension and thus heightens the sense of realism. Although the film's narrative technique is based

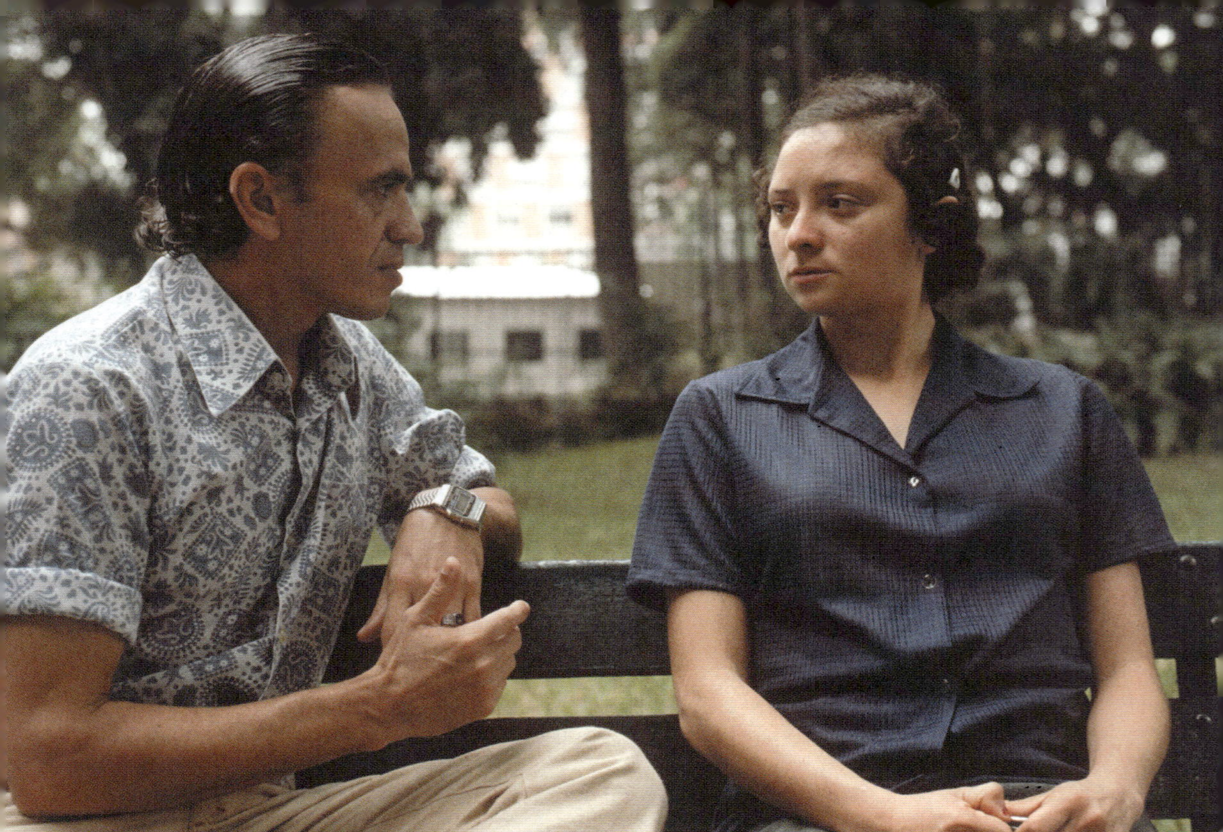

Hour of the Star

on conventional shot/reverse-shot editing and on the psychological motivations of the characters, there are original aesthetic strategies that challenge our perception of lower-class reality, mainly through the observation of details that speak for themselves. The strength of the film lies, in fact, in the depiction of Macabea's solitary moments: when she drips the sauce of her hotdog on her work place, looks at her face in old, dirt-flecked mirrors, walks dreamily through the streets of São Paulo, pees in a pot while eating a chicken leg, or when she cuts out ads from magazines.

Consequently, the film distinguishes itself from Brazil's *Cinema Novo* by lacking social allegorization or self-reflexive editing. Nonetheless, Suzana Amaral recently mentioned in a talk at the Brazilian Cinematheque in São Paulo that her film was meant to be a comment on the end of the dictatorship. She intended through her main character to show that people did not act for themselves, that they were manipulated and, ultimately, uncreative. 'Macabea is the face of Brazil,' she noted. While identity construction might have changed, the film is still what the film-maker desired it to be: an honest portrayal of the dreams and impediments of Brazil's working class.

Carolin Overhoff Ferreira

Mutum

Studio/Distributor:

Ravina Filmes, Gloria Films

Director:

Sandra Kogut

Producers:

Flávio R Tambellini
Laurent Lavolé
Isabelle Pragier

Screenwriters:

Ana Luiza Martins Costa
Sandra Kogut (adapted from the
novella Campo Geral, by João
Guimarães, 1956)

Cinematographer:

Mauro Pinheiro Jr

Art Director:

Marcos Pedroso

Editor:

Sérgio Mekler

Duration:

104 minutes

Genre:

Drama

Cast:

Thiago da Silva Mariz
Wallison Felipe Leal Barroso
João Miguel

Year:

2007

Synopsis

Mutum is based on the novella *Campo Geral*, written by João
Guimarães Rosa, 1956, considered Brazil's most important writer of
the twentieth century. Due to his verbal exuberance and linguistic
innovations, he has often been compared to James Joyce. The film
tells the story of 10-year-old Thiago who lives with his four siblings,
father, mother, grandmother, uncle, a maid and a worker in the poor
backlands of Minas Gerais, far away from any urban centre, medical
support or school. We look at the world through his eyes. The
relationships among and with the adults are often difficult and strange.
His beloved uncle leaves the farm after a fight between his mother and
his father. Thiago does not quite understand why, but we guess that his
mother and uncle are in love. His father treats him with condescension
for his dreamy nature, but Thiago defies his loyalty when the uncle
tries to get in touch with the mother. After his other son, Felipe, dies
from a fever, the already violent father starts losing control. To be safe,
Thiago is sent away to become a cowboy. Shortly after, his father kills
the farm worker and his uncle returns with him to the family. But his life
is destined to be different. A physician who passes by discovers that
his behaviour is a result of his poor eyesight and suggests taking him to
the big city where he will get medical care and an education.

Critique

The film is a delicate and sensual adaptation of Guimarães Rosa's
autobiographical book about the boy Miguilim and transposes the
story from the 1950s to the reality of contemporary times. Point-of-
view shots and extreme close-ups immerse us in Thiago's universe,
the imaginary of childhood and of the Brazilian backlands. The
simplicity of the lives of the characters and complete lack of material
distractions bring the human relationships to the fore, especially
those between Thiago and his family: his strong bond with his
mother, his desire to be loved by his father, his admiration for and
companionship with his uncle, the deep complicity with his younger
brother Felipe who dies unexpectedly after cutting his foot, and his
trust in the maid Rosa.

Albeit a fiction feature, *Mutum* blurs the line that usually separates
the documentary from the fictional, using semi-amateur actors who
not only live in the region but were also prepared for their roles
in workshops. Then they lived together for two months with the
professional actors on the small farm, where the film was shot. Sandra
Kogut had prepared the entire film for a year and a half, in which she
travelled through the region, looking for the actors and the location.
The poetic strength of the film derives, indeed, from the truthful
reconstruction of the living conditions and feelings of the characters,
as well as from low-key dramatization. The cinematography does
not aim for picturesque images but, rather, shows us how Thiago
perceives the details of the world that surrounds him and whose
mysteries he tries to comprehend.

Given Guimarães Rosa's specific literary style, it would seem
difficult to translate his descriptions and dialogues into sounds and

images. Yet the film remains not only close to the plot, but also close to its spirit. The alteration of the title from *Campo Geral* (General Field), which might be interpreted as a metaphorical indication of the universality of Miguilim's issues, to *Mutum*, the factual name of the isolated region where the main character lives, offers a clue to Kogut's adaptation strategy. 'Mutum' is less figurative but accumulates a symbolic richness, since it not only defines a place but also a bird; as a palindrome it is also an acoustic sign that suggests density or circularity. Accordingly, the tale of Thiago's transition to adulthood is engaged in a palpable reality, rendering tangible its symbolic dimension. The last scene, in which he asks to borrow glasses from the physician who will take him to the city, demonstrates this characteristic most poetically. When he puts on the glasses, Thiago smiles, and we see through point-of-view shots his family members, his house and its surroundings. It all looks as it did before, but we know that Thiago sees it differently, factually and figuratively; and so do we.

Carolin Overhoff Ferreira

Mutum

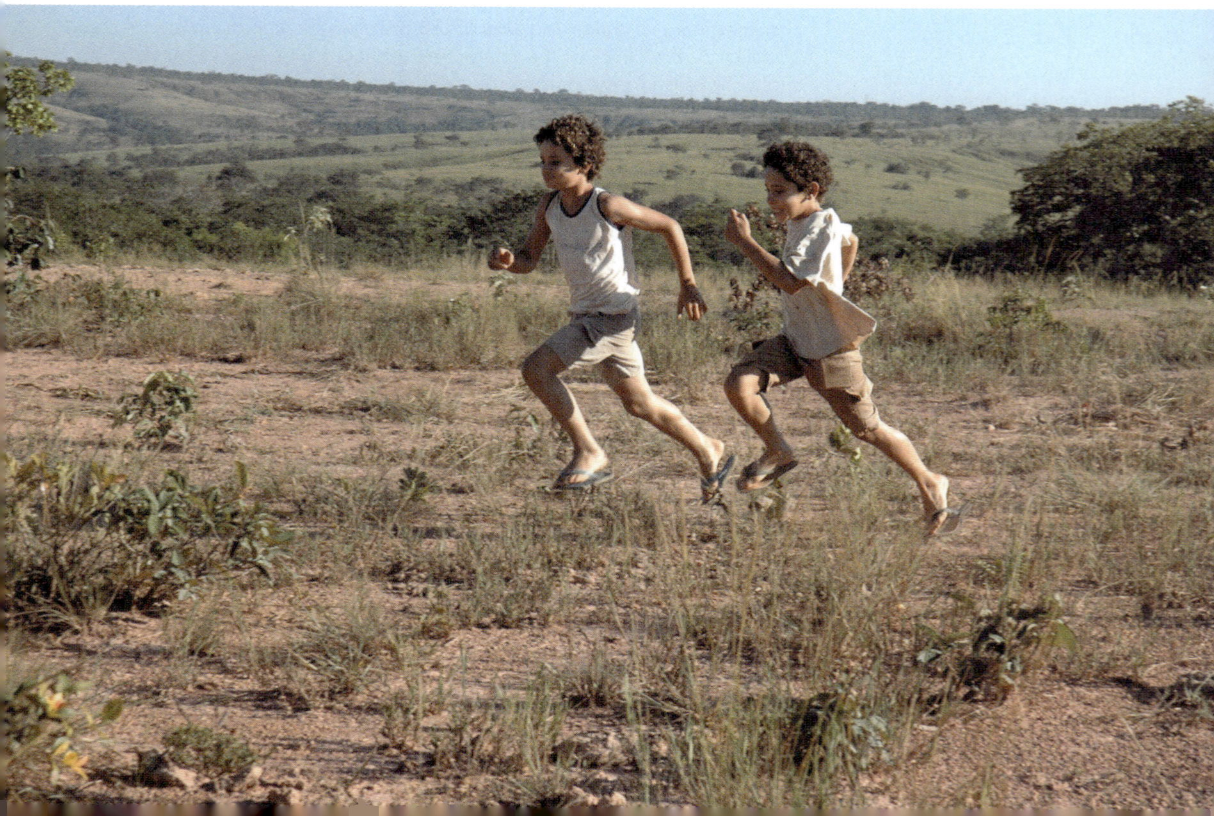

Prison Memories

Memórias do cárcere

Studio/Distributor:

Embrafilme, Luiz Carlos Barreto
Produções Cinematográficas,
Regina Filmes

Director:

Nelson Pereira dos Santos

Producers:

Lucy Carlos Barreto
Luiz Carlos Barreto
Nelson Pereira dos Santos

Screenwriter:

Nelson Pereira dcs Santos
(adapted from the eponymous
novel by Graciliano Ramos,
1953)

Cinematographers:

José Medeiros
Antonio Luiz Soares

Art Director:

Irenio Maia

Composer:

Louis Moreau Gottschalk

Editor:

Carlos Alberto Camuyrano

Duration:

185 minutes

Genre:

Drama

Cast:

Carlos Vereza
Glória Pires
Jofre Soares
José Dumont

Year:

1984

Synopsis

Prison Memories is Nelson Pereira dos Santos's powerful adaptation of Graciliano Ramos's (b.1892–d.1953) eponymous book, a first-person account of the writer's unfair imprisonment from March 1936 to January 1937, during the second phase of Getúlio Vargas's government (1934–37). Ramos was already a well-established writer living in the state of Alagoas when he was caught on the repressive wave against left-wingers and sympathizers following the *Intentona Comunista* of 1935, a failed attempt at a communist revolution against Vargas's dictatorial government, led by the leader of the Brazilian Communist Party, Luís Carlos Prestes. The film follows Ramos's account of a descent into hell, from an ordinary jail in Alagoas to a correctional facility in Rio de Janeiro and finally to a penal colony in Ilha Grande, an island off the coast of the state of Rio de Janeiro. Through his ordeal, Ramos meets a myriad of characters, instrumental in providing him with the means to keep writing inside the prison, from finding pen and paper to protecting the final manuscript. He is also supported by his wife, a faithful champion of his work and a vital connection to the outside world.

Critique

Nelson Pereira dos Santos's first adaptation of a Graciliano Ramos novel was *Vidas secas/Barren Lives* (1963), a landmark film of the aesthetically-daring *Cinema Novo* movement. In his second adaptation, made 21 years later, the director remained much closer to a classical style in its tight-weaved narrative, psychologically-rounded characters and continuity editing. The film was a box office success and received positive reviews by critics, as well as the FRIPESCI Award at the 1984 'Cannes Film Festival'.

Despite preserving the spirit of the book, the director allowed for certain changes in the original account of Ramos's incarceration, such as reducing the number of characters and situations and, at times, rearranging the order of events. One of the most significant variations from page to screen, testament to the director's creative approach, can be found at the end of the film. As Ramos finally learns that he will be released from the Penal Colony at Ilha Grande, he realizes that his manuscript is bound to be confiscated by the prison wardens, who know about his secret writing. In a touching scene, conceived by Nelson Pereira dos Santos, the manuscript is handed over from one prisoner to another, each hiding a single page and thus saving it from destruction. In reality, Ramos lost the manuscript in prison and only started writing his memories ten years after the event (the book's unfinished version was edited posthumously months after his death in 1953). The invented final scene symbolizes, however, more than a concession to melodrama: by putting the manuscript's fate in the hands of all the prisoners, the director bestowed a collective dimension upon an individual experience, highlighting the importance of common effort and of solidarity in the fight against repression. This is also in tune with the character development of Ramos and his wife in the film. Before his imprisonment, which followed his dismissal from a government post in the education department of the state of Alagoas, the couple led a conventional life in the capital Maceió. At that time, the writer still had a romantic notion of life behind bars, and even saw it as a means to escape from another prison, that is, his tedious domestic life. With time, following the series of arbitrary transfers and the gradual deterioration of prison conditions, described in detail in the book and faithfully depicted in the film, Ramos's views inevitably evolve. From a taciturn and somewhat conceited man, he gradually opens up to the other prisoners – both political and common – and this is instrumental in building his political awareness and sense of solidarity. His relationship with his wife also changes, for she proves to be a lot more than a plain housewife, taking the long trip to Rio de Janeiro to visit him in prison, providing constant support for his work and fighting for his rights. Carlos Vereza as Graciliano Ramos and Glória Pires as Heloísa Ramos give remarkable performances that greatly contribute to the film's accomplishment.

The significance of Ramos's book as a portrayal of an important period of Brazilian history, tainted by injustice and repression, gained another level of significance with Nelson Pereira dos Santos's film. Made in 1984, on the eve of the democratic opening of the country that followed more than two decades of military regime, *Prison Memories* looks at the 1930s with a nod to the equally repressive and unjust 1960s and 1970s, when history proved to be painfully cyclical. Punctuated by extracts of Gottschalk's 'Grand Fantasy on the Brazilian National Anthem' (1869), the film articulates a powerful comment on the state of the nation, ending on a hopeful note for more fraternal days.

Cecília Mello

Prison Memories/
Memórias do cárcere

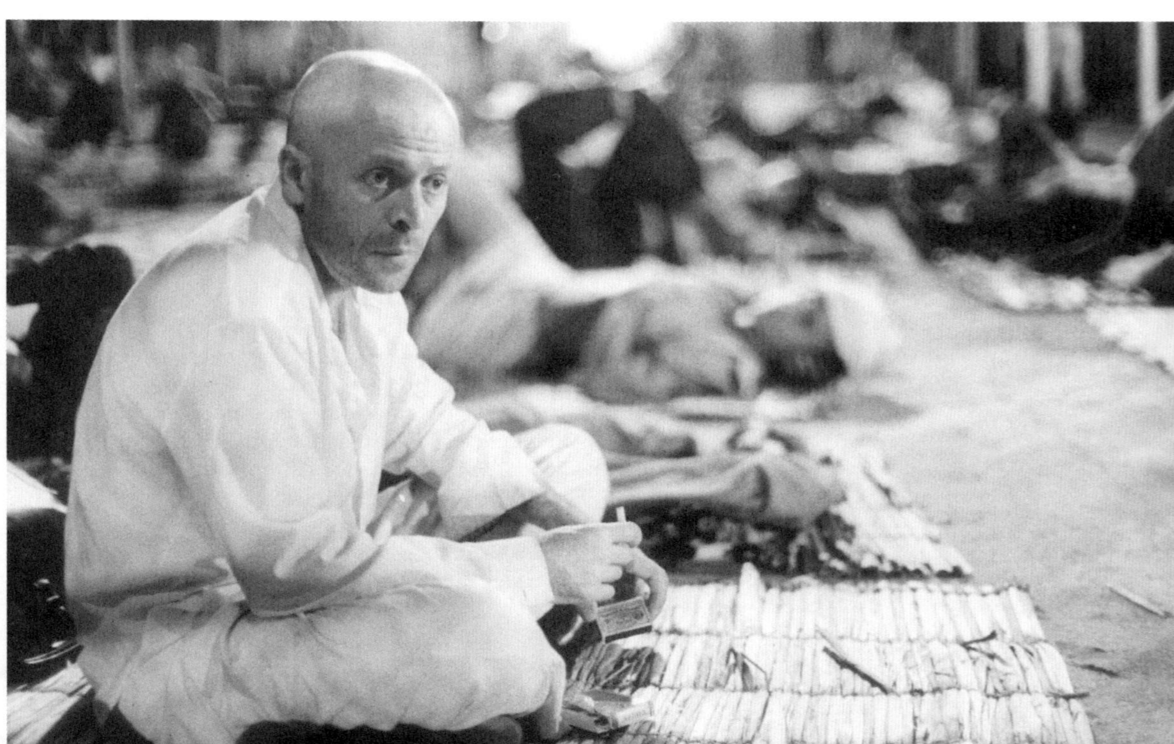

Tent of Miracles

Tenda dos milagres

Studio/Distributor:

Regina Filmes

Director:

Nelson Pereira dos Santos

Producers:

Tininho Nogueira da Fonseca
Carlos Alberto Diniz
Francisco Drummond

Screenwriters:

Jorge Amado
Nelson Pereira dos Santos
(adapted from the eponymous
novel by Jorge Amado, 1969)

Cinematographer:

Helio Silva

Art Director:

Tizuka Yamasaki

Synopsis

Tent of Miracles, based on a novel by Jorge Amado (b.1912–d.2001), shifts between the past and the present in order to make sense of the life and deeds of fictional character Pedro Archanjo. A beadle at the School of Medicine in Bahia, Archanjo begins researching and writing books which champion racial crossbreeding as the solution to the country's problems. His doctrine merges science and popular culture, the first linked to a generic European heritage and the second to Afro-Brazilian traditions. As his ideas become increasingly popular among the students, Archanjo is fired and persecuted by Professor Nilo Argolo, who is radically opposed to the notion of racial integration. Archanjo, however, continues to exert his influence by moving in different circles, from the *candomblé* celebrations to the houses of the white elite in Bahia. He remains true to his ideas to the very end, but is virtually forgotten after his death. His name is later revived by American scientist and Nobel Prize Winner Dr Livingstone, a professor of anthropology at Columbia who had come to Brazil for a series of master classes, and who celebrates Archanjo as one of the greatest intellectuals of the twentieth century.

Critique

Tent of Miracles, adapted to the screen by director Nelson Pereira dos Santos and author Jorge Amado, begins at the editing table,

ent of Miracles

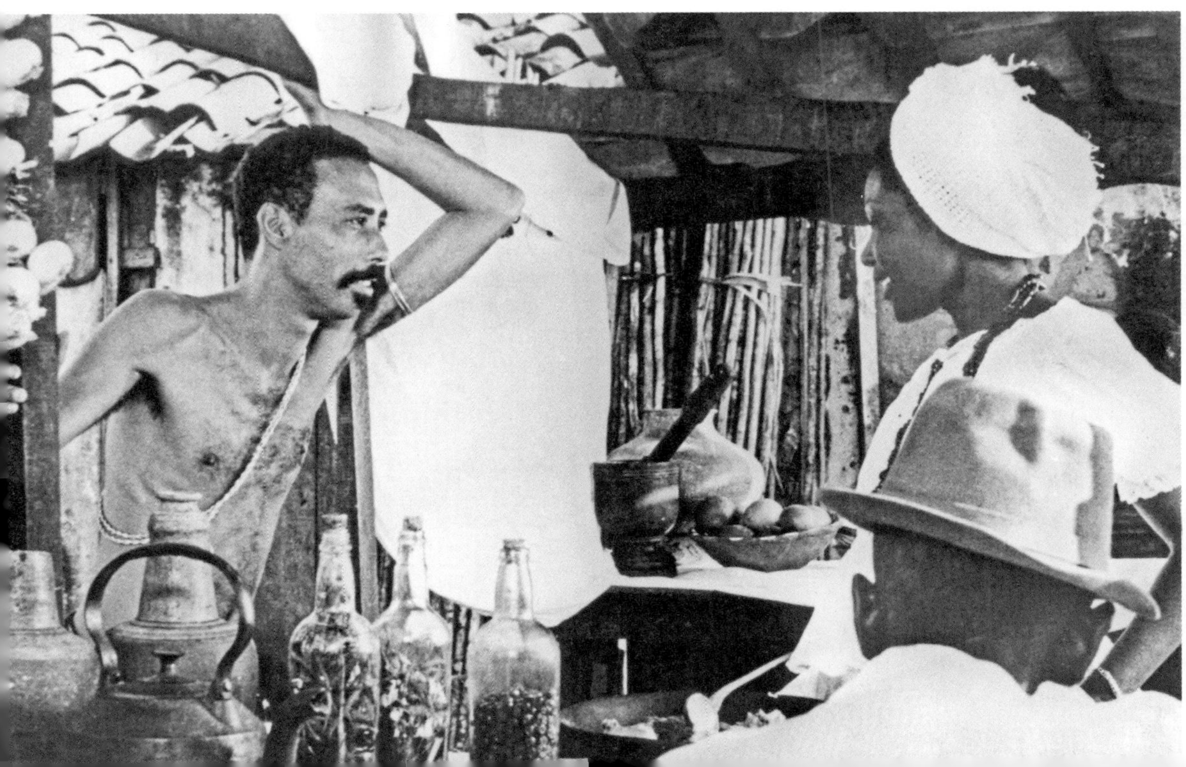

Composer:

Jards Macalé

Editors:

Raimundo Higino
Severino Dadá

Duration:

135 minutes

Genre:

Drama

Cast:

Hugo Carvana
Sonia Dias
Anecy Rocha
França Teixeira

Year:

1977

where journalist Fausto Pena and his assistant Dadá are cutting a film based on the life of Pedro Archanjo. The character is introduced by Pena as 'a *baiano* from the past, described by the police as a poor smartass mulatto, but who in fact is one of the greatest social scientists in the world'. *Tent of Miracles* then starts to shift between the present time of the edit, the recent past of Dr Livingstone's visit to Brazil that prompted the making of Pena's film, and the filmic account of Archanjo's life, which spans from the late nineteenth century to the first decades of the twentieth century. It thus incorporates a self-reflexive stance into investigation reminiscent of *Citizen Kane* (Orson Welles, 1941), which starts from a man's death (the first scene of Pena's film indeed shows Archanjo's final moments in the 1940s) and goes on to build a mosaic of a man's life. Through the film's complex *mise en abyme* structure, Archanjo, based on black intellectual Manuel Querino (b.1851–d.1923), gradually comes to life but ultimately preserves an aura of mystery. What was his real contribution to Brazilian anthropological theories and to racial equality? Is he indeed a hero or just a highly intelligent man with original ideas? In its somewhat puzzling structure, *Tent of Miracles* leaves these questions unanswered, adding a new layer of self-reflexivity by concomitantly indulging in and questioning cinema's role in the making of myths. It interrogates further to what extent Brazilian society has evolved since Archanjo's time, for it is in fact the ironically-named and caricatured American professor who reawakens interest in Archanjo's legacy, until then forgotten by his own people.

Tent of Miracles belongs to a long list of film, television and stage adaptations of Jorge Amado's work, which also includes a second film by director Nelson Pereira dos Santos, *Jubiabá* (1986) and the famous *Dona Flor e seus dois maridos/Dona Flor and Her Two Husbands* (Bruno Barreto, 1976). The author is one of Brazil's most renowned fictional writers and has been translated worldwide. Constant themes in his work, which are also central to *Tent of Miracles*, are the Afro-Brazilian syncretist religion of *candomblé* and the sensuous nature of Brazilian women, exemplified by the character Ana Mercedes and her uninhibited approach to sex in the novel and the film. It could be argued that *Tent of Miracles* largely incorporates the syncretic nature of *candomblé* and Amado's synaesthetic descriptions not only as the basis for Archanjo's original thought but also into its self-reflexive structure, colourful art direction, layered soundtrack and music, and fragmented narrative style. It is perhaps here, and not at the level of the fable – where racial tensions seem to be easily resolved or forgotten – that the film's political force resides.

Cecília Mello

To the Left of the Father

Lavoura arcaica

Studio/Distributor:

Tibet Filme
VideoFilmes

Director:

Luiz Fernando Carvalho

Producers:

Mauricio Andrade Ramos
Raquel Couto
Donald K Ranvaud

Screenwriter:

Luiz Fernando Carvalho
(adapted from the eponymous
novel by Raduan Nassar, 1975)

Cinematographer:

Walter Carvalho

Art Director:

Yurika Yamasaki

Composer:

Marco Antônio Guimarães

Editor:

Luiz Fernando Carvalho

Duration:

171 minutes

Genre:

Drama

Cast:

Selton Mello
Raul Cortez
Juliana Carneiro da Cunha
Simone Spoladore

Year:

2001

Synopsis

To the Left of the Father, based on Raduan Nassar's first novel from 1975, is the story of André, the son of a large family of Lebanese immigrants living in the Brazilian countryside during the first half of the twentieth century. His father is an authoritarian figure who keeps tight control over his sons and daughters, all of whom work on the family farm. Sitting at the head of the table, he pontificates about the virtues of a restrained and traditional life, close to God and the land. Conversely, André's mother appears as a loving, albeit passive, individual. One day, the stability of their lives is shaken by André's decision to abandon the family and move to the city. Wishing to restore order, the parents send their eldest son Pedro to find André and bring him back to the family nest. The film unfolds in a series of flashbacks, starting from the moment Pedro finds his younger brother in a dingy hotel room, and then alternating between the present time of their encounter, memories of their idyllic childhood on the farm and the events which immediately preceded André's departure.

Critique

To the Left of the Father has often been described as a variation on the Parable of the Prodigal Son. André desires to escape his father's rule but ends up returning home, with the promise to work hard and follow the path of the righteous. However, during his welcome party, it becomes clear that he still has feelings for his sister – the real reason why he left in the first place – and that she continues to tempt him. The family's destruction is complete when the father realizes what had been going on between his son and daughter, striking her in wrath with a sickle.

Luiz Fernando Carvalho has worked extensively since the 1980s for Brazilian television network Globo, directing big-budget soap operas and mini-series. *To the Left of the Father* was his cinematic debut and is to date his only feature film. His adaptation remains faithful to the original text, with minor changes to the order of events. The book is narrated in the first person by André, and the film employs a curious strategy to convey the story from his point of view: most of the flashback sequences that illustrate the brothers' conversation inside the hotel room are accompanied by a voice-over, taken verbatim from Nassar's book, but spoken by director Luiz Fernando Carvalho. The fact that his voice differs considerably in tone and in accent from actor Selton Mello's (André) creates a sense of estrangement in relation to the main character.

Nassar's book is rich in poetic language and florid descriptions which are incorporated into the film's style. The childhood sequences, for instance, are bathed in a soothing light, much in tune with André's idyllic memories of a time free from temptation and sin. From there the film moves on to the awakening of his incestuous lust, and the camera seems to get even closer to the actors' faces, hands and skin, to the leaves on the ground, to details inside the house, fragmenting the space and the bodies and lingering on each of them. The soundtrack greatly contributes to this visually rich atmosphere, combining Lebanese musical motifs with farm and city sounds, such as the wind brushing on the leaves and the whistle of a train. The flashback sequences are intercut with dark images inside the hotel room, where both brothers seem to hide in the shadows of their own fears and secrets. It is clear that the director's desire was to 'suggest' rather than to 'show'. Despite his use of the voice-over narration and of key dialogue sequences, the film is not built around the 'word'. A central character such as Ana, for instance, does not have a single line, while her whole body is constantly dissected by a tactile camera. Carvalho's over-reliance on poetic images, however, ends up replacing subtlety with excess, partly undermining the film and the novel's original take on a difficult subject.

Cecília Mello

The Trespasser

O Invasor

Studio/Distributor:

Drama Filmes

Director:

Beto Brant

Producers:

Renato Ciasca
Bianca Villar

Screenwriters:

Beto Brant
Marçal Aquino
Renato Ciasca (adapted from
the eponymous novel by Marçal
Aquino, 1997)

Cinematographer:

Toca Seabra

Art Director:

Yukio Sato

Composers:

Rica Amabis
Daniel Ganjaman
Paulo Miklos
Sabotage
Tejo

Editor:

Manga Campion

Duration:

97 minutes

Synopsis

Giba, Ivan and Estêvão, former college friends, are now partners in a construction firm. Estêvão holds the financial control of the business and is radically opposed to establishing shady deals with the government in exchange for highly lucrative building contracts. Ivan and Giba realize that Estêvão stands between them and their ambitions. Under Giba's influence, they decide to hire a hit man to kill Estêvão, making it look like a robbery-homicide. They meet the assassin Anísio in a poor suburb of the city and seal the deal. A few days later, Estêvão and his wife are found dead inside their car. All seems to have gone to plan until one day Anísio decides to show up unannounced at their construction firm. The trespasser gradually infiltrates their lives and the firm's routine, becoming an uncomfortable presence which cannot be extirpated. He also befriends Marina, Estêvão's only daughter, who lives in a mansion and spends her days in a daze of drugs, alcohol and electronic music, unaware that her new lover is in fact her parents' killer. While Giba keeps his cool, Ivan descends into an increasing paranoia, tormented by his crime, a failing marriage and an affair with a mysterious woman.

Critique

The Trespasser is based on the eponymous novel by Marçal Aquino, a journalist, screenwriter and novelist based in the city of São Paulo. It is also the third collaboration between Aquino and director Beto Brant after *Os Matadores/Belly Up* (1997) and *Ação entre amigos/ Friendly Fire* (1998). Aquino's work belongs to the crime-genre trend in contemporary Brazilian literature, inaugurated by Rubem Fonseca's narratives of urban violence from the 1960s onwards. The film follows the book quite closely, with few alterations to the plot. In an attempt to get closer to the tough reality of São Paulo's streets, it incorporates the agility of the novel's writing into its style, with a fast-paced narrative, fragmented editing structure and hand-held camera.

A lot less photogenic than other Brazilian cities and a fragmented space par excellence, São Paulo retreated to the studios during the

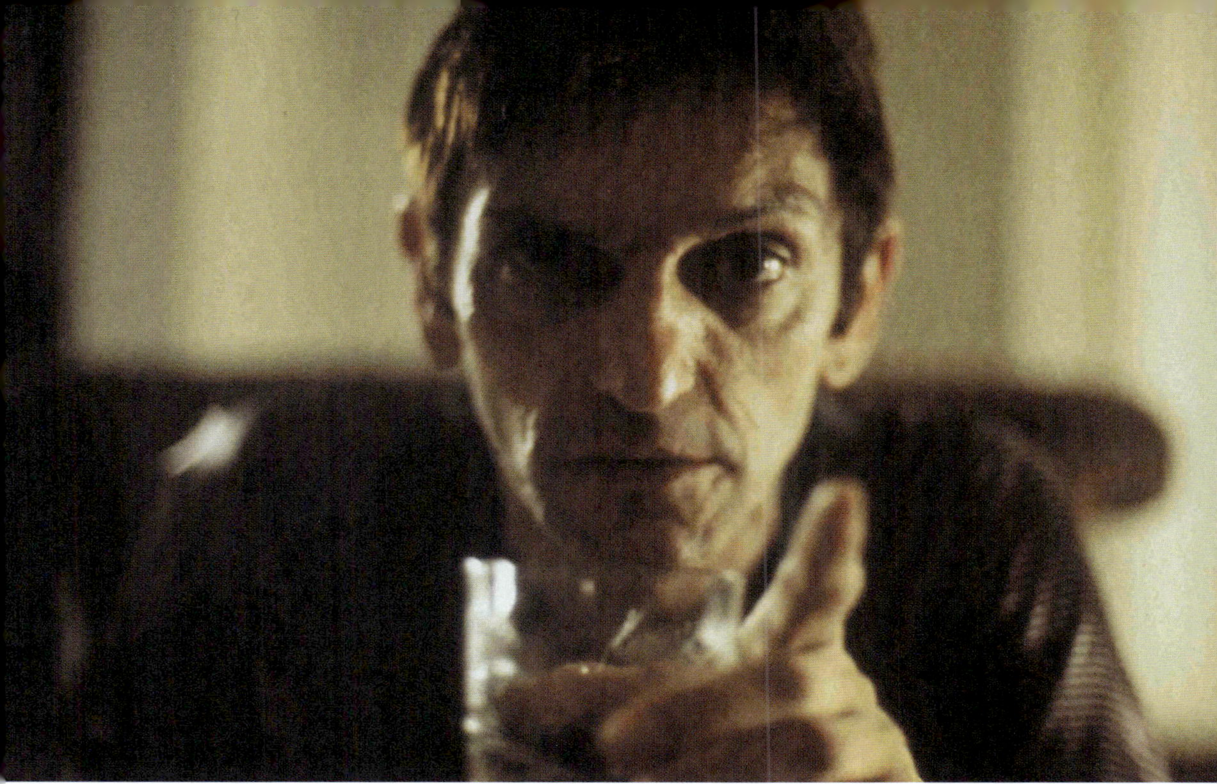

The Trespasser/O invasor

Drama

Cast:

Marco Ricca
Alexandre Borges
Paulo Miklos
Mariana Ximenes

Year:

2002

postmodern 'neon-realist' cycle of the 1980s and early 1990s, with films by the likes of Guilherme de Almeida Prado, Wilson Barros and Francisco Botelho. Conversely, *The Trespasser* is an example of the profuse use of São Paulo as a location in Brazilian films from the mid 1990s onwards, and it exacerbates the presence of the real city by featuring recognizable places, avenues and neighbourhoods. There is also a conscious choice made to magnify the abject side of the city, plagued by poverty and violence, humongous miserable suburbs and an overall lack of harmony, even in the richest areas. This is reminiscent of another cycle in São Paulo's cinema history, the so-called *Cinema Marginal* of Rogério Sganzerla, whose films celebrated the chaotic fragmentation of the metropolis in the late 1960s and early 1970s. Yet *The Trespasser* is very successful in updating its spatial treatment by including elements of street culture such as Brazilian hip hop and electronic music, which punctuate the narrative and give topicality to a story of crime and revenge with Faustian overtones. Paulo Miklos, famous singer of São Paulo's seminal band Titãs, is impeccable in the role of the trespasser/devil, and greatly contributed to the film's success especially among young audiences. *The Trespasser* also features another singer, rapper Sabotage, straight from the violent suburbs of the city where Giba and Ivan first met Anísio. Tragically, Sabotage died a few months after the film came out, another victim of the drug feuds which dominate everyday life in the periphery.

Through its implausible story about a hit man from the suburbs, who comes to the centre to claim a piece for himself, *The Trespasser* manages to capture the tragic fracture that defines a space such as the city of São Paulo, where rich and poor live apart and in fear. It also works as a comment on the degeneration of public institutions such as the police and the government, which appear, much as in reality, as corrupt and unreliable. The final image of Marina, sleeping like a baby after a heavy night out with Anísio, brings the film to an end with the suggestion that if the new generation of privileged youngsters is anything to go by, hope for political change can only exist in a very distant future.

Cecília Mello

Turbulence

Estorvo

Studio/Distributor:

D&D Audiovisuais, Instituto Cubano del Arte e Industrias Cinematográficos (ICAIC), Skylight Cinema Foto Art

Director:

Ruy Guerra

Producers:

Jom Tob Azulay
Miguel Mendoza
Ruy Guerra

Screenwriter:

Ruy Guerra

Cinematographer:

Marcelo Durst

Art Directors:

Raúl Oliva
Cláudio Amaral Peixoto

Composer:

Egberto Gismonti

Editor:

Tony de Castro
Mair Tavares

Duration:

95 minutes

Genre:

Drama

Synopsis

Ruy Guerra's *Turbulence* follows the homonymous novel by Chico Buarque de Holanda (1991) with great precision, but develops an ingenious cinematographic approach to translate the perturbation of the book's protagonist. The main character, referred to as 'I' in the casting list, is a young man who comes from a traditional upper-class family. After a failed marriage and without a job, he lives isolated in an apartment of a city that bears the traces of three metropolises from the co-producing countries: Rio de Janeiro, Lisbon and Havana. When a strange character disturbs him in his sleep, he is alarmed by a familiar gesture that he sees through the peephole and embarks on a paranoid perambulation. Looking for shelter, he visits a couple of familiar places: the posh house of his sister, the workplace and apartment of his ex-wife, the apartment block of an old friend, and the abandoned country house of his family that is now being occupied by drug dealers. It ends fatally, when he is stabbed at a bus stop, but we are uncertain if we are now at the beginning or the end of the story.

Critique [warning: this review necessarily reveals a major plot development]

The shattered family relationships in both book and film stand for Brazil's contemporary society, where alternatives to the patriarchal structure that cause the protagonist's crisis are lacking. The main character's drama derives from rejecting this patriarchal social structure after his father's death, but also from the fact that he has no supplementary project. Since he is paranoid, emotionally and financially dependent on his family, especially on his sister, he is unsuited for the defiance that he intends to enact. What is more, his revolt is restricted to a pact with criminals who live on the family property and to whom he tries to sell jewels stolen from his wealthy sibling.

The upper class, which sustains patriarchal society, is portrayed as neurotic and perverted. They lead a ghettoized lifestyle to protect themselves from the results of the social injustice they nourish and

Cast:

Jorge Perugorría
Bianca Byington
Suzana Ribeiro
Leonora Rocha
Xando Graça

Year:

2000

they react brutally to assaults on their belongings. Symptomatically, the protagonist's brother-in-law denounces not him but the criminals when he burgles their home. The character who triggers off the protagonist's roaming in fact turns out to be a policeman who ends the problem of theft and occupation by means of a massacre. With the reappearance of the strange character the narrative takes the shape of a cycle and it remains unclear if the story starts at its end.

The cyclic structure stresses that the young man's revolt leads ironically to the re-establishment of the social order. It is uncertain if he actually dies when he flees from the scene of the execution to a bus stop and runs into the knife of a startled traveller, or whether this happened before he was disturbed at home, or if everything was only a dream. In any case, the film states that patriarchy is under threat by dissidents like the protagonist, even though he proves ineffective in his anarchic action which implicates him in a crime and is, ultimately, self-destructive. The impact of both film and book lies in demonstrating this dilemma.

There are some alterations with regard to the original novel that expand the main character's crisis of belonging to a profoundly patriarchal and authoritarian society and turn his problem into a transnational issue. *Turbulence* was filmed in three different cities. Since these cities are not recognizable in the shots, this creates the impression that the film could take place in any bigger Ibero-American metropolis and that the story is valid for a larger cultural context. Another strategy to enhance the story's geographical impact occurs on the linguistic level and consists in the use of an eccentric mixture of Portuguese and Spanish by some characters, particularly by the protagonist.

There are two additional cinematographic strategies that participate in the amplification and transnationalization of the protagonist's conflict. The first consists in the duplication of the character into the performing protagonist and an auto-diegetic narrator. The result is twofold. On the one hand, it serves to express the schizophrenic state of the protagonist. On the other, the use of Ruy Guerra's own voice-over and Mozambican accent to articulate the thoughts of the protagonist bears the traces of his transnational belonging, raising multiple questions on authorship. The second strategy derives from shots and images that express the perturbation of the main character by using unfocused lenses, fast camera movements, a vast amount of close-up shots, high paced editing, to name but the most relevant.

Given this set of strategies, it might be argued that the film's aesthetic principle points towards a disturbance that is not only related to the protagonist's Ibero-American crisis, but, more generally, a result of the contemporary world. In the tradition of Franz Kafka's literature that battled with archaic authoritarian mechanisms in the modern world, the film transcends the national towards the transnational by exploring the contemporary paranoid mind.

Carolin Overhoff Ferreira

What's the Price Or Is It by Kilo?

Quanto vale ou é por quilo?

Studio/Distributor:

Agravo Produções
Cinematográficas

Director:

Sérgio Bianchi

Producers:

Patrick Leblanc
Luís Alberto Pereira

Screenwriters:

Eduardo Benaim
Newton Cannito
Sérgio Bianchi (adapted from
Machado de Assis's short story
'Father against Mother', 1906)

Cinematographer:

Marcelo Corpanni

Art Director:

Renata Tessari

Editor:

Paulo Sacramento

Duration:

104 minutes

Genre:

Drama

Cast:

Antonio Abujamra
Caio Blat
Herson Capri
Ana Carbatti
Marcelia Cartaxo
Clara Carvalho
Leona Cavalli
José Rubens Chachá
Caco Ciocler
Joana Fomm
Ênio Gonçalves
Silvio Guindane

Synopsis

The film updates the short story 'Father against Mother' by Brazil's most eminent writer, Machado de Assis (b.1839–d.1908), and uses historical chronicles based on lawsuits from the eighteenth century (compiled by Nireu Cavalcanti) as further material for its multi-narrative.

Oscillating between the colonial period and contemporary times, the story is built around two directors of non-governmental organizations set in Rio de Janeiro whose employees cross with each other constantly in the narrative: Marco Aurélio runs a double-billing scheme in his projects for technological development and Noêmia a perverse rehabilitation centre for homeless people. Arminda, a pregnant social worker from the slums, discovers Marco Aurélio's plot. She assembles proof from her friend Lurdes who is fired from Marco Aurélio's NGO. Mônica, on the other hand, works for Noêmia, whose pregnant niece gets married to Candinho. After losing his job and in an urge to sustain his young family, he becomes an assassin. When Arminda reveals publicly the incriminating material, Candinho is hired to eliminate her. Illustrating that little has changed, the contemporary version of Machado de Assis's young father who turned into a slave hunter and whose prey, a pregnant woman, dies before his eyes when she is returned to the owner, follows the historical version, shown in a flashback just before the modern Candinho kills Arminda.

Critique

The film leaves no doubt that the former slave trade has been substituted by social marketing's exploitation of misery. This argument is put forward with acid humour, irony and parody. It begins like a costume drama. A white man steals the slave of a black woman who had bought her freedom. When the woman protests, she is condemned for public disturbance. Two deeply rooted characteristics of Brazilian society are spelled out right from the beginning: exploitation is continued by the exploited and jurisdiction is based on racism. A comment on the country's perverse socio-economic dynamic is set up in another episode from colonial times: social relationships are always based on profit interest, but are disguised as solidarity. In the present-day narrative, ladies from the middle and upper class act benevolent, but benefit from their financial or social assistance through tax reduction or the possibility to make their workers do extra hours.

The working class, condemned to live at the periphery or in the slums, is neither a naïf nor passive. Arminda takes action and invades an exclusive reception in honour of Marco Aurelio, where he receives yet another award for his social engagement. He appears bandaged, because Dido, the son of his cleaning lady, Dona Judith, had kidnapped him and cut off an ear and a finger to press for ransom. Revolt and violence are, in fact, reactions that the film does not condemn as a response to corruption and exploitation. Rather, they appear as natural outcomes of these factors. That there could be true

Umberto Magnani
Noemi Marinho
Leonardo Medeiros
Cláudia Mello
Danton Mello
Zezé Motta
Bárbara Paz
Teca Pereira
Ariclê Perez
Míriam Pires
Lázaro Ramos
Odelair Rodrigues
Lena Roque
Ana Lúcia Torre

Year:

2005

solidarity among the oppressed is only suggested when the film's credits are half way through. A second ending has Arminda convince Candinho that they should share the money from the corruption scheme, which was deposited in the bank account of the illiterate Dona Judith.

The back-and-forth between different historical moments makes it possible for the spectator to grasp Sérgio Bianchi's idea about the timeless lack of true welfare and social rights. Actors who play roles in the historical episodes reappear in comparable social situations in the contemporary sequences. In part cular, Arminda takes part repeatedly in different roles as a slave. She even has visions of historical characters in modern Rio de Janeiro, as though she was haunted by her earlier existences. Another aesthetic challenge consists in the combination between different modes of storytelling, including parodies of the way in which the media usually represent violence and the disadvantaged. Daydreams may take the shape of an institutional video, directors of publicity spots set up a debate about race, and a news report turns into an ironic testimony of abuse.

Based on Machado de Assis's most thought-provoking and political short story, Bianchi's film brings up the painful suggestion that the colonialist mentality persists in contemporary Brazil.

Carolin Overhoff Ferreira

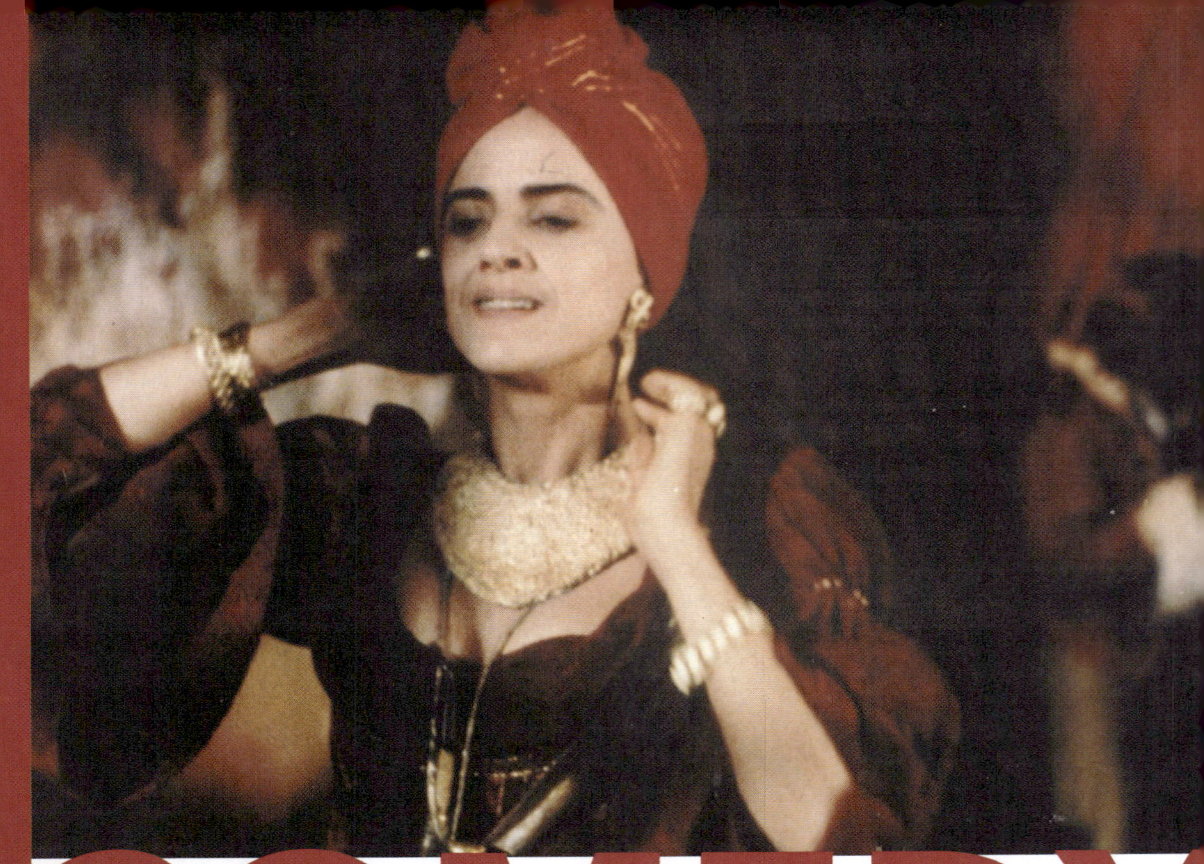

COMEDY

Humour and satire in the Portuguese language trace back to key cultural productions from the *Songs of Mockery and Slander* in the medieval troubadour tradition (1200–1350), to playwright Gil Vicente's farces, Gregório de Matos Guerra's trenchant mockery of colonial life, and Tomás Antônio Gonzaga's *Chilean Letters'* political spoofs, whose scornful spirit is comparable to that of poet Manuel du Bocage and his ridiculing of the presumptions of the Portuguese Empire. Some of the qualities recognizable in today's Brazilian comic films are also found in the Iberian picaresque – the rogue who survives social inequalities – and in Molière's disdain for human deception.

Based on stock characters of popular appeal, these seminal comedy genres share with *Commedia dell'arte* a socio-historic penetrating insight, a carnivalesque flavour, and a gallery of fixed types (*tipi fissi*) whose long-lasting lineage is reminiscent of improvisational Roman comedy. Martins Pena's (b.1815–d.1848) nineteenth-century comedies of manners, which earned him the epithet the 'Brazilian Molière', already hinted at a type of humour which starts with an amiable criticism, then evolves into self-deprecation, in a strategy aimed ultimately at winning over the public and achieving the classical *castigat ridendo mores* [to criticize mores through ridicule – eds]. Musical theatre extravaganzas at the end of the nineteenth century added to these ingredients to create the *chanchada* genre, with which we open the review section of this chapter.[1]

Journalist Arthur Azevedo was celebrated for his agile musical theatre which was inspired by French operetta, and known in Brazil as Review Theatre (*revista*) – an assessment of the preceding year's news on stage, much like the Variety Show, Burlesque and Vaudeville. *Chanchada* effectively transposes these elements to film. With the support of Presdient Getúlio Vargas , who intended to stimulate key sectors of Brazilian industry, the Press and Propaganda Department (DIP) began to set the nationalist agenda – this is when two important measures to protect the Brazilian film market were created: the requirement that a share of national films should appear in theatres and the establishment of the first national studios to produce all-Brazilian films. Thus, movies emulated Hollywood's successes and star system – but with local zest.

The perfection of the *chanchada*, perhaps the quintessential Brazilian film genre, could be said to be found in 1941 with Atlântida, its director Watson Macedo, his disciple Carlos Manga and Croatia-born JB Tanko. It was only in the 1949 Atlântida production *Carnaval no fogo/Carnival on Fire* (Watson Macedo), though, that the model *chanchada* would be crafted, finally emancipating the form from the fragmentary, Ziegfeld Follies-like recipe, and gaining praise for its incipient narrative. The key element in the film was its gallery of comedians: the double act of the well-known Grande Otelo and Spanish-born Oscarito, the former Brazil's Black Chaplin, sometimes the butt of ambiguously racist jokes; the latter offering burlesque cross-dressing numbers; heartthrob Cyl Farney and sweetheart Eliana Macedo, and finally, José Lewgoy, Wilson Grey , and Jesse Valadão as the utmost villains.

Like other *chanchadas* that lampooned Hollywood and high-culture literature – examples are Oscarito's impersonation of *Gilda*, Otelo and Oscarito's *Romeo and Juliet* skit, a caricature of Cecil B DeMille's *Samson and Delilah* (1949), to name a few – Carlos Manga's 1959 *O Homem do Sputnik/The Sputnik Man* is probably the best *chanchada* ever made. In his review, Antônio João Teixeira shows how director Carlos Manga pushes the envelope with his 1960s Cold War parody, beyond the predictable musical fun – noteworthy is TV talk show host and humorist Jô Soares's (1938) debut on the big screen.

Reviewed by Robert Anderson, 1954's *Candinho* is one of the 33 films starring Amacio Mazzaropi. A circus, radio and TV actor, Mazzaropi was introduced to cinema by Abílio Pereira de Almeida, a serious stage and film director. Playing the hillbilly (*caipira*), fish-out-of-water in the big city, Mazzaropi's *caipira* shrewdness was a smash hit in the cinema. Attaining the same level of affection with the public, due especially to her foul-mouthed humour, a circus, *revista*, TV, and film actor of 25 movies, Dercy Gonçalves– a Mae West and Lucille Ball blend – leads *A Baronesa transviada/The Deviant Baroness* (1957), directed by Macedo, where notable comedians Otello Zeloni and Renato Consorte also appeared. In her review, Angélica Coutinho focuses on its basic attraction for the greater public: a comedy of errors and mistaken identity where the commoner is exploited but wins in the end.

In the late 1950s, *chanchadas* reflected both Vargas's nationalism and the euphoria of Juscelino Kubitschek's Golden Years (1951–61), and begin to overlap with *Cinema Novo*'s critical engagement with sociopolitical problems. Directed by Victor Lima and released in 1959, *Os Três cangaceiros/The Three Outlaws* signals such an intersection as it parodies the Brazilian western revolving around the *cangaceiro*, the bandit from the deserted north-east, a true 1960s counter-culture icon – Victor Lima Barreto's 1953 *Cangaceiro* is credited with launching the *cangaço* genre. Alessandra Brandão's review suggests the film's associations with *chanchada*-like parody of another classic – Alexandre Dumas's *The Three Musketeers* (1844). Ronald Golias features here, whose sitcom *Trapo Family*'s (created by Carlos Alberto de Nóbrega and Jô Soares, 1967–71) character named Bronco – the bigmouth brother-in-law – was a 1960s favourite.

Thus, in the 1960s, television lends the popularity of its characters to film – the TV troupe of comedians the Tramps (*Os Trapalhões*), led by Renato Aragão (1935), with Dedé Santana (1936), Mussum and Zacarias are the epitome of this. The Tramps gave their own spin on classics like Ali Baba, Aladdin, Robin Hood and also the *cangaceiro*, among others, all of which were not free of a double edged racist humour, branding actor Mussum with the stereotypical masculinity of the inebriated black man. *Os Saltimbancos trapalhões/The Street Acrobats* (1981), directed by JB Tanko and the sixth out of 33 released by this group, shows the Iberian *picaro* who struggles in the interstices of society, and as Amanda Aouad points out, they reinforce the motto that for the weak only unity is the key to triumph.

Pornochanchada is the goofy risqué type of parody from the 1970s, soft-core porn which bypassed the scrutiny of the infamous 1968 Institutional Act 5 which established pre-emptive censorship of public entertainment. *Histórias que nossas babás não contavam/Stories That Our Baby Sitters Would Not Tell Us* is a piquant version of *Snow White* from 1979, directed by Oswaldo de Oliveira, a master of exploitation topics featuring women in brothels, boarding schools and prison. Presenting Adele Fátima– the archetypal sexy *mulata* – and comedian Costinha, the film also mocked current issues and indulged in homophobic jokes, as Ramayana Lira notes. *Pornochanchadas* were initially produced in São Paulo's red light zone – where prostitutes, pimps and drug dealers wandered freely at night – and was a very lucrative business eagerly supported by independent private initiative.

Like playwright Nelson Rodrigues's cynical comedy of manners, 1978's anarchic *Tudobem/All Is Well* was the sixth out of nine films directed by Arnaldo Jabor. This is a seriocomic piece that uses its domestic setting to portray the staggering Brazilian class divide. Gabriela Lírio informs the readers as much and underlines Jabor's disapproval of the contemptuous middle-class attitude towards the disadvantaged. Internationally acclaimed actor Fernanda Montenegro stars in the movie with radio, stage and TV actor Paulo Gracindo. Zezé Motta also stars, having played important Afro-Brazilian roles both on stage, film, and TV – most notably in Cacá Diegues's 1976 *Xica da Silva*.

The late 1970s is marked by the Ernesto Geisel government, processing his so-called 'dictatorship distension' which gradually led to democracy and popular elections in 1989. The Fernando Collor de Mello government that ensued was not a good one for the film industry, as Embrafilme was terminated. Via new methods of film financing and exhibition, Carla Camurati is credited with the cinema revival in Brazil, known as *retomada*, with her 1995 blockbuster *Carlota Joaquina: princesa do Brasil/Carlota Joaquina: Princess of Brazil*. Possibly incited by the number of studies reflecting upon the 500 years of the 'discovery' of Brazil, the film is a caustic satire disparaging Portuguese political leadership, as Sandra SF Erickson observes in her review. *Carlota Joaquina* stars the superb duo Marieta Severo (and Marco Nanini, also popular in their TV sitcom, *The Great Family* (2001–2013). The film drove legions of film-goers into the theatres and was truly a cultural event of national proportions.

The last two films reviewed are post-*retomada* productions.[2] *O Homem que copiava/The Man Who Copied* (2003) stars TV actors Lázaro Ramos, Leandra Leal, Pedro Cardoso and Luana Piovani. In this understated crime comedy, sarcastic and out-of-money André holds a dead-end job which he loathes and wants out of, as reviewer Patricia Fox notes. The film mixes, first, the implausible accidents and mean chance typical of a comedy of errors, second, references to Hitchcockian voyeurism and believed fidelity to the film production storyboard – André is a talented graphic designer – and, finally, the *Pulp Fiction*-like (Quentin Tarantino, 1994) spin on the bag-full-of-money quest. As such, *The Man Who Copied* may very well stand for director Jorge Furtado's preparation of his own point of view, appropriate to the comment made in *Rear Window* (Alfred Hitchcock, 1954) by Jeff's straight-thinking nurse, Stella: 'We've become a race of Peeping Toms.' Lázaro Ramos's appearance as a regular guy in dire straits consolidates him as a fine actor free of the deleterious Afro-Brazilian male stereotypes.

Lastly, the 2000 cinema version of Ariano Suassuna's 1927 play *O Auto da compadecida/A Dog's Will*, was directed by Globo Network's Guel Arraes, and stars favourites such as Fernanda Montenegro, Marco Nanini and Lima Duarte, besides the new generation double act Matheus Nachtergaele and Selton Mello. In her review below, Leslie March accurately suggests the picaresque inspiration behind Suassuna's creation, with north-eastern spice. The box office success of such productions reinforces the power of TV in the Brazilian film industry, as the major sponsor for commercial viability.

Regina R Félix

Notes
1. Comments on the order of the films refer to their chronological place in the following chapter.
2. Last two chronological, not in the alphabetical order in which they appear below.

All Is Well

Tudobem

Studio/Distributor:

Arnaldo Jabor Produções
Cinematográficas
Embrafilme
Sagitarius Produções
Cinematográficas

Director:

Arnaldo Jabor

Producer:

Arnaldo Jabor

Screenwriters:

Arnaldo Jabor
Leopoldo Serran

Cinematographer:

Dib Lufti

Art Director:

Helio Eichbauer

Editor:

Gilberto Santeiro

Duration:

110 minutes

Genre:

Political allegory

Cast:

Paulo Gracindo
Fernanda Montenegro
Luiz Fernando Guimarães
Zezé Mota

Year:

1978

Synopsis

All Is Well is a portrait of Brazilian society as seen by a middle-class family haunted by ghosts of poverty and guilt in the face of the desire for a better life. The Barata family lives in a dilapidated apartment building that is undergoing renovation and is formed by Mrs Elvira Barata, Mr Juarez Ramos Barata, and their children, Vera and Zé Roberto. There is no eventful storyline in this film as it is an allegorical theatrical rendition of class relations in Brazil and develops as juxtaposed skits illustrating these relations. Past, present and future; ethnic, social and historical types are on stage. Mr Barata represents the official discourse in which he believes that the solution for the country will come from its natural resources and the indigenous peoples. Elvira is a needy woman, deprived of affection and sex, who has fantasies of having an unfaithful spouse; a possibility that excites her. She creates an imaginary rival, a mistress named Valdete, and she incorporates the imaginary rival's mannerisms and traits to ultimately seduce her own husband into much-desired intercourse. Their son and daughter represent the future in terms of business: Zé Roberto is a director of public relations, a profession depicted as the core of marketing and Vera is engaged to a successful American whose business is satellites – he mocks the need for connectedness in the global village. Nothing is more original in the context of a country that has since the 1940s had the motto: 'Brazil, the country of the future.'

Critique

Arnaldo Jabor analyses Brazilian identity by reflecting on the cultural hybridism of a society marked by the economic abyss that separates the classes. *All Is Well* is a portrait of the Brazilian middle class in the 1970s. Jabor analyses a petit-bourgeois family chased by ghosts such as the dread of impending poverty and the fear of sexual expression as delirious ways of escaping life's miseries. *All Is Well* shows their seemingly ordinary daily lives marked by a self-centred petty outlook on the Brazilian social, political and economic difficulties of the time.

In *Tudo Bem* (everything's alright) Juarez questions the direction the country would take in times of political openness. The idealization of the Brazilian people is given a withering critique by the film-maker of the middle class, working from the imagery of a people united in their naïve ignorance and blind generosity. This acts as a way of excusing them as politically unable to transform their alleged compassion into praxis or political action. The 'strong and ignorant' people are placed in an unimpeachable position in the Brazilian imaginary: a place of humiliation and exclusion where not much can be done or achieved.

The criticism of the middle class is the agenda of almost all the film-maker's works, focusing in particular on their childish views between the utopia of belonging to the upper class, of having power and money, and the fear of decay and poverty. The decaying Barata family home is decorated with stuffed animal heads on the walls and rough replicas of statues and works of art. While it undergoes a makeover, Barata listens to Xavante-Indian chants in the living-room sound system. Barata tells Elvira that 'these civilized Indians have watches and fountain pens'. She, in turn, cannot sleep with the sound of 'cannibals in the room'.

Exclusion is a theme dear to the film-maker. When the construction workers arrive in the apartment, Elvira makes a speech about the absurd increase in prices in Brazil and affirms that in spite of it 'the people are good, very good'. During the renovation one of the workers, Piauí (José Dumont), named after the Brazilian state with the biggest poverty rates, is evicted for lack of payment and is invited to camp along with his family in the Baratas' living room for a few days. The Baratas receive them well at first but then have second thoughts and decide to find a way to get rid of them. They ask the property manager to devise a letter ordering the family's removal according to the building regulations. The theatrical scene in which this occurs shows the guilt experienced by the Brazilian middle class and its disingenuous ways of speaking. Compassion only exists as a discourse and through minor acts of kindness (such as when Piaui's family receives used clothes donated by the Baratas' neighbours) that do not contribute in any way to changing the political and economic divisions of the country.

Jabor creates an epiphany of senses with an apocalyptic tone by connecting the delusions of all in the private family space, including the Indians (through songs), blacks, mulattos, the maids, the construction workers, the whites, the middle class and the high bourgeoisie, represented by Vera's American fiancé who is the director of a big company named Thompson. Scenes that are poetically constructed show the melting pot of cultures and rituals that make up the Brazilian popular imaginary.

Gabriela Lírio

Candinho

Studio/Distributor:

Companhia Cinematográfica
Vera Cruz

Director:

Abílio Pereira de Almeida

Producer:

Cid Leite da Silva

Screenwriter:

Abílio Pereira de Almeida

Cinematographer:

Edgar Brasil

Art Director:

Antônio Gomide

Composer:

Gabriel Migliori

Synopsis

'In about 1926', an infant, accompanied by his donkey, Policarpo, and wearing a lavish medallion, appears in a basket in the river on a farm in Brazil. The landowner and his family adopt him and christen him Candinho. Candinho's place of honour is usurped, however, with the birth of the colonel's twins, so he grows up as one of the servants, known for both his good nature and mischief. The adoptive son comes under the influence of the family friend, Professor Pancrácio, who expounds philosophical optimism. He also flirts with his stepsister, Filoca, but when the patriarch discovers the couple kissing, he expels Candinho from the farm. Candinho sets off on his beloved Policarpo to find his long-lost mother, suffering misadventures en route to and in the 'big city' (São Paulo). There he befriends the homeless Pirulito (Lollipop or 'Slim'), and the two try to find work, never losing their innocence and kind-heartedness. Eventually, Candinho finds Pancrácio, who works as a false beggar to subsidize his vocation as a philosopher. Candinho also learns that Filoca has run away from home to become a taxi dancer in the big city. Candinho's loyalty convinces Filoca to return with him to the country as his

Editor:

Oswald Hafenrichter

Duration:

95 min.

Genre:

Comedy of manners

Cast:

Amácio Mazzaropi
Ruth de Souza
Adoniran Barbosa
Policarpo
the Donkey

Year:

1954

fiancée. She discovers that his medallion contains a treasure map, and the friends set off to search for the prize. The treasure is unexpected but good news for Candinho. The happy ending includes a musical celebration of a double wedding.

Critique

This film brought together Brazil's greatest comic film actor, Mazzaropi, and its first world-class studio, the Vera Cruz Film Company, founded in São Paulo in 1949. The legendary Amácio Mazzaropi was the star of this comedy, and, in *Candinho*, his third film, he debuted the film version of his big-hearted *caipira* ('hick') persona. Mazzaropi was born 9 April 1912 in São Paulo city to a modest family and was raised both in the city and in small towns in the interior – the very setting that he often parodied and celebrated. His career began at the age of fourteen, when he joined a circus. He later perfected his comic routines in theatre, on radio and on television. In all he starred in 32 feature releases before his death in 1981, all box office successes. In Brazil, DVD releases are widely available, a testament to Mazzaropi's enduring popularity.

Candinho is a reworking of Voltaire's *Candide* (1759). If the resemblance of the title and some of the plot were not enough to give this away, then the quote from Pangloss that appeared in the title frames would: 'Tudo é para o melhor neste melhor dos mundos' ('All is for the best in this best of worlds'), slightly altered from the French: 'Tout est pout le mieux dans le meilleux des mondes' ('All is for the best in the best of all [possible] worlds'). Similarly, Candinho and Pancrácio's refrain within the motto of the film is that 'Tudo que acontece de ruim é para melhorar a vida da gente' ('Everything bad that happens is to improve our lives').

The plot is the picaresque hero's journey from the country to the city and back. The work also follows the formulae of the nineteenth and twentieth century Brazilian comedy of manners, continued in the *chanchada* film genre of the cinema of the early years. *Candinho* has several musical numbers, some composed by several of Brazil's most gifted popular songwriters, sometimes performed by Mazzaropi on burro-back, as if he were the Brazilian Gene Autry. There are also regional dances and festive local colour. The comedy is situational and enriched by Mazzaropi's trademark spoken and facial expression performances. There are sight gags as well, for example, when the friends are searching for the treasure map amid papers on the police chief's desk that multiply before the viewers' eyes: the comic timing of the five-person ensemble is perfect. The supporting cast included Ruth de Souza, one of Brazil's premier black actresses, who played the house servant Miss Manuela. Although her social role is stereotyped, her character is given some room for depth and expression, extremely rare for black actors in the mid century. Songwriter Adoniran Barbosa played Professor Pancrácio, and his rendering of the philosopher's grandiose eloquence, is second only to Mazzaropi's humour in the film.

The anti-hero Candinho draws on both realist and stereotypical elements from the rural setting, including manner, dress, speech and values. The plot proposes a vision that is particular to modernizing the Brazil of the mid twentieth century: Candinho suffers reversals of fortune from the time of his childhood onwards, and he enjoys ultimate triumph in the big city. Unlike Candide, therefore, this protagonist overcomes adversity with the core values of his milieu: persistence, loyalty, kindness and authenticity. These are qualities that not even the city can dampen, and the feel-good quality of the film lies in the idea that even urban modernity can be humanized. The picaresque aspects of the story are also handled in a peculiarly Brazilian way: they are not falls from grace or losses of innocence (Candinho is already playing tricks on the farm) – they are just necessary accommodations to harsh conditions. The happy ending is not only a vindication of our picaresque hero, it is testimony to the humanity of the whole community.

Robert Anderson

Carlota Joaquina: Princess of Brazil

Carlota Joaquina: Princesa do Brasil

Studio/Distributor:

Europa Filmes

Director:

Carla Camurati

Producers:

Bianca DeFellipes
Carla Camurati

Screenwriters:

Carla Camurati
Melanie Dimantas
Angus Mitchell

Cinematographer:

Breno Silveira

Art Directors:

Richard Luiz
Bianca De Filippes

Composer:

André Abujamra

Editors:

Cezar Migliorim

Synopsis

Camurati's film thematizes the life of the Spanish Infanta Carlota Joaquina de Bourbon, narrated in voice-over by a Scotsman to the young girl Yolanda. It covers Carlota's legendary life from the age of ten, when she is chosen to marry D João de Orleans and Bragança, until her death by suicide after being alleged to have conspired against him. The plot also deals with the exile of the Portuguese royal family to Brazil (1808), its richest colony during the Napoleonic wars in Europe. Episodes of Brazilian history linked to the Europeanization of Rio de Janeiro, promoted by D João (the creation of the Bank of Brazil, of Rio de Janeiro's Botanical Garden and of the School of Fine Arts, where painter Jean-Baptiste Debret taught) are revisited in parodic and burlesque fashion. Camurati focuses on Carlota's life showing her political and sexual interests. At the same time, the film subtly demonstrates how Brazil was being converted into a monarchy and emphasizes the continued Portuguese exploitation of Brazil's resources, in such an irresponsible way that Britain's accumulation of wealth was favoured despite the colonizers' own losses.

Critique

This was Carla Camurati's first feature film to gain sufficient popular success to bring the positive attention of critics and film-makers. The film is credited with initiating a revival of the Brazilian film industry, after the extinction of the state-funded film company Embrafilme (1969–90) by the neo-liberal government of Fernando Collor de Mello. Camurati displays sophistication in her manipulation of the historical episodes which constitute the film's plot. For instance, the shift of setting from Spain, to Portugal and finally to Brazil, in which each respective language is spoken, is coupled with narration in English. This linguistic diversity conveys the 'foreignness' Brazilians have felt as a colonized people, where the prevalent perception is that foreigners founded and controlled the country for centuries.

Thus the film established a debate on Luso-Brazilian history. It

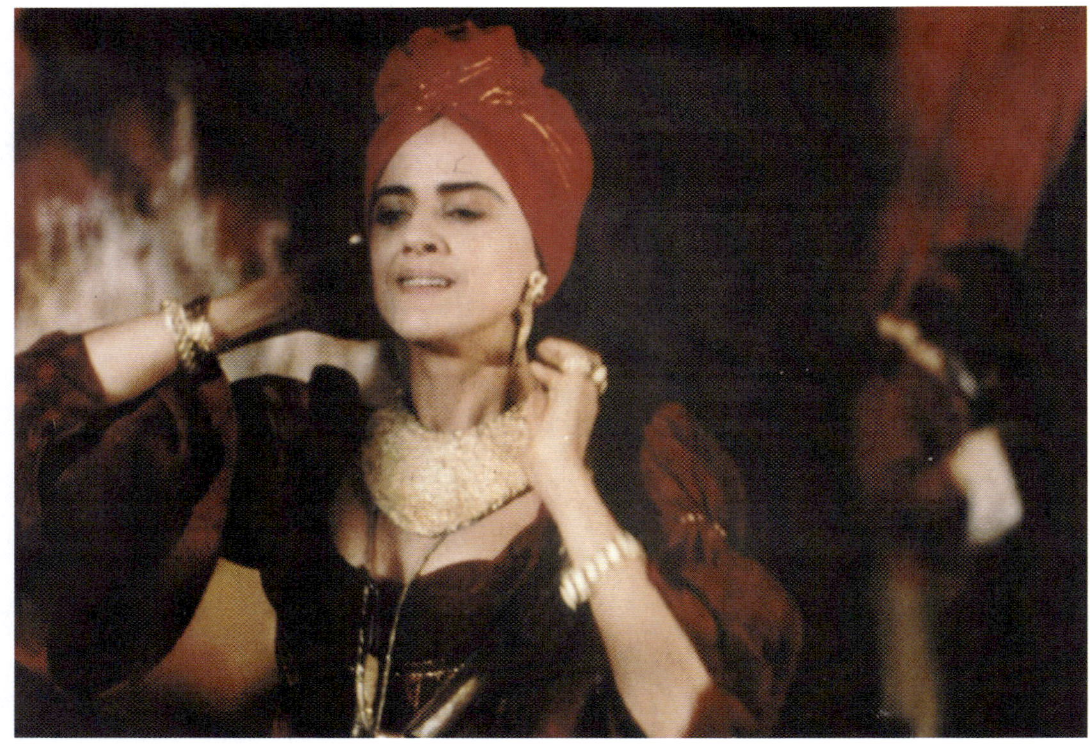

Image courtesy of Copacabana Filmes e Produções

Marta Luz

Duration:

100 minutes

Genre:

Political satire

Cast:

Marieta Severo
Marco Nanini
Marcos Palmeira
Ludmila Dayer Schuller

Year:

1995

represents an uncompromising criticism of the Portuguese colonizers as brutal and unenlightened. Representative of such an illustration of negativity and unenlightened demeanour is the darkness in which the seat of the Portuguese crown in Lisbon is presented, as opposed to both the vivacity and opulence of the Spanish court and the colourful and lavish Brazilian nature. As a result, her satire is a cathartic moment for Brazilians needing to overcome their discontent with their colonial heritage. Don João's stuffing his mouth with fried chicken throughout the film and Carlota's parading on a horse with a whip in hand, threatening pedestrians on the streets of Rio de Janeiro as if they were animals, is a caricature which addresses the way, in the mind of the colonized, the rulers managed their colonies.

The film's aggressive and pitiless portrayal condemns the project of the Portuguese colonization of Brazil, suggesting that its consequences affect Brazilians to this day. The Portuguese royalty is shown as unsophisticated and morally decayed. In exposing the miserly, concupiscent, and disloyal rule of the Orleans and Bragança exploitation of Brazil's reserves, the film broadens its criticism to the mentality of Brazilian elites across the ages, a mentality which has ruthlessly transferred riches from Brazil to other countries, looking solely after their own interests. Nonetheless, even if Carlota's extravagant and tyrannical behaviour is not excused by the movie, her intelligence, confidence, and executive shrewdness show through in the movie (albeit ultimately neutralized by a male-oriented society).

The film attracted three main critical responses. First, historians protested against its failed historicity and Camurati's distortion of 'real' and 'accurate' accounts. Secondly, some critics pointed out the 'rough' quality of the film. Third, remnants of the Orleans and Bragança Imperial Family opposed the unfair portrayal of their ancestors.

All in all, the film performs a postcolonial reading of Luso-Brazilian history in opposition to a hallowed view of historical figures. In doing so it channelled the public's feeling of outrage against Brazil's historic rulers. The clamorous success of the movie reflects the fact that for the average film-goer the film was liberating, ultimately expurgating any possible illusions that the Portuguese 'civilizing' mission was not indeed one of misuse and cruelty. Camurati thus promoted a re-signification of Brazilian colonial heritage and in doing so she might have served history better than the books that perpetuate myths which more often endorse the obscurantism of colonial power.

Sandra SF Erickson

The Deviant Baroness

A Baronesa transviada

Studio/Distributor:

Brasil Vita Filmes
Watson Macedo Produções
Cinematográficas

Director:

Watson Macedo

Producers:

Athayde Caldas
Alberto Laranja
Watson Macedo
Oswaldo Massaini

Screenwriters:

Watson Macedo
Ismar Porto
Chico Anisio

Cinematographer:

Mario Pages

Synopsis

Gonçalina is a simple woman working as a manicurist in a Rio de Janeiro beauty salon. She gets an audition from a film studio to work as an actress but is then rejected. Later, while reading a Rio newspaper, she discovers that a rich, dying Baroness is looking for her missing daughter. Who else but Gonçalina?! When the Baroness dies, despite attempts by greedy relatives eager to steal her fortune, Gonçalina goes to live in the mansion and decides to invest her entire inheritance in film production. Returning to the studio – now on the verge of bankruptcy – the producers offer her a part in a film in return for financial backing. Investing more money than she should, Gonçalina must sell inherited jewellery which she soon discovers is fake; her relatives have stolen the real ones. When she finally gets them back, they are sold to finish the movie.

Critique

An example of *chanchada*, *The Deviant Baroness*, directed by Watson Macedo, was released at the same time that another cinematic movement, *Cinema Novo*, began to emerge in Brazil. In 1957, *The Deviant Baroness* was being shown as well as Nelson Pereira dos Santos's *Rio, zona norte/Rio, Northern Zone*, one of the first films of the new movement. *Cinema Novo* rejected popular musical comedy (*chanchada*), turning instead to the cinema of political commitment.

Art Director:

Lyrio Panicalli

Composer:

Eolo C. Moura

Editor:

Mauro Alice

Duration:

100 minutes

Genre:

Chanchada

Cast:

Dercy Gonçalves
Humberto Catalano
Otelo Zeloni
Zaquia Jorge

Year:

1957

Using theatre and radio artists, *chanchada* movies attracted thousands of fans eager to see their idols on-screen. After all, one of the many definitions given by the critic Alex Viany for *chanchada* was 'popular comedy with musical interpolations', which accounts for the important participation of radio singers. At the same time, there were other more biased definitions which referred to the popular movement as 'worthless plays or vulgar movies'. Yet if the long lines at theatres were any indication, the public was not swayed by such negative criticism; in fact, it felt a strong identification, a factor which allowed Brazilian cinema to enjoy a unique moment in its history. Not only that but there was a growing film industry, the studios proliferated, and there were several other favourable factors: in 1952, Brazil had the seventh cheapest ticket prices in Latin America, was among the top ten countries in its number of theatres, and there was no competition from television – that only came in 1950.

At the time of *The Deviant Baroness*, the *chanchada* genre was already well-established and did not need any more musical pieces to attract the public. However, the fundamental elements still persisted with a comic hero who comes from the masses and is invariably fooled by the more powerful. In Watson Macedo's film, the heroine is played by Dercy Gonçalves: naïve and cunning at the same time, she fights for her rights. Her main enemies are her aunts and their husbands, curiously characterized by one wearing a Hitler-style moustache and the other a goatee à la Leon Trotsky. Gonçalina does not give up and goes to live in her mansion, bringing along her friends Marisa (Aida Campos) and Edward (Bill Farr), and becomes pals with her cousin Neco (Edayr Badaro), who raises chickens in the house, and his assistant Grande Otelo.

On the other hand, while trying to enter the film world that had rejected her, she encounters still more opportunistic people: Suely Borel, an actress who aspires to be a star, and producers who want her money to save the studio. The actress (played by Zaquia Jorge) accepts an offer from the producers (Humberto Catalano and Otelo Zeloni) who take advantage of Gonçalina's supposed *naïveté* to ask for a fortune to buy screws and other banal accessories for the movie set; she writes the cheques without question.

Although there is doubt about the producers' actions, the audience is sure of the heroine's ultimate success. After all, this is central for how the public identifies with *chanchada* protagonists: Rio's urban population was largely made up of workers who constantly faced setbacks in their lives and yet believed themselves capable of succeeding in the end. Culturally, power was represented by the influence of American cinema which was constantly parodied by popular movies in Brazil. Although there are few musical numbers in *The Deviant Baroness*, there is Bill Farr, a singer who together with Aida Campos make up a romantic duo to perform a *chanchada* version of the final scene like Fred Astaire and Ginger Rogers in *Shall We Dance* (Mark Sandrich, 1937). *Sans* the masks worn in the original version yet in a similar scenario, Dercy Gonçalves and Catalano comically dance a tango, both dressed in black like the American actors. In the film produced by Gonçalina, there is also a final scene in which she does a performance à la Josephine Baker, making for a curious convergence between the two actresses: it is common knowledge that before becoming a successful artist, Baker had an extremely hard life and was prone to a bawdy vocabulary, elements which also mark the biography of Dercy. But it is interesting that when Gonçalina is watching her own exaggerated performance on-screen, with a curious glance, she laughs at herself.

To laugh at oneself. This was, perhaps, one of the biggest lessons that *chanchada* gave its public.

Angélica Coutinho

A Dog's Will

O Auto da compadecida

Studio/Distributor:

Globo Filmes

Director:

Guel Arraes

Producer:

Guel Arraes

Screenwriters:

Guel Arraes
Adriana Falcão
João Falcão (adapted from the homonymous play by Ariano Suassuna, 1955)

Cinematographer:

Félix Monti

Art Director:

Lia Renha

Composer:

Sá Grama

Editors:

Ubiraci de Motta
Paulo Henrique Farias

Duration:

104 minutes

Genre:

Regional comedy

Cast:

Matheus Nachtergaele
Selton Mello
Denise Fraga
Marco Nanini

Synopsis

The story begins in the early twentieth century in a small town in the north-east of Brazil where João Grilo and Chicó carry signs through the streets announcing the showing of the film *The Passion of Christ*. Next to his pal Chicó, the clever, *Nordestino* (north-easterner) João Grilo struggles to survive by deceiving everyone along the way. These two picaresque characters are the central protagonists of this story alongside a colourful cast of characters. Continually searching for a way to earn money and food, the two find work at the local bakery where they must put up with the baker's stinginess and his wife's infidelities. After the death of Dona Dora's beloved dog, João Grilo concocts a plan to console the woman and, in exchange for a large sum, promises that he will get the priest to give her dog a proper Catholic burial. For the funeral to take place, he deceives the local priest and the bishop by claiming that the dog's last will and testament was to give money to the Church. João Grilo's machinations do not stop there. He weaves a web of trickery, giving money to some and taking from others to get what he needs while involving a cast of local characters. His deceptions continue until one day the local bandit Severino arrives to loot the town. In the violence that is unleashed, Severino, João Grilo, the baker and his wife as well as the priest and the bishop end up dead and find themselves before the devil, Jesus Christ and Nossa Senhora, a *Compadecida* [compassion] in their final judgment.

Critique

Director Guel Arraes has balanced his interest between comedy and romance genres. Prior to *A Dog's Will*, he primarily worked in television but has since merged directing telenovelas and cinema. Indeed, *A Dog's Will* began as a mini-series adaptation of the play by Ariano Suassuna for Rede Globo in 1999 before becoming a feature film. Arraes repeated this film-television convergence with the mini-series 'A Invenção do Brasil' (Globo TV, 2000) and the film *Caramuru – a invenção do Brasil* (2001). More recently, Arraes directed *O Bem amado* (2010), an adaptation of the popular 1970s telenovela, which was a significant box office success in Brazil and, despite far fewer copies of the film circulating, it nearly beat *Xuxa Requebra* (Tizuka Yamasaki, 2000) in its first week of exhibition.

Year:

2000

Notably, the film was also one of the first productions by Globo Filmes, the film production arm of Globo TV, and drew production funds from private investors and sponsorships rather than relying on federal incentive laws.

Based on the play by Ariano Suassuna, the film is highly faithful to the original text save a few modifications. Theatrical dialogues were shortened for the film. The art direction is commendable for capturing the look of a village located in the middle of the north-eastern *sertão* (backlands) in the early twentieth century. The addition of traditional north-eastern musical rhythms (i.e. *forró*, acoustic guitar) greatly contributes to establishing the regional setting. Only the final 'judgment scene' appears theatrical in its staging.

The film's humour emerges from the blending of a comedy of errors with the picaresque and the *Commedia dell'arte*. The two protagonists are reminiscent of picaresque characters who expose social injustices while demonstrating great cleverness, similar to Lazarrillo (*Lazarillo de Tormes* (Anon., 1554)) or Pablos in Francisco Quevedo's *El Buscón* (1626). The actors in the main roles, Selton Mello and Mateus Nachtergaele, pair a bumbling awkwardness with quick wit to disentangle themselves from the web of mistaken identities and other deceptions they initiate. Other characters show the influence of *Commedia dell'arte* in that they are fixed social types (i.e. the baker, the bandit, the local oligarch, etc.) presumed to be rooted in north-eastern Brazil. In addition, the film makes fun of the religious fervour and machismo associated with the Brazilian north-east. What is more, the film was released at a time when it was particularly important to celebrate the underling and make fun of pillars of authority. Thus, the film makes a humorous return to the north-eastern *sertão*, a nodal point in the Brazilian cultural imaginary, to offer a story of cultural resistance.

Leslie L Marsh

The Man Who Copied

O Homem que copiava

Studio/Distributor:

Globo Filmes
Casa de Cinema de Porto Alegre

Director:

Jorge Furtado

Producers:

Luciana Tomasi
Nora Goulart

Synopsis

In a Porto Alegre supermarket, André makes a routine purchase of groceries, including a box of matches. He then goes to a vacant lot and burns a pile of letters and bank notes. Voice-over narration recalls the events that led to this action. He works as a photocopy operator in a stationary store, lives with his mother and secretly loves Sílvia, the object of his harmless stalking. In order to escape his poverty and to capture her heart, he pursues various money-making schemes: playing the lottery, counterfeiting money on the new colour copier, and robbing an armoured bank car with Cardoso, boyfriend of co-worker Marinés. Unfortunately, André is unmasked and accidentally shoots a guard, Antunes, coincidentally Sílvia's father. André manages to escape and goes undetected by the authorities. The robbers discover that they have won the lottery and decide to return the stolen bank money. However, they must first deal with a blackmail attempt by Antunes.

Screenwriter:

Jorge Furtado

Cinematographer:

Alex Sernambi

Art Director:

Fiapo Barth

Composer:

Leo Henkin

Editor:

Giba Assis Brasil

Duration:

123 minutes

Genre:

Crime caper

Cast:

Lázaos Ramos
Leandra Leal
Luana Piovani
Pedro Cardoso

Year:

2003

Critique

Set in the director's native Porto Alegre, *The Man Who Copied* combines a series of paradoxes and twists by playfully melding universal film genres and conventions, a favoured Furtado device. The central character, André (Lázaos Ramos), is a painfully shy, young black man who is capable of feats of surprising daring: counterfeiting, armed robbery, murder. His bedroom wall is, like the film, a pastiche of seemingly random caricatures. These imaginative illustrations, animated by Allen Sieber for André's autobiographical flashbacks and paired with the random appearance of the colour copier, underscore the stifling lack of creativity in the 'push start, push stop' work world that contrasts to the character's dreams of a more vibrant existence.

On the lighter side, Furtado offers a screwball comedy of errors as when the hapless armoured car robbers escape on a city bus, stealthily digging through the stolen bills to pay the fare. Using conventions of romantic comedy, the film moves from humorous complications to postmodern happy union. André's initial approach to Sílvia (Leandra Leal) involves impressing her by attempting to purchase an expensive gift for his mother from the boutique in which the girl works. The pretence sets in motion his life of ever-escalating crime and consumerism. His affection is nevertheless genuine. In one particularly touching scene, André and Sílvia discuss a Shakespearean sonnet, reinforcing a thematic of *carpe diem* and the multiple ways in which the various characters reproduce themselves as replicas or facsimiles of their imagined personae.

Crime-caper conventions recall the more sombre shades of North American 1940s film noir. An opening flash-forward, explained in a meandering and matter of fact voice-over narration, and the use of low-key lighting in André's room reflect the narrative and visual styles of noir classics such as *Double Indemnity* (Billy Wilder, 1944). Marinés (Luana Piovani) and Sílvia display the qualities of incipient femmes fatales, potentially dangerous objects of desire. In the one case, blonde bombshell Marinés schemes for a rich benefactor but eventually succumbs to the persistent wooing of Cardoso (Pedro Cardoso). In the other, Sílvia assumes the voice-over towards the end of the film, leading the viewer to question the extent of her innocence and/or culpability in the story's events. Even more directly, André's voyeurism evokes Alfred Hitchcock's 'film gris' *Rear Window* (1954) where another binocular-wielding voyeur witnesses something odd in a neighbouring apartment. The witty take on the redemption to be found in criminality and violence where truths, expectations and realities are varied and relative echoes the tone of Quentin Tarantino's neo-noir *Pulp Fiction* (1994).

The film also reprises elements of specifically Brazilian genres including the *tropicalista* penchant for cannibalistically fusing genres and the optimism of *chanchada* of the 1930s–50s, ingenious parodies of North American movies. These influences contrast with the cynical pessimism of classic noir by subtly reinvigorating the social and political critique of the 1960s *Cinema Novo* movement, ultimately debunking the unfettered greed that treats money as a fetish. While reminiscent of Tarantino's idiosyncratic creations, *The Man* rejects graphic and gratuitous violence. Indeed, while criminality and violence play a part, they are made to seem incidental rather than integral to the film. For example, the decision of the partners in crime to return the stolen money after learning of the lottery windfall indicates that they have not been hopelessly corrupted by greed. In another instance, Cardoso and Marinés steadfastly distance themselves – at least verbally – from participating in violent schemes and André draws a line at selling drugs to nourish his need for money. This attitude stands in stark contrast to the gritty, urban criminality depicted in Brazilian films of the same period: *Cidade de Deus/City of God* (Fernando Meirelles and Kátia Lund, 2002) and *Carandiru* (Hector Babenco, 2003).

Patricia D Fox

The Sputnik Man

O Homem do Sputnik

Studio/Distributor:

Atlântida

Director:

Carlos Manga

Producer:

Cyll Farney

Screenwriter:

Cajado Filho

Cinematographer:

Ozen Sermet

Art Director:

Cajado Filho

Composer:

Radamés Gnatalli

Editor:

Waldemar Noya

Duration:

92 minutes

Genre:

Chanchada

Cast:

Oscarito
Cyll Farney
Zezé Macêdo
Jô Soares

Synopsis

An artificial satellite, supposedly the Soviet Sputnik, falls on the humble property of a suburban man, Anastácio. As the satellite is lined with gold, Anastácio and his wife Cleci see their chance to climb up the social ladder: the wife plans to move to a more fashionable sector of Rio de Janeiro and travel abroad. She also begins to pepper her speech with foreign words, in order to show signs of good-breeding. Anastácio is pestered by newspapermen who are interested in the scoop. Meanwhile, the most powerful nations of the time, those of the United States, the Soviet Union and France, find out about the satellite and send agents to Brazil. Anastácio and Cleci are taken to a fancy hotel in Copacabana, where the agents are also staying. That allows for some slapstick comedy as Anastácio, Cleci, a newspaper reporter, the Soviets, the Americans and the French get to meet one another: the motive of each foreign agent is to lay hands on the satellite; Cleci's purpose is to join the jet set; and Anastácio's is to be seduced by Bébé, the French female agent.

Critique

The Sputnik Man belongs to the Brazilian film genre called *chanchada*, which evolved from the musical to a farcical comedy of errors. The *chanchadas* flourished mainly in the 1940s and 1950s and attracted hordes of people to the movie theatres. At first disdained by Brazilian intellectual elites due to their uninhibited approach to comedy and enormous popular appeal, they later came to be admired as ferocious parodies of successful Hollywood films of different genres. Their carnivalesque aspect can be viewed from two different angles: literally, because they were often released shortly before the carnival season, and served to display new musical numbers; and in a Bakhtinian fashion, as they challenged notions of propriety, good taste and the established order. They tried to emulate and, at the same time, poke fun at prestigious Hollywood films. Their relation to the Hollywood film is thus ambiguous – unable to display the production values of this highly sophisticated

Year:

1959

sort of cinema, the *chanchadas* defy it by parodying those values, while simultaneously mimicking, in spite of their limited technical resources, the narrative sweep of those films.

The Sputnik Man (the title alludes to the Space Race) is not a musical, and invests heavily on satire. It ridicules the struggle for power displayed at the time by the United States, the Soviet Union and France, as indicated in the opening sequence. A stylized column of the Palace of Dawn, a world-famous symbol of Brasília and the Brazilian government, falls down to a horizontal position, taking the form of a scale. On one of the ends of this scale there appears a sickle, an indication of the communist work ethic of the Soviet Union, which is then balanced by a bed on the other end of the scale, symbolic of lustful France. The balance is regained when a bottle of Coca-Cola, which represents the capitalist United States, replaces the sickle.

The most outrageously critical sequences of the film refer to foreign agents who are sent to Brazil to get the satellite. The Soviet agents' musical theme is the traditional Russian song *Oczicziornyje*, and their leader, Karamazov, manifests his wish to rule the world. The colourful Americans, always dancing to jazz music and drinking Coca-Cola, want to exchange the Sputnik for chewing gum, nylon stockings and plastic gadgets. *La Marseillaise*, playing over shots of an imposing palace hall, announces the arrival of the French agents. In Monsieur Rififi's bedroom, the French 'weapon' is sitting on the bed: Bébé, played with verve by Norma Bengell, who will later try to seduce Anastácio in a celebrated impersonation of Brigitte Bardot.

The film does not spare the malaises in Brazilian political and social life of the time either: there is a ladies' group called the Popcorn for Dispossessed Children Movement, and no members of the Department of Interplanetary Research can be reached because they are all having a coffee break. But most criticism is devoted to foreign interference in Brazilian affairs; the stereotyping of the dominating nations is a sort of 'payback' for the formulaic representation of Brazilians in classic Hollywood films. An emblematic image is the struggle between Soviets, Americans and French, all of them holding the rope at the end of which the Sputnik is supposedly tied, pulling it towards themselves, and shouting: 'It's ours,' 'No, it's ours,' 'It's ours.' Anastácio, the simpleton who outwits them all, points out: 'Look, just like the League of Nations. Such nice diplomacy.'

Antonio João Teixeira

Stories That Our Baby Sitters Would Not Tell Us

Histórias que nossas babás não contavam

Studio/Distributor:

Cinedistri

Director:

Osvaldo de Oliveira

Producer:

Aníbal Massaini Neto

Screenwriter:

Aníbal Massaini Neto

Cinematographer:

Osvaldo de Oliveira

Art Directors:

Julian Romeo
Marineida Massaini

Editor:

José Luiz Andreone

Duration:

97 minutes

Genre:

Pornochanchada

Cast:

Adele Fátima
Costinha
Meiry Vieira
Denis Derkian

Year:

1979

Synopsis

In a land far away, a good-natured King remarries after his first wife's death. The new Queen, young and adulterous, hates the King's daughter, Clara das Neves (Snow Egg White). When the King dies, the Queen intends to marry a young Prince. The Prince, however, would rather marry Clara das Neves. Shunned, the Queen issues a Royal Institutional Act that abrogates Clara's rights to the throne and demotes her to the castle's kitchen to work as a maid. However, that is not enough to prevent Clara from meeting with the Prince. The Queen is informed of their love affair and decides to take more serious action as she hires a deer hunter to kill Clara. The hunter is seduced by Clara and lets her go. Clara runs away into the dark forest, where she eventually meets the seven dwarfs. Much hilarity ensues as they fight for Clara's attention and try to accommodate everyone's desires, especially because effeminate dwarf Nervoso (Edgy) thinks that she is bound to steal his place as the 'mistress' of the house. It is not long, though, before the Queen finds out where Clara is hiding and attempts to poison our heroine.

Critique

Stories That Our Baby Sitters Would Not Tell Us is, in a way, a paradigmatic *pornochanchada*. As with many other films of the genre, it is a parody of 'canonical' cultural works (other examples are *Bacalhau/Codfish* (Adriano Stuart, 1975), a take on *Jaws* (Steven Spielberg, 1975), and *A Banana mecânica* (Braz Chediak, 1974), a parody of *A Clockwork Orange* (Stanley Kubrick, 1971). Here, the narrative is a parodic appropriation of *Snow White and the Seven Dwarfs* (William Cottrell, et al., 1937). The term *pornochanchada* is used to designate a set of Brazilian comedies produced from the late 1960s to the early 1980s tinted with sexual overtones. The noun is derived from *chanchadas*, popular musical comedies, usually low-budget films from the 1940s to the 1960s, and the prefix *porno*, indicating its sexual content. The prefix, however, may be misleading, because only a small number of the *pornochanchadas* were overtly pornographic.

Stories That Our Baby Sitters Would Not Tell Us condenses a number of the ambiguities that marked the genre. There is a clear objectification of Adele Fátima's body, as the camera lingers on her form while she performs sensuous gestures and poses. Furthermore, as she is downgraded in the narrative to the status of maid, the film corroborates a historical association with colonial times in Brazil, evoking the figure of the colonial landowner and his dominion over female slaves' bodies. Nevertheless, this objectification is ambiguously countered by glimpses of empowerment when we consider that it is Clara das Neves's decision to stay with the remaining six dwarfs and not follow the prince, as in the traditional tale, thus reinforcing her subjectivity and sovereignty over her own body.

Stories That Our Baby Sitters Would Not Tell Us is, indeed, an ambiguous film. On the one hand we have the exploitation of Fátima's body and an evident masculinist focalization. Such focalization is expressed, for example, in the use of a female voice-over narration that is interpolated by male voices – as if from the spectator's place – that complain about the old-fashioned tale she starts telling and ask for a saucier version of the story. On the other hand, there are instances of a transgressive humour that charges the film with political overtones. For instance, the reference to a 'Royal Institutional Act' parodies the Institutional Acts issued by the Brazilian government under the military dictatorship. Moreover, the film ends in a very non-traditional way: Clara das Neves decides to stay with the dwarfs whereas the Prince leaves with Nervoso, a gay pairing that contests heteronormative values.

A strong presence in *Stories That Our Baby Sitters Would Not Tell Us* is comedian Costinha (born Lírio Mário da Costa, b.1923–d.1995). Playing the role of the huntsman, Costinha gives voice to some of the most homophobic remarks in the film. He says that he kills all 'deers' that come his way, 'deer' being a pejorative term to designate male homosexuals in Brazil. Costinha was well-known for his impersonations of *bichinhas* (effeminate gay men) and explicit jokes. He started making films in the 1950s, often playing secondary roles. His physiognomy was distinctive: slim body, trouty mouth, big nose. Costinha was also a remarkable TV actor with a mischievous smile, exploring double entendres and adding sexual overtones to every line he delivered. One of Costinha's most famous pet phrases is 'Euquero é gozar!', which could be translated as 'I want to enjoy myself', 'I want to have sexual pleasure' and 'I want to make fun', thus synthesizing his approach to humour: making fun is like having fun making sex.

Ramayana Lira

The Street Acrobats

Os Saltimbancos trapalhões

Studio/Distributor:

Renato Aragão Produções Artísticas (Distribuído por Europa Filmes)

Director:

JB Tanko

Producer:

Renato Aragão

Screenwriters:

JB Tanko
Gilvan Pereira (adapted from the eponymous stage play by Chico Buarque, Sérgio Bardotti and Luiz Bacalov, 1981)

Synopsis

Based on Chico Buarque de Hollanda's play, itself inspired by 'The Town Musicians of Bremen' by the Brothers Grimm, *The Street Acrobats* tells the story of the Bartolo circus troupe, who work for an exploitative owner called Barão. The responsibility for the circus's success and happiness is down to the talent of four friends, Didi, Dedé, Mussum and Zacarias, who have an incredible ability to make the public laugh. However, as they are too naïve to realize the power they have, they accept their exploitation by Barão, who underpays them and gives them only spaghetti to eat. Matters are made worse when the leader of the Trapalhões, Didi, falls in love with his boss's daughter and so does not want to create problems with her father. She, in turn, is in love with the new trapeze artist, whose past is connected to two villains: Assis Satã and The Gipsy, engendering a series of complicated situations that will only be overcome by the courage and unity of the four friends.

Critique

'Who has money, has power. Who has power, has money. Who does not have money or power is a miserable wretch.' This sentence is said by Barão, the owner of the circus, and sums up the situation that

Cinematographer:

Antonio Gonçalves

Composers:

Luis Bacalov, Sergio Bardotti, Chico Buarque

Editor:

Manoel Oliveira

Duration:

100 minutes

Genre:

Comedy

Cast:

Renato Aragão
Dedé Santana
Mussum
Zacarias

Year:

1981

The Street Acrobats opposes. In fact, the message conveyed by both the original story 'The Town Musicians of Bremen' and the film is the communist idea that unity is strength. Only people who are united can beat the greed of the bosses and inequality in general. When the film was first released, Brazil was experiencing political re-alignment under a military regime and the world was still in the midst of the Cold War. For this reason, only a group like Os Trapalhões could address such a theme and escape censorship. Taking advantage of their fame as circus clowns, the group contributed for years to Brazilian cinema, with popular tales, adaptations of classic literature and parodies of successful films. Always maintaining a soft and funny tone, the films conquered a wide and varied audience.

JB Tanko, a Yugoslavian of Brazilian citizenship, succeeds in balancing this humorous tone with social critique, bringing different layers to the film. Light and nicely paced, the film is fun to watch, combining humour, kitsch and musical numbers.

The director's filmography includes various Brazilian *chanchadas*, a popular genre influenced by Hollywood musicals, which in turn influenced the films he directed for Os Trapalhões. *The Street Acrobats* is his eighth film with Os Trapalhões and it is also his most mature work, in which the language and affinity with the group's style were better developed. Moreover, the influence of Chico Buarque de Holanda's text helps to move the film along, which adapts many songs from Buarque's play to the setting of the circus.

The structure of the screenplay is another key element of the film's success. Tanko and Gilvan Pereira further the dramatic trajectory through the figure of Didi, a typical clown, who at the same time is naïve, timid, a dreamer and in love. It is his dreams that we follow, believing in the possibility of conquering Karina's heart, becoming successful in the city and going to Hollywood. In fact, the sequences set in Los Angeles enrich the plot, which also has relatively good special effects for the time it was made. The story has a melancholic tone, but never turns to outright sadness, not even at the end. Particular attention should be paid to the beauty of the moment in which the troupe arrives in the city with video clips of the songs 'Alô, liberdade' (Enriquez, Bardotti and Chico Buarque, 1981) and 'A cidade dos artistas' (Enriquez, Bardotti, Chico Buarque, 1981). Another stand-out sequence is the song 'História de uma Gata' (Enriquez, Bardotti, Chico Buarque, 1977), which had already been made famous by Buarque's play.

In this film, Os Trapalhões retain their central characteristic: to provoke laughter and debate at the same time. They achieve this well and although the four of them complement each other, in *The Street Acrobats*, they are divided into pairs. On the one hand, there is Didi as the smart guy pretending to be dumb, Dedé as the dumb guy who pretends to be smart. On the other hand are Mussum and Zacarias, who function as countryside characters, shyer, un-hierarchical, and who always end badly. The rest of the casting helps create a series of stereotypical characters: the exploitative boss, the greedy magician, the femme fatale, the naïve lady, the romantic young man, all played by talented actors who raise the quality of the film. *The Street Acrobats* is, therefore, a significant work in the group's filmography.

Coherent direction (despite lacking originality), a good story, a well-defined moral with old fables, beautiful songs that stimulate the popular imagination and, of course, lots of laughter and fun for the audience.

Amanda Aouad (trans. Natália Pinazza)

The Three Outlaws

Os Três cangaceiros

Studio/Distributor:

Fama Filmes SA

Director:

Victor Lima

Producers:

Herbert Richers

Arnaldo Zonari

Screenwriter:

Victor Lima

Cinematographer:

Amleto Daissé

Art Director:

Alexandre Horvath

Composer:

Remo Usai

Editor:

Rafael Justo Valverde

Duration:

102 minutes

Genre:

Parody

Cast:

Ankito

Ronald Golias

Grande Otelo

Wilson Grey

Year:

1959

Synopsis

Aristides and Bronco are two cowardly citizens from the small town of Desterro, which is sacked by a group of violent *cangaceiros* (the historical bandits who spread terror in north-eastern Brazil mainly in the beginning of the twentieth century). They both happen to fall in love with Rosinha, who claims she can only love someone brave, like the mysterious Onça Vingadora, a masked man who fights the bandits and whose real identity is unknown. Hoping to prove themselves worthy of Rosinha's love, Aristides and Bronco decide to take action against the gang. Together with Mundico, a local trader, they dress like *cangaceiros* in order to infiltrate the group and inform the local authorities about their hiding place. Forced to act as real *cangaceiros*, however, the three men are caught by the sheriff, who is unaware of their disguise. Luckily, the sheriff's daughters, Zizi and Marisa, release them from jail. Dressed as male *cangaceiros*, the two girls join Aristides, Bronco and Mundico in their attempt to rescue Rosinha, who has just been kidnapped by the gang. They also count on the help of Onça Vingadora, whose identity is finally revealed.

Critique

Directed by Victor Lima, *The Three Outlaws* is a low-budget comedy that combines elements of Brazilian *chanchada* and carnival films with parodist overtones of the classical Hollywood western genre. The film set, for instance, cheaply reproduces the iconography of the old west towns. Yet the mythical bravery of Hollywood's cowboys is now replaced by the leading characters' awkward cowardice if compared to the ruthless violence of the 'real' *cangaceiros* in the film.

A carnivalesque spoof of mainstream westerns, Lima's film explores the popular appeal of the *chanchada* and carnival films as well as the popularity and charisma of the leading actors. Ronald Golias, for instance, became famous for his childish manners and funny way of speaking, with emphasis on his exaggerated facial gestures. His comic performance as Bronco in Lima's film, for instance, was so successful with the audience that the character was later taken to television, where he repeated the act in a show called *Família Trapo* (created by Carlos Alberto de Nóbrega and Jô Soares, 1967–1971), an overt parody of the von Trapp family from the famous musical *The Sound of Music* (Robert Wise, 1965).

As the title suggests, the film also alludes to the romantic cloak and dagger novel *The Three Musketeers*, by Alexandre Dumas (1844). It is indeed the famous musketeers' motto, 'all for one, one for all,' that the three protagonists call to seal their pact to fight against the bandits. Also, when Zizi and Marisa decide to join them in their secret mission, Bronco feels the need to reinvent the story and comes up with the idea that D'Artagnan had a 'brother'. It is amusing to notice that the two girls' performances as male *cangaceiros* demonstrate great confidence and bravery, thus being closer to the attitude of the 'real' *cangaceiros*, whereas Aristides, Bronco and Mundico provide a much more exaggerated rendering, denoting how misplaced they look among the gang.

One of the highlights in *The Three Outlaws* is the sequence in which Aristides, dressed as a country girl, dances to entertain the *cangaceiros*. Cross-dressing in such films was usually conveyed to hide secret identities. But, mostly, it represented a pause in the narrative where the spectacle took place, highlighting the connection with carnival since cross-dressing is an essential part of the festivities. It was, in fact, a common practice in Brazilian comedies and, thus, became one of the trademarks of the carnivalesque films of the period. Viewers looked forward to seeing such occasions of gender 'subversion' which indeed was acceptable only because it was not really meant as a serious challenge to gender and/or sexual identities insofar as it tended to be justified in the narrative. Another example of disguising in the film is Onça Vingadora (the Vengeful Brazilian Jaguar). Dressed with a special garment that imitates animal skin and a mask that covers the whole head, Onça Vingadora resembles comic book heroes like Spiderman. In this case, however, the film cannibalizes/carnivalizes the foreign element with the construction of a hero that is 'truly' Brazilian.

At the end, the guest appearance of actor Zé Trindade, as Rosinha's fiancé, is worthy of note. A celebrated radio performer, renowned for his caricature of the womanizer and famous for his catch phrase 'Ladies, here I am,' Trindade is the one who wins Rosinha's heart, even though both Aristides and Bronco have proved their courage. Their lonely, pathetic figures will later on resonate in the character of Didi Mocó, who is usually also denied a happy romantic ending in the series of films with the Trapalhões. But that is another chapter in Brazilian comedy.

Alessandra Soares Brandão

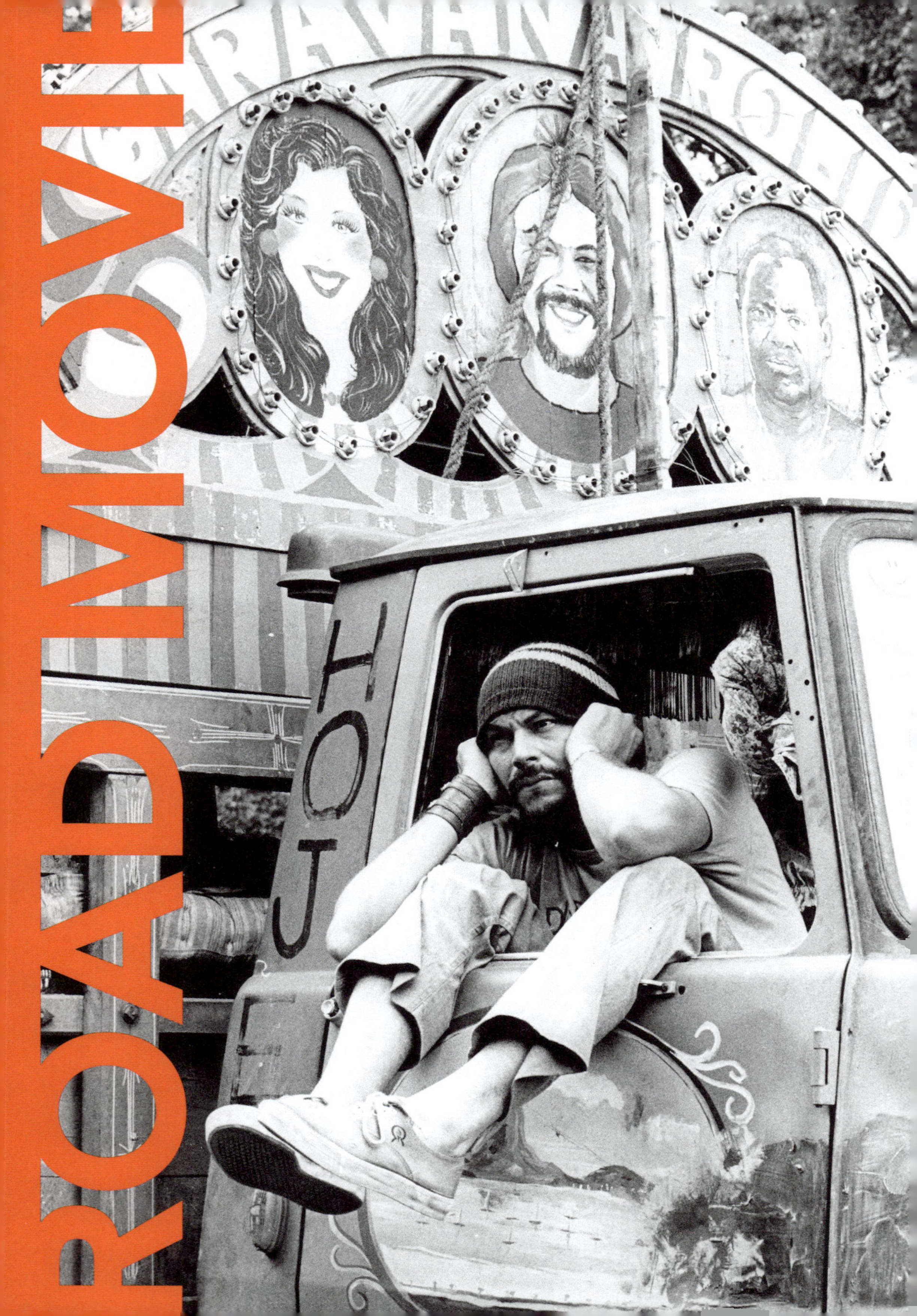
ROAD MOVIE

An increasing number of Brazilian (and more generally Latin American) films have adopted the format of the road movie, defined as 'a fluid and open-ended genre which uses the narrative trajectory of the road as an extended metaphor of quest and discovery through which to approach fundamental concepts of identity' (Everett 2004: 19). Such a preoccupation with identity is now placed within a neo-liberal context, in which culture and the postmodern condition (Harvey 1991) appear to have an impact on the subject matter and aesthetics of not only Brazilian national cinema, but also in cinemas of the world. Since Brazilian cinema's re-emergence twenty years ago, films dealing with journey narratives appear to testify to a postmodern fragmentation of both the self and of narratives of nationhood, and thus they move away from the relationship between cinema, anti-colonial thinking and national liberation that characterized *Cinema Novo*, an inevitable point of reference of Brazilian cinematic tradition. If the nation was for *Cinema Novo* the focal point of resistance for utopic struggles, the cinema that has emerged in neo-liberal Brazil transcends national projects and centres on characters as individuals rather than as actors for social mobilization. This shifted focus explains the increasing number of Brazilian road movies that use geographical and cultural displacement as a means of self-discovery. Individuals on the road enhance the opportunity for 'unexpected encounter', a motif identified by Ismail Xavier as key not only in contemporary Brazilian cinema, but in other national cinemas, in which '[w]anderers, travelling characters, unexpected cross-cultural encounters are frequent' (2003: 49).

Although most of the films reviewed in this chapter were made in the past fifteen years, Brazilian road movies are not a new phenomenon, as *Bye bye Brasil/Bye Bye Brazil* (Cacá Diegues, 1980), also reviewed here, and *Iracema, uma transa amazônica/Iracema* (Jorge Bodanzky and Orlando Senna, 1976), reviewed in the section 'The Representation of the Brazilian Indian', are two of the classics of what could be considered the 'Brazilian road movie'. Through geographical displacement, they comment on the country's uneven experience of modernity and the portrayal of multiple 'Brazils' within the national territory. *Bye Bye Brazil* says 'goodbye', as the title suggests, to both left- and right-wing utopian projects, thus indicating the changing understandings of the nation as the country began to experience the postmodern fragmentation of totalitarian grand-narratives (see Lyotard 1984) as well as suggesting what the history of the nation had in store in the 1980s (often referred to as the 'lost decade' when the country, indebted to the IMF, experienced economic stagnation and mounting social problems). Unsurprisingly, these social-economic problems affected the industrial basis of the nation's cinema, whose crisis culminated when the government of Fernando Collor de Mello brought an end to the National Film Company (Embrafilme) and the National Film Council (Concine). It is precisely during the Collor era that the next road movie, and one of the key films of the *retomada*, takes place: Walter Salles and Daniela Thomas' *Terra estrangeira/Foreign Land* (1996). The title *Foreign Land* not only refers to literal foreign lands (Portugal and Spain, other settings for the protagonist's journey), but also to Brazil, which becomes a strange environment to the protagonist after Zelia Cardoso announces the freezing of private assets and so causes an emotional shock in his elderly mother, who subsequently dies.

Displacement as a result of an unknown future after the death of a family member forms the topic also of Salles's following film, the internationally acclaimed *Central do Brasil/Central Station* (1998), another road movie reviewed in this chapter. *Central Station*, made two years after *Foreign Land*, implies a journey of national discovery from the 'centre' of Brazil and conveys a message of national conciliation. Perhaps narrating the collapse of national identity in *Foreign Land* prompted Salles's intent to reconstruct it in his following film, *Central Station*. Nagib (2006: 61) points out that the need to 're-discover' the country has shaped the work of film-makers who spent a long time abroad and began to return to Brazil in the beginning of the 1990s, most notable of whom was Salles. The manifestation of this cinematic journey to 're-discover the country' appears to be accompanied by an increase in the number of contemporary films that adopt the road movie genre. The shifted focus from public to private matters, in particular the preoccupation with paternal abandonment and the search for an absent father as a metaphor for the quest for national identity, is one of the many ruptures with film-making traditions, in particular with *Cinema Novo*. Another well-known rupture is the representation of the *sertão* (north-eastern backlands), which together with the *favelas* in Rio has been considered to be a privileged location in *Cinema Novo* films. Out of the nine films reviewed in the present chapter six take place in the *sertão*, thereby testifying to its emergence as a predominant setting for the Brazilian road movie. Nevertheless, the *sertão* does not signify in the films analysed here as the locus of social revolution that it was in *Cinema Novo*. Instead, the *sertão* in films of the past twenty years is portrayed as a setting for individualized stories and more often than not is romanticized within a clichéd binary opposition of dystopian urban area versus spiritually fulfilling countryside. As a consequence, more recent representations of the *sertão* have often been labelled 'apolitical' when analysed in relation to *Cinema Novo*, thus echoing a more general criticism of the superficiality of the postmodern condition as found for instance in Frederic Jameson's notion of the 'nostalgia film' that 'consumes the past in the form of glossy images' (1991: 287). Inserting Brazilian cinema within a wider cultural context perhaps sheds light on to the fact that films, some of them international co-productions, are now in a greater dialogue with the cinemas of the rest of the world, adopting more global aesthetics and genres like the road movie.

Like *Central Station*, *Cinema, aspirinas e urubus/Cinema, Aspirins and Vultures* (Marcelo Gomes, 2005) uses the road movie as a way to narrate the story of a city-dweller who leaves modernity and goes to the archaic *sertão*. The film situates the *sertão* in the context of world history, as it narrates the encounter between a *sertanejo*, an emblematic figure in Brazilian culture, and the German character, who immigrated to Brazil to avoid fighting in World War II. Although fantasies of pre-capitalist society also inform the spatial practices of the *sertão* in *Cinema, Aspirins and Vultures*, the film does not focus on Johann's self-discovery, as he seems to be secure of his decision not to fight the war. Unlike Dora who goes through a 'rebirth', Johann had a strong anti-war feeling prior to his experience in the *sertão*. Yet another example of protagonists that go from the city to the *sertão* is O *Céu de Suely/Suely in the Sky* (2006), directed by Karim Aïnouz, one of the screenwriters of *Cinema, Aspirins and Vultures*. The journey is of a young mother, who lives in São Paulo and decides to return to her hometown, Iguatu, in the *sertão*. Her journey, marked by various displacements, enables the exploration of issues of gender in the road movie, a genre conventionally associated with male characters. This convention is challenged by Aïnouz, whose family is from the north-east and who decides to centre on a female protagonist even though he states that displacements in his family were often experienced by men. An important point to acknowledge in Brazilian road movies is that although they frequently act as the springboard for the exploration of identity, their narratives constantly alter traditional elements of the genre. Because they tend to reflect the character's poverty, forms of transportation have a different agenda from that in traditional Hollywood road movies. They are usually multiple and precarious, as characters rarely are able to afford their own means of transportation and often depend on the kindness of strangers to complete their journey, subverting the association between transportation, speed and empowerment which was eternalized in the road movie *Easy Rider* (Dennis Hopper, 1969).

Whilst in some of the films reviewed in this chapter an experience of displacement follows the breakdown of the family unit, *O Caminho das nuvens/The Middle of the World* (Vicente Amorim, 2003) is a family road movie, in which the journey represents a metaphor for a family that is pushed to its limits by its common experience of inhospitable heat and exhaustion. Another important difference between *The Middle of the World* and the other road movies that are set in the north-east like *Central Station*, *Cinema Aspirins and Vultures* and *Love for Sale* is that the north-east is actually the point of departure. Therefore, *The Middle of the World* shares with classics of Brazilian culture such as *Vidas secas/Barren Lives* (Nelson Pereira dos Santos, 1963; based on Graciliano Ramos's 1939 novel of the same name) the migration path from north-east to south-east and seaside. The *sertão* becomes a destination in particular when it is signified either as the spiritual retreat for city dwellers as is the case of *Central Station*, or as a place of isolation and alienation like in *Viajo porque preciso, volto porque te amo/I Travel Because I Have to, I Come Back Because I Love You* (Karim Aïnouz and Marcelo Gomes, 2009).

The road movie narrative allows the film-maker and the characters to map the territory and explore its peculiarities in ways that are not limited to national boundaries, given that journeys and border-crossing became a type of cinematic manifestation of the ongoing construction of identity. At times, the films insert themselves in a transnational imaginary, engaging with its film-maker's own experiences of displacement and engaging with border crossing journeys. *Um Passaporte húngaro/The Hungarian Passport* (Sandra Kogut, 2001), a documentary that records the film-maker's own attempt to acquire a passport, is an example of a journey film that crosses many borders both physical and discursive. Because it was a record of a journey, the documentary, filmed in France, Hungary and Brazil, is imbued with images of transitional and transnational places and spaces, including train stations, seaports, vehicles and people waving goodbye on a platform. In its self-reflexive use of journey narratives and border crossing, the film explores issues of identity, migration, loss and displacement whilst simultaneously challenging dominant discourses that prevail in bureaucratic practices. Together with *Foreign*

Land and *The Hungarian Passport* another road movie that uses the cross-border experience to negotiate identities is the documentary *Pachamama* (Eryk Rocha, 2009). Like Salles's *Los Diarios de motocicleta/The Motorcycle Diaries* (2004), arguably one of the best known pan-American road movies, *Pachamama* crosses borders within the Southern Cone region as to address issues relating to modernity and transformation. Through border crossing, the film speaks both to national and regional concerns, making Bhabha's point that 'the borders between home and the world become part of each other, forcing upon us a vision that is as divided as it is disorienting' (1994: 13) highly apt.

Natália Pinazza

References

Bhabha, H (1994) *The Location of Culture*, London: Routledge.

Everett, W (2004) 'Leaving Home: Exile and Displacement in Cinema', in W Everett And P Wagstaff (eds) *Cultures of Exile: Images of Displacement*, Oxford: Berghahn, pp. 17–32.

Everett, W and Wagstaff, P (eds) (2004) *Cultures of Exile: Images of Displacement*, Oxford: Berghahn Books.

Harvey, D (1991) *The Condition of Postmodernity: An Enquiry into the Origins of Cultural Change*, Oxford: Blackwell.

Jameson, F (1991) *Postmodernism, or, The Cultural Logic of Late Capitalism*, London: Verso.

Lyotard, JF (1984) *The Postmodern Condition: A Report on Knowledge*, Minneapolis: University of Minnesota Press.

Nagib, L (ed.) (2003) *The New Brazilian Cinema*, London: I.B. Tauris.

— — (2006). *A utopia no cinema brasileiro: matrizes, nostalgia, distopias*. São Paulo: Cosac Naify

Xavier, I (2003) 'Brazilian Cinema in the 1990s: The Unexpected Encounter and the Resentful Characterer', in L Nagib (ed.), *The New Brazilian Cinema*, London: I.B. Tauris, pp. 39–63.

Bye Bye Brazil

Bye bye Brasil

Studio/Distributor:

Carnaval Unifilm

Director:

Cacá Diegues

Producers:

Luiz Carlos Barreto
Lucy Barreto

Screenwriters:

Cacá Diegues
Leopoldo Serran

Cinematographer:

Lauro Escorel

Art Director:

Anísio Medeiros

Composers:

Chico Buarque de Hollada
Dominguinhos
Roberto Menescal

Editor:

Anisio Medeiros
Mair Tavares

Duration:

100 minutes

Genre:

Drama

Cast:

José Wilker
Betty Faria
Zaira Zambelli
Fábio Júnior

Year:

1980

Synopsis

This is a road movie that follows the Rolidei Caravan across two 'Brazils': a rural and indigenous one and an urban one dominated by technology. The Caravan is initially made up of Lorde Cigano (Lord Gypsy), Salomé and Andorinha. Lorde Cigano is the Brazilian antihero, whose attempts to survive are comical. Salomé is his lover and occasional prostitute, with Lorde Cigano her pimp. Andorinha, a black character, is mute and strong, organizing everything in the Caravan and earning money by arm-wrestling. Two other characters,

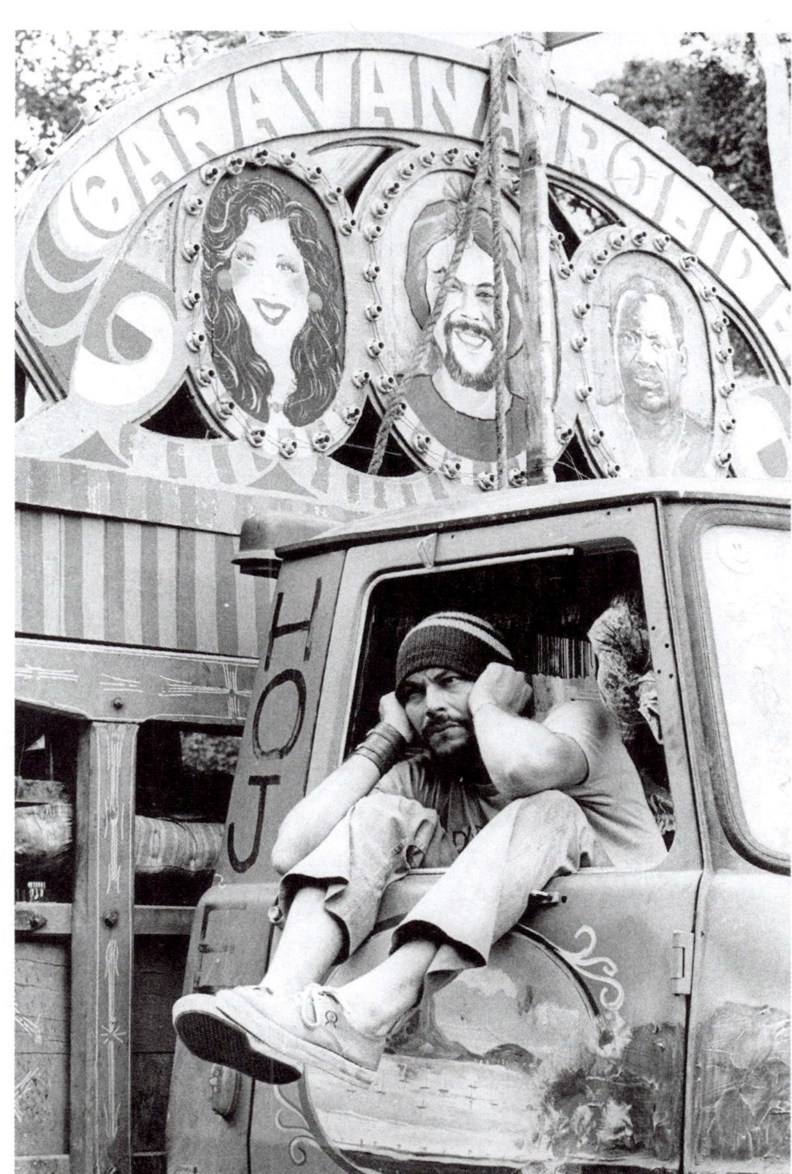

Bye Bye Brazil

Ciço and his wife Dasdô, join them to improve their lives and to see the sea, but most of all because of Ciço's love for Salomé. An interesting and affectionate relationship develops between Lorde Cigano, Ciço, Dasdô and Salomé.

Critique

Bye Bye Brazil is Cacá Diegues's masterpiece, and a film that still feels fresh and vigorous. Diegues attempts to show the integration between a new and old Brazil, but this integration seems schizophrenic in a way typical of Brazil, a country formed by a multiplicity of cultures instead of a homogenous one. Through its exploration of the countries' multiple and uneven experience of modernity, the film uncovers a complex matrix of power relations, in particular between economic periphery and centre. In following the Rolidei Caravan, we see this 'schizophrenic' Brazil, formed variously by indigenous, urban and rural cultures. Nevertheless, they try to avoid places where there is a 'fish spine', as TV antennae are called, as forms of entertainment have changed in places where people have TV, and thus a circus troupe would not be very likely to do well. In this changing Brazil, the group's hopes lie in Altamira, a supposedly paradisiacal place described by a lorry driver to Lorde Cigano.

We witness both birth and death on the way to Altamira. Dasdô's daughter is born whilst we see the devastating effects of both cultural and environmental degradation on the indigenous population. On their arrival in Altamira, the idealized place where they thought that they would find an unexploited Brazil and that would signify the ultimate fusion between rural and urban, they are actually faced with the dark side of the so-called 'progress' of the modernization processes. Altamira is a place of business dealings, dirty streets and the contraband of raw materials, where relations are based on financial interests; it is here that the Caravan breaks down and Ciço and Dasdô leave. However, they briefly meet again in a melancholic yet optimistic ending. Ciço and Dasdô play music whilst Lorde Cigano and Salomé perform a new show which relies more on technology. Their new show is called Rolidey (with a 'y' which is an Americanism) and its target audience is now the indigenous population.

Rafael Leopoldo AS Ferreira (trans. Natália Pinazza)

Central Station

Central do Brasil

Studio/Distributor:

Videofilmes
Riofilme
MACT Productions
Director:
Walter Salles

Synopsis

Isadora sits daily amongst the urban bustle of the Central Station of Rio de Janeiro writing letters dictated by illiterate all-comers. Although paid to send the letters to various loved ones and associates, she keeps them in a drawer at home and occasionally reads them for a laugh (to the discomfort of her only friend, Irene). Back at the station, 9-year-old Josué sits while his mother dictates a letter to the father he has never met. On leaving, his mother is run over by a bus and killed, and Josué suddenly finds himself alone.

Isadora sells Josué to a couple for cash but Irene makes her feel

Producers:

Martine de Clermont-Tonnerre
Arthur Cohn
Robert Redford
Walter Salles

Screenwriters:

Marcos Bernstein
João Emanuel Carneiro
Walter Salles

Cinematographer:

Walter Carvalho

Composers:

Jacques Morelenbaum
Antonio Pinto

Editors:

Felipe Lacerda
Isabelle Rathery

Duration:

113 minutes

Genre:

Drama

guilty about this; sensing some responsibility for the lad, Isadora accompanies him out of the city. Journeying ever deeper into the countryside of the *sertão* (backlands) in search of Josué's remaining family, events conspire to keep the two together at each point at which Isadora intends on leaving him. The journey into the open landscape leads both parties to reconsider their connections to home and family, as well as to each other, as the undeniable bond that starts to form changes the relationship of dependency between the two. As they reach his destination, they must confront the realities of family and separation.

Critique

Before it could even be said to be about travel, *Central Station* concerns distance, and above all the problems of separation between human beings. Against the background of the indistinct noise of the crowded central train station, the film's first word is 'Querido' (Dear/ Darling), the conventionalized start to a letter and, here, a pledge that love will endure physical distance. The station setting, grand, inert, impassive, emphasizes not the liberty of movement nor the excitement of departure but the anonymous variety of a nation collected only in transit through a Rio of aestheticized ugliness. The passengers do not speak to those they are pressed up against, but yearn instead for communication with those from whose company

Central do Brasil

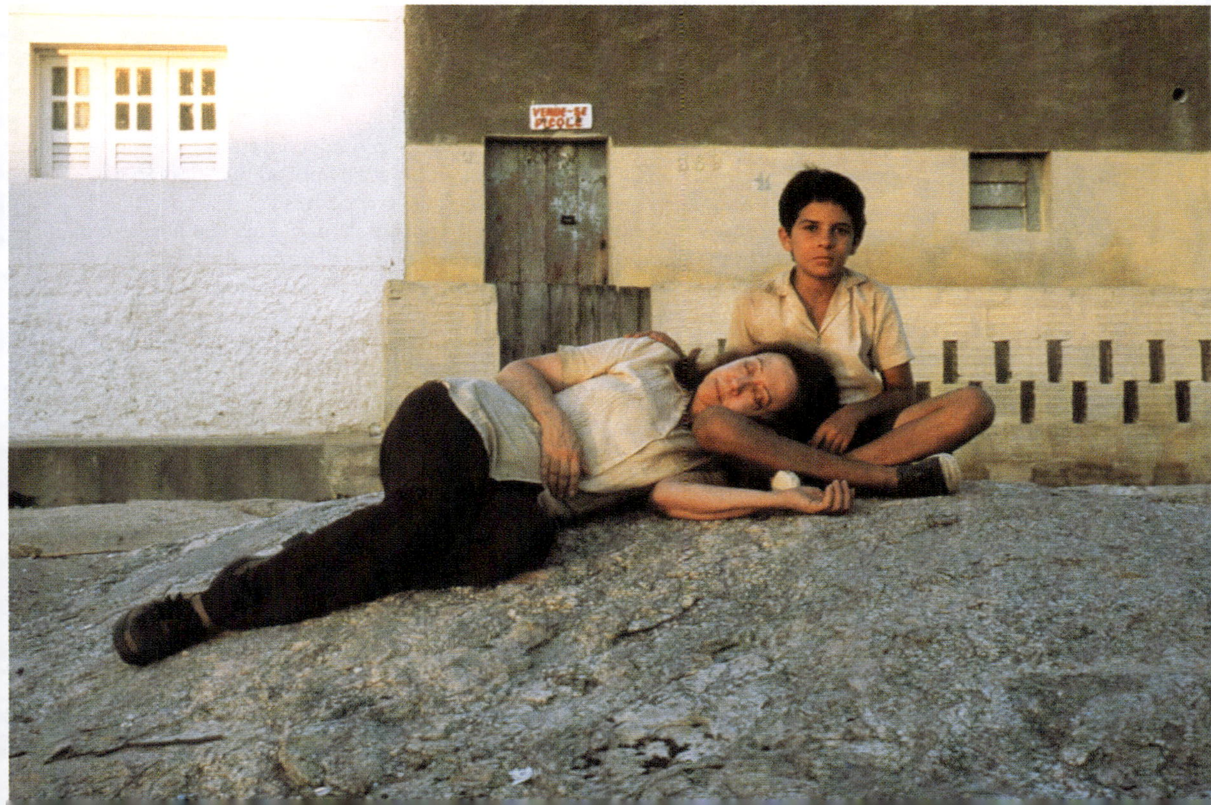

Cast:

Fernanda Montenegro
Vinícius de Oliveira
Marília Pêra

Year:

1998

they are displaced. In a series of close-ups they explain and declaim their wants, their pretentions, their meagre hopes and their grand desires, Isadora sometimes inventing for them lines in letters that contain the lies, rhetoric, simplicity, sincerity, longing – in short, the lives – of people whose words will never be read by their intended recipients. The ultimate separation is thus not only that of enunciator from addressee, but of the very act of communication from the situation which it ostensibly concerns.

What halts the urban alienation is a death; not the death of a nameless thief gunned down in a swiftly passed over occurrence of city life, but of a mother, distracted on a road by her momentarily errant son. That the son has, instinctively, been the first person to question Isadora's trustworthiness is not accidental, for he functions to bring both truth and a discovery of organic communal bonds to the narrative. These are found through the pair's ensuing journey to the *sertão*, the rural landscape where the camera is no longer caught between the protagonists and the passing crowds but glides elegantly into an expanse of silent and de-populated majesty. In this terrain, folk traditions and religious belief (faith in which is implicitly encouraged throughout the film) remain, while the uprightness of a person's character can be taken on trust.

The separation of language from communication could seem to place the film within the tradition of Brazilian modernism, but it forms instead a key moment in the recent commercial and international resurgence, the *retomada*, of the national industry. Its success, undoubtedly, promotes a much criticized conservatism by returning a city boy to a fulfilling rural traditionalism whilst maintaining the continued solitude of an aging and duplicitous female. The sentiments ascribed to childhood and the authenticity of the natural landscape place the film closer to post-war Italian neo-realism than the later, more uncompromising radicalism of the *Cinema Novo*. Meanwhile, the child's search for a mistakenly idealized father – a carpenter, Jesus, described (in a near-mystical connection of man to environment) as having one day 'vanished into the wilderness' – positions the film within an industrially successful strategy in modern festival-circuit cinema which combines an implied questioning of cinematic heritage with moving tales of domestic loss.

A film about return, it ends on separation, but also on a resolution of the opening motifs. On her way back to the city, Isadora finally finds both voice and sincerity as she reads out her own letter to Josué. Writing – over which Isadora maintains control – is here reconnected to meaning, bridging the distance between city and country, past and present, the longing of desire and the acceptance of reality. Her voice-over plays on images of her tearful, then laughing, face, as the editing maintains her association with the now geographically distant Josué who has found his home in the *sertão*. Certainly, a plea for conservation through bonds of personal loyalty. Also, a return to the film's first word, emanating from a tearful face, the dearness it holds now transcending communication to become a defiance of physical separation.

Louis Bayman

Cinema, Aspirins and Vultures

Cinema, aspirinas e urubus

Studio/Distributor:

Dezenove Filmes, Rec
Produtores Associados Ltda.

Director:

Marcelo Gomes

Producer:

Maria Ionescu

Screenwriters:

Karim Aïnouz
Paulo Caldas
Marcelo Gomes

Cinematographer:

Mauro Pinheiro Jr

Art Director:

Marcos Pedroso

Composer:

Tomaz Alves Souza

Editor:

Karen Harley

Duration:

99 minutes

Genres:

Adventure
Drama
Road movie

Cast:

Hermila Guedes
João Miguel
Peter Ketnath

Year:

2005

Synopsis

Johann is working as an aspirin salesman in Brazil in 1942, in order to escape the war in his native Germany. He drives his truck through the arid Brazilian north-east and uses short promotional films to attract customers from the villages he visits, to sell his medicine. During his journey he meets Ranulpho, a sort of drifter looking for a better life. Johann gives him a ride and Ranulpho offers his services as Johann´s assistant. Johann accepts the offer and although at the beginning the two men have some disagreements, they develop a close friendship. The turning point of the film happens when Brazil declares war on Germany, and all German nationals are required to hand themselves over to the authorities. At this point Johann faces two alternatives: to return to Germany and fight a war he rejects, or to stay in Brazil and end up in a concentration camp. He decides to choose a third alternative.

Critique

In this road movie Marcelo Gomes explores the role that things out of our control have in shaping our lives. Johann (Peter Ketnath) is in Brazil escaping the war in Europe. He is working hard to make the best of his life, therefore trying to create his own destiny. However, everything falls apart when Brazil declares war on Germany. It seems that fate is catching up with him. He then decides to reclaim his destiny, by taking the train to Amazonia and hiding there. The film uses powerful imagery to represent the omnipresence of the threat posed by the authorities that try to control Johann's fate, such as the vultures, or more literally the soldiers in the train station where he will take the train to Amazonia.

Cinema, Aspirins and Vultures is part of a group of road movies produced in Latin America in the last fifteen years or so, including the Mexican *Y Tu mamá también/And Your Mother Too* (Alfonso Cuarón, 2001) and the Brazilian *Central do Brasil/Central Station* (Walter Salles, 1998) and the international co-production *Los Diarios de motocicleta/The Motorcycle Diaries* (Walter Salles, 2004). All these films revolve around the introspection and journey of personal discovery undertaken by the central character/s. For example in *Central Station* Dora (Fernanda Montenegro) is a selfish and bitter woman at the beginning of the film. She meets Josué (Vinícius de Oliveira) and then goes on a journey that will take her back to her roots and to a rediscovery of who she really is. In *Cinema, Aspirins and Vultures*, Johann will also go on a voyage of personal discovery, escaping from a war he rejects. His friendship with Ranulpho (João Miguel) will help him make up his mind about who he really is and what he wants to do with his life. Johann´s whole situation seems to be a metaphor for millions of Europeans who were trapped in the middle of a terrible war.

As in other road movies, it is not just the actors that play a role in *Cinema, Aspirins and Vultures*, it is the country, the landscape and the people, in this case the people from the north-east of Brazil. The reality of that part of Brazil is presented in a very naturalistic and realistic way. The way the film presents this reality has many realist elements, including the use of natural settings, non-professional actors, the use of handheld camera, long takes, unexpected camera movements and angles, etc. All of these techniques create a documentary feel and form part of a Brazilian cinematic tradition that goes back to the *Cinema Novo* movement and film-makers like Glauber Rocha.

José Antonio Ureña Muñoz

Foreign Land

Terra estrangeira

Studio/Distributor:

Videofilmes
Animatógrafo

Directors:

Walter Salles
Daniela Thomas

Producer:

Flávio R Tambellini

Screenwriters:

Daniela Thomas
Marcos Bernstein
Walter Salles
Millor Fernandes

Cinematographer:

Walter Carvalho

Art Director:

Daniela Thomas

Composer:

José Miguel Wisnik

Editors:

Walter Salles
Felipe Lacerda

Duration:

100 minutes

Genre:

Drama

Cast:

Fernanda Torres
Fernando Alves Pinto
Luís Melo
Alexandre Borges

Synopsis

Paco is a physics student in São Paulo. His life takes a turn when his mother, a seamstress originally from San Sebastián in Spain, dies. Unable to find a job during the recession and struggling to finance his mother's funeral, Paco goes to a bar to drown his sorrows. There, he is engaged by a smuggler, who persuades him to go to Lisbon, from where he can easily reach Spain and honour his mother's unfulfilled wish to return to her hometown. Not aware of the real purpose of his trip, Paco flies to Portugal carrying in his luggage a violin full of diamonds, which he is supposed to sell. Upon his arrival, however, no one contacts him. Alone in Lisbon, he meets Alex, a Brazilian migrant working in a restaurant. As Paco and Alex realize they are involved in a complex criminal plot, they try to escape, driving through Portugal's secondary routes on their way to San Sebastián.

Critique

A Luso-Brazilian co-production, *Foreign Land* marks the beginning of a successful collaboration between film-makers Walter Salles and Daniela Thomas. In comparison with *Central do Brasil/Central Station* (1998) and *Los Diarios de motocicleta/The Motorcycle Diaries* (2004), films for which Salles is more widely known, *Foreign Land* has a more modernist style. The use of black and white and hand-held camera gives the film a quasi-documentary look, with close-ups, jump cuts and jazz music referencing the new cinemas of the 1960s. Genre conventions are also parodied, namely those of film noir, as in Alex's presentation as a femme fatale. Although as a crime film *Foreign Land* includes a number of vigorous action scenes, dialogue takes prominence throughout, with a reflexive tone allowing characters to talk about their feelings and emotions. For instance, in the first sequence Paco recites Goethe's *Faust*, with the passage 'Yes, if a magic cloak were mine, that / Would carry me off to foreign lands' (1808), thus introducing the film's main topic.

Featuring real footage of President Fernando Collor de Mello, the film clearly establishes its historical and political context, namely the economic crisis that hit Brazil in the early 1990s. While *Foreign Land* begins by editing two plotlines (Paco's [Fernando Alves Pinto] life in Brazil and Alex's [Fernanda Torres] life in Lisbon) in parallel, it is precisely the crisis that brings them together, with scenes set in the two countries showing us how characters on both sides of the Atlantic

Laura Cardoso
João Lagarto
Year:
1996

keep their money in drawers rather than a bank. Of course, language also unites the film's protagonists – but problems with their lusophone identities are equally stressed. Hence, Alex tells her husband she feels like a foreigner in Lisbon, where she is constantly scorned because of her accent. Showcased prominently throughout *Foreign Land*, the sea (or images that evoke the sea, such as shots of the river Tagus) also reminds the viewer of the significant cultural gap between Portugal and Brazil – especially through the striking image of a stranded boat (that Paco and Alex spot en route to Spain), clearly reminiscent of the Portuguese 'discoveries'. Another vivid spatial opposition contrasts São Paulo (where the film, despite being co-funded by the mayor of Rio de Janeiro, is partly set) and Lisbon. Whereas the former is represented by the 'Minhocão', hinting at the poverty and chaotic development of the city, the latter emerges as peaceful and historical. The introduction of the Portuguese capital takes place through a postcard-perfect shot of the river Tagus, accompanied by a Portuguese guitar solo; throughout, trams and painted tiles contribute to a stereotypical view of 'the white city'. The overwhelming majority of films shot in Lisbon by non-Portuguese film-makers include a scene devoted to *fado* and *Foreign Land* is no exception, featuring 'Estranha forma de vida', one of the musical genre's iconic songs (here curiously performed by jazz singer Maria João).

As borders and passports are significant elements of its narrative and visual composition, *Foreign Land* depicts a changing Europe where the migrant and the tourist (here embodied by the film's privileged directors) coexist. Almost two decades later, it is worth noting the changes that have occurred both in Portugal and Brazil, as well as the inversion of their roles; in 2011, due to the European debt crisis, over 100,000 Portuguese citizens moved to the Southern American nation, today the sixth largest economy in the world.

Mariana Liz

A Hungarian Passport

Um Passaporte húngaro

Studio/Distributor:

Zeugma Filmes
Arte France
Hunnia Filmstudio
Cobra Films
RTBF Bruxelles
CICV Pierre Schaeffer
Director:

Sandra Kogut
Producer:

Michel David

Synopsis

Um passaporte húngaro, a documentary filmed over the course of two years (May 1999-May 2001), as the final credits reveal, follows director Sandra Kogut, a Brazilian Jew of Hungarian descent living in Paris at the time, as she pursues an application for Hungarian nationality and passport. The film charts the often Kafkaesque bureaucratic process of application, involving navigating through sometimes conflicting sets of requirements from authorities in France, Brazil and Hungary. Dovetailed with footage of the director's meetings with officials as well as archival staff in Brazil and abroad, aiding her search for documentary proof of her European heritage, is more personal footage of her conversations with her grandmother in Rio de Janeiro, Mathilde Lajta, to whom the film is dedicated, and of meetings with her extended family back in Budapest, with whom Kogut reconnects over the course of her travels throughout the process. The film takes us on a spatio-temporal journey as we discover, for instance, the human story behind Kogut's grandparents' move to Brazil as the threat from Nazi Germany was looming. Stories

Screenwriter:

Sandra Kogut

Cinematographers:

Florent Jullien
Florian Bouchet
Sandra Kogut

Art Director:

Sandra Kogut

Editors:

Monica Almeida
Sandra Kogut

Duration:

111 minutes

Genre:

Documentary
Persons:
Kogut family, et al.

Year:

2001

of present and past transnational migrations are thus intertwined, drawing us into the complexity of personal and national identities, inevitably shown to be far from monolithic.

Critique

Early shots of *Um passaporte húngaro* taken from a moving train, with the rail tracks trailing behind the engine in motion, point to the experience of departing. Intercut with these shots of a journey, Sandra Kogut's conversations with her grandmother about her experience of migration introduce the question of displacement and its implications for any sense of personal identity which the film explores. Thus, from early on *Um passaporte húngaro*, a documentary 'on the road', fittingly explores the potential for enquiry into fundamental human concerns about the self and its place in the world that the theme of the journey opens up.

The documentary was filmed in three different countries – France, Brazil and Hungary - and continually bridges national and linguistic borders. In so doing, it creates a space for a polyphony of voices in which that of the director and prime interlocutor (who only makes two fleeting and understated appearances on the screen) systematically allows its subjects to take centre stage in front of the inconspicuous camera.

Indeed, this is one of the ways in which *Um passaporte húngaro* places hybridity at the very heart of its narrative and its construction: seen too in the intercutting of disparate film styles, the exploration of static and moving, hand-held cameras, for example, as well as in the privileging of different voices and subject positions. Embodiment of this is found in Kogut's main interviewee, her own grandmother, whom Kogut discovers is an Austrian Jew by birth who lost her nationality upon marrying, thereby acquiring Hungarian nationality and subsequently a Brazilian one. Her testimony, delivered in fluent but accented Portuguese, can be seen to crystallize the question Kogut probes in her documentary.

In this way, the image of the passport is of the essence, as *Um passaporte húngaro* explores the profound disjuncture between official constructions of identity and human experience. Thus, we might understand Kogut's careful use of the static device of black-on-white intertitles to punctuate the narrative. Each of these intertitles reproduces a different bureaucratic requirement, items on application forms, stages in the application process which Kogut needs to satisfy to be successful in her request. The static nature of these vis-à-vis the preponderance of mobility throughout the documentary illustrates the contrast between the rigidity (and seeming randomness) of the Law (often associated with fixed camera location shots) and the fluid, shifting nature of real life experience.

As the film draws to a close, we are again taken on a train journey, and again it is a departure, this time Kogut's journey from Budapest after having obtained her passport. Here, Kogut poignantly explores the open-ended nature of this situation rather than dwell on a sense of closure. As a discreet, low-angle camera captures the towering figure of the suspicious border control official who queries Kogut's possession of Hungarian documentation in a long sequence shot, the sense of control and surveillance is conveyed effectively. Yet, equally, when, in the light of her failure to understand him when he addresses her in Hungarian, he absurdly asks her for ID Kogut's mastery at deploying real life situations in defense of human agency becomes apparent once more. And in this way, the camera's tongue-in-cheek unnoticed gaze directed at authority exemplifies the tension on which much of the film's success hinges.

Sara Brandellero

I Travel Because I Have to, I Come back Because I Love You

Viajo porque preciso, volto porque te amo

Studio/Distributor:

Rec Produtores Associados Ltda.

Directors:

Karim Aïnouz
Marcelo Gomes

Producer:

João Vieira Jr

Screenwriters:

Karim Aïnouz
Marcelo Gomes

Cinematographer:

Heloísa Passos

Composer:

Chambaril

Editor:

Karen Harley

Duration:

75 minutes

Genre:

Drama

Cast:

Irandhir Santos

Synopsis

Geologist Renato journeys across the dry harsh backland of north-west Brazil to survey the area which will be affected by a project to build a new canal. He films the journey as a travel journal, however the commentary of the unseen man behind the camera soon turns to anguish and pain over his separation with his wife. Travelling across the expanse of barren land, the pretense of the geological mission breaks down and the road trip slips into wanderings amongst the wilderness and his own emotional desolation. As his journey turns into a search for the miracle that will let him come to terms with life, his camera turns to the lives of the local residents of the isolated settlements, villages and towns he passes on his travels. Ultimately though, the search to find meaning in his life is a challenge he must undertake alone.

Critique

In 1999 the film director Karim Aïnouz and fellow film-maker Marcelo Gomes took a two month road trip across Brazil. Along the way they captured images, recording the scenery, people and places they encountered on Super-8, 16mm and photographic stills. A decade later, having shot the highly acclaimed *Madame Satã/Madam Satan* (2002) and *O Céu de Suely/Suely in the Sky* (2006), Aïnouz teamed up with Gomes again to make a feature film from those images. Their own personal filmic record of their road trip developed into an intensely personal and intimate story told through the film journal of the unseen narrator-protagonist. This narration serves almost like a musical score, giving emotional expression to the images, which in turn come to embody the unseen self of this soul-searching story. As the director himself openly admits, narration was only there to complement and assist the images. Originating in images rather than a written script, *I Travel Because I Have to, I Come back Because I Love You* is nevertheless no less of a character-driven drama than Aïnouz's previous films, with the images of the road trip transforming into a story of the self.

Aïnouz and Gomes's experimental film is an intimate and searching exploration of character in which the inner landscape of the unseen protagonist is made visible through the physical landscape in which he travels. While the film is explicitly recognizable as a travel journal, as the story unfolds this reveals itself as a record of a journey of human experience. The experience of overwhelming loss established

Year:

2009

in the first part of the film becomes a search for reunification – the miracle – through which redemption might be found. This theme is underscored by highly symbolic images and resonant parallels to the Biblical story of Adam's expulsion from the Garden of Eden. This, together with filmic techniques such as the use of photographic still images and double exposures, gives *I Travel Because I Have to, I Come back Because I Love You* an aesthetic which has more in common with the visual arts and poetry than the storytelling techniques of mainstream cinema. Through the device of an intimate and personal filmic travel journal, Aïnouz and Gomes's experimental film succeeds in offering a psychoanalytic portrait which situates the audience in the emotional experience of the main character. Concern with questions of identity, renewal of self and the interplay of symbolically resonant landscape with the psychological alienation of the protagonist gives the film an evocative presence which makes the film worthy of serious critical attention.

Asako Kobayashi

The Middle of the World

O Caminho das nuvens

Studio/Distributor:

Disney/ Buena Vista

Director:

Vicente Amorim

Producers:

Bruno Barreto
Angelo Gastal

Screenwriter:

David França Mendes

Cinematographer:

Gustavo Hadba

Art Director:

Jean-Louis Leblanc

Composer:

André Cibelli Abujamra

Editor:

Pedro Amorim

Duration:

83 minutes

Genre:

Drama

Synopsis

Based on true events, *The Middle of the World* tells the story of a family that decides to relocate to Rio de Janeiro. Guided by the father Romão, they must ride away from their home in Paraíba, and towards his dream of a higher salary to enable him to take care of his family. Romão is an unemployed truck driver, and Rose, his wife, a simple woman who accepts the changes her husband makes. They are poor, with five children: a baby and four others aged between six and fourteen.

The film starts on the road. The family has four bicycles and a 3,200 kilometre journey between their city and Rio de Janeiro. Along the way they see the Brazilian countryside and its different sights and locations. Along country roads, dirt paths and highways they follow their goal. The difficulties of the challenging journey cause problems and many conflicts in the pursuit of their hopes.

Critique

The Middle of the World is the debut feature-length fiction of Vicente Amorim, who had previously made a documentary and worked as an assistant director for a number of well-respected Brazilian directors including Hector Babenco, Bruno Barreto and Cacá Diegues. His debut concerns a phenomenon familiar to Brazil: migration to the big cities, a common subject in Brazilian literature, soap opera, music and films. Oppression, powerlessness, mortality, and the transitory nature of life in the dry Brazilian north-east force people to move south to big cities like Rio de Janeiro and São Paulo. Narratives on this theme populate Brazilian culture, but *The Middle of the World* displays some marked peculiarities. The family makes their journey by bicycle, instead of the more usual migrant transportation of truck, car or bus. According to Amorim it took six months for the family on which the

Cast:

Cláudia Abreu
Wagner Moura
Ravi Ramos Lacerda

Year:

2003

film is based to undertake the whole journey. It shows, in his opinion, their 'directness and ability to adapt'. He also felt that their history was his own story too, as during his youth he had moved country several times.

The film begins on a blue sky as the camera moves through white and soft clouds rendered in CGI to give the impression of flight. The sequence reaches the protagonists on earth in a background of unending open space and in front of a sign that reads 'Square in the middle of the world'. The family is introduced, member by member, whilst looking for the baby who has suddenly disappeared. From this moment on the film frequently uses tight close-ups on the protagonists' faces, including during dialogue scenes, to evoke the feeling of enclosure which persists even during long sequences of silence. The family do not speak much but use short sentences and intense looks through which to speak, evaluate, approve or disapprove, and sometimes smile. As the plot unfolds the editing follows a slow rhythm. The film conveys an idea of effort, the family journey, within a static environment of the *sertão* (backlands). The repetitive sound of their bicycles reinforces the rhythm of the film. The horizon divides the screen into two halves: the upper half shows the bright yellow light of the sun and the movement of clouds while on the lower half lies the expanse of dry land intersected by roads and highways and the movement of the four bicycles at the bottom. A popular Brazilian singer, Roberto Carlos, plays on the slushy romantic soundtrack. Finally, when the family arrives in Rio de Janeiro their faces show disappointment. They enter the city through a slum and the following scenes show the work they will need to do so as to make a living. Later, however, when they climb up the hill of Christ the Redeemer, they see the sea, liquid, sparkling, coming and going in constant motion. Looking towards the end of the bridge, Romão's thoughts seem far away. The bridge is a metaphor, and connects Rio de Janeiro to the other states back in the direction of north-eastern Brazil.

Fabiana Ghiringhello

Pachamama

Studio/Distributor:

Urca Filmes

Director:

Eryk Rocha

Producers:

Leonardo Edde
Daniela Martins

Screenwriter:

Eryk Rocha

Cinematographer:

Eryk Rocha

Synopsis

Pachamama, whose title refers to the goddess 'Mother Earth' of the indigenous people of the Andes, is a road movie documentary which follows the director's journey from Brazil's Atlantic coast, in Rio de Janeiro, across the country's continental expanses and beyond its borders, into Peru and Bolivia. With a small crew organized into two jeeps, he sets off on a journey lasting thirty days, in search of the 'open heart' of the South American sub-continent, as he tells us in voice-over at the film's incipit. The film's focus is firmly on the disenfranchised indigenous communities, historically relegated to the fringes of society. The crew's arrival in Iñapari, on the Peruvian border, and subsequent stops in Puerto Maldonado, Mazuko, Cuzco and later in La Paz and beyond are punctuated by interviews with locals, often in tense circumstances of political or social unrest, and often speaking

Art Director:

Eryk Rocha

Composer:

Aurélio Dias

Editors:

Eryk Rocha
Eva Randolph

Duration:

105 minutes

Genre:

Documentary

Persons:

Various, from archival footage

Year:

2009

from opposite ideological perspectives, centred on issues of social justice, such as land distribution, environmental justice, defense of indigenous cultures and labour rights. The urgency of such issues is often supported by reference to media coverage of such topical issues: through the diegetic sound of radio broadcasts or excerpts from television programmes – a speech by President Evo Morales defending traditional use of coca leaves and visibility of indigenous identities in modern day Bolivia being a case in point. As the journey progresses, footage of social tensions from different locations seems to intercut, heightening the connections between local specificities, constructing the image of a sub-continent in turmoil.

Critique

Suggesting the need to underline the film's commitment to reality, a voice-over by the director-cum-traveller (who remains faceless, underscoring the film's pursuit of other subjectivities and places) informs us early on of the date of departure – 2 January 2007 – and of the purpose of the journey: to reach the frontiers and to 'bring down the frontiers' in order to understand Brazil within its South American context. The question Rocha poses is thus: 'What continent is this?'

Early close-up shots of the road surface, taken from the moving vehicle, accompanied by the sound of what seems to be a beating heart and the rolling of film footage seem to synthesize the relationship between the moving image and the experience of being on the road. This early self-reflexive moment draws our attention to the significance of the genre at hand. Indeed, as it searches for answers and sharpens its focus on the plight of the disenfranchised indigenous people of the continent, the road movie proves a powerful medium for a socially committed cinema. As the director informs us in the film's initial sequence: 'there are no boundaries between journey and film.' Following a tradition established by trailblazing Brazilian films such as Jorge Bodansky and Orland Senna's docudrama *Iracema/Iracema, uma transa amazônica* (1976), the journey and the encounters it facilitates probe important questions about the sub-continent, such as the exploitation of labour, the land and its resources, colonialism and its legacy, the representation of indigenous people.

The opening sequences of the film shot from within the moving vehicle are strongly subjective, as conveyed for instance by the monotonous movement of the windscreen wipers which becomes the camera's focus as the jeep makes headway through the driving rain. The travellers' sense of isolation and even fatigue, as their concentration wanders, is thus poignantly conveyed. This attention to the subjectivities behind the camera soon shifts to what lies beyond it once the vehicle truly hits the road after leaving the urban space of Rio de Janeiro behind. The camera is committed to pursuing a closeness with its subjects, and an early long-take of a face of a young boy encountered on the road, looking directly at the camera, suggests the film's commitment. Its engagement with social and political issues is paramount, and a striking experience of this is provided by the camera's recording, once it has reached Mazuko, of the protests of a group of Aymara Indians who condemn the existence of national borders which have 'carved up' their traditional lands into modern nations (Peru, Bolivia, Argentina and Chile) which they do not recognize. The film's incorporation of speakers of Andean indigenous languages, beside Portuguese and Spanish, further supports its questioning of issues of national and regional identities.

As it reflects on these issues and searches for answers, the camera's gaze, often supported by powerful indigenous-inspired music, constantly returns to the land: through long takes of varied breathtaking landscapes, the need for social justice through respect for a land that knows no borders – Pachamama – is defended.

Sara Brandellero

Suely in the Sky

O Céu de Suely

Studio/Distributor:

Celluloid Dreams, Fado Filmes, Shotgun Pictures

Director:

Karim Aïnouz

Producers:

Walter Salles
Maurício Andrade Ramos
Hengameh Panahi
Thomas Häberle
Peter Rommel

Screenwriters:

Karim Aïnouz
Felipe Bragança
Maurício Zacharias

Cinematographer:

Marcos Pedroso

Art Director:

Marcos Pedroso

Composers:

Berna Ceppas
Kamal Kassin.

Editors:

Tina Baz Le Gal
Isabela Monteiro de Castro

Duration:

88 minutes

Genre:

Drama

Synopsis

Hermila is a 21-year-old woman who, after eloping with her boyfriend Mateus and going to São Paulo, returns to her home town Iguatu in the interior of the state of Ceará in the north-east of Brazil with Mateuzinho, the son she has had with her boyfriend. Although she says that her boyfriend will return in a month, this does not happen and she loses contact with him. She then gets close to João, a former lover who clearly loves her dearly. Hermila does different things to make ends meet, such as raffling a bottle of whiskey and washing cars at a gas station. Eventually, she has an idea to make the money she needs to once again leave the town in which she clearly no longer belongs. She adopts the *nom de guerre* Suely and decides to raffle an unconventional prize – 'a night in paradise' (with her) – which, needless to say, causes a furore among many males but attracts much condemnation from the other townspeople, particularly the women.

Critique

Suely in the Sky is a film that we may call 'an off-road road film'. It is mostly set in the intermittent period in which Hermila (Hermila Guedes) returns from São Paulo and tries to readapt to where she comes from, before embarking on a new journey. Travel in the film serves as a way for Hermila to undergo an internal as well as an external journey during which she constructs her selfhood and her sense of being in the world. This is suggested through the film's subversion of the staple hegemonic binaries in road movies, particularly in relation to gender. That is, most road movies have served as an experience for the male character to explore the world and develop his identity, which echoes to some extent the traditional migration pattern from the north-east to the south-east of Brazil, common during many decades of the last century. In this pattern it was normally the males who migrated in search of work whereas the wives were left behind in the dry north-east to raise their children and survive on their own. However, in the case of *Suely in the Sky*, it is the female character that embarks on a physical journey: first, with her boyfriend (as the audience finds out through the protagonist's conversations with her aunt), then on her own at the end of the film,

Cast:

Hermila Guedes
João Miguel
Maria Menezes
Zezita Matos
Marcelia Cartaxo

Year:

2006

which suggests her development into an independent woman.

The road becomes a way for Hermila to escape the traditional domestic sphere to which she clearly does not belong. Her non-belonging to the latter is implied in the 'unconventional' tasks she fulfils on her return to Iguatu. At first, she intends to set up a stall to sell fake DVDs, videogames and CDs; she then starts selling raffle tickets in areas of the town frequented mostly by males (in many scenes she is the only woman among the men); and later she starts washing cars in a gas station – all tasks that subvert the roles associated with women in her society. For example, the female prostitute Georgina (Georgina Castro), with whom Hermila becomes acquainted, tells the latter: 'This is the first time I've ever seen a woman washing cars!' Even more subversive is when Hermila decides to sell the raffle for which the prize is a 'night in paradise' as this causes a scandal in Iguatu, and people threaten to get her prosecuted for it.

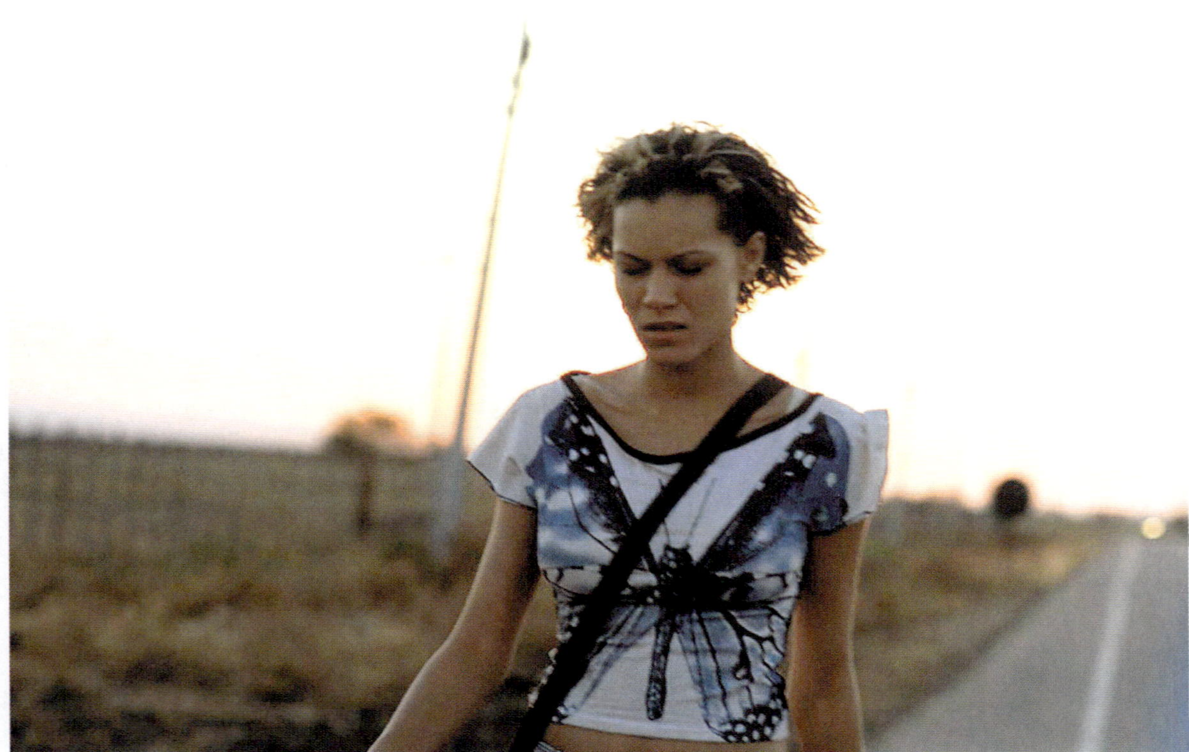

Suely in the Sky

All the problems Hermila encounters clearly result from her travelling and having experiences that may be seen as normal in other contexts, particularly in a big urban centre such as São Paulo where she had been living, but not in Iguatu. Moreover, this travelling not only conveys her own experience but also hints at many aspects of a national Brazilian identity, particularly in terms of gender, sexuality and social relations. Nevertheless, one danger that people may find in this road movie is that the female's experience of travelling results in her adopting behaviour considered immoral and promiscuous (when viewed through patriarchal lenses), evident, for instance, when one of the women who is against her raffle confronts her saying: 'I've seen people raffling many things, but a whore, I never did!' Hermila, however, rejects the idea that what she is doing is prostitution. In her view, a prostitute goes with everyone, but she will go with one man only. She concludes: 'I do not want to be a whore; I want to be fuck all!' Hermila is conscious of her acts and the results she wants to achieve through doing what she does.

A further result of Hermila's travelling experience concerns the fact that Iguatu becomes 'too small' for her; she is alienated from (and bored with) the place, which again indicates that she has developed and changed her identity through 'being on the road'. Her sense of non-belonging to Iguatu makes her decide to leave and embark on a new journey, to a place that is 'the furthest the coaches can go' from Iguatu, as she says to the attendant at the ticket office in the coach station. Such a place ends up being Rio Grande do Sul, the last state in the south of Brazil, which is located in the extreme geographical opposition to that of Ceará.

Hence, *Suely in the Sky* adopts the road as a means of development for the female character's identity. By doing so, the film adapts the genre to the Brazilian context and gives the woman opportunities to develop her adult identity through her experience of the road. Moreover, it converges spaces of movement (the road) and static locations (the home) as places that, although normally opposed to each other, still play an intersecting role in the female character's construction of her selfhood, especially through its challenge to hegemonic roles – particularly those associated with the traditional road movie genre.

Antônio Márcio da Silva

RECOMMENDED READING

Altmann, E (2010) *O Brasil imaginado na América Latina: a crítica de filmes de Glauber Rocha e Walter Salles*, Rio de Janeiro: Contra Capa.

Bentes, I (ed.) (1997) *Cartas ao mundo*, São Paulo: Companhia das Letras.

Bernadette, JC (2011) *Trajetória crítica*, São Paulo: Polis.

Butcher, P (2005) *Cinema Brasileiro Hoje*, São Paulo: Publifolha.

Catani, AM and Melo Souza, José I (1983) *A chanchada no cinema brasileiro*, São Paulo: Brasiliense.

Dennison, S and Shaw, L (2004) *Popular Cinema in Brazil*, Manchester: Manchester University Press.

Ferreira, CO (2012) 'Identity and Difference: Postcoloniality and Transnationality in Lusophone Films', Münster: Lit Verlag.

Foster, DW (1999) 'Gender and Society in Contemporary Brazilian Cinema', Austin: University of Texas Press.

Gatti, AP (2005) 'Distribuição e Exibição na Indústria Cinematográfica Brasileira (1993–2003)', PhD thesis, Campinas: Universidade Estadual de Campinas.

Hart, SM (2004) *A Companion to Latin American Film*, Woodbridge: Tamesis.

Johnson, R (1987) *The Film Industry in Brazil: Culture and State in Latin America*, Pittsburgh: University of Pittsburgh Press.

Johnson, R and Stam, R (eds) (1995) *Brazilian Cinema*, New York: Columbia University Press.

Lyra, B and Santana, G (eds) (2006) *Cinema de Bordas 1*, São Paulo: Editora A Lápis.

Nagib, L (2002) *O cinema da retomada: depoimentos de 90 cineastas dos anos 90*, São Paulo: Editora 34.

Nagib, L (ed.) (2003) *The New Brazilian Cinema*, London: I.B. Tauris.

Nagib, L (2007) *Brazil on Screen: Cinema Novo, New cinema, Utopia*, London: I.B. Tauris.

Oricchio, LZ (2003) *Cinema de novo: um balanço crítico da retomada*, São Paulo: Estação Liberdade.

Ortiz, R (1999) *Cultura brasileira e identidade nacional*, São Paulo: Brasiliense.

Ramos, F and Miranda, LF (eds) (1997) *Enciclopédia do Cinema Brasileiro*, São Paulo: Editora Senac.

Rego, C and Rocha, C (eds) (2010) *New Trends in Argentine and Brazilian Cinema*, Bristol: Intellect.

Salles Gomes, PE (1996) *Cinema: trajetória no subdesenvolvimento*, Rio de Janeiro: Paz e Terra. Shaw, D (ed.) (2007) *Contemporary Latin American Cinema: Breaking into the Global Market*, Plymouth: Rowman and Littlefield.

Shaw, L and Dennison, S (eds) (2007) *Brazilian National Cinema*, Oxon: Routledge.

Soares, MC and Ferreira, J (eds) (2001) *A história vai ao cinema: vinte filmes brasileiros comentados por historiadores*, Rio de Janeiro: Record.

Stam, R (1997) *Tropical Multiculturalism: A Comparative History of Race in Brazilian Cinema and Culture*, London: Duke Press.

Viany, A (1993) *Introdução ao cinema brasileiro*, Rio de Janeiro: Revan.

Xavier, I (1997) *Allegories of Underdevelopment: Aesthetics and Politics in Modern Brazilian Cinema*, Minneapolis: University of Minnesota Press.

BRAZILIAN CINEMA ONLINE

ANCINE (Agência Nacional do Cinema)
http://www.ancine.gov.br/
Portuguese website of the Brazilian National Cinema Agency that provides data and information about Brazilian cinema.

CinePipocaCult
http://www.cinepipocacult.com.br/
Portuguese website which provides a wide range of film reviews.

Criticos.com.br
Portuguese website which offers a wide range of film reviews.

Revista Cine Cachoeira
http://www.ufrb.edu.br/cinecachoeira/
Online film magazine of the Universidade Federal do Recôncavo da Bahia.

Contracampo Revista de Cinema
http://www.contracampo.com.br/
Online film magazine Contracampo.

Canal Brasil
http://canalbrasil.globo.com/
Portuguese website of Canal Brasil, the principal TV channel promoting Brazilian cinema.

Cinemateca Brasileira
http://www.cinemateca.gov.br/
Portuguese website of the Cinemateca Brasileira, a film library and archive of Brazilian cinema.

SOCINE (Sociedade Brasileira de Estudos de Cinema e Audiovisual)
http://www.socine.org.br/
Portuguese website of the Brazilian Society of Cinema and
Audiovisual Studies (SOCINE), which provides information about their
annual conference and recent publications.

O Cinema do Brasil
http://www.cinemadobrasil.org.br/
Portuguese website of O Cinema do Brazil, an initiative that aims to
promote Brazilian cinema in the world and gives information related
to film production and distribution.

Memória da Censura no Cinema Brasileiro
http://www.memoriacinebr.com.br/historico_do_projeto.asp
Portuguese website of Memória da Censura no Cinema Brasileiro, a
project that aims to preserve and democratize the access to footage
and material censured during the military dictatorship.

Filme Cultura
www.filmecultura.org.br
Website of the film magazine Filme Cultura.

Questions

1. What is the Portuguese-language term for the era in cinema that emerged in Brazil in the early to mid 1990s?

2. Which Brazilian composer was used in the musical score of *O Descobrimento do Brasil/ The Discovery of Brazil* and *Di/Glauber*?

3. Which major national production company made the biggest investment in the Brazilian industry's history with its first film *Caiçara*, whose long and accident-prone location shoot occurred while the company's studios were still being built in São Bernardo do Campo and was described as 'a picnic on Ilhabela' and whose crew was made up of a multinational team headed by Alberto Cavalcanti and included the so-called 'black belt in cinema', cinematographer Chick Fowle?

4. What cannibal ritual was employed as an anti-colonial metaphor in Brazilian arts and literature and would be later used in films such as *Macunaíma* and *Como era gostoso o meu francês/How Tasty Was My Little Frenchman*?

5. Which film is based on a book written by a physician who volunteered to work in one of the largest jails in Brazil?

6. Which Brazilian film-maker coined the motto 'A camera in the hand and an idea in the head'?

7. Which Brazilian director became internationally renowned for his films, in particular, road movies such as *Los Diarios de motocicleta/The Motorcycle Diaries* and, more recently, *On the Road*?

8. Which historical parody featuring the Spanish and Portuguese royal families uses comedy to address colonial issues?

9. Which film star, named the 'most popular figure in Brazilian cinema' in 1935, helped to turn the samba from its associations with a criminal underclass into the musical symbol of Brazil?

10. Which Glauber Rocha film title contains the greatest number of different languages per word of any internationally distributed title?

11. Artistically and sexually ahead of its time *Ganga bruta* was neglected for decades after its release due to its adherence to which technological anachronism?

12. Which area of São Paulo gave its name to a national strain of marginal cinema?

13. Which late 1990s commercial success for Brazilian cinema had its international distribution secured by the participation of producer Robert Redford?

14. Which Hollywood star is parodied by the sawmill worker Aldenir Coti in films whose subtitles variously describe him as 'o rapto do jaraqui dourado' and 'o boxeador da Amazônia'?

15. To which 1962 product of the *Cinema Novo* does the 2010 cinematic project *5 × favela, agora por nós mesmos/5 × Favela: Now By Ourselves* refer?

16. Which key industry decision in the early 1990s caused a crisis which led to Brazil's film

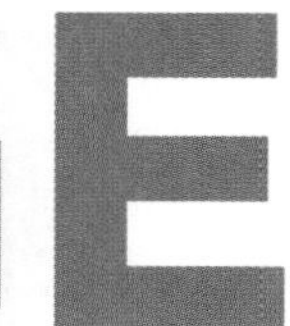

festival circuit running out of national entrants for competition?

17. Which text is taken as a statement of intent not only for the *Cinema Novo* but as a manifesto for Latin American cinema?

18. What, to date, is the only Brazilian film to have won the Palme d'Or at the 'Cannes Film Festival', and for a bonus point, in which year did it win?

19. Carmen Miranda and many other music stars feature in which Brazilian film genre?

20. Which film genre most fertile in the 1970s originates from a merging of the popular musical entertainment of the *chanchada* with the new possibilities opened up for pornographic representation?

21. At what time, according to the film directed by Jose Marins, is Coffin Joe going to take your soul?

22. Which production company has played a key role in Brazil's most recent domestic commercial successes, in part through its connection to the TV company Rede Global and its stable of A-list soap stars?

23. What is *forró* ?

24. Founder of the *Tropicália* music movement Caetano Veloso proclaimed which rebellious rock star, topic of an eponymous biopic, 'the greatest poet of his generation'?

25. What do Dona Flor's husbands have in common with Francisco's sons, and the people lost in a dirty night?

26. Which Brazilian city is home to the infamous City of God area?

27. Which German explorer gives his name to the film of an account written in Hesse in the mid sixteenth century of an expedition first on a Portuguese ship to Pernambuco and then with a Spanish armada which sunk off the Santa Catarina coast, was nominated 'commander of the Bertioga Fortress', threatened with cannibalism in an anthropophagic ritual by the Tupinambás of the Cunhambebe settlement, and rescued by the French?

28. Which famous British police killing led to a biopic on the conditions of Brazilian immigrants?

29. Which documentary of the 1979 strike of 150,000 steel workers, banned for its Marxist imagery of militant workers' autonomy, includes the future Brazilian president Luis Inácio Lula da Silva amongst its collective cast of workers?

30. The dribble of which right-winger engendered the 'joy of the people', according to the left-wing cineastes of the *Cinema Novo*?

31. Which politically controversial playwright's story of a tubercolic suburban housewife's obsession with her own death in the face of her husband's preoccupation with the local football derby formed the basis for Leon Hirszman's 1965 *A Falecida/The Deceased*, a film whose commercial failure left both the playwright and his son dismayed and indebted?

32. In its updating of Voltaire's *Candide*, what is the reason, according to Candinho, for everything bad that happens?

33. The Brothers Grimm's 'The Town Musicians of Bremen', filtered through Chico Buarque de Hollanda's play, forms the basis for which carnivalesque troupe's filmic celebration of collective solidarity?

34. Based on a true story, which method of transport does a seven-member family use to travel 3,200 kilometres in *O Caminho das nuvens/The Middle of the World*?

35. To what does the title *Pachamama* refer?

Answers

1. *Cinema da retomada*
2. Heitor Villa-Lobos
3. Vera Cruz Studios (Companhia Cinematográfica Vera Cruz)
4. Anthropophagy
5. *Carandiru*
6. Paulo César Saraceni
7. Walter Salles
8. *Carlota Joaquina: princesa do Brasil/Carlota Joaquina: Princess of Brazil*
9. Carmen Miranda
10. *Der Leone Have Sept Cabeças*
11. Vitaphone, which by the film's release in 1933 had been overtaken by synchronous sound but that the Brazilian industry of the time found difficulty affording.
12. Boca do Lixo
13. *Central do Brasil/Central Station*
14. Sylvester Stallone
15. *Cinco vezes favela/Five Times Favela*
16. The government's decision to withdraw funding for Embrafilme.
17. Glauber Rocha's 'An Aesthetic of Hunger'.
18. *O Pagador de promessas/The Given Word* (in 1962)
19. *Chanchada*
20. *Pornochanchada*
21. Midnight
22. Global Filmes
23. A north-eastern musical genre celebrated in films from Glauber Rocha's *Antônio das Mortes/O Dragão da maldade contra o santo guerreiro* to Andrucha Waddington's *Eu, tu, eles/Me, You, Them* (2000).
24. Cazuza
25. There are two of them, at least according the titles of the films *Dona Flor e seus dois maridos/Dona Flor and her Two Husbands*, *2 Filhos de Francisco/Francsico's Two Sons* and *Dois perdidos numa noite suja/Two Lost in a Dirty Night*.
26. Rio de Janeiro
27. Hans Staden
28. Jean Charles
29. *ABC da greve/ABC of Strike*
30. *Garrincha, a alegria do povo/Garrincha, Joy of the People*
31. Nelson Rodrigues
32. To improve our lives.
33. *Os Saltimbancos trapalhões/The Street Acrobats*
34. Bicycle
35. The goddess 'Mother Earth' of the indigenous people of the Andes.

NOTES ON CONTRIBUTORS

The Editors

Louis Bayman lectures in the film studies department at King's College, London and has research interests in melodrama, aesthetics, popular culture and Italian cinema. He is author of *The Operatic and the Everyday in Italian Postwar Film Melodrama* (Edinburgh University Press, forthcoming) and co-editor of *Popular Italian Cinema* (Palgrave MacMillan, forthcoming), as well as editor of *The Directory of World Cinema: Italy* (Intellect, 2011).

Natália Pinazza completed a PhD at the University of Bath and has research interests in postcolonial theory particularly as applied to Luso-Hispanic visual cultures. She graduated from the University of São Paulo and obtained an MA from the University of Bath. She has taught at the University of Sheffield and undertaken research at the University of Ottawa. She is currently co-editing with Louis Bayman *World Film Locations: São Paulo* (2014, Intellect).

The Contributors

Gonzalo Aguilar is Professor of Literature in the Department of Philosophy and Letters at the University of Buenos Aires. In 2005 he received a Guggenheim fellowship. Currently he is a researcher at the Consejo Nacional de Investigaciones Científicas y Técnicas (CONICET). He has authored *Other Worlds: New Concepts in Latin American Cultures* (Palgrave, 2010) and a number of publications in Argentine and Brazilian literature and culture.

Alice Allen is studying for a PhD in Contemporary Brazilian Visual Culture at the University of Cambridge, where she obtained her MA in European Literature and Culture. Her forthcoming article 'Shifting Perspectives on Marginal Bodies and Spaces' will appear in the *Bulletin of Latin American Research*. Current research interests include space and ethics in Brazilian documentary film and photography.

Eliska Altmann is Professor at the Universidade Federal Rural do Rio de Janeiro, in the Graduate Program in Social Sciences. She gained her PhD in Sociology from the Universidade Federal do Rio de Janeiro, with overseas training at the Universidad Autónoma Metropolitana (México, DF). She develops work in the areas of sociology of culture, anthropology and the image.

Jens Andermann is Professor of Latin American Studies at the University of Zurich and editor of the *Journal of Latin American Cultural Studies*. His latest publication on Latin American film is *New Argentine Cinema* (I.B. Tauris, 2011); forthcoming from Palgrave is his and Álvaro Fernández Bravo's *New Argentine and Brazilian Cinema: Reality Effects*.

Robert Anderson is Associate Professor at WSSU and Director for the US-Brazil Higher Education Consortia Program 'Legacies of the African Diaspora in Brazil and the United States: Persistent Inequalities'. Recent publications are 'Yorùbá Culture in Brazilian Culture: Carlos Diegues's *Quilombo* and Other Expropriations' in *Festschrift Oyèláràn*, edited by Oyètádé and Sheba (forthcoming).

Amanda Aouad is a film critic and editor of the site *CinePipocaCult*. She studied cinema at the Universidade Católica do Salvador before completing an MA in Communication and Culture at the Universidade Federal da Bahia. She teaches audiovisual culture at Faculdade Ibes. She has four years of experience working in an advertising agency as assistant director. She is also a qualified screenwriter by Unijorge, for which she has received awards and appraisals in festivals.

Luciana Corrêa de Araújo is Lecturer at Universidade Federal de São Carlos, Brazil. She received a BA in Mass Comunication from Universidade Federal de Pernambuco (1987), an MA in Cinema from Universidade de São Paulo (1994) and a PhD in Cinema from Universidade de São Paulo (1999). She has experience in Arts and in the following subjects: cinema, Brazilian cinema, Brazilian cinema history, silent film and cinema from Pernambuco.

Ivana Bentes is a lecturer on the Programa de Pós-Graduação em Comunicação da Universidade Federal do Rio de Janeiro (UFRJ), a researcher and curator in the field of audiovisual, digital culture and communication.

Sander Berg obtained an MA in French and General Linguistics from the University of Amsterdam in 1995. In 2004 he moved to England and received a BA in Spanish and Portuguese from Birkbeck, University of London in 2010. Currently he is doing a PhD at Birkbeck on the supernatural in the novellas of María de Zayas. Apart from his studies, he teaches languages at Westminster School.

Laura Bojneagu is a final year BA student of Spanish and Portuguese languages and culture at Birkbeck University of London. Her academic interests revolve around the representation of women in contemporary Brazilian cinema and psychoanalysis in relation to film and literature. She wrote her final year dissertation on the cinematic representation of young prostitutes in contemporary Brazilian cinema.

Dário Borim Jr is Associate Professor in Brazilian Literature and Culture at UMass Dartmouth as well as a translator, creative writer and radio programmer. His books are *Antonio Carlos Jobim: An Illuminated Man*, translated from Helena Jobim's memoir (Hal Leonard, 2011), *Perplexidades: raça, sexo e outras questões sociopolíticas* (EdUFF, 2004) and *Paisagens humanas* (Papiro, 2002).

Alessandra Soares Brandão, PhD, teaches at the Ciências da Linguagem's Graduate Program at UNISUL. Her research deals with issues of transit and (im)mobility in film and literature. She is co-editing a book on the political and aesthetic configurations of Latin American cinemas. Dr Brandão is University of Leeds's Visiting Research Fellow until March 2013.

Sara Brandellero is Lecturer in Brazilian Studies at Leiden University (Netherlands) having previously taught at the Universities of Oxford and Leeds (United Kingdom). Her publications include the book *On a Knife-Edge: The Poetry of João Cabral de Melo Neto* (Oxford University Press, 2011) and the edited volume *The Brazilian Road Movie: Journeys of (Self)Discovery* (University of Wales Press, 2013).

Marcus Brasileiro is Assistant Professor of Portuguese at Utah State University. His current research interest is in the representation of displacement and migratory experience in contemporary Brazilian literature and cinema. He has published articles on the works of Torquato Neto, João Gilberto Noll and Silviano Santiago.

Anna M Brígido-Corachán is a lecturer in the Department of English and German Studies at the University of Valencia, Spain and a member of the research groups 'Culture and Development', Red MEIRCA, IULMA and ANGLOTIC. Her interests include indigenous literatures in the Americas, representational politics, audiovisual languages and intercultural education.

Kristin Brown holds an MA in Portuguese from Brigham Young University, where she completed her thesis work on the writings of Carolina Maria de Jesus. She has a special interest in Afro-Brazilian topics, the writings of marginalized authors, and contemporary socio-economic issues represented in Brazilian literature and film.

Reinaldo Cardenuto is a PhD candidate in Media and Audiovisual Process at ECA–USP and lecture of cinema history at Fundação Armando Alvares Penteado. He graduated in social sciences from USP and Journalism from Pontifícia Universidade Católica, he was the cinema programmer and assessor for the Secretaria Municipal de Cultura de São Paulo (between 2005 and 2007).

Fernando Morais da Costa is Professor of the Cinema and Video Department and a member of the Graduate Program (MA and PhD) in Communication at Fluminense Federal University (UFF).

Daniel Caetano is Professor of Film Studies at Universidade Federal Fluminense (UFF). He is co-editor of *Filme Cultura*, and maintains a blog at http://passarim.zip.net/. He has edited two books about Brazilian films and has made a feature film (*Conceição – autor bom é autor morto*), a documentary and a short film.

Michael Chanan is a film scholar and seasoned documentarist whose involvement with Latin American cinema goes back to the 1970s. He is Professor of Film & Video at the University of Roehampton, London. He blogs as Putney Debater (www.putneydebater.com).

Angélica Coutinho, PhD, created the Bachelor of Film at the University Estácio de Sá, which produced 500 short films during her tenure. Coutinho has several articles on the topics of film and TV, and has also authored literary fiction and plays. She is one of ANCINE's specialists in film and audiovisual regulation.

Mariana AC da Cunha received an MA in Cultural and Critical Studies (2004) and a PhD (2010), which focused on the aesthetics of landscape in Brazilian cinema, from Birkbeck, University of London. She taught Brazilian Portuguese and Culture at Queen Mary, University of London (2005–09), and at the University of Oxford (2010–11).

Anita DeMelo, PhD in Romance Languages and Literatures, is originally from Brazil and teaches in the United States. DeMelo's interest primarily focuses on the practice and study of teaching methodologies and approaches. Furthermore, her research focuses on the Portuguese poet Fernando Pessoa, as well as on Brazilian film and Mozambican literature.

Stephanie Dennison is Reader in Brazilian Studies at the University of Leeds. She is co-author of two books on Brazilian cinema (*Popular Cinema in Brazil* [Manchester Uuniversity Press, 2004] and *Brazilian National Cinema* [Routledge, 2007]). She co-edited *Remapping World Cinema: Identity, Culture and Politics on Film* (Wallflower, 2006) and *Latin American Cinema: Essays on Modernity, Gender and National Identity* (MacFarland, 2005). She is editor of *Contemporary Hispanic Cinema: Interrogating Transnationalism in Spanish and Latin American Film* (forthcoming with Tamesis Press).

Alexander Dent received his PhD in anthropology from the University of Chicago (2003). *River of Tears: Country Music, Memory, and Modernity* (Duke, 2009) is the first ethnography of Brazilian rural music. Dr Dent is working on a book about the relationship between intellectual property and media piracy in Brazil.

Jack A Draper III is Associate Professor of Portuguese at the University of Missouri-Columbia. He has authored *Forró and Redemptive Regionalism from the Brazilian Northeast* (Peter Lang, 2010) and various chapters/articles on Brazilian cinema, popular music and literature. His current research analyses these forms of cultural production within the field of emotion/affect studies, focusing on the sentiment of *saudade*.

Sandra SF Erickson is Associate Professor of Modern Foreign Languages at Universidade Federal do Rio Grande do Norte. Her publications include the books *A melancolia da criatividade na poesia de Augusto dos Anjos* (Editora Universitária, 2003), *Euclides da Cunha, Vargas Llosa & Cunningham Graham: Thrice Told Tales* (Editora Universitária, Universidade Federal da Paraíba, 2006), *Logos & poesis: literatura & neoplatonismo* (EDUFRN, 2005) and *ideia&mimesis* (EDUFRN, 2009).

Priscila Faulhaber is a researcher at the Museum of Astronomy and Related Sciences/CNPq and Professor at the University of Rio de Janeiro (UNIRIO), Brazil.

Regina R Félix is Associate Professor of Luso-Brazilian Studies at University of North Carolina Wilmington. Her research includes postcolonial and women's studies philosophical perspectives on literary and film criticisms. She is preparing a co-edited volume titled *Face-à-Face: Brazil-France Liaisons Exposed-Art-History-Politics*, a collection of articles written by scholars from Brazil, Europe and the United States.

Rogério Ferraraz graduated in journalism (Unesp–Bauro), completed an MA in Multimedia (Unicamp) and is a PhD in Communication (PUC–SP). He was a visiting researcher at University of California, Los Angeles in 2002 funded by CAPES (Coordenação de Aperfeiçoamento de Pessoal de Nível Superior). He was a member of the deliberative committee of SOCINE (Sociedade Brasileira de Estudos de Cinema e Audiovisual). He is now Director of Studies of the MA in Communication at the Universidade Anhembi Morumbi (São Paulo).

Carolin Overhoff Ferreira teaches Contemporary Cinema at the Federal University of São Paulo. She is the author of *Identity and Difference: Postcoloniality and Transnationality in Lusophone Films* (Lit Verlag, 2012), and editor of *O Cinema Português Através dos Seus Filmes* (Campo das Letras, 2007), *Dekalog – On Manoel de Oliveira* (Columbia University Press, 2008), *Diálogos Africanos: um Continente no Cinema* ((Unifesp, 2012) and *Manoel de Oliveira – Novas Perspectivas sobre a Sua Obra* (Unifesp, forthcoming).

Vanessa C Fitzgibbon is Assistant Professor of Portuguese at Brigham Young University. Her research focuses on Luso-Brazilian literature and film with an emphasis on historical and contemporary aspects of race and discrimination in the establishment of Brazilian identity. Currently she is working on a book manuscript on racial resentment in Brazilian literature and film.

David William Foster is Regents' Professor of Spanish and Women and Gender Studies at Arizona State University, where he coordinates the Portuguese program. His research focuses on urban culture in Latin America, with specific reference to women's lives, gender identity, and Jewish diaspora culture and with specific emphasis on the cities of Buenos Aires and São Paulo. His book *São Paulo: Perspectives on the City and Cultural Production* appeared in 2011 published by University Press of Florida.

Patricia D Fox, PhD, is an independent scholar, translator and editor. Her book *Being and Blackness in Latin America: Uprootedness and Improvisation* (University Press of Florida, 2006) and her articles analyse Afro-Latin and Caribbean popular cultures in historical and philosophical perspectives within both the national context and that of the wider black diaspora and Africa.

Mariana Baltar Freire is Lecturer in Film and TV in the Media Studies Department at Fluminense Federal University (UFF) in Rio de Janeiro, Brazil. Her recent research addresses body genres and their influence on contemporary audiovisual culture. She is the author of 'Weeping Reality: Melodramatic Imagination in Contemporary Brazilian Documentary' in the book *Latin American Melodrama: Passion, Pathos, and Entertainment* (University of Illinois Press, 2009).

Rafael de Luna Freire has a PhD in Communication from the Universidade Federal Fluminense, during which he also researched at the University of California, Los Angeles. He was Coordinator of Documentation at the Cinemateca of the Museum of Modern Art in Rio de Janeiro and he acts in the field of film preservation. As a researcher, his interests centre on Brazilian film history and technologies of the moving image.

André Gatti teaches a wide range of courses for undergraduates and postgraduates at Fundação Armando Alvares Penteado, primarily related to Brazilian film history and the circulation of national audiovisual production. He has published regularly in magazines, books and journals with a particular focus on questions regarding the film industry and its developments.

Fabiana Ghiringhello is a journalist with an MA in European Cinema from the University of Bath and specializes in documentary at the Città del Teatro. She worked for five years as a journalist. Currently, she lives in Pisa where she collaborates with the arthouse cinema Arsenale and works as a coordinator of culture at Association Pisa incontra Brasile.

Talía Guzmán-González teaches Portuguese language, Brazilian literature and culture, and Latin American studies at the University of Maryland. She is currently working on a book manuscript on the articulations of masculinity and male friendship in nineteenth century Brazilian literature. Her areas of research are Luso-Brazilian literature and culture, masculinity studies and Brazilian theatre.

Roberta Gregoli is a doctoral student at the University of Oxford, where she investigates the representation of gender and sexuality in Brazilian popular cinema. Roberta is the recipient of the Clarendon and Santander Scholarships and the Queen's College Cyril and Phyllis Long Studentship. She holds an MA from the Erasmus Mundus Crossways in the Humanities programme.

Scott Jordan Harris writes for *The Spectator* and edits its arts blog. He is Senior Editor of *The Big Picture* magazine; Roger Ebert's UK correspondent; and the editor of the *World Film Locations* books on New York, New Orleans, Chicago and San Francisco.

Luz Horne is Professor of Literature at the Humanities Department at Universidad de San Andrés in Buenos Aires. She has published articles in different journals and her book, *Literaturas reales: Transformaciones del realismo en la literatura latinoamericana contemporánea*, was published in 2012 by Beatriz Viterbo Editora. She is starting work on a project that researches the documentary tradition and the links between ethnography and aesthetics in twentieth and twenty-first century Latin American literature, photography and film.

Laura Rodríguez Isaza is currently conducting PhD research about film festivals and the international circulation of Latin American cinemas at the Centre for World Cinemas of the University of Leeds. With a background in art history, she gained an MA degree in Film Studies from the University of Nottingham in 2008 and has worked in different cultural institutions.

Marcelo Janot has been a journalist and movie critic since 1992. He presided the Brazilian FIPRESCI (International Critics Association) section and is currently a critic for the newspaper *O Globo* and cable TV channel Telecine, and editor-in-chief of the website *Criticos.com.br*. He also teaches film theory at Polo do Pensamento Contemporâneo, in Rio de Janeiro.

Robert M Jeffery is a graduate student at Brigham Young University, pursuing an MA in Luso-Brazilian Literature. He has been previously published on Portuguese romanticism, with three other works that have been accepted for publication on various subjects. He is expected to defend his thesis on Teolinda Gersão's *O silêncio* in late 2012.

Berkeley Kershisnik is a graduate student studying Luso-Brazilian Literature at Brigham Young University. Having spent over twenty months living in the north and north-eastern regions of Brazil, her focus of study deals with historical and modern examples of social stigmas in Brazilian society based on race and economic circumstance.

Kerstin Knopf has a PhD in Indigenous Film and has widely published on this topic. She teaches North American literature, media and film at the University of Greifswald in Germany and is currently writing her second book on Canadian nineteenth-century gothic literature.

Asako Kobayashi has a BA in English Literature (Shinshu University, Japan), and is studying Linguistics and Culture at Birkbeck University of London. Her interest is in dimensions of identity in language, culture and social practices, with particular interest in identity in multilingualism and multiculturalism.

Rafael Leopoldo AS Ferreira graduated in philosophy from Pontifícia Universidade Católica de Minas Gerais. He did a postgraduate course at the Faculdade Latino-Americana de Ciências Sociais. He is the author of two books *Temporadas de Abandono* (Bartlebee, 2012) and *Veludo Íntimo* (Penalux, 2013).

Lorraine Leu is Associate Professor in the Lozano Long Institute of Latin American Studies and the Department of Spanish and Portuguese at the University of Texas, Austin. She is the author of *Brazilian Popular Music: Caetano Veloso and the Regeneration of Tradition* (Ashgate, 2006), and has been an editor of the *Journal of Latin American Cultural Studies* since 2000.

Consuelo Lins is a Brazilian film-maker, as well as professor at the Federal University of Rio de Janeiro, Brazil. She received a PhD from Université Paris 3 (Sorbonne Nouvelle), having written her thesis on documentary films. She writes regularly on cinema, video and television, having published a book on the work of Eduardo Coutinho, considered the leading Brazilian documentary film-maker.

Ramayana Lira, PhD, teaches Film and Cultural Studies at Ciências da Linguagem's Graduate Program at UNISUL. Her numerous publications deal with violence, the interfaces between aesthetics and politics, and gender issues in film. Her current project looks at the reconfigurations of politics in recent Brazilian films made by young film-makers.

Gabriela Lírio is Associate Professor in the School of Communication at Universidade Federal do Rio de Janeiro with specialization in theatre at Université de Paris III. Dr Lírio has papers published in the magazines *Artciência.com*, *O percevejo*, *Concinnitas*, and has co-edited the book *Interseções: Cinema e Literatura* (7 Letras, 2010). Her new book *Theater and Film in Peter Brook* is soon to be published.

Mauricio Lissovsky was born in Rio de Janeiro, Brazil, 1958. He is a historian, screenwriter, and has a PhD in Communication. He is the professor and coordinator of the postgraduate course at the School of Communications/Federal University of Rio de Janeiro. His main field of research is visual history (History and Theory of Photography). He has published many books and essays about photography, cinema and architecture.

Mariana Liz is a PhD candidate and teaching assistant in the film studies department at King's College London. Her research interests include European cinema, film policy and transnational cinemas.

Bernadette Lyra has a PhD in Film Studies from the University of São Paulo and undertook postdoctoral research at Université René Descartes/Sorbonne. She is a professor at the Universidade Anhembi Morumbi, co-founding member of SOCINE (Sociedade Brasileira de Estudos de Cinema e Audiovisual) and the curator of the Mostra Itaú Cultural de Cinema de Cinema de Bordas. She has authored various books and articles about cinema and audiovisual media as well as fiction books, for which she received a number of awards.

Kátia Augusta Maciel holds a PhD in Film Studies (University of Southampton) and an MA in Film and Television Production (University of Bristol). She also has a degree in Journalism (Universidade Federal de Pernambuco) and has worked as a journalist and film-maker since 1995. She is currently a lecturer at the Federal University of Rio de Janeiro, where she is conducting research on contemporary Brazilian cinema.

Maria Ignês Carlos Magno is a professor of the MA in Communication at the Universidade Anhembi Morumbi, São Paulo, Brazil. She has a PhD in Sciences of Communication from ECA (Escola de Comunicações e Artes), University of São Paulo, and an MA in Cultural History from PUC/SP. Her research interests centre on critique, cinema, history, culture and identity.

Leslie L Marsh is Assistant Professor at GSU and is a specialist in Brazilian cinema with a focus on women's film-making. Dr Marsh published 'Taking Initiative: Brazilian Women's Film-making Before and After the Retomada' (*New Trends in Brazilian and Argentine Cinema*, Intellect, 2010) and completed the manuscript *Revisioning Citizenship: Brazilian Women's Film-making from Dictatorship to Democracy* (University of Illinois Press, 2012).

Fernanda Aguiar Carneiro Martins is Professor in Cinema and Audiovisual Department at Universidade Federal do Recôncavo da Bahia – UFRB, and is also a researcher with a project financed by the Conselho Nacional de Desenvolvimento Científico e Tecnológico – CNPq, with a doctorate in Études Cinématographiques et Audiovisuelles at Université Paris III – Sorbonne Nouvelle.

Luciana Martins is Director of the Centre for Iberian and Latin American Visual Studies at Birkbeck, University of London. Her publications include *O Rio de Janeiro dos Viajantes* (2001), *Tropical Visions in an Age of Empire* (co-edited with Felix Driver, University of Chicago Press, 2005), and *Photography and Documentary Film in the Making of Modern Brazil* (forthcoming, Manchester University Press, 2013).

Carlos Alberto Mattos is a film critic and researcher. He is a member of Fipresci – International Film Critics Association and author of six books on Brazilian film-makers. He is currently editor of *Filme Cultura* magazine and writes regularly for his blog *www.carmattos.com* and the website *www.criticos.com.br*.

Bryan McCann is Associate Professor of History at Georgetown University. He has published works on the history of radio, popular music, politics and journalism in Brazil. He is currently researching a book on the neighbourhood association movement that reshaped urban space and politics in Rio de Janeiro in the second half of the twentieth century.

Alessandra Meleiro is Lecturer at Universidade Federal Fluminense, in Rio de Janeiro, and holds a post-doctorate at the Media and Film Studies Programme (University of London). He is editor of the book series *World Cinema: Industry, Politics and Market* (Escrituras, 2007) including five books on Africa, Latin America, Asia, Europe and United States and the Brazilian Film Industry and until now, six books on cinema and the market, cinema and political economy, cinema and politics of state.

Cecília Mello is FAPESP (Foundation for Research Support of the State of São Paulo) Senior Research Fellow in the Department of History of Art, Federal University of São Paulo, Brazil. Her research focuses on issues of audiovisual realism, cinema and urban spaces, and intermediality. She has co-edited with Lúcia Nagib the book *Realism and the Audiovisual Media* (Palgrave, 2009).

Luís Alberto Rocha Melo is Professor of Cinema and the Audiovisual at Universidade Federal de Juiz de Fora, an independent film-maker, and a researcher. He has produced, scripted and directed, among other works, the films *Nenhumafórmula* *para a contemporânea visão do mundo* (82', 2012) and *Legiãoestrangeira* (70', 2011).

Cezar Migliorin is head of the Cinema and Video Department and member of the graduate program (MA and PhD) in communication at Fluminense Federal University (UFF) – Brazil. He writes articles on Brazilian cinema and on aesthetic and political matters of the audiovisual in contemporary society.

Chandra Morrison is completing her PhD at the Centre of Latin American Studies, University of Cambridge, where she also received an MPhil in Latin American Studies (2007). Her research explores urban art (especially graffiti and street art), youth culture, and transformations of urban space in Brazil, Chile and Argentina.

José Antonio Ureña Muñoz received a BA in Film and Media Studies (2010) from Birkbeck, University of London and is currently studying Brazilian Portuguese at the same university. He is interested in world cinema, especially from Latin America and Iran. He is particularly interested in representations of gender and sexuality in Latin American cinema.

Simplício Neto is a documentary film-maker, TV writer and film studies researcher. She was a member of the selection committee of the 'Rio de Janeiro International Short Film Festival' in 2007 and 2008. She was curator and organizer of the exhibition 'Film-makers and Images of the People' as well as editor of the catalogue of this retrospective study of Brazilian documentaries, which took place in Rio de Janeiro, São Paulo and Brasília in 2010.

Luigi Patruno earned his undergraduate degree in Spanish from the University of Salento. Later, he studied Latin American Literature at the University of Buenos Aires. He is now a PhD candidate at Harvard University. Among others, he has published academic articles on writers such as Juan José Saer, Pablo Neruda and Gabriel García Márquez.

Antônio Márcio da Silva is the Brazilian lector at Birkbeck, University of London. He is completing a PhD at the University of Bristol and received an MRes from the University of Leeds (2008–09). His postgraduate research focused on representations of gender and sexuality in Brazilian cinema through depictions of women in prison films (MRes) and the femme fatale (PhD).

Patrícia Rebello da Silva has an MA and PhD in Social Communicantions by the Federal University of Rio de Janeiro. She is a film critic and researches on cinema, focusing on documentary films. She is a member of the selection board of the 'It's All True International Documentary Film Festival'.

Cacilda Rêgo is Associate Professor at Utah State University. She co-edited *New Trends in Argentine and Brazilian Cinema* (Intellect, 2011) and is the author of several book chapters and articles on telenovelas (soap operas), as well as Brazilian television and film.

Luiz Augusto Rezende received his first degree in Film Studies (1995) and a PhD in Media Studies (2005); he is Lecturer on the Doctoral Studies Programme on Health and Science Education (NUTES) at the Federal University of Rio de Janeiro. He is head of NUTES' Media Lab and coordinator of the graduate programme on educational video.

Carolina Rocha is Associate Professor of Spanish at Southern Illinois University – Edwardsville. She specializes in contemporary Southern Cone literature and film. She co-edited with Cacilda Rêgo *New Trends in Argentine and Brazilian Cinema* (Intellect, 2011) and is the author of *Masculinities in Contemporary Argentine Popular Cinema* (Palgrave, 2012).

Jara M Ríos Rodríguez is working on her PhD dissertation at the University of Wisconsin-Madison which focuses on animals and post-humanist studies in Brazilian and Luso-African literature. She works as an editorial assistant to the *Luso-Brazilian Review*. She holds an MA in Comparative Literature from the University of Puerto Rico-Río Piedras.

Mauro Rovai is a professor of sociology at the Department of Social Sciences – UNIFESP (Federal University of São Paulo – Brazil). He is the author of two books: *Os saberes de si* (Annablume, 2001), about the poetic images of Fernando Pessoa (Álvaro de Campos); and *Imagem, tempo e movimento* (Editora Humanitas, 2005), an analysis of the film *Triumph of the Will/Triumph des Willens* directed by Leni Riefenstahl, 1935.

Daniel Serravalle de Sá is Lecturer of English Literature at the Federal University of Santa Catarina, Brazil. In recent years, Daniel has written about the Gothic and its manifestations in different cultural contexts. He is the author of the book *Tropical Gothic* (Aracne, 2010).

Isis Sadek is an assistant professor at the University of South Carolina. Her work focuses on the relations between place, spatial practices, cultural identity and power in film and literature, with a focus on Brazil and Argentina from the 1950s onward.

Martin Schlesinger studied Media Culture at the Bauhaus-University Weimar, Germany (2002–08) and Social Communication at the Federal University of Minas Gerais, Brazil (2005–06). Since 2009 he has been a scientific co-worker at the Ruhr-University Bochum, writing a doctoral thesis on Brazilian cinema. He is author of *Brasilien der Bilder/Brazil of the Images* (VDG Weimar, 2008).

Sheila Schvarzman has a post-doctorate in Multimedia and a PhD in Social History from the Universidade Estadual de Campinas. She is a lecturer of the MA in Communications at University Anhembi Morumbi and has co-authored with Samuel Paiva the book *Viagem ao Cinema Silencioso do Brasil* (Azougue, 2011).

Deborah Shaw is Reader in Film Studies at the University of Portsmouth. She is founding co-editor of *Transnational Cinemas*. Her publications include *The Three Amigos: The Transnational Film-making of Guillermo del Toro, Alejandro González Iñárritu, and Alfonso Cuarón* (2012, forthcoming); and *Contemporary Latin American Cinema: Ten Key Films* (Continuum International Publishing Group Ltd., 2003).

Lisa Shaw is Reader in Portuguese and Brazilian Studies at the University of Liverpool and has just completed a book on Carmen Miranda for the BFI/Palgrave Macmillan's Stars series. She is co-author of *Popular Cinema in Brazil, 1930-2001* (Manchester University Press, 2004) and *Brazilian National Cinema* (Routledge, 2007).

Juliano Gonçalves da Silva is a researcher and PhD candidate in Anthropology Universidade Federal Fluminense (UFF). He obtained an MA in Multimedia from Unicamp and completed a dissertation titled *O índio no cinema brasileiro* *e o espelho recente*. He is currently a researcher at the Laboratory of Visual Anthropology of the UFF and blogs at *www.antrocine.blogspot.com.br/*. He is a member of Socine and Antropologia do Cinema (ABA).

Steven K Smith is Associate Director of Global Studies at the University of Wisconsin-Madison. He holds an MA in International Affairs from Columbia University and a PhD in Lusophone Literature from the University of Wisconsin-Madison. His dissertation examined the burgeoning alternative theatre scene in São Paulo, Brazil.

Carlos Roberto de Souza is a film archivist and cinema historian. He teaches in the postgraduate programme in Image and Sound at the Universidade Federal de São Carlos. He completed his PhD at ECA, University of São Paulo and was granted a postdoctoral fellowship by the Fundação de Amparo à Pesquisa do Estado de São Paulo.

Antonio João Teixeira, PhD, teaches at UEPG. His recent publications are 'The Construction of National Identity in Shakespeare's *King Lear* and its filmic adaptation by Peter Brook' (2006), 'The Direct Image of Time and Interstices: Jean-Luc Godard's *King Lear*' (2007), 'Woman of the West – Genre, Gender, and Politics in *Johnny Guitar*' (2009); 'A Will that Will not Bend – Mise-en-Scène in *The Nun's Story*' (2010).

Orfeu (Cacá Diegues, 1999) **141**

Pachamama (Eryk Rocha, 2009) **267**

The Plantation Owner's Daughter/Sinhá Moça (Tom Payne and Osvaldo Sampaio, 1953) **143**

Playing/Jogo de cena (Eduardo Coutinho, 2007) **199**

Porto das Caixas (Paulo César Saraceni, 1962) **75**

Possible Loves/Amores possíveis (Sandra Werneck, 2001) **96**

Prison Memories/Memórias do cárcere (Nelson Pereira dos Santos, 1984) **219**

Prisoner of the Iron Bars/O Prisioneiro da grade de ferro (auto-retratos) (Paulo Sacramento, 2004) **200**

A Public Opinion/A Opinião pública (Arnaldo Jabor, 1967) **76**

O Quatrilho (Fábio Barreto, 1995) **180**

Quilombo (Cacá Diegues, 1984) **145**

Rio, Northern Zone/Rio, zona norte (Nelson Pereira dos Santos, 1957) **124**

Saudate for the Future/Saudade do futuro (Marie Clémence and César Paes, 2000) **182**

Santiago/Santiago (Uma reflexão sobre o material bruto) (João Moreira Salles, 2007) **203**

São Bernardo (Leon Hirszman, 1972) **78**

São Paulo, Symphony of a Metropolis/São Paulo, a sinfonia da metrópole (Rodolpho Rex Lustig and Adalberto Kemeny, 1929) **54**

Song of the Sea/O Canto do Mar (Alberto Cavalcanti, 1953) **55**

The Sputnik Man/O Homem do Sputnik (Carlos Manga, 1959) **244**

Stories That Our Baby Sitters Would Not Tell Us/Histórias que nossas babás não contavam (Oswaldo de Oliveira, 1979) **246**

The Street Acrobats/Os Saltimbancos trapalhões (JB Tanko, 1981) **247**

Suely in the Sky/O Céu de Suely (Karim Aïnouz, 2006) **269**

Super Woman/A Super fêmea (Aníbal Massaini Neto, 1973) **98**

Tent of Miracles/Tenda dos milagres (Nelson Pereira dos Santos, 1977) **221**

The Three Outlaws/Os Três cangaceiros (Victor Lima, 1959) **249**

To the Left of the Father/Lavoura arcaica (Luiz Fernando Carvalho, 2001) **223**

The Trespasser/O Invasor (Beto Brant, 2002) **224**

Turbulence/Estorvo (Ruy Guerra, 2000) **226**

The Turning Wind/Barravento (Glauber Rocha, 1962) **79**

Twenty Years Later/Cabra marcado para morrer (Eduardo Coutinho, 1984) **205**

Two Lost in a Dirty Night/Dois perdidos numa noite suja (José Joffily, 2002) **183**

The Two Sons of Francisco/2 Filhos de Francisco (Breno Silveira, 2005) **125**

Vera (Sérgio Toledo, 1986) **99**

Viramundo (Geraldo Sarno, 1964) **206**

What's the Price Or Is It by Kilo?/Quanto vale ou é por quilo? (Sérgio Bianchi, 2005) **228**

Women in Fury/Fêmeas em fuga (Michele Massimo Tarantini, 1984) **101**

Xica da Silva (Cacá Diegues, 1976) **146**

The Year My Parents Went on Vacation/O Ano em que meus pais saíram de férias (Cao Hamburger, 2006) **184**